500 BIBLE STUDY OUTLINES

TITLES BY F.E. MARSH

Devotional Bible Studies
Discipler's Manual
Emblems of the Holy Spirit
500 Bible Study Outlines
Illustrated Bible Study Outlines
Major Bible Truths
1000 Bible Study Outlines
Why Did Christ Die?
Practical Truths From First Thessalonians

500 BIBLE STUDY OUTLINES

by

F.E. Marsh

KREGEL PUBLICATIONS
Grand Rapids, Michigan 49501

First Kregel Publications edition...........1980
Reprinted 1985, 1986

Library of Congress Cataloging in Publication Data

Marsh, Frederick Edward, 1858-1919.
500 Bible study outlines.

Reprint of the 1897 ed. published by Marshall Bros., London, under title: Five hundred Bible readings.
Includes index.
1. Bible — Indexes, Topical. 2. Bible — Miscellanea. I. Title.
[BS432.M36 1980] 251'.02 79-2549
ISBN 0-8254-3248-0 (pbk)

Printed in the United States of America

CONTENTS

Publisher's Preface ... xi
Introductory Note ... xii
God's Word to His Children ... xv

1 Abel ... 1
2 A Blessing to all Nations ... 2
3 Abounding ... 4
4 Abraham and Sodom ... 4
5 A Bright Promise ... 6
6 Abundance ... 6
7 A Golden Chain of Blessing 6
8 Alive for Evermore ... 7
9 All Grace ... 8
10 All Saints ... 8
11 "Alls" of Separation ... 9
12 All Times ... 9
13 Alphabet on the Holy Spirit 9
14 Alphabet on the Second Coming of Christ... 11
15 Alphabet on what God is to His People... 14
16 Always... 16
17 Amen ... 16
18 Angelic Ministry ... 16
19 An Illustration of Grace ... 17
20 Anna ... 17
21 As He is *versus* As He was... 19
22 Asking ... 20
23 Aspects of the Gospel ... 21
24 Atonement of Christ... 21
25 Authority of Christ ... 21

26 Being Saved ... 22
27 Believer's attitudes and relations to Christ... 22
28 Believers have a common interest in Christ ... 22
29 Benefits of Christ's Resurrection ... 23
30 Better ... 23
31 Beware... 25
32 Biography of Sin ... 25
33 Blamelessness... 26
34 Blessing ... 26
35 Blinded ... 27
36 Blood of Christ ... 27
37 Blood of Christ ... 28
38 Boasting ... 28
39 Bondage of Sin ... 28
40 Born of God ... 29
41 Bread of Life ... 30

42 Cain, the Man of Unbelief ... 31
43 Caleb ... 32
44 Caleb, or Whole-heartedness 32
45 Caleb's Reward ... 34
46 Call of Abraham ... 35
47 Chain of Good Things ... 37
48 Chastisement ... 37
49 Cherubim, Illustrative of the Believer's union with Christ ... 37
50 Children of God ... 38
51 Cleaving to Christ ... 39
52 Christ's Ability ... 39
53 Christ and the Children ... 39
54 Christ above the Believer ... 41
55 Christ as the Opener and the Shutter ... 41
56 Christ as the Possessor of the Key of David ... 42
57 Christ as the Son of Man ... 43
58 Christ before the Believer ... 44
59 Christ behind the Believer ... 44
60 Christ beneath the Believer... 45
61 Christ beside the Believer ... 45
62 Christ for us ... 45
63 Christ's Glory... 46
64 Christ in a Sevenfold Character ... 46

65 Christ in Isaiah lii. and liii. 47
66 "Christ Jesus" in Philippians 49
67 Christ needs us 40
69 Christ occupied for us ... 59
70 Christ our Example... ... 50
71 Christ our Hiding-Place ... 51
72 Christ our Life 52
73 Christ our Object 52
74 Christ our Substitute ... 53
75 Christ's Peaceful Reign ... 53
76 Christ's Perfection 55
77 Christ's Prayer in Gethsemane 55
78 Christ's Resurrection ... 55
79 Christ's Voice 57
80 Christ, the Bread of Life ... 57
81 Christ, the Earnest Worker 59
82 Christ, the Light of the World 59
83 Christ, the Needy One ... 60
84 Christ, the Prophet... ... 61
85 Christ, the True One ... 61
86 Christ, the Way 61
87 Christ within the Believer... 61
88 Christians are to be filled ... 62
89 Christian Work 62
90 Circle of Blessing 63
91 Come 63
92 Commands of Christ ... 63
93 Committal 64
94 Compassion of the Lord ... 65
95 Compromise 66
96 Conditions of Power ... 66
97 Confession, the Forerunner of Blessing 67
98 Contrasts 67
99 Conversion 67
100 Conviction of Sin 68
101 Countenance of the Lord ... 68
102 Courage 68
103 Covetousness... 69
104 Covetousness... 69
105 Crossing the Jordan... ... 70

106 David and Goliath 71
107 David and Goliath 73
108 David King over Israel ... 74
109 David's Threefold Anointing 75
110 Days of Scripture 76
111 Death of Christ 76
112 Death of Christ 77
113 Degrees of Faith 77
114 Deity of Christ 77
115 Deliverance 78
116 Deliver us from Evil ... 78
117 Diligence 79
118 Disciple whom Jesus loved... 79
119 Doors 80
120 Down-grade-ism of Asa ... 80

121 Ebed-Melech 81
122 Endurance 82
123 Esau 82
124 Escape from 83
125 Eternal Blessings of the Believer 84
126 Eternal Life 84
127 "Even as" in Ephesians ... 85
128 Every "Though" has its "Yet" 85
129 Example in Service... ... 86

130 Face of Jesus... 86
131 "Faint not" 87
132 Faith 87
133 Faith 88
134 Faith 88
135 Faith 89
136 Faith 90
137 Faith 90
138 Faithful Servant 91
139 Faithfulness of God ... 91
140 Feasts of Jehovah 91
141 Feeding the Five Thousand 92
142 Fervour of the Holy Spirit... 94
143 Fire 94
144 Firstfruits 95
145 First Things First 95
146 Following Christ 95
147 Following the Lord... ... 96
148 "Forget not" 96
149 Forgiveness 67
150 For Him 97
151 Found 97
152 Four Good Workers ... 98
153 Four "If so be's" 99
154 Fourteen Appearings of Christ 99
155 Fruit bearing... 100
156 Fruit of the Spirit 101
157 Fulness of Supply 101

158 "Gathered Together" ... 101
159 "Gave Himself for" ... 102
160 Genesis xxviii. 15 102
161 Gift of the Holy Spirit ... 102
162 Glorious Protection... ... 104
163 Glory of Jesus 104
164 "Go" 105
165 God's care for His people ... 105
166 God's charge to Abram ... 105
167 God's Covenant with Abram 107
168 God's Judgment on Sodom 107
169 God's Creative Acts Typical of His New Creation ... 109
170 God's Covenant with Noah... 110
171 God's desire for the welfare of man 111

172 God's Dwelling-place ... 111
173 God's Remembrance ... 113
174 God's Workmen 114
175 God's Written Word ... 115
176 Grace 117
177 Grace 117
178 Graciousness of Jesus ... 117
179 Groans 118

180 Half-heartedness 118
181 Hallelujah! What a Saviour 119
182 Hands of Christ 120
183 Hand of the Lord 120
184 Hear 120
185 Heavenly People 121
186 Help of the Lord 121
187 Hidden 122
188 Him 122
189 His Love 122
190 His Name 123
191 His Presence... 123
192 Holiness 123
193 Holy Spirit and Christ ... 125
194 Honey... 126
195 House of the Lord 126
196 How to Serve 127

197 "I am" 127
198 Ignorance 128
199 I knows of Paul 129
200 Inclusiveness of "In Christ" 129
201 Incorruptible Things ... 130
202 Increasing 131
203 Indwelling 131
204 "In Him" 132
205 "In Love" 132
206 "In Me" 133
207 "In My Name" 133
208 "In no Wise" 133
209 Inquiring—Directed ... 134
210 "In the Light" 134
211 "In the Lord" 134
212 In the Lord's Hands ... 135
213 "In the Midst" 135
214 "In the Spirit" 136
215 Israel's Bondage in Egypt ... 136
216 "I will" 138
217 "I wills" in Psalm cxxxii.... 138
218 "I wills" of Grace 139
219 "I wills" of John xiv. ... 139

220 Jacob 139
221 Jacob's Blessing 140
222 Jacob's Isolation 141
223 Jacob's Journey 141
224 Jacob's Prayer 143
225 Jehoshaphat's Prayer ... 144
226 Jehovah in Psalm xxvii. ... 145
227 Jehovah-Jireh 146
228 Jehovah's Presence 146
229 Jesus 147
230 Jesus 148
231 Jesus and John 148
232 Jesus at the grave of Lazarus 149
233 Jesus before the High Priest 150
234 Jesus cleansing the Temple 152
235 Jesus saw 153
236 Jesus 154
237 John and Herod 154
238 Jonah 155
239 Joseph's Name 156
240 Joseph sold into Egypt ... 157
241 Joshua and Service 160
242 Joy 161
243 Joy of the Lord 162
244 Joyful Ones 162
245 Justification 162

246 Keep 163
247 Keep 163
248 Keeping Christ's Words ... 164
249 Keeping God's Word ... 164
250 Kept 165
251 Kept and Keeping 166
252 Kept by the Lord 167

253 Landmarks 168
254 Learn 168
255 Learn 169
256 Learning from Christ ... 169
257 Liberty 169
258 Liberty 170
259 Listening to Christ 170
260 Living Water 170
261 Look Back 171
262 Looks of Christ 171
263 Love 172
264 Love 172
265 Love 172
266 Love of God 173
267 Love of God—Its Character 173
268 Love of Jesus 173
269 Love's Character 174
270 Love's Picture 174
271 Love's Sevenfold Cord ... 174

272 Made in Christ 175
273 Man full of Grace 175
274 Man of Faith 176
275 Manifestations of the Lord... 176
276 Manner of God's Love ... 177
277 Melchisedec 177
278 Mercy of the Lord, The ... 178
279 Mighty God 179

280 Mind of Christ 179
281 Ministry of Angels 179
282 Moriah 180
283 Must 182

284 Names of Believers... ... 182
285 Nine Nots 183

286 Obedience 184
287 Obedience 184
288 "Once" 185
289 Oneness of Believers ... 185
290 "Only" 187
291 Open Things... 187
292 Oughtness of the Christian Life 187
293 Our God 188
294 Our Speech 188

295 Paths 189
296 Past and present walk of the one who now believes in Christ 189
297 Wisdom's start and separation. 190
298 Paul's Experience 191
299 Peace 192
300 Peace 193
301 Peace in Isaiah 193
302 People of God 194
303 Personality of the Holy Spirit 195
304 Places of Blessing 196
305 Pleasing the Lord 196
306 Position of Christ 196
307 Power... 197
308 Power... 197
309 Power of Darkness 198
310 Practical Power of Christ's Resurrection 199
311 Prayer 199
312 Prayer of Faith 201
313 Preparation 201
314 Presence of Christ 201
315 Presence of God with David 202
316 Presence of the Lord ... 202
317 Preservation 203
318 Prevailing Prayer 203
319 Pride 204
320 Pride 205
321 Priesthood of Christ ... 205
322 Provision of the Gospel ... 206
323 Put on 206

324 Redemption 207
325 Relation of Christ to the Father 207
326 Responsibility regarding the Word of God 208
327 Rest 209
328 Results of Abiding in Christ 210
329 Resurrection of Christ ... 210

330 Sacrifice of Christ 211
331 Sacrifice the Ground of Blessing 211
332 Safeguards 212
333 Safety 212
334 Salvation 213
335 Salvation 213
336 Sameness of Christ 213
337 Samson, a Type of Christ ... 214
338 Sanctification of the Levites 215
339 "Sanctify yourselves" ... 215
340 Satan, a Serpent 216
341 Saved 216
342 Saviour 217
343 Saviour of Life or Death ... 219
344 Seeing... 219
345 Seeing the Lord 220
346 Self-confidence 220
347 Self-will 221
348 Sent Forth 221
349 Separation 223
350 Service 223
351 Seven "I have's" of Paul to Timothy 225
352 Seven L's in relation to the Home in Bethany 225
353 Seven Looks 226
354 Seven Positions the Lord holds for His People ... 226
355 Seven "It is enough's" ... 226
356 Seven men in a hurry ... 227
357 Seven moments 228
358 Strange Things 229
359 Seven Resurrections ... 229
360 Seven Spirits... 230
361 Seven Suppers 231
362 Seven Tables... 231
363 Seven "Thats" 231
364 Seven Things it pleased God to do... 232
365 Seven Things the Lord does for the Believer in Ps. xxiii. 232
366 Seven Things the Word of God does in Psalm xix. ... 232
367 Seven Times the words "in the Lord" occur in Eph.... 233
368 Seven Times Christ is said to speak to His Father ... 233
369 Seven "Thou Hasts" in Psalm xxx. 233
370 Shadow 234
371 Sin 234

372 Sin 235
373 Sin 236
374 Sin 236
375 Sin and Grace 237
376 Sin—Its Extent and Nature 238
377 Snares... 239
378 Songs of Degrees 239
379 Sparrows 240
380 State of the Sinner 240
381 Star 241
382 Steps in the Christian Life... 241
383 Steps in True Consecration 242
384 "Steps of Faith" 243
385 Strength of the Lord ... 244
386 Strong Drink... 245
387 Substitution of Christ ... 246

388 Take 248
389 Take Heed 248
390 Tactics of Satan 248
391 "Ten Men with one Cry"... 249
392 The Agony in Gethsemane 249
393 The Ark 251
394 The Believer in relation to the Flesh 252
395 The Book of Genesis (Book of Absolute Facts)... ... 252
396 The Book of Genesis (Book of Typical Persons) ... 253
397 The Book of the Revelation 254
398 The Bridge of Sighs ... 255
399 The Cities of Refuge ... 256
400 The Cries of Christ 258
401 The Death of Christ ... 258
402 The Divine Helper 259
403 The Eyes of the Lord ... 260
404 The Exclusiveness of "In Christ" 260
405 The Father's Sevenfold Gift to Christ 261
406 The Good Samaritan's Action in regard to the man who fell among thieves... ... 262
407 The Gospel 263
408 The Gospel proclaims ... 263
409 The Holy Spirit in Rom. viii. 264
410 The Happy Man in Ps. xxxii. 264
411 The Lord around His people 265
412 The Lord as the Helper ... 265
413 The Lord as Shield in the Psalms 266
414 The Lord's Prayer 267
415 The Lord's Preservation ... 267
416 The Lord's Supper 267
417 The Man of Faith 269
418 The Man of God 269
419 The Mercy-seat 270
420 The Most Comprehensive Verse in the Bible... ... 271
421 The New Birth 272
422 The New Home in Caanan... 272
423 The Observant Christ ... 274
424 The Passover Instituted ... 274
425 Touch of the Lord 277
426 The Passage of the Red Sea 278
427 The Prince of Peace .. 279
428 The Report of the Spies ... 280
429 The Rich Young Ruler ... 282
430 The Secret of Victory ... 284
431 The Son of God 284
432 The Tempter 285
433 The Temptation of Jesus ... 286
434 The First Disciples of Jesus 288
435 The Temptation of Jesus ... 289
436 The Thirst of Christ ... 291
437 The Thorny-ground Hearer 292
438 The Test 293
439 The Transfiguration ... 294
440 The Twelve sent forth ... 295
441 The Word of Life 297
442 Things that Differ 298
443 Things which we obtain by Faith 299
444 Thorny-ground Hearers ... 299
445 Three Appearings 300
446 Three Crosses of Calvary ... 300
447 Threefold Death 301
448 Three Looks 301
449 Three Representative Women 302
450 Three Sights 304
451 The Word of the Lord ... 305
452 Then 306
453 Things of Christ in Philippians 307
454 Towardness of our Beloved 307
455 Treasures of the New Testament 307
456 Trial of Abraham's Faith ... 308
457 Trinity 310
458 Twelve Apostles 311
459 Two Adams 313
460 Two Followings 315
461 Two Siftings 315
462 Two Wants 316
463 Typical Colours 317

464 Understanding Heart ... 319
465 Unfailing Things 319
466 Unfaithfulness 319
467 Unity 320
468 Unsurpassed Glory of the Lord... 321
469 Unto Him 321
470 "Upon" 321
471 Upper-room Meetings ... 322

472 Walk 322
473 Walk of the Believer ... 323
474 Watchfulness 323
475 Weak ones 324
476 " We have" 325
477 Well pleasing 325
478 Went down 326
479 What Christ was made ... 326
480 What does it mean to be saved? 327
481 What an Imperfect Heart means 327
482 What does it mean to follow Jesus? 329
483 What every man needs ... 330
484 What is a Christian? ... 330
485 What is a Christian? ... 331
486 What is a Christian? ... 332
487 What is a Christian? ... 333
488 What is a Christian? ... 333
489 What love does, as illustrated in David and Jonathan ... 334
490 What shall I do? 335
491 What we are to do with the Word of God 336
492 Where Blessing is found ... 336
493 " White as Snow" 337
494 " Whose I am" 337
495 " With Him" 338
496 Wisdom 338
497 What the Tongue can do ... 338
498 Wonderful Gems for setting 340
499 Workmen's Material ... 344
500 Wedges fof driving... ... 350
501 Whetstones to sharpen ... 354
502 Weapons for using 358
503 Weighty Words of comfort 362

Scripture Text Index 367

PUBLISHER'S PREFACE

How best can one find delight in meditation on God's Word and be instructed and guided to make its teachings personal and practical? The author's response would be to use Scripture to explain Scripture. F.E. Marsh believed that the best commentary on the Bible is the Bible. Those who are acquainted with his writings admire his skill in bringing together various parts of the Bible bearing on different subjects. His writings reflect his patient, long and prayerful study of God's Word, together with his faith in its Divine inspiration and his submission to the teaching ministry of the Holy Spirit to enlighten and guide him.

In *500 Bible Study Outlines,* you will see how he shared his skilled wisdom. In these skeleton outlines, there are a variety of subjects treated in a variety of ways. Some are expository; others are topical. The more extensive outlines are on great personalities from the Scriptures.

There are sufficient practical, yet fascinating subjects for a year's daily devotions enabling one to meditate on God's Word and find exceptional delight in using this desk-top handy reference work as a companion to the Scriptures.

These rays of light from God's lamp of truth will illumine one's Bible study. There are suggestive and helpful thoughts, both devotionally and scholastically, to aid the preacher and public speaker in the preparation of many messages.

Amid the moral and spiritual darkness around us, *500 Bible Study Outlines* offers us light from the Bible and increases our knowledge of Christ, Who is the way, the truth and the light.

INTRODUCTORY NOTE

THE best commentary on the Bible is the Bible. Important help may be received from devout scholarship in the accurate translation of Hebrew and Greek words, when the student is not familiar with the original languages in which the Scriptures were written; but beyond that, men can give very little assistance in the elucidation of the text.

The Bible is a plain Book, intended for a plain people. Hence the Westminster Assembly of Divines, 1647 A.D., wisely said: "All things in Scripture are not alike plain in themselves, nor alike clear unto all; yet those things which are necessary to be known, believed, and observed, for salvation, are so clearly propounded, and opened in some place of Scripture or other, that not only the learned, but the unlearned, in a due use of the ordinary means, may attain unto a sufficient understanding of them." Not only the learned, but the unlearned, can say to God in adoring gratitude, "Thy Word is a lamp unto my feet, and a light unto my path. . . The entrance of Thy words giveth light; it giveth understanding unto the simple" (Psalm cxix. 105, 130).

It is the purpose of this book of "Bible Studies" to use Scripture to explain Scripture. Those who have read the author's previous writings, need not be told, that by long, patient, and prayerful study of God's Word, by thorough conviction of its Divine inspiration in every part, by humble reliance upon the Holy Spirit to enlighten and guide him, he has, through grace, obtained a wonderful skilled wisdom in putting together various portions of the Bible, bearing upon different subjects. His book, therefore, must be more valuable than any commentary, to all who accept the following rules of Bible study:—

First. Be fully persuaded that "all Scripture is given by inspiration of God, and is profitable for doctrine, for reproof, for correction, for instruction in righteousness; that the man of God may be perfect, throughly furnished unto all good works" (II. Timothy iii. 16, 17). The profound reverence paid to the very words of Scripture by our Lord Jesus Christ, and His inspired apostles, shows how true it is that "the prophecy came not in old time by the will of man; but holy men of God spake as they were moved by the Holy Ghost" (II. Peter i. 21).

Second. Be humble as you sit face to face with God's inerrant Word. "To this man will I look, even to him that is poor and of a contrite spirit, and trembleth at My Word" (Isaiah lxvi. 2). Few, alas! can say in these days with the Psalmist, "My heart standeth in awe of Thy Word" (Psalm cxix. 161). Never forget, in reading the Bible, that "God resisteth the proud, but giveth grace to the humble" (James iv. 6).

Third. Recognizing your dependence upon the Holy Spirit, you will be led earnestly to seek His blessing, "that we might know the things that are freely given to us of God. Which things also we speak, not in the words which man's wisdom teacheth, but which the Holy Ghost teacheth; comparing spiritual things with spiritual. But the natural man" (even in a believer) "receiveth not the things of the Spirit of God; for they are foolishness unto him; neither can he know them, because they are spiritually discerned" (I. Cor. ii. 12-14).

Fourth. Learn to find the Lord Jesus Christ everywhere in the Bible. "Search the Scriptures; for in them ye think ye have eternal life; and they are they which testify of Me" (John v. 39). "Beginning at Moses and all the prophets, He expounded unto them in all the Scriptures the things concerning Himself" (Luke xxiv. 27).

Fifth. Do not neglect the Old Testament; "for whatsoever things were written aforetime were written for our learning, that we through patience and comfort of the Scriptures might have hope" (Romans xv. 4). "Now all these things happened unto them for ensamples (margin, types); and they are written for our admonition, upon whom the ends of the world are come" (I. Corinthians x. 11).

Sixth. Peruse this book of "**Bible Studies**" with a desire to make its teachings personal and practical. "Thy Word have I hid in mine heart, that I might not sin against Thee" (Psalm cxix. 11). "Whosoever heareth these sayings of Mine, and doeth them, I will liken him to a wise man, which built his house upon a rock" (Matthew vii. 24). "Why call ye Me, Lord, Lord, and do not the things which I say?" (Luke vi. 46).

Seventh. Remember that, by the Word of God you are begotten, James i. 18; you are born again, I. Peter i. 23; you grow, I. Peter ii. 2; you are cleansed, John xv. 3; you are sanctified, John xvii. 17; you are built up, Acts xx. 32; you are prepared to be presented to Christ, Ephesians v. 26, 27; you are defended amid the perils of the way, Ephesians vi. 17; and you patiently wait, "until the day dawn, and the day star arise in your hearts," II. Peter i. 19. The blessed Bible is the only lamp which God swings out in the darkness of the future.

GOD'S WORD TO HIS CHILDREN

BY F. E. MARSH

THE Word is *Milk* to feed (1. Peter ii. 2),
  Th' imparted life (1. Peter i. 23);
This is the fare we need (Jer. xv. 16),
  In peace and strife (1. John ii. 14).

The Word is *Food* to mould (Acts xx. 32),
  The man within (Eph. iii. 16);
And makes him strong and bold (Joel ii. 11),
  The fight to win (Rev. xii. 11).

The Word is *Honey* sweet (Psalm cxix. 103),
  Refined and pure (Psalm xviii. 30, M.).
It fills with joy complete (1. Thess. i. 6).
  Unspoil'd and sure (Psalm xciii. 5).

The Word's a *Living Fount* (Psalm xxxvi. 9),
  'Tis pure and clear (Psalm xii. 6);
It makes the soul to mount (Isaiah xl. 31)
  To Christ most dear (1. Peter ii. 4-6).

The Word's a *Running Stream* (Isaiah xxxiii. 21),
  'Tis broad and deep (Psalm lxv. 9);
His love in it doth gleam (Jer. xxxi. 3),
  The soul to keep (Jude 21).

The Word's a *Fire of Love* (Jer. xx. 9),
  To make aglow (Psalm xxxix. 3)
The soul, to things above (Col. iii. 1),
  While here below (Prov. xv. 24).

The Word's a *Lamp* to light (Psalm cxix. 105),
  Through life's dark way (Prov. vi. 23).
It guides us safe and right (Isaiah lviii. 11),
  To realms of day (Psalm xliii. 3).

The Word's a *Safe Guide Book* (Psalm lxxiii. 24)
To map the way (Psalm cxix. 9).
To this we need to look (James i. 25),
Lest we should stray (Psalm cxix. 11).

The Word's a *Mirror bright* (James i. 25),
In which is seen (Job xlii. 5, 6)
Dark self—a hideous sight (Rom. vii. 18);
The flesh—unclean (Isaiah lxiv. 6).

The Word's a *Hammer hard* (Jer. xxiii. 29),
The heart it breaks (II. Kings xxii. 11-13).
Its force can none retard (John v. 25),
The soul it shakes (Jer. xxiii. 9).

The Word's a *Balm* to heal (Psalm cvii. 20),
The broken heart (Psalm cxlvii. 3);
New life, and strength, and zeal (John vi. 63)
It doth impart (I. Kings xviii. 1).

The Word's a *Girdle sure* (Eph. vi. 14)
To brace the loins (Luke xii. 35);
It girds us to endure (Psalm xviii. 39),
What truth enjoins (I. Peter i. 13).

The Word's the *Spirit's sword* (Eph. vi. 17),
As sharp as steel (Heb. iv. 12),
To kill unholy words (I. Thess. ii. 13);
Its power we feel (Acts xix. 20).

The Word's the *Pilgrim's Stay* (Isaiah l. 10),
While here below (Isaiah l. 4, R.V.);
It helps us on our way (Psalm cxix. 54),
As home we go (II. Cor. v. 8, R.V.).

The Word's a *Casket rare* (Psalm cxxxix. 17),
Its gems are great (II. Peter i. 4);
Its cost can none declare (Job xxviii. 16)
On earth's estate (Psalm cxix. 72).

500 BIBLE STUDY OUTLINES

1. ABEL

MANWARD, the Bible is a history of the children of God and the children of the Wicked One. As there are to be seen near Interlaken, in Switzerland, two streams which run into each other, the one a dirty colour, and the other a blue colour; so the two seeds are plainly distinguished in the Word of God. The saved and the unsaved. The justified and the condemned. The sheltered and the exposed, as the Israelites and the Egyptians in Egypt. The righteous and the unrighteous, as Cain and Abel. Abel is the man of faith, and Cain is the man of unbelief.

ABEL, THE MAN OF FAITH. Faith in God is the indicator that tells out a man's attitude towards Him. Three C's sum up the life of faith, namely, confidence in God, consecration to God, and communion with God.

1. **The Man of Faith acts according to God's Word.** "By faith Abel offered," &c. (Heb. xi. 4). Presumption always acts upon its own authority, as in the case of the Egyptians when they would cross the bed of the Red Sea. Faith is guided by God's utterance; from this we may infer that God had made known His will as to the manner in which He was to be approached.

2. **The Man of Faith is regarded by God** (Genesis iv. 4). The word "respect" is rendered "regard" in Exodus v. 9. We might, therefore, translate the words, "The Lord had regard," &c. The Lord took special notice of Abel and his offering by looking upon them with delight. Christ is the One who is well-pleasing to God (Matt. iii. 17), and in Him the believer is accepted (Eph i. 6).

3. **The Man of Faith is envied by others** (Genesis iv. 4). Cain would not bring the right offering himself, and he was envious of Abel, who did as God directed. It is the old story of the dog in the manger. The dog cannot eat the hay, nor will he allow the cow, who can.

4. **The Man of Faith condemns the unrighteous** (1. John iii. 12). If there is anything that rouses the enmity in the natural heart, it is when one acts in such a way as to condemn another. This was the cause of the hatred and malice of the Jews against the Lord Jesus. The clear, holy light of His life condemned the dark uncleanness of their conduct.

5. The Man of Faith is noted by God (see Matt. xxiii. 35; Luke xi. 51; Heb. xi. 4; xii. 24; 1. John iii. 12). No one can touch the man of faith without God making special note of it, for believers are His special treasure, and are as dear to Him as the apple of the eye to a person. Besides, the man of faith is regarded, as he is obedient, with the love of complacency by God.

2. A BLESSING TO ALL NATIONS

GENESIS xviii. 17-21

SEEING that Christ is of the "Seed of Abraham" (Matt. i. 1), the promise to Abraham is specially fulfilled in Him, for He is the channel of all blessing.

I purpose giving an acrostic on the word *Blessing*, as illustrating how we are a blessing to others, or the class of people that are a blessing to others.

B. Blessed Ones. "I have known," or "chosen him" (Genesis xviii. 19). We cannot possibly be a blessing without first being blessed. We must receive to give, as when the disciples received the bread and fish from the hands of Christ, and then gave them to the multitude. We must know, to make known, as when the apostles had seen Christ, the Risen One, then they were able to witness of Jesus and the Resurrection; and those who have met with Christ are able to invite others to meet with Him, as the woman of Samaria, who invited the Samaritans to come and see Christ, with whom she had conversed.

L. Living Ones. Abraham was one who was in touch with the Living God, therefore he had life from Him, even as the branch of the tree owes its being and well-being to the tree. It is those who have life *from* Christ (John v. 24), life *in* Christ (Romans viii. 2), life *with* Christ (Gal. ii. 20), and Christ *as* their Life, that are able to "hold forth the Word of Life" to others (Phil. ii. 16), to their quickening and blessing (James i. 18), even as exemplified in Peter on the day of Pentecost, when the Holy Spirit ministered through him.

E. Empowered Ones. In Matthew xxviii. 18-20, we are told that Christ has "all power," and "therefore" He bade His disciples to go and make disciples of all nations. All authority is vested in Christ, therefore He has authority to bid His disciples to act according to His instructions. His servants only have authority as they are under His authority. The centurion said he was "a man under authority," therefore he said to one, "Come," and he came, and to another "Go," and he went (Matthew viii. 9). It was because the centurion was under authority that he had authority. In like manner, as we are in the line of the Divine power by obedience to Christ, and as Christ the Power of God thus lives in us, we have power over others, even as the electric wire communicates the electricity because of its connection with the dynamo.

S. Sent Ones. The word of the Lord Jesus to His disciples was "Go." When the Lord bids us go on any errand, there should be prompt and persistent obedience (John xx. 21).

S. Sanctified Ones. The disciples were to baptize in the name of the Father, Son, and Holy Spirit. The spiritual meaning of baptism into the Father, Son, and Holy Spirit is the entering into all they are. Into the Father, into His grace and love, to make us loving and gracious; into the Son, that is, into His life and liberty, that His liberty may free us, and that His life may energize us; and into the Holy Spirit, that His holiness and power may touch every part of our life. The immersion in water was but an illustration of the deeper truth of immersion into the blessings of the grace of the Gospel. Therefore it presupposes that those who were sent to baptize, knew the spiritual meaning and practical outcome of the ordinance they enjoined upon others.

I. Initiated Ones (Genesis xviii. 17, 18). Those who fear the Lord are sure to be in the secrets of the Lord (Psalm xxv. 14). The Lord delights to make known His ways to us if we are in touch with Himself, even as He did to Moses (Psalm ciii. 7). It was to Daniel that God revealed the king's dream and the interpretation. The wise men of Babylon were baffled, but Daniel, the man of God, made known the forgotten dream (Daniel ii.). Again, Joseph was the one who interpreted Pharaoh's dream. There are many illustrations in Holy Writ, to prove that it is only to God's own people, and those of them who are in fellowship with Him, that God makes known the mysteries of the kingdom and of His Word (Matthew xiii. 11; I. Cor. ii. 9-14), that they may proclaim them to others (I. John i. 1-3).

N. Nothings. Abraham confessed he was "dust and ashes" in the sight of the Lord (Genesis xviii. 27). It is easy to say we are "nothing," but to know it in reality is to be like Christ, who "made Himself of no reputation." Notice Paul's growth in grace.
"Least of the apostles" (I. Cor. xv. 9).
"Less than the least of all saints" (Eph. iii. 8).
"Chief of sinners" (I. Tim. i. 15),
"Nothing" (II. Cor. xii. 11).

G. Godly Ones. Those who know the God of blessing, by walking in fellowship with Him, as Enoch did, shall surely be a blessing from God to others. To be in touch with the God of Holiness, by union with Himself, must result in the holiness of God being transmitted in the presence of others, even as the atmosphere transmits the light. Those who know the God of Love by acting like Him, have the love of God. When a lady put a number of cakes into the dirty, ragged frock of a poor shoeless, hatless, hungry lassie, she was so filled with astonishment that she exclaimed, "Be you God's wife, ma'am?" She knew God loved her, and she therefore thought that the God-like action of the lady indicated a near relative of His. It is not what we *say*, but how we *serve*, that shows our sanctity.

3. ABOUNDING

1. **Abound in Hope.** "That ye may *abound* in hope" (Romans xv. 13).
2. **Abound in Love.** "That your love may *abound*" (Phil. i. 9).
3. **Abound in Faith.** "As ye *abound* in everything, in faith" (II. Cor. viii. 7).
4. **Abound in our Walk.** "Ye ought to walk . . . so ye would *abound*" (I. Thess. iv. 1).
5. **Abound in Grace.** "If these things be in you and *abound*" (II. Peter i. 8).
6. **Abound in every Good Work.** "In all things may *abound* to every good work" (II. Cor. ix. 8).
7. **Abound in Suffering.** "The sufferings of Christ *abound* in us" (II. Cor. i. 5).

4. ABRAHAM AND SODOM

GENESIS xviii. 22-33

I. Abraham's Question relating to Sodom. "Wilt thou also destroy the righteous with the wicked?" God never destroys the righteous with the wicked, as the following illustrations will evidence.

1. *Noah and the Antediluvians. When* Noah and his family were safely housed in the ark, then the flood-gates were opened, and the waters swept away all outside the vessel of safety (Gen. vii. 13, &c.).

2. *The firstborn of Israel and Egypt.* After the protecting blood of the lamb was sprinkled upon the door-posts of the Israelites, *then* the Lord smote the first-born of Egypt (Exodus xii. 28, 29).

3. *Israel and Korah.* It was *after* Israel had withdrawn from the tents of Korah and his followers, that the earth clave asunder and engulfed them (Numbers xvi. 26, &c.).

4. *The believer and unbeliever.* Before the Lord comes in judgment to banish the unbeliever from His presence, He will have gathered His redeemed to Himself; hence they are seen coming with Him (Rev. xix. 14), and sitting in judgment as well (Rev. xx. 4; I. Cor. vi. 2, 3).

Matthew Henry says upon Abraham's question, "First. The righteous are mingled with the wicked in this world. Amongst the best there are, commonly, some bad; and among the worst, some good. Even in Sodom, one Lot. Second. Though the righteous be among the wicked, yet the righteous God will not, certainly He will not, destroy the righteous with the wicked. Though in the world, they may be involved in the same calamities, yet, in the great day, a distinction will be made."

II. Abraham's Plea regarding Sodom. Abraham's plea was,

that wicked Sodom should be spared for the sake of the righteous ones in it. There are two things suggested by the plea.

1. *That righteous men are preventative of judgment.* "Ye are the salt of the earth," said Christ to His disciples. The saints are the salt of the earth, that keep the rest from rotting and putrefying. Many an ungodly man has been prevented from doing evil in the presence of one who was walking with God. I well remember a man hiding himself, one Sunday morning, in the bulrushes that were growing by the river Avon, because he had been working in his garden on the Lord's Day; but his conscience smote him at the sight of a follower of Christ.

2. *The law of substitution suggested.* Ten righteous men would have been the salvation of Sodom, but Sodom would have been spared for others' sake, and not for its own sake. Even so with the believer; he is saved and forgiven for the sake of Christ (Eph. iv. 32; I. John ii. 12), who has borne all judgment for him. God sought in vain for a man to stand in the gap with reference to staying judgment upon Judah, and there was none (Ezek. xxii. 30; Jer. v. 1); but in Christ, there is One who stands in the breach, and takes the place of those who believe in Him.

III. Abraham's Communion with the Lord about Sodom (verses 17, 33). God says more to Abraham about the destruction of Sodom than to anyone else, and herein God let him into His secrets. It was not to Lot, who is typical of a half-hearted Christian, that the purpose of God was made known, but to the faithful separated friend. To be initiated into Divine secrets and the wonders of God's Word, we must be in whole-hearted fellowship with the Lord, even as the beloved John, being "in the Spirit," was able to see and apprehend the wondrous symbols of the book of Revelation. It was not to the Sodomites that God's purpose was revealed. They had long since dulled their moral sense by sin, and therefore were unable to hear the voice of God. The one thing that impresses me by this incident is, that God says more to His children about the punishment of the wicked, than to the wicked themselves. God told Noah about the Flood. The Lord informed Moses about the coming destruction of the first-born of Egypt. It was to Daniel that it was revealed that Christ should overthrow the world powers, as seen in the stone crushing the image to pieces (Daniel ii.). It was to the disciples that Christ depicted the punishment of the wicked, who should "go away into eternal punishment" (Matt. xxv. 46). To the church at Thessalonica, was revealed the fact, that "eternal destruction is to be the portion of those who obey not the Gospel" (II. Thess. i. 9); and it was to the Apostle John that the scene of the last judgment was depicted (Rev. xx. 11-15). There seems to be two reasons why the Lord tells His children so much about punishment, and these are, that they may realise the awful doom from which they have been rescued; and, second, that they may tell out with burning heart and lip, the wrath that is coming upon the ungodly.

5. A BRIGHT PROMISE

"I WILL never leave thee, nor forsake thee" (Heb. xiii. 5).

The frequency of the promise of God's unfailing presence is very marked in God's Word.

1. The **Promiser** of this promise—Jehovah (Gen. xxviii. 15).

2. The **ground** of this promise—covenant (Deut. iv. 31).

3. The **power** of this promise in conflict (Deut. xxxi. 6).

4. The **suitability** of this promise for special work (Deut. xxxi. 8).

5. The **certainty** of this promise (Joshua i. 5).

6. The **reason** of the fulfilment of this promise (I. Sam. xii. 22).

7. The **stimulus** of this promise (I. Chron. xxviii. 20).

8. The **condition** to be fulfilled to know the truth of this promise (I. Kings vi. 12, 13).

9. The **presentness, perfectness,** and **perpetuity** of this promise (Psalm xxxvii. 28-33).

10. This promise is **valid,** although saints may not always realize it (Psalm xciv. 14).

11. The **class of people** that appreciate this promise (Is. xli. 17).

12. The **immutability** of this promise (Heb. xiii. 5, 6).

6. ABUNDANCE

1. **Saved in abundant grace.** "Where sin *abounded*" (Rom. v. 20).

2. **Blessed according to abundant mercy.** "Which according to His *abundant* mercy hath begotten us again" (I. Peter i. 3).

3. **Energised with abundant life.** "That they might have life, and that they might have it more *abundantly*" (John x. 10).

4. **Calmed in abundant peace.** "*Abundance* of peace as long as the moon endured" (Psalm lxxii. 7).

5. **Rejoiced with abundant joy.** "Your joy may be more *abundant* in Christ Jesus" (Phil. i. 26).

6. **Satisfied with abundant goodness.** "They shall be *abundantly* satisfied with the goodness of Thy house" (Ps. xxxvi. 8).

7. **Prayer answered in abundant manner.** "Able to do exceeding *abundantly*" (Eph. iii. 20).

7. A GOLDEN CHAIN OF BLESSING

"BLESS the Lord, O my soul, and forget not all His benefits: Who *forgiveth* all thine iniquities; Who *healeth* all thy diseases; Who *redeemeth* thy life from destruction; Who *crowneth* thee with *lovingkindness* and *tender mercies;* Who *satisfieth* thy mouth with good things; so that thy youth is *renewed* like the eagle's" (Psalm ciii. 1-5). Notice seven things in these verses that the Psalmist blesses God for:—

1. **Forgiveness.** All, not some of, the past sins forgiven, and not only so, but forgotten. In the eleventh of Hebrews, where we have recorded what faith has done, there is not a single word about the failures of these Old Testament saints. Why is this? Because, in the tenth chapter, God had said, "Your sins and iniquities I will remember no more."

2. **Healing.** It is the privilege of the child of God to know, that He can, if He wills, heal us of all our bodily as well as spiritual diseases.

3. **Redemption.** Not only past sins forgiven, but deliverance from the power of sin, and soon from its presence.

4. **Lovingkindness.** Some people will do a kindness out of mere benevolence, but there is no love with it; not so with our Father. Recently, we saw an advertisement of a certain paper, which said it was the brightest, biggest, and best. Whether that is so or not, it is not for us to say; but we do know this, that our Heavenly Father gives the brightest, biggest, and the very best He has to give to us. Hence, in speaking, we have to get all the adjectives we can to express in some measure what He gives. His love is *great* love; His kindness is *lovingkindness;* His mercy is *tender*, *great*, *plenteous*, and *everlasting*.

5. **Tender Mercies.** Not doles of charity, but mercies given out of His loving, Fatherly heart, by virtue of His Son's work, and enjoyed in the Spirit.

6. **Satisfaction.** One of the Puritans has said that "man's heart is a triangle, so that if the whole world were in it, there would be still three corners left unfilled." But the believer has the work of Christ to satisfy his conscience, the word of the Father to assure his mind, and the presence of the Holy Spirit to fill his heart, so that there is not a single corner unoccupied.

7. **Renewing.** I remember a friend saying once, when going to a place to hold special meetings, "We are looking for a revival;" and I replied that it showed they were in a bad state, as the Christian should *live in a revival.* Our inward man is, or should be, renewed day by day, not only when an evangelist is holding special meetings.

8. ALIVE FOR EVERMORE

1. **Alive to quicken.** "*Living* Stone" (I. Peter ii. 4).
2. **Alive to satisfy.** "*Living* Bread" (John vi. 51).
3. **Alive to refresh.** "*Living* Water" (John iv. 10).
4. **Alive to keep.** *Living* High Priest (Hebrews vii. 25).
5. **Alive to save.** "Saved in His *life*" (Romans v. 10, R.V., M.).

6. **Alive to reproduce.** "Christ *liveth* in me" (Gal. ii. 20).

7. **Alive to glorify.** "When Christ, who is our *Life*" (Col. iii. 4)

9. ALL GRACE

1. **God is able to make all Saving Grace to abound towards us, in its sufficiency to deliver us at all points.** "God is able to make *all grace abound* towards you" (II. Cor. ix. 8).

2. **All Sanctifying Grace in its hallowing all our being.** "Seen the *grace* of God . . . . exhorted them all, that with purpose of heart" (Acts xi. 23).

3. **All strengthening Grace in its empowering us to delight in suffering.** "My *grace* is sufficient for thee . . . . . . I glory in mine infirmities" (II. Cor. xii. 9).

4. **All Sustaining Grace to uphold us at all times.** "God is able to make all *grace abound* . . . always" (II. Cor. ix. 8).

5. **All Stablishing Grace in making us steadfast.** "It is a good thing that the heart be established with *grace*" (Heb. xiii. 9).

6. **All Serving Grace to enable us to minister.** "And His *grace* which was bestowed upon me was not in vain; but I laboured" (I. Cor. xv. 10).

7. **All Supplying Grace to meet every need.** "And of His fulness have all we received, and *grace for grace*" (John i. 16).

10. ALL SAINTS

THE late Henry Dyer was once asked where he worshipped. He replied "that he attended three churches, viz., 'Holy Trinity,' 'Christ's Church,' and 'All Saints.'"

1. In reference to the **Lord's Coming.** "The coming of our Lord Jesus Christ with *all* His *saints*" (I. Thess. iii. 13).

2. Refers to **Paul** when he says: "Who am less than the least of *all saints*" (Eph. iii. 8).

3. **Paul's salutations.** Salute . . . . . *all* the *saints*" (Rom. xvi. 15; Hebrews xiii. 24).

4. **The saints' salutations.** "*All* the *saints* salute you" (II. Cor. xiii. 13; Phil. iv. 22).

5. **Paul's Epistle to the Philippians.** "*All* the *saints* in Christ Jesus" (Phil. i. 1).

6. **Paul's Prayer for the Ephesians.** "May be able to comprehend with *all saints*" (Eph. iii. 18).

7. **Paul's Exhortation to the Ephesians.** "Praying always . . . . . for *all saints*" (Eph. vi. 18).

8. **Love to the saints.** "Love unto *all* the *saints*" (Eph. i. 15; Philemon, 5).

11. ALLS OF SEPARATION

We have the life of good king Josiah summed up under seven "alls."

1. The "all" of **separation.** "*All* the abominations ..... did Josiah put away" (II. Kings xxiii. 24).

2. The "all" of **affection.** "Turned to the Lord with *all* his heart" (II. Kings xxiii. 25).

3. The "all" of **soul** or **life.** "Turned to the Lord with *all* his soul" (II. Kings xxiii. 25).

4. The "all" of **strength.** "*All* his might" (II. Kings xxiii. 25).

5. The "all" of **fidelity.** "According to *all* the law of Moses" (II. Kings xxiii. 25).

6. The "all" of **perseverance.** "*All* his days they departed not from following the Lord" (II. Chronicles xxxiv. 33).

7. The "all" of **influence.** "The king commanded *all* the people, saying, Keep the passover unto the Lord" (II. Kings xxiii. 21).

12. ALL TIMES

1. **Praise.** "I will bless the Lord at *all times*" (Psalm xxxiv. 1).

2. **Trust.** "Trust in Him at *all times*" (Psalm lxii. 8).

3. **Righteousness.** "Blessed ..... he that doeth righteousness at *all times*" (Psalm cvi. 3).

4. **Longing.** "My soul breaketh for the longing that it hath unto Thy judgments at *all times*" (Psalm cxix. 20).

5. **Friendship.** "A friend loveth at *all times*" (Prov. xvii. 17).

6. **Zeal.** "Good to be zealously affected at *all times*" (Galatians iv. 18, R.V.).

7. **Peace.** "The Lord of peace Himself give you peace at *all times*" (II. Thess. iii. 16, R.V.)

13. ALPHABET ON THE HOLY SPIRIT

A. Advocate, to plead in us. "I will pray the Father, and He shall give you another *Advocate*" (John xiv. 16, R.V., M.).

Anointing, for power. "Hath *anointed* us" (II. Cor. i. 21).

B. Baptism, to unite to Christ. "By one Spirit are we all *baptised* into one body" (I. Cor. xii. 13).

C. Comforter, to cheer. "He shall give you another *Comforter*" (John xiv. 16).

Convincer, to alarm. "He will *reprove* the world of sin" (John xvi. 8).

D. Director, to guide. "*Led* by the Spirit of God" (Rom. viii. 14).

Dew, to refresh. "I will be as the *dew*" (Hosea xiv. 5).

E. **Earnest**, to assure. "Which is the *Earnest* of our inheritance" (Ephesians i. 14).

Enlightener, to reveal. "The true *Light* now shineth" (I. John ii. 8).

F. **Fulness**, to enrich. "*Be filled* with the Spirit" (Eph. v. 18).

Fruit, to manifest. "The *fruit* of the Spirit is" &c. (Gal. v. 22).

G. **Guide**, to lead. "He will *guide* you into all truth" (John xvi. 13).

Spirit of **Glory**, to remind. "The *Spirit of Glory* and of God resteth on you" (I. Peter iv. 14).

H. **Helper**, to enable. "The Spirit also *helpeth* our infirmities" (Romans viii. 26).

Holy Spirit, to sanctify. "Grieve not the *Holy Spirit* of God" (Eph. iv. 30).

I. **Indweller**, to occupy. "The Spirit of God *dwelleth* in you" (I. Cor. iii. 16).

Illuminator, to reveal. "He will *show* you things to come" (John xvi. 13).

J. **Joy**, to gladden. "Fill you with all *joy* . . . through the power of the Holy Ghost" (Romans xv. 13).

K. **King**, to rule. "The *Lord* is that Spirit, and where the Spirit of the Lord is, there is liberty" (II. Cor. iii. 17).

L. **Life**, to ennoble. "The Spirit of *Life*" (Romans viii. 2).

Liberator, to free. "Hath made me *free* from the law of sin and death" (Romans viii. 2).

M. **Mark** of God, that we are His. "Also *sealed* us and given us the *earnest* of the Spirit" (II. Cor. i. 22).

N. **New** nature Begetter. "That which is *born* of the Spirit is spirit" (John iii. 6).

O. **Oil** of gladness. "God hath anointed thee with the *oil of gladness*" (Psalm xlv. 7).

P. **Power**, to strengthen. "*Strengthened* with *might* by His Spirit" (Eph. iii. 16).

R. **Renewer**, to invigorate. "The inward man is *renewed* day by day" (II. Cor. iv. 16).

S. **Searcher**, to search. "The Spirit *searcheth* all things" (I. Cor. ii. 10).

Sanctifier, to separate. "*Sanctified* by the Holy Ghost" (Romans xv. 16).

T. **Teacher**, to instruct. "He shall *teach* you all things" (John xiv. 26).

Spirit of **Truth** to arm. "The *Spirit of Truth*" (John xv. 26).

U. Unction, to empower. "Ye have an *unction* from the Holy One" (I. John ii. 20).

Understanding, to discern. "The Spirit of *Wisdom and Understanding*" (Isaiah xi. 2).

W. Witness, to establish. "The Spirit Himself beareth *witness*" (Romans viii. 16, R.V.).

Well of Living Water. "The water that I shall give him shall be in him a *well of water*" &c. (John iv. 14).

Z. Zeal, to inspire. "I will *pour* out of My Spirit upon all flesh" &c. (Acts ii. 17).

14. ALPHABET ON THE SECOND COMING OF CHRIST

THERE are many ways by which we may arrive at the importance of any given subject. The person who is an authority as a specialist makes his utterance of value when he speaks upon a topic; the issues that are involved, give weight and interest to a discussion; the probable results will influence to a certain course of action; and the frequency with which a truth is brought before us in Holy Writ, will make itself felt to the prayerful student of the Word of God. All the above pleas may be applied to the blessed hope of Christ's second coming. He who says "I come again" is the Son of God—God the Son—therefore His word is valid. The issues at stake are of pressing importance. The overthrow of evil, the binding of Satan, universal peace, righteousness exalted, and God glorified, are issues that are involved as the truth of Christ's return is pondered in its wider aspect. The results of the apprehended fact of Christ's near approach will make the believer holy in life; and the blessings attendant upon Christ's arrival, to the Church, and the world, are beyond our telling and ken. The frequency with which reference is made to a truth must have the effect of awakening our interest and riveting our attention. This is remarkably true in relation to the topic before us, viz., the return of our Lord. As illustrating the repeated utterance of the Holy Spirit in speaking of this subject, and the results produced, and the commands incumbent upon us in looking for our Lord Jesus, we shall give the following alphabetical outline:—

A. Abiding in Christ is the position that He should find us in when He comes. "And now, little children, *abide* in Him; that when He shall appear, we may have confidence, and not be ashamed before Him at His *coming*" (I. John ii. 28).

B. Blamelessness of life is the normal condition in which we should seek to be when Christ arrives. "He may stablish your hearts *unblameable* in holiness before our God and Father at the *coming* of our Lord Jesus Christ" (I. Thess. iii. 13). "Your whole spirit and soul and body be preserved *blameless* unto the *coming* of our Lord Jesus Christ" (I. Thess. v. 23; I. Cor. i. 8; II. Peter iii. 14; Jude 24, R.V.).

C. Comfort in bereavement is found in the truth of Christ's return. "But I would not have you to be ignorant, brethren, concerning them which are asleep, that ye *sorrow not*, even as others which have no hope. For if we believe that Jesus died and rose again, even so them also which sleep in Jesus *will God bring with Him*. For this we say unto you by the word of the Lord, that we which are alive and remain unto the coming of the Lord shall not prevent them which are asleep. For the Lord Himself shall descend from heaven with a shout, with the voice of the archangel, and with the trump of God: and the dead in Christ shall rise first: then we which are alive and remain shall be caught up together with them in the clouds, to meet the Lord in the air: and so shall we ever be with the Lord. Wherefore *comfort one another* with these words" (I. Thess. iv. 13-18).

D. Deliverance to the groaning creation from the bondage of corruption will be given at Christ's arrival. "For the earnest expectation of the creature *waiteth* for the manifestation of the sons of God." "Because the creature itself also shall be *delivered* from the *bondage of corruption* into the glorious liberty of the children of God" (Rom. viii. 19, 21).

E. Encouragement to endure amid persecution is one of the supports that Christ's coming gives. "So that we ourselves glory in you in the churches of God for your patience and faith in all your *persecutions* and *tribulations* that ye *endure*: which is a manifest token of the righteous judgment of God, that ye may be counted worthy of the kingdom of God, for which ye also suffer: seeing it is a righteous thing with God to recompense tribulation to them that trouble you: and to you who are troubled rest with us, when the Lord Jesus shall be revealed from heaven with His mighty angels, in flaming fire taking vengeance on them that know not God, and that obey not the gospel of our Lord Jesus Christ" (II. Thess. i. 4-8).

F. Faithfulness in Christian service is one of the marks of belief in Christ's return. "Moreover it is required in *stewards*, that a man be found *faithful*. But with me it is a very small thing that I should be judged of you, or of man's judgment: yea, I judge not my own self. For I know nothing by myself; yet am I not hereby justified: but He that judgeth me is the Lord. Therefore judge nothing before the time, *until the Lord come*, Who both will bring to light the hidden things of darkness, and will make manifest the counsels of the hearts: and then shall every man have praise of God" (I. Cor. iv. 2-5).

G. Gladness of spirit is a result now and hereafter, as we are looking for the approach of Christ. "Inasmuch as ye are partakers of Christ's sufferings, rejoice; that at the revelation of His glory also ye may rejoice with exceeding joy" (I. Peter iv. 13).

H. Holiness of life is the outcome of living in the expectancy of Christ. "The God of peace Himself *sanctify* you wholly; and may your spirit and soul and body be preserved entire at the *coming of our Lord Jesus Christ*" (I. Thess. v. 23, R.V.).

I. Immortality and incorruptibility are assured blessings when our Lord comes back. "Now this I say, brethren, that flesh and blood cannot inherit the kingdom of God; neither doth corruption inherit incorruption. Behold, I shew you a mystery; We shall not all sleep, but we shall all be changed, in a moment, in the twinkling of an eye, at the last trump: For the trumpet shall sound, and the dead shall be raised *incorruptible*, and we shall be changed. For this corruptible must put on *incorruption*, and this mortal must put on *immortality*. So when this corruptible shall have put on *incorruption*, and this mortal shall have put on *immortality*, then shall be brought to pass the saying that is written, death is swallowed up in victory" (I. Cor. xv. 50-54).

J. Justly shall we act in all our dealings if we are looking for Christ's return. "The grace of God which bringeth salvation . . . teaching us, that . . . we should live soberly, righteously" (same word translated "*justly*" in I. Thess. ii. 10), "and godly, in this present world, looking for that *blessed hope*," &c. (Titus ii. 11-13).

K. Keeping to the confession of the Lord's coming should characterize all who believe in Him. "*Hold fast*" (the same word is rendered "keep" in Luke viii. 15) "the *confession* of your hope that it waver not" (Heb. x. 23, R.V.).

L. Likeness to Christ is produced as we are looking for Him. "Every man that hath this hope set on Him *purifieth himself*, even as *He is pure*" (I. John ii. 3, R.V.).

M. Manifestation in glory with Christ is brought before us as we think of His return. "When Christ, who is our Life, shall be *manifested*, then shall we be *manifested* with Him in *glory*" (Col. iii. 4, R.V.).

N. Nearness of the believer's completed salvation is proclaimed as we think of Christ's coming. "Now is our salvation *nearer* than when we believed" (Rom. xiii. 11).

O. Occupation for Christ in trading with the pound of the Gospel is our work till He returns. "*Occupy till I come*" (Luke xix. 13).

P. Patience is a grace that is to be exercised till our Lord arrives. "Ye have need of *patience*, that after ye have done the will of God, ye might receive the promise" (Heb. x. 36, 37). "*Be patient* . . . brethren, unto the *coming* of the Lord" (James v. 7).

Q. Quietude of heart is ministered to us as we think of our returning Lord; for He shall adjust all things when He arrives (I. Thess. v. 1-11). "Let us, who are of the day, be *sober*, putting on the breastplate of faith and love: and for a helmet, the hope of salvation" (I. Thess. v. 8).

R. Redemption of the body will take place when our Lord comes: for this we are waiting. "Waiting for the adoption, to wit, the *redemption of our body*" (Rom. 8. 23).

S. Stimulus to Christian service is imparted as we keep in memory our Lord's return. "I charge thee in the sight of God, and of Christ Jesus, Who shall judge the quick and the dead, and by *His appearing* (R.V.) and kingdom: *preach the word; be instant in season, out of season*," &c. (II. Tim. iv. 1, 2).

T. Threefold work of Christ will be complete when He appears. See the threefold appearing mentioned in Heb. ix. 24-28.

U. Untilness of Scripture will be fulfilled when Christ comes back. See the seven "Untils" in Luke xix. 13, Acts iii. 21 (R.V.), Rom. xi. 25, I. Cor. xi. 26, I. Cor. iv. 5, Phil. i. 6, and Rev. ii. 25.

V. Vigilance is commanded by Christ till He comes. "Take ye heed, *watch* and pray: for ye know not when the time is. For the Son of man is as a man taking a far journey, who left his house, and gave authority to his servants, and to every man his work, and commanded the porter to watch. *Watch ye* therefore: for ye know not when the Master of the house *cometh*, at even, or at midnight, or at the cockcrowing, or in the morning: lest coming suddenly He find you sleeping. And what I say unto you I say unto all, *Watch*" (Mark xiii. 33-37).

W. Waiting for Christ is to be our attitude. "*Wait* for His Son" (I. Thess. i. 10). "We *wait* for the Saviour" (Phil. iii. 20). "To them that *wait* for Him" (Heb. ix. 28, R.V.).

X. 'Xcellent glory is that into which we shall enter at the coming of Christ. "We made known unto you the power and *coming* of our Lord Jesus Christ . . . *excellent glory*" (II. Peter i. 16, 17).

Y. Yieldingness is a grace that is begotten by the apprehended fact of Christ's coming. "Let your *moderation*" (yieldingness) "be known unto all men. The Lord is at hand" (Phil. iv. 5).

Z. Zeal is inspired as we are expecting Christ. "Looking for and *earnestly desiring* the coming of the day of God" (II. Peter iii. 12, R.V.).

15. ALPHABET ON WHAT GOD IS TO HIS PEOPLE

A. Almighty God, to bless us. "I am the *Almighty God*" (Gen. xvii. 1).

B. Blessed God, to cheer us. "Glorious gospel of the *blessed God*" (I. Tim. i. 11).

C. Compassionate God, to bear with us. "For the Lord's portion is His people," &c. (Deut. xxxii. 9-13).

D. Defending God, to protect us. "The Lord is my Strength," &c. (Exodus xv. 2, 3).

E. Eternal God, to secure us. "The *eternal God* is thy Refuge" (Deut. xxxiii. 27).

F. Faithful God, to assure us. "Judged him *faithful* Who had promised" (Heb. xi. 11).

G. **Gracious** God, to bless us. "Thou art a *gracious God*, and merciful, slow to anger," &c. (Jonah iv. 2).

H. **Holy** God, to sanctify us. "I am God . . . the *Holy One*" (Hosea xi. 9).

I. **Indwelling** God, to establish us. "God is *in the midst* of her; she shall *not be moved*" (Psalm xlvi. 5).

J. **Just** God, to clear us. "A *just God* and a *Saviour*" (Isaiah xlv. 21).

K. **Kind** God, to supply us. "Who crowneth thee with *loving-kindness*" (Psalm ciii. 4).

L. **Loving** God, to cherish us. "Yea, I have *loved thee*" (Jer. xxxi. 3).

M. **Mighty** God, to deliver us. "With His *mighty power*" (Deut. iv. 37).

N. **Near** God, to sustain us. "He is *near* that justifieth me" (Isaiah l. 8).

O. **Omniscient** God, to watch over us. "Behold He that *keepeth* Israel," &c. (Psalm cxxi. 4-7).

P. **Powerful** God, to strengthen us. "The Lord stood with me and *strengthened* me" (II. Tim. iv. 17).

Q. **Quickening** God, to change us. "Hath *quickened* us together with Christ" (Ephesians ii. 5).

R. **Righteous** God, to justify us. "Establish the *just*: for the *righteous God* trieth the hearts and reins" (Psalm vii. 9).

S. **Saving** God, to free us. "This is our God . . . . . and He will *save* us" (Isaiah xxv. 9).

T. **Truth-keeping** God, to encourage us. "Which keepeth *truth* for ever" (Psalm cxlvi. 6).

U. **Unchanging** God, to secure us. "I am the Lord, *I change not*" (Malachi iii. 6).

V. **Victorious** God, to overcome for us. "Thanks be to God, which giveth us the *victory*" (I. Cor. xv. 57).

W. **Wise** God, to enlighten us. "If any lack *wisdom*, let him *ask* of God," &c. (James i. 5).

Y. **Yearning** God, to look after us. "Yet will I not *forget* thee. Behold I have *graven* thee upon the palms of My hands" (Isaiah xlix. 15, 16).

Z. **Zealous** God, to keep us. "According to His Divine power hath given unto us all things," &c. (II. Peter i. 3).

16. ALWAYS

SEVEN things the believer in Christ is always to do:—

1. **Jehovah is to be always the Object before the soul for salvation and strength.** "I have set the Lord *always* before me" (Psalm xvi. 8).

2. **The garments of the life are always to be kept white by righteousness.** "Let thy garments be *always* white" (Ecclesiastes ix. 8).

3. **The commandments of the Lord are always to be obeyed.** "Thou shalt love the Lord thy God, and keep His charge, and His statutes, and His judgments, and His commandments, *alway*" (Deuteronomy xi. 1).

4. **Holiness to the Lord is to be the feature in the character.** "Holiness to the Lord . . . *always*" (Ex. xxviii. 36-38).

5. **Prayer is the oil that keeps the believer always running smoothly on the rails of truth.** "Praying *always*" (Eph. vi. 18).

6. **Joy is always the outcome of the recognition of the Lordship of Christ.** "Rejoice in the Lord *alway*" (Phil. iv. 4).

7. **The lamp of testimony will always burn brightly if fed by the oil of the Spirit.** "Oil . . . . to cause the lamp to burn *always*" (Exodus xxvii. 20).

17. AMEN: ITS DIFFERENT MEANINGS

1. **Affirmation.** So it is. "*Verily*,* *Verily*" (John vi. 47).
2. **Supplication.** So let it be. "*Truth*,* Lord" (Matt. xv. 27).
3. **Expectation.** Let it be. "*Surely*,* I come" (Rev. xxii. 20).
4. **Confidence.** It shall be. "*Verily*,* *Verily*" (John v. 24).
5. **Necessity.** It must be. "*Verily*,* I say" (John iii. 3).
6. **Certainty.** It is. "Promises in Him, *Amen*"* (II. Cor. i. 20).
7. **Acquiescence.** Let it be. "*Even** *so*, Father" (Matt. xi. 26).

18. ANGELIC MINISTRY

1. ANGELS **point** out the way we should go (Ex. xxiii. 20; xxxii. 34).

2. Angels **prepare** us for coming conflict (Judges vi. 11-22).

3. Angels **provide** for our need in times of discouragement (I. Kings xix. 5).

4. Angels **protect** us in times of danger (II. Kings vi. 17; Psalm xxxiv. 7).

5. Angels **prevent** harm from coming to us (Dan. iii. 28; vi. 22).

6. Angels **pull us out** of difficulties (Gen. xix. 16; Acts xii. 7-11).

7. Angels **preserve** us in all our journeyings (Gen. xxiv. 7, 40; Isaiah lxiii. 9).

---

* Same word in Greek.

19. AN ILLUSTRATION OF GRACE

MATTHEW xxi. 1-7

As the Lord needed the colt upon which He rode into Jerusalem, so He needs every sinner. "Not a very complimentary simile to compare us to an ass!" says one. We often find that man is compared to animals in the Scriptures. He is compared to a sow for uncleanness (II. Peter ii. 22), to a sheep for stupidity (Isaiah liii. 6), to a dog as an object of contempt (Matt. xv. 26), and to an ass for his wildness and wilfulness (Job xi. 12). I am, therefore, warranted in taking the ass as illustrating the condition the sinner is in, and what the Lord is willing to do for him.

1. As the ass was "tied" (verse 2), so the sinner is under the bondage of sin (Gal. iii. 22).

2. As the ass was "without" (Mark xi. 4)—not in a comfortable stable—so the sinner is without the blessings of the covenant (Eph. ii. 12).

3. As the ass was in a place where two ways met (Mark xi. 4), so the sinner is where two paths are found in this life—the broad and the narrow way (Matt. vii. 13).

4. As the colt had never been ridden on, therefore, had been of no use (verse 2); so the sinner is useless to God, for they who are in the flesh cannot please Him (Rom. viii. 8).

5. As the colt was known by Christ before it was brought to Him (verse 2), and He directed where and how it would be found; so Christ knew us before we knew Him, and He gives in detail our natural character in Rom. iii.

6. As the colt was loosed by a power outside itself (verse 2), so the grace of God is the only power that can free us from the consequence and control of sin (Eph. ii. 5).

7. As the colt was brought to Christ (verse 7), so the Holy Spirit is the Power that leads us to the Lamb of God, who takes away our sin (Acts xxvi. 18).

8. As the colt was used by Christ (verse 7), so those who are brought to Christ are used by Him (Col. i. 29).

9. As the colt was needed by Christ (verse 3), so He needs all His people to carry out His purpose, even as the head needs the members of the body to accomplish its will (I. Cor. xii. 12).

20. ANNA

"SOMETIMES the sun seems to hang for half an hour in the horizon, only just to show how glorious it can be. The day is gone, the fervour of the shining is over, and the sun hangs golden—nay, redder than gold—in the west, making everything look unspeakably beautiful with the rich effulgence which it sheds on every side. So God seems to let some people, when their duty in this world is done, hang in the west, that men may look on them, and see how beautiful they are." Such was the aged Anna.

1. **Anna was a prophetess** (Luke ii. 36). As a prophet was one who received messages from God, through being in immediate communication with Him, so a prophetess was the same. Dr. Bullinger says, "The usage of the word is clear, it signifies one on whom the Spirit of God rested (Num. xi. 17, 25, 26, 29); one to whom and through whom God speaks (Num. xii. 2); one to whom God makes known His mysteries (Amos iii. 7, 8). Hence it means one to whom God reveals His truth, and through whom He speaks" (Gen. xx. 7, 17, 18).

2. **Anna was a servant of God** (verse 37). It it said of her that she "served God." What better epitaph could one have, than a testimony of having served the Lord? "Ye serve the Lord Christ" (Col. iii. 24) was the apostle's word to the Christian slaves at Colosse as he urged them to do their menial tasks as unto the Lord Himself. A carpenter was once asked why he troubled to finish off a magistrate's bench so carefully. His reply was, "I can't do otherwise; besides, I may have to sit on it one of these days." A better reply was given by the little servant girl when she was asked why she took such pains in washing the doorstep, "I am doing it for the Lord Jesus." Ah! if anything be done for, and as to Him it will be done well.

3. **Anna was self-denying.** It is said she fasted (verse 37). Anna did not fast, as some do, to obtain favour with God, but, knowing the grace of the Lord, she was willing to deny herself food that she might serve the Lord better.

4. **Anna was prayerful** (verse 37). Her prayers ascended to God "night and day." She was incessant in her pleading, and attentive in her attendance at the means of grace. An old writer says, "Prayer is the *key* of the morning and the *lock* of the evening." If we pray each morning before we go out on life's pathway, we shall unlock the mercies God has for us; and if we look to Him at the close of the day, we shall know that we are locked in with God from all harm and evil, as Noah was when the Lord shut him in the ark.

5. **Anna was thankful.** Simeon was not alone in his thanksgiving, for Anna "gave thanks likewise unto the Lord" (verse 38). Praise is comely to the Lord. Those who bless God with their praises are sure to be blessed by God with His mercies. A thankful man is full of blessing. To be thankless is to be graceless, but to be thankful is to be graceful.

6. **Anna was a true witness.** "She spake of Him" (verse 38). Her testimony of Christ as the Redeemer, is implied in that she "spake of Him to all that looked for *redemption* in Jerusalem." A true witness always tells out what Christ is, what He has done, and what He is able to do, as known from personal experience.

21. AS HE IS, *versus* AS HE WAS

1. As He *is*. He is walking in majesty in the midst of the Churches. "Who walketh in the midst of the seven golden candlesticks" (Rev. ii. 1).

As He *was*. He was seen in humiliation, and in the midst of two thieves, crucified. "They crucified Him, and two other with Him, on either side one, and Jesus in the midst" (John xix. 18).

2. As He *is*. He is girt about the breast, signifying His priestly kingship. "And girt about the paps with a golden girdle" (Rev. i. 13).

As He *was*. He was seen girded about the loins, signifying Him who came not to be ministered to, but to minister. "Took a towel, and girded Himself" (John xiii. 4).

3. As He *is*. He is seen in garments of glory, representing the glory of His person. "Clothed with a garment down to the foot" (Revelation i. 13).

As He *was*. He was stripped of His garments, and made a spectacle to men, demons, and angels. "Took His garments, and made four parts" (John xix. 23).

4. As He *is*. We see His head, and His hairs are white—telling us of His glory and eternity. "His head and His hairs were white like wool" (Revelation i. 14).

As He *was*. That head was crowned with thorns—telling us of Him who bore the cross and curse for us. "The soldiers platted a crown of thorns, and put it on His head" (John xix. 2).

5. As He *is*. His eyes are as flames of fire—reminding us of His all-seeingness. "His eyes were as a flame of fire" (Rev. i. 14).

As He *was*. Those eyes lost their brightness in death, and closed under the load of sin. "And He bowed His head, and gave up the ghost" (John xix. 30).

6. As He *is*. His feet are as burning and polished brass—telling us of His durability and deity. "His feet like unto fine brass, as if they burned in a furnace" (Rev. i. 15).

As He *was*. Those feet were nailed to the Cross. "Behold My hands and My feet" (Luke xxiv. 39).

7. As He *is*. His voice is as the sound of many waters, reminding us of the power of His word. "His voice as the sound of many waters" (Rev. i. 15).

As He *was*. His voice was hushed in death. "Saw that He was dead" (John xix. 33).

8. As He *is*. His hand is mighty to hold, and to help us. "He had in His right hand seven stars" (Rev. i. 16).

As He *was*. Those hands were pierced, and nailed to the accursed tree. "They pierced My hands" (Psalm xxii. 16).

9. As He *is*. Out of His mouth, goes a sharp twoedged sword—telling us of His power to destroy His enemies. "Out of His mouth went a sharp twoedged sword" (Rev. i. 16).

As He *was*. He opened not His mouth, but was smitten by the officer over the mouth. "Yet He opened not His mouth" (Is. liii. 7).

10. As He *is*. His face is as the sun shining in his strength. "His countenance was as the sun shineth in his strength" (Rev. i. 16).

As He *was*. That face was marred, spit on, the hair plucked from, and the rude hand of man insulted. "His visage was so marred more than any man" (Isaiah lii. 14).

22. ASKING

1. **Who to ask—**

   Our Heavenly Father. "Whatsoever ye shall *ask* of the *Father* in My name" (John xv. 16).

2. **How to ask—**

   In the name of Christ. "Whatsoever ye shall *ask* in *My name*, I will do it" (John xiv. 13).

   In the power of the Spirit. "Likewise the *Spirit* also *helpeth* our infirmities" (Rom. viii. 26; Eph. ii. 18).

   In faith. "And all things, whatsoever ye shall *ask* in prayer, *believing*, ye shall receive" (Matt. xxi. 22; James i. 6).

3. **What to ask for—**

   Help of the Lord. "And Judah gathered themselves together, to *ask help of the Lord*" (II. Chron. xx. 4).

   Fulness of the Spirit. "How much more shall your heavenly Father give the *Holy Spirit* to them that *ask* Him" (Luke xi. 13).

   Fulness of **joy.** "*Ask*, and ye shall receive, that your *joy* may be *full*" (John xvi. 24).

   Wisdom. "If any of you lack *wisdom*, let him *ask* of God" (James i. 5).

   Anything. "If ye shall *ask anything* in My name, I will do it" (John xiv. 14).

4. **The Condition—**

   Abiding in Christ. "If ye *abide* in Me, and My words abide in you, ye shall *ask* what ye will" (John xv. 7; I. John iii. 22).

5. **Encouragements to ask—**

   Promise of Christ. "I say unto you, whatsoever ye shall *ask* the Father in My name, *He will give it*" (John. xvi. 23).

   He heareth us. "If we *ask* anything according to His will, *He heareth us*" (I. John v. 14, 15).

   Christ praying. "*I will pray* the Father for you" (Jno. xvi. 26).

23. ASPECTS OF THE GOSPEL

1. **Gospel of God.** "Separated unto the *gospel of God*" (Rom. i. 1).

2. **Gospel of the grace of God.** "I have received of the Lord Jesus, to testify the *gospel of the grace of God*" (Acts xx. 24).

3. **Gospel of Jesus Christ.** "The beginning of the *gospel of Jesus Christ*" (Mark i. 1).

4. **Gospel of Christ.** "I am not ashamed of the *gospel of Christ*" (Rom. i. 16).

5. **Gospel of uncircumcision.** "When they saw that the *gospel of the uncircumcision* was committed unto me" (Gal. ii. 7).

6. **Gospel of peace.** "Your feet shod with the preparation of the *gospel of peace*" (Eph. vi. 15).

7. **Everlasting Gospel.** "Having the *everlasting gospel* to preach unto them that dwell on the earth" (Rev. xiv. 6).

24. ATONEMENT OF CHRIST

THE atonement that Christ made upon the cross when He died is the

1. **Source** of all our spiritual blessing (Eph. i. 7).
2. **Separating** power in holiness (Heb. xiii. 12).
3. **Spring** in service (II. Cor. v. 14).
4. **Success** in conflict (Rev. xii. 11).
5. **Solace** in trouble (Heb. xii. 2, 3).
6. **Stay** in bereavement (I. Thess. iv. 14).
7. **Sufficiency** in glory (Rev. vii. 14).

25. AUTHORITY OF CHRIST

1. CHRIST has authority over all flesh (John xvii. 2, R.V.).

2. Christ has all authority given to Him in heaven and earth (Matt. xxviii. 18, R.V.).

3. Christ had authority from His Father to lay down His life (John x. 18). The word "*power*" in this verse is the same that is rendered "authority" in John xvii. 2, R.V.

4. Christ has authority to forgive sins (Matt. ix. 6, margin, R.V.).

5. Christ gives authority to those who receive Him, to be the children of God (John i. 12). The word "power" is the same as "authority" in John v. 27.

6. Christ gave His disciples authority over disease and demons when He was here on earth (Matt. x. 1, R. V.).

7. Christ has authority to execute judgment (John v. 27).

26. BEING SAVED

"Saved in His life" (Romans v. 10, M.).

THE remedy against all sin is Christ. As Ulysses, in the Odyssey, was safe from the enchantments of Circe, because of a certain herb which he possessed; so those who have Christ, and whom Christ has, possess an antidote against all inconsistencies.

1. The **Meekness** of Christ shall save from intemperance in dress, as His Word is followed (1. Peter iii. 3-5).

2. The **Love** of Christ shall save from evil habit, as that love fills the being by obedience (Luke vii. 47; John xiv. 21).

3. The **Power** of Christ shall save from stumbling into the snares of sin, as we trust in Him (Jude 24, R.V.).

4. The **Spirit** of Christ shall save from failure, as we are filled with Him, through waiting upon Him (Acts iv. 33).

5. The **Holiness** of Christ shall save from unlikeness to Christ, as we abide in Him (John xv. 5).

6. The **Zeal** of Christ shall save from laziness in the Lord's service, as we are fired by Him (1. Cor. xv. 58).

7. The **Coming** of Christ shall save us from discouragement, as we are looking for Him (James v. 7).

27. BELIEVERS' ATTITUDES & RELATIONS TO CHRIST

1. **Walking with Him,** as the two disciples to Emmaus (Luke xxiv. 15), is *revelation.*

2. **Talking with Him,** as Moses and Elias did on the mount of transfiguration (Luke ix. 30), is *fellowship.*

3. **Listening to Him,** as Mary of Bethany (Luke x. 39), is *instruction.*

4. **Abiding with Him,** as the two disciples mentioned in John i. 39, is *joy.*

5. **Living with Him,** as the disciples of John, is *oneness* (Jno. i. 39).

6. **Waiting upon Him,** as the early Christians, is *power* (Acts iv. 31).

7. **Watching for Him,** as the people were waiting for Christ, is *expectancy* (Luke viii. 40).

28. BELIEVERS HAVE A COMMON INTEREST IN CHRIST

1. PARTAKERS from Him of one **common life.** "Quickened *us* together with Christ" (Eph. ii. 5).

2. In Him they have a **common interest in His atonement.** "In whom *we* have redemption" (Col. i. 14).

3. Saved in Him by a **common salvation.** "To write unto you of the *common* salvation" (Jude 3).

4. Related through Him to one **common Father.** "*All* the children of God by faith in Christ Jesus" (Gal. iii. 26).

5. Sheep by Him in one **common flock.** "There shall be *one* flock" (John x. 16, R.V.).

6. Stones on Him in one beautiful and **common temple.** "*Ye* also, as lively stones, are built up a spiritual house" (I. Peter ii. 5).

7. Branches in Him as partaking of a **common life.** "I am the Vine, *ye* are the branches" (John xv. 5).

8. Sharers with Him of one **common glory.** "Be with Me where I am; that *they* may behold My glory" (John xvii. 24).

29. BENEFITS OF CHRIST'S RESURRECTION

THERE are so many benefits associated with the resurrection of Christ, that we can only give a few. The following seven are among the many:—

1. Blessing (Acts iii. 26).
2. Justification (Romans iv. 24, 25).
3. Holiness (II. Cor. v. 15).
4. Power (Eph. i. 20).
5. Fruit-bearing (Romans vii. 4).
6. Quickening (Romans viii. 11).
7. Pledge of our loved ones who have fallen asleep coming with Christ (I. Thess. iv. 14).

30. BETTER

THE key word of the Epistle to the Hebrews is the term "*Better.*" It occurs no less than *thirteen* times (i. 4; vi. 9; vii. 7, 19, 22; viii. 6; ix. 23; x. 34; xi. 16, 35, 40; xii. 24). The word is rendered "*Best*" in I. Cor. xii. 31, and, as it will be seen, it means that which is of greater power and effect. It will be noticed that prophets, angels and men are placed in contrast with Christ, and as the stars pale in the presence of the sun, so all these are eclipsed by Him.

I. **Christ is better than the prophets because He is The Prophet.**

1. Christ is better in His *utterance*, because He is the Living Word of God, and God the Word (i. 2).

2 Christ is better in His *relation* to God. He is the Son of God, God the Son, and "Heir of all things" (i. 2).

3. Christ is better in His *person*. The prophets were creatures. Christ is Creator: "He made the worlds" (i. 2).

4. Christ is better in His *glory*. The prophets were but men; Christ is "The brightness of God's glory" (i. 3).

5. Christ is better in His *likeness to God*. He is the "express image," &c. The image of God in Him is not blurred by sin (i. 3).

6. Christ is better in His *power*. The prophets were upheld: He upholds (i. 3).

7. Christ is better in His *work* (i. 3). The prophets could not take away their own sins, leave alone others, but He could take away the sins of others.

8. Christ is better in His *place* (i. 3). He is seated at the right hand of God: the prophets could only occupy the servant's place.

II. **Christ is better than the angels.**

1. Christ is better because He is the Son, and they are servants (i. 5).

2. Because He is the Object of the angels' worship, and they are the worshippers (i. 6).

3. Because He rules, and they are ruled (i. 7, 8).

4. Because He is on the throne to reign, and they are before the throne to serve (i. 8-14)

III. **Christ is better than the best, if we think who He is.**

He is the Son of God: God the Son to accomplish (i. 2).

The Heir of all things, to occupy (i. 2).

The Creator, with Almighty power (i. 2).

The Brightness of God's glory in beauty (i. 3).

The Personification of God's Person in character (i. 3).

The Sustainer of all things in power (i. 3).

The Sacrifice to purge away sins (i. 3).

The Exalted One at the right hand of God in honour (i. 3).

The Object of angels' worship (i. 4).

The Delight of the Father (i. 5).

The Righteous King in rule (i. 8).

The One above His fellows in eminence (i. 9).

Unchanging One in immutability (i. 10-12).

Jesus in humiliation (ii. 9).

Grace in death (ii. 9).

The End to which all things converge (ii. 10).

The Source of all things (ii. 10).

The Captain of Salvation in endurance (ii. 10).

The Sanctifier in holiness (ii. 11).

The Brother among His brethren in adversity (ii. 11.)

The Leader in praise (ii. 12).

The Kinsman in redemption (ii. 14).

The Redeemer in avenging (ii. 14).

The Deliverer in emancipation (ii. 15).

The Merciful and Faithful High Priest to represent (ii. 17).

The Reconciler in atonement (ii. 17).

The Tried One in sympathy and succour (ii. 18).

31. BEWARE

"Beware lest thou forget the Lord" (Deut. vi. 12).

We often see such notices as these:—"Beware of the Dog," or "Beware of Pickpockets;" but there is one we never see, and that is, "Beware of Self." "Let him that thinketh he standeth, take heed lest he fall." We read recently of the author of a book on the "Dangers of Alpine Climbing, with Practical Advice to Tourists," having himself lost his life while ascending a mountain. Beware, worker, lest you should fall into the things that you warn others against.

1. Beware of the **word** of the Lord to do it (Deut. vi. 12; viii. 11).
2. Beware of **wine**—the symbol of earthly pleasure (Jud. xiii. 4-13).
3. Beware of the **wiles** of self-righteousness (Matt. xvi. 6).
4. Beware of the **world** of covetousness (Luke xii. 15).
5. Beware of the **wickedness** of wicked men (Phil. iii. 2).
6. Beware of the **wisdom** of man (Col. ii. 8; Matt. vii. 15; x. 17).
7. Beware of **wresting** the Scriptures (II. Peter iii. 16, 17).

32. BIOGRAPHY OF SIN

In Psalm lxxviii. we have a summary by the Holy Spirit as to the continued sinning of Israel in the wilderness.

"Stubborn" (verse 8).

"Rebellious" (verse 8).

"Set not their heart aright" (verse 8).

"Spirit not stedfast with God" (verse 8).

"Turned back in the day of battle" (verse 9).

"Kept not the covenant of God" (verse 10).

"Refused to walk in His law" (verse 10).

"Forgat His works" (verse 11).

"Sinned yet more" (verse 17).

"Provoking the Most High" (verse 17).

"Tempted God" (verse 18).

"Spake against God" (verse 19).

"Believed not in God" (verse 22).
"Trusted not in His salvation" (verse 22).
"Not estranged from their lust" (verse 30).
"They sinned still" (verse 32).
"They lied unto Him" (verse 36).
"Their hearts not right with Him" (verse 37).
"Not stedfast in His covenant" (verse 37).
"How oft did they provoke Him" (verse 40).
"Grieve Him" (verse 40).
"Turned back (verse 41).
"Tempted God" (verse 41).
"Limited the Holy One of Israel" (verse 41).
"Remembered not" (verse 42).

33. BLAMELESSNESS

BLAMELESS. Faultless we can never be; blameless we must be.

1. Blamelessness of **Heart.** "To the end that He may stablish your hearts *unblameable*" (I. Thess. iii. 13).

2. Blamelessness of **Life.** "*Unblameably* we behaved ourselves" (I. Thess. ii. 10).

3. Blamelessness in **Testimony.** "That ye may be *blameless* and harmless . . . . . in the midst of a crooked and perverse nation" (Phil. ii. 15).

4. Blamelessness in **Service.** "Walking in all the commandments and ordinances of the Lord *blameless*" (Luke i. 6).

5. Blamelessness in the **Whole Being.** "I pray God your whole spirit and soul and body be preserved *blameless*" (I. Thess. v. 23).

34. BLESSING

THE blessing of existence is good, but the best of all blessings is to have the Embodiment of all blessing, even Christ.

1. The **source** of blessing is the *Father* (Eph. i. 3).
2. The **channel** of blessing is *Christ* (Luke xxiv. 30).
3. The **power** of blessing is the *Holy Spirit* (Gal. iii. 14).
4. The **promise** of blessing is in the *Scriptures* (Heb. vi. 14).
5. The **reception** of blessing is by *faith* (Gal. iii. 9).
6. The **path** of blessing is *obedience* (Matt. v. 3-11).
7. The **character** of blessing is *spiritual* (Eph. i. 3).
8. The **outcome** of blessing is *separation* (Acts iii. 26).
9. The **consummation** of blessing is at *Christ's return* (Titus ii. 13).

35. BLINDED

II. Cor. iv. 4

Some are blinded with—

1. **Pride,** as Naaman (II. Kings v. 11, 13).
2. **Self-righteousness,** as the Pharisee (Luke xviii. 11).
3. **Riches,** as the Rich Ruler (Luke xviii. 23).
4. **Worldliness,** as Demas (II. Tim. iv. 10).
5. **Covetousness,** as Balaam (Jude 11).
6. **Self-will,** as Saul (I. Sam. xv. 22, 23).
7. **Prejudice,** as the Rulers (John vii. 47).
8. **Lust,** as Esau (Heb. xii. 16, 17).

36. BLOOD OF CHRIST

Fourteen distinct and direct blessings that come to the believer through the Blood.

1. **Remission.** "For this is My *blood* . . . . . shed for many, for the remission of sins" (Matt. xxvi. 28).

2. **Redemption.** "In Whom we have redemption through His *blood*" (Eph. i. 7; Col. i. 14; I. Peter i. 19).

3. **Reconciliation.** "Peace through the *blood* of His cross, by Him to reconcile all things unto Himself" (Col. i. 20).

4. **Justification.** "Much more then, being now justified by His *blood*" (Romans v. 9).

5. **Removal.** "How much more shall the *blood* of Christ . . . . purge your conscience from dead works" (Heb. ix. 14).

6. **Meetness.** "Made white in the *blood* of the Lamb" (Rev. vii. 14).

7. **Access.** "Boldness to enter into the holiest by the *blood* of Jesus" (Heb. x. 19).

8. **Nearness.** "Made nigh by the *blood* of Christ" (Eph. ii. 13).

9. **Liberty.** "Loosed us from our sins by His *blood*" (Rev. i. 5, R.V.).

10. **Sanctification.** "That He might sanctify the people with His own *blood*" (Heb. xiii. 12).

11. **Cleansing.** "The *blood* of Jesus Christ His Son cleanseth us from all sin" (I. John i. 7).

12. **Claimed.** Purchased. "Which He hath purchased with His own *blood*" (Acts xx. 28).

13. **Communion.** "The communion of the *blood* of Christ" (I. Cor. x. 16).

14. **Victory.** "Overcame him by the *blood* of the Lamb" (Rev. xii. 11).

37. BLOOD OF CHRIST

"This Man's blood" (Acts v. 28).

MANY have found that the "Blood of this Man" is—

1. The **harbinger of peace.** "Made peace through the blood of His cross" (Col. i. 20).

2. The **harbour of refuge.** "Who have fled for refuge to lay hold upon the hope set before us" (Heb. vi. 18).

3. The **herald of mercy.** "The blood of sprinkling, that speaketh better things than that of Abel" (Heb. xii. 24).

4. The **heritage of redemption.** "In Whom we have redemption through His blood" (Eph. i. 7).

5. The **highway of blessing.** "God sending His own Son in the likeness of sinful flesh, by a sacrifice for sin" &c. (Rom. viii. 3, 4, margin).

6. The **hewer of sin.** "He died unto sin once . . . . likewise reckon ye yourselves to be dead indeed unto sin" (Rom. vi. 10, 11).

7. The **holder of saints.** "He died for all, that they which live should not henceforth live unto themselves, but unto Him" (II. Cor. v. 15).

38. BOASTING

1. BOASTING **in God.** "We also *joy* (boast) in God" (Rom. v. 11).

2. Boasting **in Christ Jesus.** "*Rejoice* in Christ Jesus" (Phil.iii.3).

3. Boasting **in the Cross.** "God forbid that I should *glory* save in the cross of our Lord Jesus Christ" (Gal. vi. 14).

4. Boasting **in the glory of God.** "*Rejoice* in hope of the glory of God" (Rom. v. 2).

5. Boasting **in the grace that is seen in others.** "Great is our *glorying* in you" (II. Cor. vii. 4; II. Cor. ix. 2; II. Thess. i. 4).

6. Boasting **in infirmities.** "*Glory* in mine infirmities" (II. Cor. xii. 9).

7. Boasting **in apostleship.** "I have therefore whereof I may *glory*" (Rom. xv. 17).

The words of the above Scriptures which are in italics are one and the same in the original, and is rendered "*boast*" in II. Cor. ix. 4; x. 8, 13, 15, 16.

39. BONDAGE OF SIN

Israel's bondage in Egypt is an illustration of the sinner's bondage in sin. Egypt is a type of the world; Pharaoh is a type of Satan; and the bondage an illustration of the enslaving power of sin. Different men are in bondage to different sins. Let me give seven sample cases.

1. **The Pharisee.** He was in bondage to self-righteousness. He thought he was free, and behold he was bound. He thanks God he is not as other men, and behold he is worse than other men, because of what he is not, and being proud of it (Luke xviii. 11).

2. **Esau.** He was in bondage to sensual satisfaction (Genesis xxv. 32; Heb. xii. 16). He did not care about the future or spiritual things so long as his present need was supplied, and his desire granted. He had enough when his appetites were met.

3. **Balaam.** He was in bondage to the love of money. He loved the wages of unrighteousness. It was of little moment to him who suffered if only he could obtain his own ends (Jude 11; Numbers xxii.).

4. **Demas.** He was in bondage to worldliness (II. Tim. iv. 10). Love of the world fascinated Demas to his destruction. It was a wrecker's light that lured him on to the rocks of error, where he made shipwreck of faith and of a good conscience.

5. **Korah.** Korah and his followers were guilty of rebellion against God in coveting the priesthood; hence, they were in bondage to pride (Numbers xvi.). Pride is self-assertion and self-will in opposition to God's word and will. Pride is a hideous power to be under. It is a very octopus that will suck the life-blood out of any man, and lead him to eternal death.

6. **Nadab and Abihu.** It seems that these sons of Aaron, being under the influence of strong drink, brought strange fire into the Lord's presence, as after their death the priests were prohibited from drinking strong drink when in the service of the tabernacle (Lev. x. 9). The sons of Aaron were in bondage to strong drink, hence, their rash action which brought such a terrible judgment upon them. How many there are who are in bondage to intemperance. It is a blight that kills everything that is bright, beautiful, noble, and moral.

7. **Lord of Samaria.** The lord of Samaria was in bondage to unbelief. He did not believe that God could meet the need of Samaria. The consequence was, he was punished by death for his want of faith (II. Kings vii. 2, 19, 20). Unbelief is a cloud that hides the sun from view.

There is only one Person who can free the one who is in bondage, and that One is Christ.

40. BORN OF GOD

WHAT is the evidence that we are born of God? We have the question answered in John's first Epistle. Seven times we find the words "Born of God" occurring.

1. **Righteousness of life.** "Every one that doeth righteousness is born of Him" (ii. 29).

2. **Not practising sin.** "Whosoever is born of God doth not commit sin" (iii. 9).

3. **New nature implanted.** "He cannot sin, because he is born of God" (iii. 9).

4. **Loving one another.** "Every one that loveth is born of God" (iv. 7).

5. **Faith in Christ.** "Whosoever believeth that Jesus is the Christ, is born of God" (v. 1).

6. **Victory over the world.** "Whatsoever is born of God overcometh the world (v. 4).

7. **Kept by Christ.** "Whosoever is born of God sinneth not; but He that was begotten of God keepeth him" (v. 18, R.V.).

5 Grace

41. BREAD OF LIFE

Bread is expressive of the Atonement of Christ, in the process it undergoes. From its birth, till it is consumed, the corn of wheat preaches to us.

1. **The corn of wheat has to die,** before it can bring forth more wheat. Christ uses this very fact as an illustration of the necessity of His death for us (John xii. 24). He would have been for ever alone in His holiness and blessedness, if He had not died for us; and we should have been for ever alone in our sinfulness and misery.

2. **When the corn is ripe it has to be cut down;** even so, when the fulness of time was come, Christ was cut off out of the land of the living (Isaiah liii. 8); cut off by the justice of God in dying for our sins (Zech. xiii. 7); and cut off by death, that He might conquer the king of terrors, and overthrow him who had the power of death, which is the devil (Heb. ii. 14).

3. **Then the wheat has to be threshed.** How intensely Christ was maltreated. He gave His back to the smiters, and His cheeks to them that plucked off the hair (Isaiah l. 6). "The chastisement of our peace was upon Him" (Isaiah liii. 5). How much Christ suffered at the hands of wicked men! We have only to go over the scenes that immediately precede His death for illustration on this point.

4. **The corn has to be ground.** Whether we think of the corn being bruised between the mill-stones as used in the East (Isaiah xxviii. 28), or think of the corn as it is ground in the modern machinery of to-day, we are reminded of the bruising of Christ. "He was bruised for our iniquities" (Isaiah liii. 5). Who can analyze such expressions as "He was made sin for us" (II. Cor. v. 21). "He was made a curse" (Gal. iii. 13)? Who can weigh that soul agonizing cry of Christ, "My God, My God, why hast Thou forsaken Me?" Well might Luther sit for hours pondering that mysterious exclamation, and at last burst forth in the following words, "God, forsaken by God!"

5. **When the flour has been made into loaves, it has to be baked.** The fire makes it into bread, so that we can eat it with pleasure. This reminds us of Christ, who has undergone the fire of God's judgment for our sins. He passed through the fiery baptism of God's wrath (Matt. xx. 22), when He was condemned in our stead (Rom. viii. 3, margin). It is because the fire has fed upon the God-appointed sacrifice that the coals from off the altar have a cleansing virtue, as is illustrated in the case of Isaiah, when the seraph applied the live coal to the unclean lips of the prophet, and said, "Thine iniquity is taken away, and thy sin is purged" (Isaiah vi. 7).

6. **When the bread is eaten, then the nutriment of the bread becomes part of the one who eats**; and when Christ is received by faith, then we possess Him, and He becomes the life of our being (John vi. 54).

42. CAIN, THE MAN OF UNBELIEF

As faith and obedience are synonymous, so are disobedience and unbelief.

1. The man of unbelief **acts in his own way.** "The way of Cain" (Jude 11) is Cain acting according to his own thought, which was in direct opposition to the Word of God. "There is a way that seemeth right unto man, but the end thereof is death" (Prov. xiv. 12; Isaiah lv. 8).

2. The man of unbelief is **rejected** (Gen. iv. 5). Jehovah did not regard the offering of Cain. Abel's offering was accepted, because fire from heaven fell upon it, which was a sign of its acceptance on behalf of the offerer, as may be gathered from Lev. ix. 24; Judges vi. 21; I. Kings xviii. 38; I. Chron. xxi. 26, and II. Chron. vii. 1. On the other hand, when no fire fell, it was an evidence that the offering was not acceptable to God; hence, the offerer is rejected with his offering.

3. The man of unbelief is **angry** (Gen. iv. 5). When man is in the wrong, he often vents his spite in angry words and actions. The word "wroth" is translated "kindled" in Job xxxii. 2, 3; thus to be angry is to be consumed as with a fire, or a burning disease. The same term is rendered "fret" in Psalm xxxvii. 1, 7, 8; Prov. xxiv. 19. Beware of anger, especially anger against the Lord, as Jonah (Jonah iv. 1, 4, 9), when the men of Nineveh repented; or, as in the case of Cain, when he was angry because his brother was accepted, and he rejected.

4. The man of unbelief is **self-willed** (Gen. iv. 7). When Cain had the opportunity to bring the offering that was pleasing, he refused to do so. The more correct rendering, undoubtedly, is not "sin," but a "sin-offering croucheth at the door." The Preacher's Homiletical Commentary paraphrases the verse as follows:—"A sin-offering is crouching at the door of thy brother's fold, though, in order to do well, thou must needs own thyself a sinner, and be

indebted to thy brother for a sin-offering out of his fold; yet this will not destroy thy rights as firstborn, notwithstanding to thee shall be his desire, and thou shalt rule over him. Let not pride, therefore, deter thee from this better—this only proper—way. Let no obstinacy, no groundless fears, keep thee from thus doing well."

5. The man of unbelief is an **unhappy** man. With sullen looks Cain broods over his rejection. "His countenance fell," is the Divine comment, and, in addition, the Divine question, "Why is thy countenance fallen?" The word "fell" is translated "rot" in Numbers v. 21. As a disease will rot away the vital part of the human body, and will show itself in the face of its victim; so pride was a cancer that was eating out the love that Cain should have had for his brother, which showed itself in his unhappy looks.

6. The man of unbelief is **hateful** (Gen. iv. 8; 1. John iii. 12). The Holy Spirit takes the case of Cain hating and slaying his brother, as an example of the hatred the world has for the Christian.

7. The man of unbelief is **punished** (Gen. iv. 11-13). As unbelief is the mother of all sin, so unbelief is the harbinger of coming wrath. They who live in unbelief are laying up wrath against the day of wrath.

43. CALEB

THERE are seven things that characterise Caleb.

1. He was a **thorough believer,** for he followed the Lord fully (Num. xiv. 24).

2. He was a **courageous witness,** for he would not listen to the popular voice (xiii. 30).

3. He was a **separated saint,** for he was of "another spirit" than the others (xiv. 24).

4. He was a **prompt actor.** "Let us go up at once and possess the land," is his cry (xiii. 30).

5. He was a **confident man.** "We are well able to overcome," is his unhesitating cry (xiii. 30).

6. He was a **persecuted servant.** The people are not willing to hearken to Joshua and Caleb, but want to stone them (xiv. 10).

7. He was a **rewarded disciple** (xiv. 24; xxxii. 11, 12), for he was privileged to see, enter, and enjoy the land of promise (Joshua xiv).

44. CALEB, OR WHOLE-HEARTEDNESS

SEVEN times we are told that Caleb wholly followed the Lord, or more correctly, the term "*wholly*" is found in association with Caleb seven times. Once the same Hebrew word is rendered "*fully*" (Num. xiv. 24).

It is of interest to know that the word "*wholly*" is the same as is rendered "*consecrate*" in the setting apart of Aaron and his sons for the priesthood (Ex. xxviii. 41; xxix. 9). The word means, to be full, and is again and again translated "*full*" in the Psalms (Ps. xxxiii. 5; lxv. 9; civ. 24; cxix. 64).

I. The **essential** to wholly following the Lord. In Deut. i. 36, we read that Caleb "wholly followed the Lord," or, as the margin gives it, "fulfilled to go after the Lord." The words seem to indicate his willingness to follow the Lord. The main thing in consecration is, that the will is adjusted to the will of God, as the clock is adjusted to the sun for correctness of time. Christ says, "if any man willeth to do His will, he shall know of the teaching, whether it be of God" (John vii. 17, R.V.). If the will is right the walk will be right too, for what the regulator is to the watch, so the will is to the life.

II. The **meaning** of wholly following the Lord. In Num. xiv. 24, the Lord says, "Caleb . . . . followed me fully," or as Young translates the words, "he is fully after Me." To be fully after the Lord signifies that we are so close to Him that there is not anything between Him and us, and that we seek to act like Him in all things, in that we carry out His word in every particular.

III. Caleb is seen in **contrast** to those who did not wholly follow the Lord (Num. xxxii. 11). One reason why Christ was hated, was because the holy light of His pure life showed up the unholy lives of His enemies, and made them to stand out in unmistakable contrast. When our lives are like the beautiful rainbow, it will cause those who are like the dark cloud to be seen in vivid contrast.

IV. The Lord delights to commend the **thoroughness** of whole-heartedness. Num. xxxii. 12, is one of the many places where Caleb is commended for wholly following the Lord. God delights in all men with the *love of compassion* (John iii. 16), but it is only those whose hearts and lives are right with Him that He can delight in with the *love of complacency* (Col. i. 10). He ever delights to commend what He can. The widow's mite (Luke xxi. 3); the cup of cold water (Mark ix. 41); the Samaritan's kindness (Luke x. 37); the pot of ointment (John xii. 7); the woman's tears (Luke vii. 44); the faith of the Thessalonians (1. Thess. i. 8); and the seven traits of character in the Ephesian saints (Rev. ii. 2, 3), are a few things He commends.

V. The **courage** of whole-heartedness (Joshua xiv. 8). As Caleb says, the rest of those, excepting Joshua, who went to spy the land, were entirely over-awed by what they saw, but not so Caleb. He knew the Lord, and was fully confident of His ability to give the entire victory. Faith reckons not on outward appearances, but looks at matters through the telescope of God's truth. Faint heart, want of courage, and unbelief are sure to see the lions in the way, as Timorous and Mistrust in *Pilgrim's Progress* did, but they do not see, as Christian did, that the lions are chained.

VI. The **possession** of whole-heartedness (Joshua xiv. 9). Caleb had been promised that he should see the land of Canaan, and now he claims the fulfilment of the inheritance that had been promised him. We are not promised an earthly inheritance as a reward of faith, but we have an incorruptible inheritance (1. Peter i. 4), which we may enjoy now in some measure (Eph. i. 3), as we have already received the earnest (Eph. i. 13, 14).

VII. The **reward** of whole-heartedness (Joshua xiv. 14). Hebron became the reward of Caleb's faithfulness. Hebron means "fellowship." Fellowship with Christ is the reward of walking in the light of His presence now (i. John i. 7), and fellowship with Him in a peculiar sense, in the eternity to come, is the reward of faithfulness (Rev. iii. 4).

45. CALEB'S REWARD

JOSHUA xiv. 5-14

THE men of the Bible have generally one trait in their character which is more prominent than another. Moses is the man of meekness; Abraham, the man of separation; David, the man of courage; Joseph, the man of purity; John, the man of love; Peter, the man of zeal; and Caleb, the man of faith.

I shall call attention to a sevenfold aspect of faith, as brought out in Caleb.

1. **Claim of Faith** (verse 6). Faith's claim is always based on God's promise. "The thing the Lord said concerning me," is ever the language of faith. Faith has nothing to say about itself, other than "The Lord says." When men claim that which God has not promised, it is presumption, and not faith.

> "Faith, mighty faith, the promise sees,
> And looks to God alone,
> Laughs at impossibilities,
> And cries 'It shall be done.'"

2. **Consecration of Faith** (verse 8). The word "*consecrate*" in Exodus xxviii. 41, and xxix. 9, is the same as we have rendered "*wholly*" in describing Caleb's obedience. Trapp remarks, "The Hebrew signifies 'I fulfilled after the Lord.' A metaphor taken from a ship under sail carried strongly with the wind, as if it feared neither rocks nor sands. Thus he commended himself, that none might tax him with injustice or ambition for that which he now required from Joshua." Caleb's devotion in following the Lord fully is noted in Deut. i. 36; Num. xiv. 24, xxxii. 11; Josh. xiv. 8, 9, 14. Faith's consecration is summed up in one word—"Obedience." Consecration on the Godward side of it, is the indwelling presence of Christ acting within to reproduce His own behaviour in the life (Gal. ii. 20); and on the manward side, consecration is the response of the believer to the word of God's grace in simple, whole-hearted obedience (1. Peter i. 14-21).

3. **Confession of Faith** (verse 10). "The Lord hath kept me," is ever the glad confession of faith. "No might" (II. Chron. xx. 12) is the plea of faith in prayer for the Lord's protection. Caleb had kept himself in the Lord's keeping by his whole-heartedness, and now, as a consequence, he can proclaim what the Lord had done for him. As the electricity runs along the wire that is connected with the battery, so the Lord's keeping grace is found along the line of faith (I. Peter i. 5), which faith shows itself in obedience; and when we have experienced the keeping power of God's grace, then we can bear our testimony to His faithfulness, and not otherwise.

4. **Courage of Faith** (verse 11). Caleb feels that he is still able to go to war, for his strength, like that of Moses (Deut. xxxiv. 7), was not abated. His health of soul (III. John 2) had conduced to healthiness of body. Godliness is profitable from this standpoint (I. Tim. iv. 8). The secret of courage in the Christian life for warfare and witnessing is found in walking with the Lord. If we can look up into the face of God with an uncondemning heart (I. John iii. 20, 21), then we shall be able to look into the faces of men in faithful testimony (Acts iv. 13).

5. **Company of Faith** (verse 12). The presence of Jehovah was Caleb's joy. He felt he could do anything, be anything, and go anywhere, if only the Lord was with him. If the Lord is with us, victory is sure (I. Sam. xiv. 6), our feet are kept from slipping (Psalm xviii. 32, 33), our faith is bold (Psalm xxvii. 1-3), our soul is comforted (Psalm xxiii. 4), and we are encouraged (Phil. iv. 13).

6. **Confidence of Faith.** "I shall be able to drive them out, as the Lord said" (verse 12). Caleb had the Divine promise of victory over his enemies (Josh. iii. 10), and therefore he was confident of success. The difference between faith and presumption is this: presumption acts on its own authority, but faith always depends on "Thus saith the Lord" (Heb. xi. 29). Self-confidence is man acting without God, but faith-confidence upon the Lord (I. Sam. xvii. 45, 46).

7. **Compensation of Faith** (verses 13, 14). Caleb is rewarded because of his faithfulness. Hebron becomes his inheritance. Hebron means fellowship. Fellowship with the Lord is the reward of walking with the Lord now (I. Cor. i. 9), and, in the hereafter, a crown. An "incorruptible crown" for diligently running the race (I. Cor. ix. 25), a "crown of life" for endurance (James i. 12), a "crown of righteousness" for those who love Christ's appearing (II. Tim. iv. 8), a "crown of rejoicing" for those who bring others to Christ (I. Thess. ii. 19), and a "crown of glory" for faithful service (I. Peter v. 4).

46. CALL OF ABRAM

GENESIS xii. 1-9

IF we take in the last two verses of Gen. xi., we find that Abram is connected with three places, namely, "Ur," "Haran," and "Canaan." "Ur," as associated with Abram in his idolatry; "Haran," as connected with Abram's partial obedience; and "Canaan," as identified with Abram's communion with God.

Ur. Ur means in Hebrew "Light," and was probably so called because of the idolatrous custom of fire worship among the Persians. Very little, if anything, is known of the history of "Ur," other than it was in Chaldea, as it is specially designated "Ur of the Chaldees," but of this we are plainly told, that it was associated with idolatrous worship, for the ancestors of Abram are said to have "dwelt beyond the river," the river Euphrates, and "served other gods" (Joshua xxiv. 2, R.V.). It was from this place that the Lord called Abram. There are several expressions which bring out what God did for Abram in bringing him out of idolatry, which illustrate what God does for the believer in Christ.

1. God **chose** Abram. "The Lord thy God chose Abram" (Neh. ix. 7). As God chose Abram to be for Himself, so He has chosen the believer in Christ (Eph. i. 4).

2. God **called** Abram. "By faith Abraham, when he was called," &c. (Hebrews xi. 8). As God called Abram out of idolatry, so He has called the believer out of the darkness of sin, into the life, light and liberty of the Gospel (I. Peter ii. 9).

3. God **commanded** Abram. "The Lord had said unto Abram, Get thee out of thy country," &c. (Gen. xii. 1). As God commanded Abram to be separated from his old surroundings and relations, so He directs the believer not to be yoked with unbelievers and the world (II. Cor. vi. 14-18).

4. God **taking** Abram. "I took your father Abraham," &c. (Joshua xxiv. 3). As God took Abram from the old position and condition that he was in, so He has taken the believer from the course of this wicked age, and the death of sin, and made him to be seated with Christ in heavenly places (Eph. ii. 1-6).

5. God **bringing** Abram. "I am the Lord that brought thee out" (Gen. xv. 7; Neh. ix. 7). God's action to Abram was not only a command to "come out" of Ur, not only an exhibition of His power in taking him out, but a gracious act in leading him, as the mother leads her child out of danger. In like manner the Lord has dealt with us (Col. i. 13).

6. God **redeemed** Abram. "The Lord, who redeemed Abraham" (Isaiah xxix. 22). All the Old Testament saints (Rom. iii. 24, 25, R.V.), as well as ourselves (Eph. i. 7), owe their redemption to the blood of Christ (I. Peter i. 18, 19). To redeem, means to set at liberty by virtue of a price paid.

7. Abram **obeyed** God (Heb. xi. 8). Obedience was a proof of his election, and ours (II. Peter i. 10).

47. CHAIN OF GOOD THINGS

THE believer in Christ ever says, with the Psalmist, "I have no good beyond Thee" (Psalm xvi. 2, R.V.).

1. In ourselves there is no good thing (Rom. vii. 18).
2. But the good that has been planted within us (II. Tim. i. 14).
3. Which is the outcome of the good work of the Lord (Phil. i. 6).
4. Is productive of good works (Eph. ii. 10).
5. So that by His grace we have a good conscience (I. Tim. i. 19).
6. And fight a good warfare (I. Tim. vi. 12).
7. Thus are we good soldiers of Jesus Christ (II. Tim. ii. 3).

48. CHASTISEMENT

THE purposes of chastisement are many, but they may be classified under the following seven heads:

1. **Illuminative.** To discover faults and failings. "I speak not with your children which have not known, and which have not seen the chastisement" (Deut. xi. 2).

2. **Preventative.** To keep from failure and self exaltation. "God hath seen mine affliction, and the labour of my hands, and rebuked (chastened) thee yesternight" (Gen. xxxi. 42).

3. **Instructive.** To cause us to know His way and will. "The prophecy his mother taught him" (Prov. xxxi. 1).

4. **Curative.** To prevent us from failing, where we have failed before. "Behold, I have given thy brother a thousand pieces of silver . . . thus she was reproved" (Gen. xx. 16).

5. **Corrective.** To drive away that which is not helpful. "Foolishness is bound up in the heart of a child; but the rod of correction shall drive it far from him" (Prov. xxii. 15).

6. **Illustrative.** To let others see the divine grace and patience exemplified in us. "Happy is the man whom God correcteth; therefore despise not thou the chastening of the Almighty" (Job v. 17).

7. **Punitive.** To punish for misdeed or disobedience. "To deliver such an one unto Satan" (I. Cor. v. 5).

49. CHERUBIM, ILLUSTRATIVE OF THE BELIEVER'S UNION WITH CHRIST

WE will take, as illustrating the believer's union with Christ, the cherubim on the veil, the covering, in the mercy-seat, and in the throne.

1. **On the veil** (Ex. xxxvi. 35). "The veil of the temple was rent in the midst" (Luke xxiii. 45); and in this we see that, in the person of our Representative, we have borne the punishment due to sin, satisfied Divine justice, and hence we are said to be baptised into His death (Rom. vi. 3).

2. **On the covering of twined linen, &c.** (Ex. xxxvi. 8). This covering was the ceiling of the tabernacle, and when the priest went in, he would see the cherubim inwrought on the beautiful covering. As it was above, so, in a spiritual sense, we are risen in and made to sit with Christ in heavenly places; or, as we are told in another place, "Buried with Him in baptism, wherein also ye are *risen with Him*, through the faith of the operation of God, who hath raised Him from the dead" (Col. ii 12).

3. **In the mercy-seat.** The cherubim were made out of the same piece of gold as the mercy-seat, as we read in Ex. xxv. 19: "And make one cherub on the one end, and the other cherub on the other end; even of *the matter of the mercy-seat* (margin) shall ye make the cherubim on the two ends thereof." This reminds us that "both He that sanctifieth and they which are sanctified are one;" that we are made partakers of the Divine nature; that we are accepted, blest, risen, and seated in the heavenlies in the person of our Lord.

4. **In the throne** (Rev. iv. 6, and v. 6, R.V.). We cannot do better than quote the words of another on this point: "These living ones not only stand before the throne and serve, as redeemed unto God by the blood of the Lamb; they are one with the Lamb in the midst of the throne, 'members of His body, of His flesh, and of His bones,' raised up together and made to sit together in Him and with Him in the heavens. For when God 'raised Him up from the dead, and set Him on His own right hand in the heavenlies,' He 'gave Him to be Head over all things to the Church, which is His body, the fulness of Him that filleth all in all.'"

50. CHILDREN OF GOD

1. We are children of God **instrumentally,** by faith in Christ. "Ye are all the children of God by faith in Christ Jesus" (Gal. iii. 26).

2. We are children of God by **birth,** as to our right. "As many as received Him, to them gave He power to become the sons of God" (John i. 12, 13).

3. We are children of God by **acknowledgment,** for He acknowledges us as such. "We should be called children of God, and such we are" (1. John iii. 1, R.V.).

4. We are children of God by **adoption,** as to our security. "Having predestinated us unto the adoption of children" (Eph. i. 5).

5. We are children of God **consciously,** because He, by the Spirit in the Word, tells us so. "Because ye are sons, God hath sent forth the Spirit of His Son into your hearts, crying, Abba, Father" (Galatians iv. 6).

6. We are children of God **manifestly** before the world, as we walk in practical obedience to Him. "As obedient children, not fashioning yourselves according to the former lusts in your ignorance" (1. Peter i. 14-17).

7. We are children of God in **reality**, as we are led by the Spirit. "As many as are led by the Spirit of God, they are the sons of God" (Rom. viii. 14).

51. CLEAVING TO CHRIST

ACTS xi. 23

THE following seven ways will indicate how we can cleave to Christ:—

1. By prayerful dependence upon Him (Phil. iv. 6).
2. By being taught by Him (Matt. xi. 29).
3. By ready response to His word (John xiv. 21).
4. By whole-hearted surrender to Him (Rom. xii. 1).
5. By separation from the ungodly (II. Cor. vi. 17).
6. By living a life of faith upon Him (Gal. ii. 20).
7. By waiting for Him (I. Thess. i. 10).

52. CHRIST'S ABILITY

1. HE is **able to establish** us according to the Gospel. "That is *able* to stablish you according to my gospel" (Rom. xvi. 25).

2. He is **able to supply** our every conceivable and inconceivable need. "That is *able* to do exceeding abundantly above all that we ask or think" (Eph. iii. 20).

3. He is **able to succour** the tempted under every condition of temptation. "He is *able* to succour them that are tempted" (Hebrews ii. 18).

4. He is **able to save** to the uttermost. "Wherefore He is *able* also to save them to the uttermost" (Heb. vii. 25).

5. He is **able to guard** from stumbling. "That is *able* to guard you from stumbling" (Jude 24, R.V.).

6. He is **able to make** us sufficient in service. "Who also made us *sufficient* as ministers of a new covenant" (II. Cor. iii. 6, R.V.).

7. He is **able to subject** all things to Himself. "He is *able* even to subdue all things unto Himself" (Phil. iii. 21).

53. CHRIST AND THE CHILDREN

MATTHEW xviii. 1-14

"IT is not the will of your Father in heaven that one of these little ones should perish" (Matt. xviii. 14).

The expression, "The kingdom of heaven," is far more comprehensive than "The Church of God." There are many that are in the kingdom who are not in the Church, while all who are in the Church are in the kingdom. The Church has to do with heavenly things (Eph. ii. 6; Phil. iii. 20). The kingdom has to do with earthly things (Matt. x. 7). The Church is made up of those who are the members of Christ's body (Eph. i. 23). The kingdom is composed of those who *profess* to be the followers of Christ.

1. **Conversion is the door of the Kingdom** (verse 3). Conversion means a turning round. In the Biblical sense conversion means a turning to God, which necessitates a turning from that which has occupied His place before (1. Thess. i. 9). This is far more than a change of opinion or religious views. "God forbid that I should change my religion!" said an ignorant old woman, when she was exhorted to leave her self-righteousness and to believe in Christ. "You object to change your religion," said the friend who was speaking to her, "but has your religion changed you?"

2. **Humility is the law of the Kingdom** (verse 4). As there are certain great laws in the realm of nature which govern this earth, such as the law of gravitation, so there are certain laws in the kingdom of heaven, and chiefest among them is humility. Humility is the grace that holds all the other graces together. "The Greek word imports that humility is the ribbon or string that ties together all those precious pearls, the rest of the graces. If this string breaks they are all scattered." Augustine was once asked, "What is the first article in the Christian religion?" and he replied, "Humility." "What is the second?" "Humility." "And what is the third?" And again he answered, "Humility." Humility is the *evidence* that we have learnt of Christ (Matt. xi. 29). Humility is the *attitude* to receive more grace (Jas. iv. 6). Humility is the *garment* that the Lord loves to see us wear (1. Peter v. 5). Humility is the *place* where God can reach us to exalt us (Luke xviii. 14).

3. **Doing good to others is the evidence of being in the Kingdom** (verse 5). To receive one of the little ones, is to receive Christ Himself; that is, anything that is done for Christ's sake to one of the little ones, Christ reckons it as being done to Himself. What an incentive this should be to do good to others! For there is nothing done as to the Lord, which escapes His notice. A cup of cold water given (Matt. x. 42), a prophet received (Matt. x. 41), a garment made (Acts ix. 39), alms given (Acts x. 4), a sick one visited (Matt. xxv. 36), a hungry one supplied (Matt. xxv. 35), and an offering sent (Phil. iv. 18), will always be noted by Christ, and shall surely be rewarded.

4. **Offences, the excluder from the Kingdom** (verses 6-10). The word rendered "*offence*" in verse 7, is translated "*fall*" in Romans xiv. 13, and "*stumbling-block*" in Rev. ii. 14. Its meaning is evident if we take the latter Scripture. As Balaam taught Balak to cast a stumbling-block in the way of Israel (Num. xxv.), in causing them to fall by the sin into which he led them, so to cast an offence in the way of a child is to cause it to sin, and he who does so has the "woe" of Christ resting upon him.

5. **Angelic ministry, the privilege of the Kingdom** (verse 10). Children are the special regard of heaven, in that they have the angels to watch over them, and to care for them, who evidently give a report of all that men do in relation to them.

6. **Salvation, the purport of the Kingdom** (verses 11-13). Even the children are "lost," hence, the needs be, that the Son of Man should come and save them. All have sinned (Rom. iii. 23), all have gone astray (Isaiah liii. 6), all are under sin (Gal. iii. 22), and, therefore, all are lost; but God sent His Son to save (Jno. iii. 17), Christ has come to save (I. Tim. i. 15), He died to bring us to God (I. Pet. iii. 18), He has made peace by the blood of His cross (Col. i. 20), and receiving Christ as our Saviour we are "saved" (Eph. ii. 5), made new creatures in Christ Jesus (II. Cor. v. 17), and become the children of God (John i. 12).

The word "*save*," in verse 11, is translated "*healed*" in Mark v. 23; "*made whole*," in Mark v. 34; "*do well*," in John xi. 12; and "*preserve*" in II. Tim. iv. 18. Sin is a disease; therefore, Christ heals us. Sin has broken us; therefore, Christ makes us whole by re-making us. Sin made us do ill; therefore, Christ makes us do well. Sin made us perverse in self-doing, Christ preserves us by His doing.

7. **Love is the basis of the Kingdom** (verse 14). God's will is our welfare. He could never desire that any should perish. This is plainly stated by Christ in John iii. 16. But, on the other hand, there is a possibility of even one of the little ones perishing, if he lives in the ways of sin and self. Love's provision for all is salvation; well for all if they accept the provision.

54. CHRIST ABOVE THE BELIEVER

1. As the **Finisher** of His work on our behalf. "After He had offered one sacrifice for sins for ever, sat down" (Heb. x. 12).

2. As the **Conqueror** over His and our enemies. "He might destroy him" (Heb. ii. 14).

3. As our **High Priest**, to represent. "To appear in the presence of God for us" (Heb. ix. 24).

4. As our **Advocate**, to plead. "We have an Advocate" (I. John ii. 1).

5. As the **Firstfruits** of the harvest. "Christ the Firstfruits" (I. Cor. xv. 23).

6. As the **Sun** to warm. "The Lord God is a Sun" (Ps. lxxxiv. 11).

7. As the **Shield**, to protect. "I am thy Shield" (Gen. xv. 1).

55. CHRIST AS THE OPENER AND SHUTTER

"HE that openeth, and no man shutteth" (Rev. iii. 7).

1. Christ, as the **Convincer of sins, opens our eyes to see ourselves.** "I the Lord have called Thee (Christ) in righteousness, and will hold Thine hand, and will keep Thee, and give Thee for a

covenant of the people, for a light of the Gentiles, to *open the blind eyes*" (Isaiah xlii. 6, 7).

2. **Christ as the Deliverer from sin: He opened the prison-house of sin and gave us liberty.** The first time that Christ preached in the Synagogue at Nazareth, He opened the book or scroll of the Scriptures, and turned to the place having reference to Himself as the Deliverer, and said, "The Spirit of the Lord is upon Me, because He hath anointed Me to preach the Gospel to the poor; He hath sent Me to heal the broken-hearted, to preach deliverance to the captives" (Luke iv. 18). As He delivered Israel out of the hand of Pharaoh, so He has delivered us out of the power of the god of this world. As He delivered Peter out of prison, so He has delivered us out of the prison-house of sin, and brought us into the glorious liberty of the Gospel.

3. **He opens the heart to receive Himself as the possessor.** We read in Acts xvi. 14, how He opened Lydia's heart. Again our Lord says, "Behold I stand at the door and knock; if any man hear My voice, and open the door, I will come in to him and sup with him, and he with Me" (Rev. iii. 20).

4. **He opens our understanding by opening the Scriptures to us, as the Teacher.** When Christ appeared to His disciples after His resurrection, in the upper room, we read that "He opened their understanding, that they might understand the Scriptures." Also the confession of the two disciples who were on their way to Emmaus was, "Did not our heart burn within us while He talked with us by the way, and while He opened to us the Scriptures?" (Luke xxiv. 32, 45).

5. **He has opened the sources of heaven for our supply.** "He opened the rock and the waters gushed out" (Psalm cv. 41); "Thou openest Thy hand, they are filled with good" (Psalm civ. 28).

56. CHRIST AS THE POSSESSOR OF THE KEY OF DAVID

"HE that hath the key of David. He that openeth, and no man shutteth; and shutteth, and no man openeth" (Rev. iii. 7).

"The Key of David." The key represents power, authority, office.

A person who has the key can unlock the door, and thus reveal what is in the room. Christ has power to show what sin has done. Sin is like Ehud slaying Eglon, king of Moab; after Ehud had slain the king, he shut the door and escaped (Judges iii. 23); sin has slain us, and naturally we are dead in trespasses and sins.

Christ is the Revealer of the Father. He had to say to the lawyers when here on earth, "Ye have taken away the key of knowledge: ye entered not in yourselves, and them that were entering in, ye hindered." But it was not, and is not so with Christ. He was faithful in speaking out the Father's words, and instead of hindering, He has laid down His life for us, and opened up a new and living way into the Father's presence.

A person who has the key has the power to admit into the house or to let out. Christ says, "I have the keys of hell (hades) and the grave" (Rev. i. 18). Satan seems to have had the keys before Christ died. We have a picture given to us of the state of things in Luke xi. 21, 22. Satan had the keys—the authority over the unseen world—before Christ came, but Christ was manifest to destroy the works of the devil.

A person who has the key of the house has authority over the house, and hence a right to enter into all the rooms. Christ has authority over His Church, for we are all His house.

There are two words rendered "power" in the New Testament, one meaning strength, and the other authority.

In reference to the past. "I have power (authority) to lay it (life) down, and I have power (authority) to take it again. This commandment have I received from My Father." Christ was sent by the Father to die. He had His authority from His Father for all that He did; hence when Pilate boasted of the authority he had, and said to Him, "Knowest thou not that I have power (authority) to crucify Thee, and have power (authority) to release Thee?" Christ replied, "Thou couldest have no power (authority) at all against Me except it were given thee from above" (John xix. 10, 11).

In reference to the present. Christ is the Head of all principality and authority (Col. ii. 10), and because He is such, He has authority to make those who believe in Him children of God, for "As many as received Him, to them gave He power (authority) to become the children of God" (John i. 12). Yea, all authority in heaven and on earth has been given to Him, as He says, "All power (authority) is given unto Me in heaven and on earth" (Matt. xxviii. 18), and that was the reason He gave His disciples for sending them forth to preach the Gospel and make disciples.

In reference to the future. Christ having the key of David, has reference to the fact that He is yet to reign over the House of David (see Psalm cxxxii. 11; Acts ii. 30; Isaiah ix. 6, 7; Ezek. xxxiv. 23, 24; xxxvii. 24, 25; Luke i. 32, 33). Christ shall literally stand upon the Mount of Olives, overcome the enemies of Israel, gather out everything that offends, and reign over this earth one thousand years.

57. CHRIST AS THE SON OF MAN

A SEVENFOLD view given to us of Christ as the Son of Man.

1. As the Son of Man He is seen in His **suffering** (Matthew xvii. 12, 22; xx. 18, 19; xxvi. 2, 24, 45).
2. In His **poverty** (Matt. viii. 20).
3. In His **authority** (ix. 6; xii. 8; xiii. 41; xvi. 13).
4. In His **work** (xiii. 37; xviii. 11).
5. In His **death** (xii. 40).
6. In His **resurrection** (xvii. 9).

7. In His **coming glory** (xvi. 27, 28; xix. 28; xxiv. 27, 30, 37, 44; xxv. 13, 31; xxvi. 64).

When Christ is spoken of as the "Son of Man" it is always in relation to the earth. He is never once said to be such in the epistles in relation to the Church, for the Church has to do with heaven, and not earth. Not once in the epistles is He said to be the Son of Man. Once He is said to be the Son of Man in the Acts (vii. 56), and twice in the Revelation (Rev. i. 13; xiv. 14).

58. CHRIST BEFORE THE BELIEVER

1. As the **Object** of faith. "Looking unto Jesus the Author and Finisher of our faith" (Heb. xii. 2).

2. As the **Light,** to direct. "He that followeth Me shall not walk in darkness" (John viii. 12).

3. As the **Lord,** to obey. "If I then, your Lord and Master, have washed your feet; ye also ought to wash one another's feet" (John xiii. 14).

4. As the **Shepherd,** to follow. "My sheep hear My voice and I know them and they follow Me" (John x. 27).

5. As the **Master,** to serve. "Ye call Me Master and Lord: and ye say well; for so I am" (John xiii. 13).

6. As the **Prize,** to win. "For whom I have suffered the loss of all things, . . . that I may win Christ" (Phil. iii. 8-14).

7. As the **Goal,** to reach. "Know ye not that they which run in a race run all, but one receiveth the prize? So run, that ye may obtain" (1. Cor. ix. 24).

59. CHRIST BEHIND THE BELIEVER

1. As the **Suffering One** for us. "Once . . . He appeared to put away sin" (Heb. ix. 26).

2. As the **Pillar of fire,** for light and protection. "It was a cloud and darkness to them, but it gave light by night to these" (Ex. xiv. 20).

3. As the **Voice, to direct.** "Thine ears shall hear a word behind thee, saying, this is the way" (Isaiah xxx. 21).

4. As the **Beloved, to encourage.** "He looketh forth at the windows, shewing Himself" (Solomon's Song ii. 9).

5. As the **Goodness and mercy, to follow.** "Surely goodness and mercy shall follow me all the days of my life" (Psalm xxiii. 6).

6. As the **Lord, to reveal.** "I heard a voice behind me" (Rev. i. 10).

7. As our **Rereward, for separation** between us and the world. "The God of Israel will be your Rereward" (Isaiah lii. 12).

60. CHRIST BENEATH THE BELIEVER

1. As the **Foundation** on whom we are built. "For other Foundation can no man lay" (1. Cor. iii. 11).

2. As the **Way** to walk in. "I am the Way" (John xiv. 6).

3. As the **Shoes** of Peace, to protect. "Your feet shod with the preparation of the Gospel of peace" (Eph. vi. 15).

4. As the **Arms** to carry. "Underneath are the everlasting arms" (Deut. xxxiii. 27).

5. As the **Shoulders** to bear. "Layeth it on His shoulders" (Luke xv. 5).

6. As the **Bosom** to rest in. "Which also leaned on His breast" (John xxi. 20).

7. As the **Staff** to support. "Thy rod and Thy staff" (Psalm xxiii. 4).

61. CHRIST BESIDE THE BELIEVER

1. As the **Strength,** to uphold. "I will uphold thee with the right hand of My righteousness" (Isaiah xli. 10).

2. As the **Companion,** for fellowship. "Did not our heart burn within us, while He talked with us by the way" (Luke xxiv. 32).

3. As the **Friend** to counsel. "The sweetness of man's friend by hearty counsel" (Prov. xxvii. 9).

4. As the **Guide,** to direct. "When He, the Spirit of Truth, is come, He will guide you into all truth" (John xvi. 13).

5. As the **High Priest,** to succour. "We have not an High Priest which cannot be touched with the feeling of our infirmities" (Hebrews iv. 15).

6. As the **Comforter,** to cheer. "He shall give you another Comforter, that He may abide with you for ever" (John xiv. 16).

7. As the **Teacher,** to teach. "He shall teach you all things, and bring all things to your remembrance" (John xiv. 26).

62. CHRIST FOR US

Different characters in which Christ appears for us in Heb. ix. & x.

1. As the **Propitiation,** to atone (Heb. ix. 12).
2. As the **Purifier,** to cleanse (ix. 14).
3. As the **Mediator,** to act (ix. 15).
4. As the **Priest,** to represent (ix. 24).
5. As the **Sin-Remover,** to bless (ix. 26).
6. As the **Substitute,** to suffer (ix. 28).
7. As the **Saviour,** to deliver (ix. 28).

8. As the **Willing One** in obedience (x. 5-9).
9. As the **Sanctifier,** to separate (x. 10).
10. As the **Sin-offering,** to save (x. 11, 12).
11. As the **Exalted Man** in glory (x. 12).
12. As the **Expectant One,** to triumph (x. 13).
13. As the **Perfecter** of His people (x. 14).
14. As the **Fore-runner,** to procure (x. 19, 20).
15. As the **High Priest,** to represent (x. 21).

63. CHRIST'S GLORY

JOHN ii. 11

As the first ray of the morning sun is the harbinger of the sunshine of the day, so this first miracle was the forerunner of the many wondrous deeds that Christ was about to perform.

There are many rays in the sun of Christ's glory:—

1. The **moral** glory of His **life** proclaims the **spotlessness** of His **holiness** (John i. 14).

2. The **majestic** glory of His **person** speaks forth the **excellence** of His **worth** (II. Peter i. 17).

3. The **mysterious** glory of His **Deity** tells out the **wonder** of His **Godhead** (Psalm xxiv. 7, 10; Heb. i. 3).

4. The **munificent** glory of His **grace** reminds us of the **greatness** of His **mercy** (Eph. i. 6).

5. The **many-sided** glory of His **truth** declares the **immutability** of its **infallibility** (Psalm cviii. 4, 5).

6. The **marvellous** glory of His **Gospel** tells out the **sufficiency** of His **atonement** (II. Cor. iv. 6).

7. The **mighty** glory of His **miracles** speaks of the **strength** of His **power** (Eph. iii. 16, 19).

64. CHRIST IN A SEVENFOLD CHARACTER

CHRIST is seen in seven characters in Luke ii. 25-34.

1. **Consolation of Israel** (verse 25). Christ in this character is One who is alongside to encourage and comfort.

An old Christian, as he was lying on what proved to be his death-bed, said

"My soul most surely prizes
The sin atoning Lamb;
Thence all my hope arises,
Unworthy though I am."

2. **Lord's Christ** (verse 26). Jesus as the "Christ" signifies God's Anointed (John i. 41, margin). Jesus being anointed with

the Holy Spirit was the evidence that He was the Sent of God (Acts x. 38), and the Baptizer with the Holy Spirit (John i. 32, 33).

3. **Jesus** (verse 27). The name "Jesus" means "Saviour," and is always associated with Him in His humiliation, as is illustrated in His being circumcised. Godet says upon the presentation of Christ in the Temple, "After the circumcision there were two other rites to observe. One concerned the mother. Levitically unclean for eight days after the birth of a son, and for fourteen days after that of a daughter, the Israelitish mother, after a seclusion of thirty-three days in the first case, and of double this time in the second, had to offer in the Temple a sacrifice of purification (Lev. xii.). The other rite had reference to the child; when it was the firstborn it had to be redeemed by a sum of money from consecration to the service of God and the sanctuary. In fact, the tribe of Levi had been chosen for this office simply to take the place of the firstborn males of all the families of Israel; and in order to keep alive a feeling of His rights in the hearts of the people, God had fixed a ransom to be paid for every firstborn male. It was five shekels, or, reckoning the shekel at 2s. 4d., nearly 12s. (Ex. xiii. 2; Num. viii. 16; xviii. 15). Verses 22 and 23 refer to the ransom of the child, verse 24 to Mary's sacrifice.

4. **Salvation** (verse 30). Salvation is here personified. It is well to let all our blessings resolve themselves into Christ, as He Himself said when He went into the house of Zaccheus, "To-day is salvation come to thy house" (Luke xix. 9).

5. **Light** (verse 32). He is Light to discover evil *to* us: He is Light to remove the consequence of evil *from* us, through cleansing by His blood; and He is Light in showing us the path in which to walk.

6. **Glory of Thy people Israel** (verse 32). Israel, alas! would have none of Him; hence they are wanting in glory, but when they shall look upon Him whom they have pierced, and receive Him as their Messiah, then Christ shall be their glory indeed.

7. **Sign** (verse 34). Christ is the Rise or Fall of every being. They who speak against Him shall find He is opposed to them, and a Sign of their eternal condemnation.

65. CHRIST IN ISAIAH LII. AND LIII

1. **The Prudent Servant.** "My Servant shall deal prudently" (lii. 13).

2. **The Marred Man.** "His visage was so marred" (lii. 14).

3. **The Kingly Silencer.** "The kings shall shut their mouths at Him" (lii. 15).

4. **The Rejected Messiah.** "Who hath believed our report?" (liii. 1).

5. **The Arm of Jehovah.** "To whom is the Arm of the Lord revealed?" (liii. 1).

6. **A Tender Plant.** "He shall grow up before Him as a Tender Plant" (liii. 2).

7. **Independent Root.** "As a Root out of a dry ground" (liii. 2).

8. **The Uncomely Saviour.** "He hath no form nor comeliness" (liii. 2).

9. **The Rejected King.** "He is despised and rejected of men" (liii. 3).

10. **A Man of Sorrows.** "A Man of sorrows and acquainted with grief" (liii. 3).

11. **Companion of Grief.** "Surely He hath borne our griefs" (liii. 4).

12. **The Unesteemed One.** "Yet we did esteem Him stricken, smitten of God, and afflicted" (liii. 4).

13. **The Divine Substitute.** "The chastisement of our peace was upon Him" (liii. 5).

14. **The Burden-bearer.** "The Lord hath laid on Him the iniquity of us all" (liii. 6).

15. **The Afflicted Christ.** "He was oppressed and He was afflicted" (liii. 7).

16. **The Dumb Sufferer.** "He opened not His mouth" (liii. 7).

17. **The Severed Branch.** "He was cut off out of the land of the living" (liii. 8).

18. **The Stricken Shepherd.** "For the transgression of My people was He stricken" (liii. 8).

19. **The Seeming Felon.** "He made His grave with the wicked" (liii. 9).

20. **The Holy Lord.** "He had done no violence, neither was any deceit in His mouth" (liii. 9).

21. **The Sin-offering.** "Thou shalt make His soul an offering for sin" (liii. 10).

22. **The Prosperous Servant.** "And the pleasure of the Lord shall prosper in His hand" (liii. 10).

23. **The Satisfied Redeemer.** "He shall see of the travail of His soul, and be satisfied" (liii. 11).

24. **The Righteous Mediator.** "My righteous Servant shall justify many" (liii. 11).

25. **The Rewarded Jesus.** "Therefore will I divide Him a portion with the great" (liii. 12).

26. **The Conquering Hero.** "He shall divide the spoil with the strong" (liii. 12).

27. **The Drink Offering.** "He hath poured out His soul unto death" (liii. 12).

28. **The Interceding Priest.** "Made intercession for the transgressors" (liii. 12).

66. "CHRIST JESUS" IN PHILIPPIANS

1. "**Saints** in *Christ Jesus*" (i. 1). Our standing.
2. "Let this **mind** be in you which was also in *Christ Jesus*" (ii. 5). Our example.
3. "**Rejoice** in *Christ Jesus*" (iii. 3). Our rejoicing.
4. "**Apprehended** of *Christ Jesus*" (iii. 12). Our aim.
5. "**High calling** of God in *Christ Jesus*" (iii. 14). Our goal.
6. "**Peace** of God keep your hearts and minds through *Christ Jesus*" (iv. 7). Our rest.
7. **Need** supplied according to God's "riches in glory by *Christ Jesus*" (iv. 19). Our supply.

67. CHRIST NEEDS US

Christ needs His people, now in this life, to accomplish His purposes.

He needs our *lips* to preach His Gospel, as He told His disciples (Matt. xxviii. 19).

He needs our *hearts* to perfume with His presence (Eph. iii. 17), as He needed the tabernacle of old (Ex. xxv. 8).

He needs our *company* for fellowship, as may be gathered from His talk and walk with the two disciples who were journeying to Emmaus (Luke xxiv. 15).

He needs our *ear* to reveal to us. His secrets, as He did in the case of Abram regarding Sodom (Gen. xviii. 17).

He needs our *hands* to minister to the needs of others, as may be gathered from Matt. xxv. 34-37.

He needs our *love* to gladden Him, as is illustrated in His regard and pleasure in Mary anointing Him with the precious ointment (John xii. 3-7).

He needs our *obedience* to glorify Him, as is shown in His commendation of Job to the devil (Job i. 8).

He needs our *wills*, to mould them, as is plainly expressed in His invitation to take His yoke upon us (Matt. xi. 29).

He needs our *talents* to speak for Him, as is represented in His appreciation of the workmen of the tabernacle (Ex. xxxi. 2, 3).

He needs our *life* to reproduce His own, as it may be observed from the apostle's words in Gal. ii. 20.

He needs our *praise* to honour Him, as He clearly states in His words to the thankful Samaritan leper (Luke xvii. 17).

He needs our *whole being*, spirit, soul, and body, to sanctify, that like the temple of old, "every whit may utter His glory" (Psalm xxix. 9, M.).

Our need is met, as we meet the need of Christ. The ass's colt has been honoured for all time in carrying Christ into Jerusalem. In like manner, those who honour God are honoured by Him (Prov. iv. 8); those who give to God, receive from God (Luke vi. 38); those who yield to God, He yields Himself to them (Rom. vi. 13, 14); those who obey God, have the power of God (Acts v. 32); and those who endure for God have a crown of righteousness as a reward (II. Tim. iv. 7, 8).

69. CHRIST OCCUPIED FOR US

THE activities of the Lord Jesus, as He is occupied in His present service, is a fruitful subject. Fruitful in more ways than one. It is fruitful because it reminds us of His love in His present ministry for us; and of our love to Him, which should be expressed in a similar way to His love to us.

1. His **heart** is occupied in His loving sympathy for us, as our **Faithful Friend.** "He groaned in spirit and was troubled . . . . behold how He loved him" (John xi. 33, 36).

2. His **mind** is occupied in His constant thought of us, as our **Divine Lover.** "He thinketh upon me" (Psalm xl. 17).

3. His **eyes** are occupied in His watchful care over us, as our **Vigilant Shepherd.** "Behold He that keepeth Israel shall neither slumber nor sleep" (Psalm cxxi. 4).

4. His **hands** are occupied in His untiring labour for us, as our **Unfailing Strength.** "I will uphold thee with the right hand of My righteousness" (Isaiah xli. 10).

5. His **ears** are occupied in His unceasing attention to us, as our **Gracious Lord.** "His ears are open unto their cry" (Ps. xxxiv. 15).

6. His **lips** are occupied in His earnest pleading for us, as our **Great High Priest.** "He ever liveth to make intercession for them" (Hebrews vii. 25).

7. His **feet** are occupied in His ministry for us, as our **Sustaining Companion** (Luke xxiv. 15).

70. CHRIST, OUR EXAMPLE

"Do likewise" (Judges vii. 17).

GIDEON bids his men to look to him and to act as he acts, so that there may be united action. When he blew his trumpet they were to blow theirs; when he brake his pitcher they were to break theirs; and when he shouted they were to shout too. The Lord Jesus also says to His followers, "Look on Me and do likewise."

1. He bids us **love** as He loves (John xiii. 34).

2. He calls us to **suffer** wrongfully as He suffered (1. Pet. ii. 20-23).

3. He tells us to go out in **service**, as He went (John xx. 21).

4. He directs us to **deny** ourselves as He denied Himself (John xii. 24, 25).

5. He commands us to **minister** to each other as He ministers to us (John xiii. 14, 15).

6. He calls us to be **humble**, as He was (Phil. ii. 5-8).

7. He demands that we should **walk** as He walked (1. John ii. 6).

71. CHRIST, OUR HIDING PLACE

1. He is a **Safe** Hiding Place. "A Covert from the tempest" (Isaiah xxxii. 2). "Thou shalt hide them in the secret of Thy presence from the pride of man; Thou shalt keep them secretly in a pavilion from the strife of tongues" (Psalm xxxi. 20).

Note the three "froms" in the above verses as showing that from which the Lord saves.

2. He is a **Sure** Hiding Place. "In the time of trouble He shall hide me in His pavilion; in the *secret* * of His tabernacle shall He hide me" (Psalm xxvii. 5). Note the two "*Shalls*." There is no uncertainty.

3. He is a **Secret** Hiding Place. "Thou art my *Hiding Place;* Thou shalt preserve from trouble" (Psalm xxxii. 7). The word "Hiding" in the above is rendered "Secret" in some of the Scriptures before us, and is so given in 1. Samuel xix. 2, which may be taken as an illustration.

4. He is a **Comfortable** Hiding Place. "I will abide in Thy tabernacle for ever; I will trust in the *covert* of Thy wings" (Psalm lxi. 4). The young birds find the covert of the mother bird's wings a place of comfort.

5. He is a **Strong** Hiding Place. "He that dwelleth in the *secret place* of the Most High, shall abide under the shadow of the Almighty (Psalm xci. 1). Note, it is the "*Almighty*" who is the Shelterer.

6. He is a **Secure** Hiding Place. "Thou art my *Hiding Place* and my Shield; I hope in Thy Word" (Psalm cxix. 114). He assures us in His Word what He is, hence our security.

7. He is a **Communing** Hiding Place. "O, my dove, thou art in the clefts of the rock, in the *secret places* of the stairs, let me see thy countenance, let me hear thy voice," &c. (Cant. ii. 14). The Lord is not a cold hard rock in which we hide; He is a living Person, with whom we hold converse.

---

* The *words in the texts in italics* are so given to indicate that in the Hebrew they are one and the same.

72. CHRIST, OUR LIFE

THERE are many words and phrases that are peculiar to John; for instance, the double "verily," "excepts," and "true" things. John's Gospel is peculiar in itself. Matthew shows us Christ as "King," Mark as the "Servant," Luke as the "Man," and John as the "Life." This may be traced right through John.

Chapter i. The **Source** of life (verse 4).
,, ii. The **Glory** of life (verse 11).
,, iii. The **Power** of life (verse 5).
,, iv. The **Gift** of life (verse 14).
,, v. The **Assurance** of life (verse 24).
,, vi. The **Bread** of life (verse 48).
,, vii. The **Blessings** of life (verse 38).
,, viii. The **Liberty** of life (verse 36).
,, ix. The **Testimony** of life (verse 37).
,, x. The **Security** of life (verse 28).
,, xi. The **Energy** of life (verse 43).
,, xii. The **Union** of life (verse 24).
,, xiii. The **Holiness** of life (verse 13-15).
,, xiv. The **Hope** of life (verse 3).
,, xv. The **Fruitfulness** of life (verse 4).
,, xvi. The **Spirit** of life (verse 13).
,, xvii. The **Abode** of life (verse 24).
,, xviii. The **Rejection** of life (verse 40).
,, xix. The **Humility** of life (verse 17).
,, xx. The **Peace** of life (verse 19).
,, xxi. The **Instructions** of life (verse 15).

73. CHRIST, OUR OBJECT

1. HE is the Object of God's **Counsels.** "I was daily His delight" (Prov. viii. 30).

2. He is the Object of the **Scriptures.** "Search the Scriptures . . . . and they are they which testify of Me" (John v. 39).

3. He is the Object of our **Faith.** "Behold the Lamb of God" (John i. 29, 36).

4. He is the Object of our **Worship.** "And he worshipped Him" (John ix. 38).

5. He is the Object of our **Life.** "Should not henceforth live unto themselves, but unto Him" (II. Cor. v. 15).

6. He is the Object of our **Imitation.** "Christ also suffered for us, leaving us an Example" (I. Peter ii. 21).

7. He is the Object of our **Hope.** "Lord Jesus Christ, which is our Hope" (I. Tim. i. 1).

74. CHRIST, OUR SUBSTITUTE

WE must know Christ "for us" as our Substitute, before we can know Christ "in us" as our Strength, and before we can be with Him in the glory.

1. Christ is the **God-appointed** Substitute (Romans v. 8).

2. Christ is the **God-approved** Substitute (Eph. v. 2).

3. Christ is the **God-satisfying** Substitute (II. Corinthians v. 21; Galatians iii. 13).

4. Christ is the **Protecting** Substitute from Divine wrath (I. Cor. v. 7).

5. Christ, as our Substitute, **places** us in an **unparalleled position** (I. Thessalonians v. 9, 10).

6. As our Substitute, Christ has **procured** for us **unlimited blessings** (Romans viii. 32).

7. Christ, in being our Substitute, had a **practical** end in view (Titus ii. 14; I. John iii. 16; I. Peter ii. 20, 21; I. Peter iv. 1).

In all the above Scriptures the words "*for us*" will be found.

75. CHRIST'S PEACEFUL REIGN

ISAIAH xi. 1-9

THE term "The kingdom of God" is like a majestic river which is made up of three tributary rivers, hence the three rivers make the one what it is, in its flow and force. There is the kingdom of grace, or the spiritual realm into which the believer in Christ is introduced (Col. i. 13); there is the kingdom of glory, or the millennial reign of Christ over the earth (Rev. v. 10); there is the kingdom of God, or the eternal government of the Father, Son, and Holy Spirit as the one God (I. Cor. xv. 24). In the first, "*Grace* reigns through righteousness unto eternal life" (Rom. v. 21); in the second, "A *King* shall reign in righteousness" (Isaiah xxxii. 1); and in the third, Righteousness shall *dwell* (II. Peter iii. 13).

Christ is now seated upon His Father's throne (Rev. iii. 21), but He will yet sit upon His own throne (Matt. xxv. 31). It is after His appearing in judgment with His saints, that Christ sets up His kingdom, as the Holy Spirit implies when He speaks of Christ's "appearing and kingdom" (II. Tim. iv. 1). His appearing first, and then His kingdom. There can be no millennium without the King. There is a time coming when the kingdoms of this world shall have become the kingdoms of the Lord and His Christ (Rev. xi. 15). It is also stated that at the end of the thousand years of Christ's millennial reign (Rev. xx. 4-6) He will give up the kingdom to His Father (I. Cor. xv. 24).

The Scriptures are occupied with two main facts, namely, Christ's sufferings and His glory (Luke xxiv. 26), and these two facts are like two mighty girders of a bridge, which are the main factors in the bridge, and to which the rest of the bridge is related. Thus, all truth is related to Christ's suffering and glory. Or, to change the figure, Christ's suffering and glory are the Jachin and Boaz, the supporting pillars of the great temple of truth (I. Kings vii. 21). Now, as Christ has actually and literally suffered and died, so He will as actually and as surely reign in glory, and on the earth where He was rejected and where He suffered.

In the points before us we have one or two intimations as to the character of Christ's Kingship.

1. **Royal King** (verse 1). He comes from the royal line of David, for He is to be a stem out of Jesse. Christ is the Son of Man as to His humanity; the Son of God as to His Deity; the Son of David as to His royalty. It is as the latter He is to sit on the throne of His father David (Luke i. 32; Ps. cxxxii. 11; Isa. ix. 6, 7).

2. **Regal King** (verse 2). Many an earthly king has been royal as to the place he occupied, but has not been attired in the regal robes of moral worth as far as his life was concerned. It is in this sense that I use the word "regal," for the regalia of moral and spiritual worth were ever seen in the life of Christ, and will be seen in Him as King, as is indicated in the sevenfold characteristic of the Holy Spirit resting upon Him.

3. **Regarding King.** The Revised Version of verse 3 reads, "His delight shall be in the fear of the Lord." As Christ delighted to do the will of God in His humiliation (Psalm xl. 8), so the same delight shall fill Him in His glory.

4. **Righteous King** (verses 4, 5). No unrighteousness shall be in Him, and no unrighteous action shall ever be done by Him. No bribe shall buy Him, and no action shall blind Him.

5. **Resolute King** (verse 4). He shall smite the wicked. Saul lost his kingdom through his hesitation to slay the enemy of God (I. Samuel xv. 22, 23), but with Christ there will be no hesitation, for resolutely and faithfully shall He put down the wicked one mentioned in II. Thess. ii. 8, and all who, like him, are guilty of self-will.

6. **Rest-giving King** (verses 6-8). The whole creation, which now groaneth and travaileth in pain, is to be delivered into the glorious liberty of the children of God (Romans viii. 21, 22). The animal creation is to share in the peace of the peaceful reign of Christ (Isaiah lxv. 25).

7. **Regenerating King** (verse 9). The earth, which has been cursed and blighted by sin, is to share in the blessing of Christ's rule. The time of regeneration (Matt. xix. 28), the time of the restoration of all things (Acts iii. 21, R.V.), is when Christ reigns in millennial glory. The presence of Christ is the great factor in this reign of peace. In like manner, as Christ is known now, and allowed to reign in our hearts, so we have peace.

76. CHRIST'S PERFECTION

CHRIST was perfect in all He was, in all He said, in all He did, and in all His life.

1. There was no rift in the lute of His character, for He did always the things which were pleasing to His Father (Matt. iii. 17).

2. There was no flaw in the devotion of His life, for He knew no sin (II. Cor. v. 21).

3. There was no fault in the consecration of His service, for He finished the work given Him to do (John xvii. 4).

4. There was no stain in the texture of His nature, for He was without sin (I. John iii. 5).

5. There was no alloy in the gold of His holiness, for He was the Holy One of God (Mark i. 24).

6. There was no spot in the sun of His testimony, for He did no sin (I. Peter ii. 22).

7. There was no want in the obedience of His love, for He was faithful to death (Phil. ii. 8).

77. CHRIST'S PRAYER IN GETHSEMANE

THE characteristics of the prayer of Christ are:—

1. It was a **lonely** prayer. He withdrew Himself about a stone's cast from His disciples, as He went to prayer (Luke xxii. 41).

2. It was a **humble** prayer. In Mark, we are told Christ "knelt," and in Matthew, that He fell upon His face. The attitude of His body in an indication of the posture of His spirit.

3. It was a **filial** prayer. He does not say here, as He did afterwards, "My God," &c., but "Abba Father." The former reminds of God's dealing in judgment with sin: the latter is the Father making known His will (Mark xiv. 36).

4. It was an **earnest** prayer (Luke xxii. 44; Heb. v. 7).

5. It was a **repeated** prayer. He used "the same words" (Matthew xxvi. 44).

6. It was a **persevering** prayer. He prayed three times (Matt. xxvi. 44).

7. It was a **resigned** prayer. "Not My will," &c. (Luke xxii. 42). "'My will, not Thine, be done,' turned Paradise into a desert; and 'Thy will, not Mine be done,' turned the desert into a Paradise."

8. It was an **answered** prayer. In Luke xxii. 43, we are told an angel came and strengthened Him.

78. CHRIST'S RESURRECTION

No one can over-estimate the importance of the truth of Christ's resurrection. If this be overthrown, Christianity is a farce, Christ is a liar, the apostles were deluded, the martyrs were deceived, the believer is in the darkness of despair, God is unknown, and our loved ones are for ever lost. As Dr. Kennedy says:—"Blot the resurrection out of the story of Christ, and you may as well blot out Christ Himself. Blot out Christ, and you may as well blot out God. For all our true conceptions of Him, and all our true affections towards Him, grow out of the filial relation to Him, to which Christ lovingly restores us. And 'God added to, or deducted from the sum of existence,' makes existence an altogether different thing from what it would otherwise be. Save us, by any means, from the conclusion of the sceptic, who could only see an 'empty heaven looking down upon a soul-less earth.'"

What light is to the earth, Christ's resurrection is to the believer.

1. **The risen Christ is Christ's attestation to the reality of His claims.** Again and again He said that He would rise again from the dead. After His transfiguration He told His disciples that He would die and rise again, but they did not understand Him, and we find them questioning among themselves as to what this rising from among the dead could mean (Matt. xvii. 9; Mark ix. 9-10). As Christ is journeying towards Jerusalem, He takes them apart, and seeks to impress upon them the same truth (Matt. xx. 19). And at the sepulchre the angels reminded the women of what He had told them (Luke xxiv. 7).

2. **The risen Christ is the Clue to the understanding of the Scripture.** When Mary Magdalene told Peter and John that the tomb of Christ was empty, they did not believe her, so they ran to the tomb to see for themselves. The Divine comment upon this is, "For as yet they knew not the Scripture, that He must rise from the dead" (John xx. 9). See John ii. 22; Acts ii. 24-32; Acts xiii. 32, 35.

3. **The risen Christ is the fulfilment of His own word as to the necessity of His resurrection to complete His atoning work.** After Peter's confession of faith as to the Person of Christ, at Cæsarea Philippi, we read that Christ began "to shew unto His disciples He must go unto Jerusalem," &c. (Matt. xvi. 21; Acts iii. 18).

4. **The risen Christ is the Channel of blessing** (Acts v. 30, 31; x. 40; xiii. 37, 38).

5. **The risen Christ is the Object of our faith** (Rom. x. 9; I. Peter i. 21).

6. **The risen Christ is the Assurance of our justification** (Romans iv. 25).

7. **The risen Christ is our Answer to every accusation** (Romans viii. 34).

8. **The risen Christ is put to the believer's account** (Rom. vi. 5; Col. ii. 12).

9. **The risen Christ is the Model, Aim, and End of the believer's life** (II. Cor. v. 15).

10. **The risen Christ is the ground of Christ's claim to the believer, and His protection of him** (Rom. xiv. 8, 9).

11. The risen Christ is the Pledge of our inheritance (I. Peter i. 3).

12. The risen Christ is the Earnest of our being glorified with Christ (Romans viii. 11).

13. The risen Christ is the guarantee that our loved ones, who have fallen asleep, shall be raised (I. Cor. xv. 20).

14. The risen Christ is God's bond that we shall see our loved ones again (I. Thess. iv. 14).

15. The risen Christ is the exhibition of God's power (Eph. i. 20).

16. The risen Christ is the worker's theme in testimony (Acts iii. 15, 16; iv. 10).

17. The risen Christ is our Commissioner for service (Gal. i. 1).

18. The risen Christ is the positive proof that God will judge the world in righteousness (Acts xvii. 31).

19. The risen Christ should be the desire of all our life (Phil. iii. 10).

79. CHRIST'S VOICE

1. **Powerful Voice.** "His voice as the sound of many waters" (Revelation i. 15).

2. **Convicting Voice.** "Heard a voice saying unto him, Saul, Saul, why persecutest thou Me?" (Acts ix. 4).

3. **Quickening Voice.** "He cried with a loud voice, Lazarus, come forth" (John xi. 43).

4. **Inviting Voice.** "If any man thirst let him come unto Me and drink" (John vii. 37).

5. **Comforting Voice.** "Jesus saith unto her, thy brother shall rise again" (John xi. 23).

6. **Guiding Voice.** "My sheep hear My voice . . . . and they follow Me" (John x. 27).

7. **Pleading Voice.** "If any man hear My voice" (Rev. iii. 20).

80. CHRIST, THE BREAD OF LIFE

JOHN vi. 27-35

AMONG the many "I Am's" of the Gospel of John, is the one that speaks of Christ as the Bread of Life. There are seven things that relate to Christ as the Bread of Life.

1. Christ is the **Sealed** Bread, as attesting His genuineness (ver. 27). In the East, bakers who were found selling bread that was not of good quality, were severely punished. In Turkey, not very long since, cheating bakers were nailed up by the ear; and in Persia they have

been roasted in their own ovens. The Oriental bakers are in the habit of stamping their name upon their bread, or, as they would say, "sealing it," as a measure of precaution, lest they should be made to suffer for the sins of their neighbours, and also as attesting its good quality. "The Talmudic word for baker is *nakhtom*, or *nakhtoma*, which has been connected with *khatham*, to seal." Christ was sealed by His Father, at His baptism, with the Holy Spirit, and His works afterwards by the Holy Spirit's power told out in unmistakable language that He was the Sealed of God (Acts x. 38).

2. Christ is the **Sent** Bread, as to the authority of His coming (vi. 32, 33). If there was one thing more than another that Christ affirmed again and again, it was, that He was sent from God to do a specific work. As proof of this, look through the Gospel of John, and mark the word "sent," which occurs over forty times.

3. Christ is the "**True** Bread," in contrast to everything that is false and fleeting (verse 32). He is the "True Light" (John i. 9), in contrast to the false lights of earth; He is the "True Vine" (John xv. 1), in contrast to Israel, who proved to be a false vine; and He is the "True Bread," because He is unlike the manna that fell in the wilderness, which only satisfied for a time, whilst He saves and satisfies for ever. Man-invented theories and pursuits are all false and misleading. Pleasure with its fascination, money with its glitter, honour with its applause, worldliness with its charm, lust with its seeming satisfaction, pride with its ambition, and self with its assertiveness, are all disappointing, delusive, and destructive. Christ alone is the "True Bethlehem" (House of Bread) where salvation and satisfaction are found (Ruth i. 19).

4. Christ is the **Living** Bread as to His enduringness (verse 35). Those who live upon Him partake of His life; and those who do not are spiritually dead. "There is a pathetic story which comes to us from the earlier explorers of Australia. There grows there a strange plant called the nardoo, bearing leaves like clover. The Britishers, Burke and Wills, who were making these explorations, in the failure of other food, followed the example of the natives, and began to eat the leaves and roots of the nardoo. It seemed to satisfy them; it seemed to fill them with a pleasant sense of comfort and repletion. But they grew weaker every day, and more emaciated; they were not hungry, for the plant seemed to satisfy. But all the effects of an unfulfilled hunger began to appear in them; their flesh wasted from their bones, their strength failed till they scarcely had the energy of an infant; they could not crawl on in their journey more than a mile or two a day. At last one of them perished of starvation; the other was rescued when in the last extremity. On analysis, it was discovered that the bread made of this plant lacked an element essential to the sustenance of a European. And so, even though they seemed fed, the explorers wasted away, and one of them died, because they were feeding on a sustenance inappropriate." In like manner, those who feed on anything else

than Christ will find that they have been deceived, and will enter into that state described as the "second death."

5. Christ must be the **Sought** Bread (verse 27). Christ rebukes the people who were following Him for the sake of the food they obtained, and urges them to labour for that food which is imperishable. Those who seek, have the promise that they shall surely find, but those who are listless and careless have no promise.

6. Christ must be the **Received** Bread (verse 29). To receive Christ is to believe in Him (John i. 12), even as the disciples received Him into the boat, and thus showed their confidence in Him, by placing themselves absolutely in His hands (John vi. 21).

7. Christ is the **Satisfying** Bread (verse 35). Fuller has well said, "The old Grecians that had fed altogether on acorns before, after bread came in amongst them they made no reckoning of their mast any more, but kept it only for swine. And leathern and iron money began to grow out of request amongst the Lacedemonians after gold and silver came into use. So, when a man hath once found the favour of God in his heart, and the love of God in Christ hath once lighted on it, and got assurance of it, he ceaseth then to be greedy of the world's trash, which is, in regard of it but dross or pebble stones to gold and diamonds, as mast to the best bread corn; yea, rather of far less worth or value to that, than either of these is to it."

81. CHRIST, THE EARNEST WORKER

(JOHN ix. 4)

CHRIST'S *authority* for working was because He was "sent;" His *model* in working was according to the "works of Him" who commissioned Him, and the *necessity* that was laid upon Him is seen in the "I must." If the following Scriptures are pondered, it will be seen how Christ viewed His life and death as an absolute necessity. Constantly Christ uses the term "*must*."

1. The must of **work** (Luke ii. 49; John ix. 4; x. 16).
2. The must of **walk** (Luke xiii. 33).
3. The must of **death** (John iii. 14; xii. 34).
4. The must of **preaching** (Luke iv. 43).
5. The must of **seeking** (John iv. 4).
6. The must of **resurrection** (John xx. 9).
7. The must of **increase** (John iii. 30).

82. CHRIST, THE LIGHT OF THE WORLD

(JOHN ix. 5)

THERE are two things, among the many, that light does. It reveals the wrong and makes known that which is right. These two features of light are abundantly illustrated in the life of Christ. As to the first, when the Pharisees brought the woman to Christ, He said to them, " He that is without sin among you, let him first cast a stone at her," and " being convicted by their own conscience," they all slunk out of His holy presence (John viii. 7, 9). And as to Christ's making known the good, the right, the true, no one can prayerfully ponder John iii. 16 without seeing the light of His love flashing out in its sevenfold perfection.

1. There is the **red** light of Christ's atonement in the *given Son* (Acts xx. 28).

2. There is the **blue** light of heaven in the "*God gave*" (II. Corinthians ix. 15).

3. There is the **yellow** light of heaven's glory in the "*everlasting life*" (Col. iii. 4).

4. There is the **green** light of faith in the "*believe*" (John iii. 36).

5. There is the **orange** light of safety in the "*shall not perish*" (John x. 28).

6. There is the **purple** light of the eternal state in the "*everlasting*" (I. Peter i. 3, 4).

7. There is the **white** light of the *effulgence of God* in the "*only begotten Son*" (Heb. i. 5).

83. CHRIST, THE NEEDY ONE

Does He who made all things need anything? No, in one sense, as we read in Acts xvii. 24, 25; but He became a needy One, as we shall see.

Christ was a needy Man when on earth.

1. He had no **home** in which to be born (Luke ii. 7).

2. No **place** to lay His head (Matt. viii. 20).

3. No **money** to pay the tax (Matt. xvii. 27).

4. No **comforter** in Gethsemane agony (Matt. xxvi. 40).

5. No **friend** to plead for Him when He was falsely accused (Mark xiv. 50).

6. No **God** to befriend Him when suffering for sin (Matt. xxvii. 46).

7. No **grave** of His own in which to be buried (Matt. xxvii. 60).

Christ became a needy Man that He might meet our need. "Though He was rich, yet for your sakes He became poor, that ye through His poverty might be rich" (II. Cor. viii. 9).

He had no home, that we might have an eternal inheritance (I. Peter i. 4).

He was poor, that we might have all spiritual blessing (Eph. i. 3).

He had no comforter, that we might have the Comforter (John xiv. 16).

He had no friend, that we might have an abiding Friend (Proverbs xvii. 17)

He was made sin, that we might become the righteousness of God (II. Cor. v. 21).

84. CHRIST, THE PROPHET

JESUS was recognised as the Prophet that Moses had spoken of and promised to Israel (Deut. xviii. 15-18).

P owerful	prophet	(Matt. xiii. 54).
R oyal	,,	(Matt. xvi. 16).
O mnipotent	,,	(Luke vii. 16).
P enetrating	,,	(John iv. 19).
H ealing	,,	(Mark v. 29).
E nlightening	,,	(John vii. 40).
T ruthful	,,	(John iii. 34).

85. CHRIST, THE TRUE ONE

1. HE is the True **Light,** to illuminate (John i. 9).
2. He is the True **Bread,** to satisfy (John vi. 32).
3. He is the True **Vine,** to fructify (John xv. 1).
4. He is the True **God,** to assure (I. John v. 20).
5. He is the True **Witness,** to speak (Rev. iii. 14).
6. He is the True **Judge,** to determine (Rev. xix. 11).

86. CHRIST, THE WAY

JACOB'S ladder is a type of Christ (John i. 51), the only Way between God and man. Christ is—

1. An **Opportune** Way, for the man in danger, even as the manslayer found the way to the city of refuge to be (Deut. xix. 3).
2. An **Open** Way, for He has removed the barrier of sin away, by the sacrifice of Himself (Heb. ix. 26).
3. An **Original** Way, for there never was such a way opened as Christ has made by His death (Heb. x. 20).
4. An **Omnipotent** Way, as they who walk in it find, for they are protected by the Saviour's presence and power (Isa. xxxv. 8, 9, margin).
5. The **Only** Way to God (John xiv. 6), blessing, salvation, and usefulness (John x. 9).

87. CHRIST WITHIN THE BELIEVER

1. As the **Life,** to live out. "I live; yet not I, but Christ liveth in me" (Gal. ii. 20).
2. As the **Power,** for walk and service. "I will dwell in them, and walk in them" (II. Cor. vi. 16).

3. As the **Source** of fruit-bearing. "Cannot bear fruit of itself except it abide in the vine" (John xv. 4).

4. As the **Word,** to teach. "Let the word of Christ dwell in you richly in all wisdom" (Col. iii. 16).

5. As the **Peace,** to rule. "Let the peace of God rule in your hearts" (Col. iii. 15).

6. As the **Joy,** to fill. "That your joy might be full" (John xv. 11).

7. As the **Hope** of glory, to cheer. "Christ in you the Hope of Glory" (Col. i. 27).

88. CHRISTIANS ARE TO BE FILLED

1. With the **Spirit.** "Be *filled* with the spirit" (Eph. v. 18).

2. With **comfort.** "I am *filled* with comfort" (II. Cor. vii. 4).

3. With **joy.** "Greatly desiring to see thee, being mindful of thy tears, that I may be *filled* with joy" (II. Tim. i. 4).

4. With **fruits of righteousness.** "Being *filled* with the fruits of righteousness, which are by Jesus Christ, unto the glory and praise of God" (Phil. i. 11).

5. With the **knowledge of His will.** "*Filled* with the knowledge of His will in all wisdom and spiritual understanding" (Col. i. 9).

6. With **good things.** "He hath *filled* the hungry with good things" (Luke i. 53).

7. With all the **fulness of God.** "That ye might be *filled* with all the fulness of God" (Eph. iii. 19).

89. CHRISTIAN WORK

This has reference to what we do and are for Christ. The quality of our works is to be good.

1. **Christ** is our Example. "I have finished the *work*" (John xvii. 4).

2. **Faith** is the principle. "If ye were Abraham's children, ye would do the *works* of Abraham" (John viii. 39).

3. **Love** is the motive. "She hath wrought a good *work*" (Matt. xxvi. 10).

4. **Word** of God is our authority. "Let your light so shine . . . . . . see your good *works*" (Matt. v. 16).

5. **Holy** Spirit is our power. "Created in Christ Jesus unto good *works*" (Eph. ii. 10).

6. **Good** is their character. Dorcas—"Full of good *works*" (Acts ix. 36).

7. **Evidence** of faith in Christ. Rahab—"Justified by *works*" (James. ii. 25).

8. **Tested** at the judgment seat. "The fire shall try every man's *work*" (I. Cor. iii. 13).

90. CIRCLE OF BLESSING

SATAN said that the Lord had put a hedge about Job on every side (Job i. 10), so that he could not touch him. The Lord has put a hedge of blessing around the believer, so that he can say—

1. Isaiah xliv. 22, is the **Pledge** of my forgiveness.
2. Gal. ii. 20, is the **Confession** of my faith.
3. John v. 24, is the **Assurance** of my salvation.
4. Isaiah xli. 10, is the **Comfort** of my life.
5. Psalm lv. 22, is the **Joy** of my unceasing privilege.
6. Luke xix. 13, is the **Burden** of my present responsibility.
7. Phil. iii. 20, 21, is the **Outlook** of my constant expectation.

91. "COME"

Note some of the "*comes*" of Christ as illustrating the fulness and freeness of His Gospel.

1. **Regard.** "*Come* down" (Luke xix. 5).
2. **Rest.** "*Come* unto Me, and I will give you rest" (Matt. xi. 28).
3. **Refreshment.** "*Come* and drink" (John vii. 37). "*Come* and take" (Rev. xxii. 17).
4. **Re-animation.** "*Come* forth" (John xi. 43).
5. **Responsibility.** "*Come* after Me" (Mark viii. 34).
6. **Reward.** "*Cometh* to Me shall never hunger" (John vi. 35).
7. **Response.** "*Come* and see" (John i. 39).

Mr. Spurgeon says of the last come, this is a "loving invitation," and says, "At the beginning of the Gospel, Christ said, 'Come and see;' at the close, 'Come and dine.' The first is for babes in Christ, the second for strong men."

92. COMMANDS OF CHRIST

There were many commands that the Lord Jesus gave His disciples. The following seven peaks are to be seen in the mountain range of His directions:—

1. "**Repent**" (Luke xiii. 3). Change of mind.
2. "**Believe**" (John iii. 16). Rest of soul.
3. "**Love**" (John xiii. 34). Affection of heart.
4. "**Follow**" (John xii. 26). Walk of feet.
5. "**Abide**" (John xv. 4). Attitude of spirit.
6. "**Tarry**" (Luke xxiv. 49). Pleading of faith.
7. "**Go**" (Matt. xxviii. 19). Testimony of lips.

93. COMMITTAL

"GLASS, with anxiety!" Strange expression this! What does it mean? These words accompanied a parcel sent from Norway to England, and they were intended to indicate that the sender feared, from the fragile nature of its contents, that some mishap might befall it.

Is there not a lesson here for Christians? Might not some of us be rightly labelled—

"Christians, with anxiety?"

In many instances there is no need for a label, as anxiety is only too plainly stamped upon the countenance, although the apostolic injunction is, "in nothing be anxious" (Phil. iv. 6, R.V.). Some obey this command in certain circumstances only, while others reverse the reading, and live as though they were to be anxious for everything. The Lord wishes His children to carry their worries and anxieties to Him; and to leave them with Him. Here are seven things which He bids us cast upon Him, or commit unto Him.

1. **Commit yourself unto Him.** "He is able to keep that which I have *committed* unto Him against that day" (II. Tim. i. 12). Paul deposited himself in the hands of the Heavenly Banker; and, as the money in the Bank of England is kept safe in the strong rooms within and by the guard without, so was the apostle, for he was kept by the Holy Spirit within, and by the Lord who encamped round about him.

2. **Commit your soul unto Him.** "Wherefore let them that suffer according to the will of God *commit* the keeping of their souls to Him in well doing, as unto a faithful Creator" (I. Peter iv. 19). Suffering we shall have, but if we commit the keeping of our souls unto the Lord in well doing, as the three Hebrew young men did, we shall, like them, but lose our bonds, and gain the company of Jesus.

3. **Commit your spirit unto Him.** "Into Thine hand I *commit* my spirit" (Psalm xxxi. 5). If the Lord has the control of our spirit, He will control us altogether.

4. **Commit your way unto Him.** "*Commit* thy way unto the Lord; trust also in Him; and He shall bring it to pass" (Psalm xxxvii. 5). If we commit our way unto Him, we shall never stray from Him.

5. **Commit your works unto Him.** "*Commit* thy works unto the Lord" (Proverbs xvi. 3). If the Lord controls the works and the workers, there will be no clashing in the working.

6. **Commit your burden unto Him.** "*Cast* thy burden upon the Lord" (Psalm lv. 22). If the Lord is our Burden-bearer, we shall be free to bear one another's burdens.

7. **Commit your care unto Him.** "*Casting* all your care upon Him, for He careth for you" (I. Peter v. 7). One John Careless, a

martyr, in writing to a friend, said, "Now my soul is turned to her old rest again, and has taken a sweet nap in Christ's lap. I have cast my care upon the Lord, who careth for me, and will be *careless*, according to my name." If we cast all our care upon Him, He will take all care off us.

94. COMPASSION OF THE LORD

WHEN Pharaoh's daughter saw the fair child, Moses, weeping, she had compassion upon him, and manifested her love in the kindly interest she took in him, and the loving care she exercised on his behalf. The word "*compassion*" is the same that occurs in Malachi, where it speaks of God sparing those who feared His name: "I will *spare* them, as a man *spareth* his own son that serveth him" (Mal. iii. 17). The same term is used in speaking of God's gracious action in His forbearance towards Israel, when He is said to have "had *compassion* on His people" (II. Chron. xxxvi. 15). In Joel ii. 18, the word is translated "*pity*," and is so given again and again. As Pharaoh's daughter pitied Moses, so the Lord has graciously had compassion upon us, for "God commendeth His love toward us, in that while we were yet sinners Christ died for us" (Rom. v. 8).

This fact may be further illustrated by the several instances where Christ is said to have had compassion upon people.

1. The **Shepherd** having compassion upon the scattered sheep, and being willing to save them (Matt. ix. 36; Mark vi. 34).

2. The **Divine Physician** having compassion upon the sick, and healing them (Matt. xiv. 14).

3. The **Miracle-worker** having compassion upon the hungry multitude, and supplying their need (Matt. xv. 32; Mark viii. 2).

4. The **Restorer** having compassion upon the blind men, and giving them their sight (Matt. xx. 34).

5. The **Cleanser** having compassion upon the unclean leper, and cleansing him (Mark i. 41).

6. The **Comforter** having compassion upon the sorrowing mother, and raising her son to life (Luke vii. 13).

7. The **Good Samaritan** having compassion upon the helpless traveller, and taking care of him (Luke x. 33).

8. The **Almighty Deliverer** having compassion upon the demon-possessed man, and liberating him (Mark v. 19).

9. The **Father** having compassion upon the prodigal, and giving him a royal welcome (Luke xv. 20).

The **One** who had compassion upon the people when on earth, is the same One with Whom we have to do.

95. COMPROMISE

I. KINGS XX. 31-43

1. *Compromising is* **listening to the enemy instead of listening to God** (verses 31-33). Ahab should not have listened to the overtures of the King of Syria in the face of the definite instructions that he had received from God. Neither must the Christian pay attention to the suggestions of Satan, as Eve did; nor listen to the longings of the natural heart, as Achan did when he coveted the forbidden things; nor must we pay heed to what half-hearted Christians say. We must follow the Lord fully, as Caleb, and be willing to be thought "eccentric," "odd," "extreme," "faddist," "peculiar," &c.

2. *Compromising is* **receiving favours from those who are God's enemies** (verse 34). It would have been perfectly right for Ahab to have received the cities that his father had lost from the hand of God, but to receive them from Ben-hadad was wrong. In like manner, for the believer in Christ to receive anything from the world in the shape of money to carry on God's work (III. John 7; I. Cor. ix. 15-18; II. Cor. viii. 5), or to adopt methods that are of the world, is to put the unconverted in a wrong position, and to bring discredit on the name of Christ.

3. *Compromising is to* **enter into a covenant with those who are not the Lord's** (verse 34). II. Cor. vi. 14-18 is very plain as to the attitude the believer in Christ should maintain. The only place of safety is separation unto Christ. Separation unto Christ! Not separation for separation's sake, for that would be Phariseeism, but separation for Christ's sake, because He commands it; for we cannot have fellowship with Him and the world too.

4. *Compromising* **does not pay** (verses 42, 43). Ahab had to pay very dearly for his self-will and disobedience. To be "out and out" is the best policy, looking at the question from policy's standpoint, which is not the Christian's ground. Better for our own sakes to keep to the lines of God's truth, for then we shall surely make progress, even as the train does by keeping on the metals.

96. CONDITIONS OF POWER

1. **Saved by Christ's grace.** "Thou hast neither part nor lot in this matter, for thy heart is not right in the sight of God" (Acts viii. 21).

2. **Standing in Christ's acceptance.** "The Gospel . . . . which also ye have received and wherein ye stand" (I. Cor. xv. 1).

3. **Obedience to Christ.** "The Holy Ghost, whom God hath given to them that obey Him" (Acts v. 32).

4. **Fellowship with Christ.** "By Whom ye were called unto the fellowship of His Son, Jesus Christ our Lord" (I. Cor. i. 9).

5. **Waiting upon Christ.** "These all continued with one accord in prayer and supplication" (Acts i. 14).

6. **Expecting from Christ.** Tarry ye in the city of Jerusalem until ye be endued with power from on high" (Luke xxiv. 49).

7. **Faith in Christ.** "Doeth he it by the works of the law or by the hearing of faith?" (Gal. iii. 2, 5).

97. CONFESSION, THE FORERUNNER OF BLESSING

CONFESSION is the forerunner of blessing.

1. **Abraham** said, "I am dust and ashes" (Gen. xviii. 27), and got all he asked for.

2. **Isaiah,** "I am unclean," and got cleansed (Isa. vi. 5).

3. **Job,** "I am vile," and got blessing (Job xl. 4).

4. **David,** Born in sin, and got covered (Ps. li. 5; xxxii. 1).

5. **Peter,** "I am a sinful man," and received the keys of the kingdom (Luke v. 8; Matt. xvi. 19).

6. **Publican,** "the sinner," and went home justified (Luke xviii. 13, R.V., M.).

7. **The prodigal,** "I am not worthy," and was feasted (Luke xv. 21).

98. CONTRASTS

As the world is full of contrasts—light and darkness, joy and sorrow, calm and storm, riches and poverty, cleanliness and filth, health and sickness, life and death—so the Scriptures present to us many opposites.

1. Abel, the man of **confidence**; and Cain, the man of **conceit** (Gen. iv. 3-7).

2. Abraham, the man of **faith**; and the king of Sodom, the man of the **world** (Gen. xiv. 22-24).

3. Isaac, the man of **promise**; and Ishmael, the man of the **flesh** (Gal. iv. 29).

4. Jacob, the man of **prayer**; and Esau, the man of **pleasure** (Hosea xii. 4; Heb. xii. 16).

5. Moses, the man of **God**; and Pharaoh, the man of **stubbornness** (Num. xii. 3; Exodus viii. 32).

6. David, the man of **consecration**; and Saul, the man of **compromise** (Acts xiii. 22; I. Samuel xv. 26).

7. John, the man of **fearlessness**; and Herod, the man of **vacillation** (Matt. xiv. 1-12).

99. CONVERSION

THE following sevenfold contrast will demonstrate what conversion is:—

1. "Dead in sins" (Eph. ii. 1). "Passed from death" (John v. 24).

2. "Condemned" (John iii. 18). "Justified" (Rom. v. 1).
3. "Lost" (Luke xix. 10). "Saved" (Eph. ii. 8).
4. "Under sin" (Gal. iii. 22). "Under grace" (Rom. vi. 14).
5. "Without Christ" (Eph. ii. 12). "In Christ" (II. Cor. xii. 2).
6. "Sinners" (I. Tim. i. 15). "Saints" (I. Cor. i. 2).
7. "Astray" (Isaiah liii. 6). "Abiding" (John xv. 4).

100. CONVICTION OF SIN

THE things that come to the heart and produce conviction of sin are a consciousness of—

1. The law broken by us (Gal. iii. 10).
2. The heart defiled by sin (Matt. xv. 19, 20).
3. The nature wrong (John iii. 6).
4. Failure to come up to God's glory (Rom. iii. 23).
5. Helpless condition (Rom. v. 6).
6. Hopeless state (Eph. ii. 12).
7. Indebtedness to God (Luke vii. 41-42).

101. COUNTENANCE OF THE LORD

1. **The grace of His countenance.** "The Lord lift up His *countenance* upon thee, and give thee peace" (Num. vi. 26).

2. **Reflection of His countenance.** "Lord, lift Thou up the light of Thy *countenance* upon us" (Psalm iv. 6).

3. **Joy of His countenance.** "Thou hast made him exceeding glad with Thy *countenance*" (Psalm xxi. 6).

4. **Saving of His countenance.** "For the help of His *countenance*" (Psalm xlii. 5, 11).

5. **Renewing of His countenance.** "Who is the health of my *countenance* and my God" (Psalm xliii. 5).

6. **Power of His countenance.** "Neither did their own arm save them . . . . . but the light of Thy *countenance*" (Ps. xliv. 3).

7. **Place for the believer to walk in.** "They shall walk, O Lord, in the light of Thy *countenance*" (Psalm lxxxix. 15).

8. **Discernment of His countenance.** "Our secret sins in the light of Thy *countenance*" (Psalm xc. 8).

102. COURAGE

1. COURAGE is the Divine **nerve** that enables us to go forward at the Lord's bidding in spite of all obstacles, as seen in the case of Joshua (Joshua i. 6, 7, 9, 18).

2. Courage gives **fibre** to the moral nature, so that we gladly keep the Lord's Word (Joshua xxiii. 6).

3. Courage is the **helm** that keeps the soul according to the Divine compass of God's truth, and makes us regardless of the storms we may encounter (Deut. xxxi. 6, 7).

4. Courage is the **secret** of a true life, for the God of Grace and Power is the feeder of it (I. Chron. xxii. 13; xxviii. 20).

5. Courage is the **fire** that shall make us burn with a holy zeal for the Lord's honour and glory, as we are acting under the Lord's instructions (II. Chron. xv. 8; Ezra x. 4).

6. Courage is the **forerunner** of blessing, for as we wait on the Lord in good courage, He comes in His grace and strengthens us (Psalm xxvii. 14; xxxi. 24).

7. Courage is the **steadfastness of faith,** which looks up to the Lord, and counts upon Him to give the victory in conflict (II. Sam. x. 12).

103. COVETOUSNESS

I. KINGS xxi

1. COVETOUSNESS always seeks to take away from another that which would be to the other's advantage (verses 1, 2).

2. Covetousness is regardless of God's Word (ver. 3; Lev. xxv. 23).

3. Covetousness is displeased when it does not accomplish its purpose (verse 4).

4. Covetousness will allow dishonest and diabolical means to obtain its end (verses 5-9).

5. Covetousness will lie, by bearing false witness to get its desire (verses 10-13, 16).

6. Covetousness is noted by God (verses 17-19).

7. Covetousness is not allowed to go unrebuked (verses 20-25).

8. "Covetousness is idolatry" (verse 26; Col. iii. 5).

9. Covetousness brings evil on others (verse 29).

10. Covetousness brings punishment (ver. 21; Hab. ii. 9-12).

104. COVETOUSNESS

COVETOUSNESS is the root of all evils. It—

1. **Blunts** the sensitive nerve of love (Jude 11).

2. **Blurs** the picture of life (II. Tim. iv. 10).

3. **Banishes** the companionship of generosity (Matt. xiii. 22).

4. **Breeds** the evil worm of discontent (I. Tim. vi. 5-8).

5. **Burdens** the spirit with the load of sorrow (I. Tim. vi. 10).

6. **Blinds** the eyes to the beauty of Christ (Luke xviii. 22-24).

7. **Blasts** the unscrupulous devotee with an unholy passion and endless misery (I. Tim. vi. 9).

105. CROSSING THE JORDAN

JOSHUA iii. 5-17

ISRAEL'S crossing the Jordan was a new epoch in their history. The wilderness with its zigzag path of unbelief was to be left behind, while Canaan with its abundant supply was about to be possessed. The typical teaching for the believer in Christ is, that when he sees the river of God's judgment rolling over his old sinful self, as the stones which represented Israel were placed in the bed of the Jordan (Josh. iv. 9), and as he beholds himself seated with Christ in heavenly places, as illustrated in the stones which were placed in Gilgal (Josh. iv. 20), then he is enabled to walk in newness of life (Rom. vi. 4).

1. **A Sanctified People** (ver. 5). It was essential that the people should be sanctified, before the Lord could do wonders among them. The wonders of God's power are performed through a people who are separated to Himself; and the wonders of His grace are exhibited when He is sanctified as Lord in the heart (1. Pet. iii. 15).

2. **The Obedient Priests** (verses 6-17). The priests acted according to the instructions given to them by Joshua. They were to take up the ark, pass over before the people, and stand in the bed of the Jordan till all the people had gone over. The priests in their priestly service were first and they were last. Thus, those who are believers in Christ are to remember that the priestly service of prayer, supplication, thanksgiving, and communion with the Lord come before more active service, and must come after it. As the ark of the covenant was seen by the people because it was on the shoulders of the priests, so Christ should always be seen in our work for the Lord.

3. **An Honoured Leader** (verse 7). Joshua had been a faithful servant of the Lord, and now the Lord is about to honour him by working a wondrous miracle through him in causing the Jordan to roll back. Those who magnify the Lord by their loving obedience and praise (Psalm xxxiv. 3; 1. Chron. xvii. 24), the Lord will magnify with His favour and power (Joshua iv. 14; 1. Chron. xxix. 25).

4. **A Listening Servant** (verse 8). Joshua listens attentively to the voice of the Lord as He directs him what he is to do. We must wait before we run (Isaiah xl. 31), tarry (Luke xxiv. 49) before we are empowered (Acts ii. 1, 2), receive before we can give (Acts i. 8), be taught before we can teach (Isaiah l. 4, R.V.), and listen before we speak (Luke x. 39).

5. **A Faithful Messenger** (verse 9). Having received the message, Joshua gives it to Israel. There were no deductions or additions, there was simply a reproduction. In like manner, when we receive the message of the Lord, as given in His Word, we must not add to it nor take from it (Deut. xii. 32; Rev. xxii. 18). People are apt to do one of three things in connection with God's Word, namely, take from, add to, or alter. Notice that Eve did all three. She *took from* when she left out the word "freely" (see

Gen. iii. 2, and ii. 16); she *added to* when she put in the word "touch" (see Gen. iii. 3, and ii. 17); and she *altered* when she said, "lest ye die" (Gen. iii. 3), when God had said, "Thou shalt surely die" (Gen. ii. 17).

6. **The Almighty Conqueror** (verse 10). The living God was to be the One who would drive out their enemies. It was not a question of their skill or of their power, but of the Lord's doings. The one essential is to be strong in the power of His might (Eph. vi. 10), and to have faith in Him to overcome (1. John v. 4), then no giant can stand before us (1. Sam. xvii. 45).

7. **The Symbolic Ark** (verse 11). The ark is the symbol of Jehovah's presence. Six times the ark is called "the ark of the covenant" (verses 3, 6, 8, 11, 14, 17); twice it is called "the ark" (verse 15); once it is called "the ark of the Lord" (verse 13); once it is called "the ark of the covenant of the Lord of all the earth" (verse 11); and once there is the addition to the words "the ark of the Lord" of the expression, "The Lord of all the earth." "*The* ark" is so called because there is only one; "the ark of the *covenant*" is so called because it contained the law; "the ark of the covenant of the Lord of all the earth" is so designated because He possesses all things; and "the ark of the Lord, the Lord of all the earth," is so described because no power can stand before Him. All this can be applied to Christ.

8. **Representative Men** (verse 12). The twelve men taken from the twelve tribes, from each tribe a man, signifies that these men were each acting in the place of the tribe. Christ is the Representative Man for the believer. He acts on our behalf (Hebrews ix. 24).

9. **The Supreme Power** (verses 13-17). The waters of Jordan could not stand before the *fiat* and presence of Jehovah (Ps. civ. 7); neither can the waters of judgment nor the waters of trouble (Isaiah xliii. 2) immerse the child of God. "No condemnation" and "no separation" are the two pillars of the temple of truth. As long as we are behind the omnipotent power of Jehovah no force of earth, no might of hell, and no weapon forged by man can touch or harm us.

106. DAVID AND GOLIATH

1. Samuel xvii. 38-51

In the valleys mentioned in Scripture, there have been enacted many wonderful scenes, and not least among them is the Valley of Elah (1. Sam. xvii. 2). A valley is suggestive of lowliness, fruitfulness, and fertility. The valleys of Scripture bloom with the truths of graces, and are fruitful with the triumphs of God.

1. **Trained.** The central figure of this reading is David. Up to the time of the incident before us, he had appeared very little in public, but the Lord had been fitting him for His service. He had learnt to know God in secret, hence he can now bear testimony of

Him in public. David knew that the Lord, whose strength had proved sufficient in giving him the victory over the lion and the bear, would give him the victory over the Philistine (verses 36, 37). "The Lord had been preparing an instrument for this new and difficult work. He trains in secret those whom He is about to use in public. He makes His servants acquainted with Himself in the secret solemnity of His sanctuary, and causes His greatness to pass in review before them, that they may be able to look with a steady gaze at the difficulties of their path. Thus it was with David. He had been alone with God while keeping the sheep in the wilderness; his soul had become filled with the thought of God's power; and now he makes his appearance in the Valley of Elah, in all the self-renouncing dignity of a man of faith."

2. **Trammelled** (verses 38, 39). Saul arms David with his armour, but David is only trammelled by the coat of mail, and puts it off. He cannot go to the Lord's battle with man's equipment. Satan often seeks to tempt the Lord's servants to put on some suit of mail out of his armoury. He endeavours to influence the man of prayer to adopt the covering of half-heartedness; he will try to induce the separated man to wear the robe of worldly conformity, and he will seek to trammel the Christian warrior with fleshly armour.

3. **Taunted** (verses 42-44). The Philistine taunts David with jeers and sneers. As with David, so with the Christian. The man of faith is sure to be taunted with the scantiness of his implements of war, with the unwisdom of his methods, and with the foolishness of his faith in an Unseen Power; but let them laugh that lose, they are sure to who win. The only thing that Christ has told us we shall receive from the world is persecution (John xvi. 33). They who live godly in Christ Jesus will have to suffer for it (II. Timothy iii. 12), but that only brings us into closer fellowship with Him who suffered (I. Peter iv. 1) on our account, and gives us a great blessing of happiness (I. Peter v. 10).

4. **Trusting.** The man of faith does not trust in his weapons (verse 40), but in the Lord Himself (verse 45), and in His action on behalf of the trustful one (verses 46, 47). "It is interesting to observe David's address to Goliath. He does not say, 'I come to thee with a sling and a stone.' No; but, 'in the name of the Lord of Hosts.' With him the means were nothing—God everything." Thus faith ever honours God, taking no credit to itself; and God honours faith in consequence, by giving complete victory.

5. **Triumph** (verses 50, 51). The triumph of David is a type of David's Son and Lord triumphing over all the power of the enemy, as one has remarked, "The claims of justice could not be met—death and judgment frowned in the distance, and man could only tremble at the prospect. But, blessed be the God of all grace, a Deliverer has appeared—One mighty to save, the Son of God, the true David, the anointed King of Israel, and of all the earth. He

has met the need, filled up the gap, satisfied the yearnings of the heart. But how? When? Where? By His death on Calvary, in that terrible hour when all creation was made to feel the solemn reality of what was being transacted. . . . . . The poor trembling sinner may stand by and behold the conflict, and the glorious issue thereof—may behold all the power of the enemy laid low by one stroke of his glorious Deliverer, and feel the crushing burden rolled, by the same stroke, from his struggling spirit. The tide of Divine peace and joy may flow into his soul, and he walk abroad in the full power of his emancipation, purchased for him by the blood, and proclaimed in the Gospel."

107. DAVID AND GOLIATH

I. SAMUEL xvii. 38-51

DAVID, in his triumph over the giant, illustrates the power and victory of faith.

1. **Renunciation of faith** (verse 39). Saul is an illustration of the man of the flesh, who counts upon a good armour for protection, and he seeks to encumber the man of faith with a like protection. The man of faith tries on the armour, but finds that he cannot act in it, and therefore puts it off. Earth resources are not God's resources, hence the man of faith must not depend on the former, but on the latter. The man of faith puts off the weights that would hinder him (Heb. xii. 1), the clothing of the old man (Eph. iv. 22; Col. iii. 8), and the weapons of earth's warfare (II. Cor. x. 4).

2. **Weapons of faith** (verse 40). A staff, a sling, and five smooth stones out of the brook Kidron, are all the weapons that faith takes. The staff of the Lord's presence (Isaiah l. 10; Psalm xxiii. 4), the sling of God's Word, and the five smooth stones which are found in the stream of Christ's mediatorial action and Person are the weapons of faith. The five smooth stones are—

Christ *is*, Christ *can*, Christ *has*, Christ *will*, Christ *does*.

"*Christ is.*" His living presence is our confidence and consolation (Isaiah xli. 10).

"*Christ can.*" He can conquer, for He stooped to conquer, and accomplished His purpose (Luke xi. 22; Heb. ii. 14; Col. ii. 15; I. John iii. 8).

"*Christ has.*" All power is His, and He has all power for us (Luke x. 19; Mark xvi. 17).

"*Christ will.*" He has promised the victory, therefore it is sure (I. John v. 4, 5).

"*Christ does.*" Faith makes His promise a present effect, and a continuous reality (Eph. vi. 16; Rev. xii. 11).

3. **Courage of faith.** David did not wait till the giant came up to him, he advanced towards the enemy (verse 40). The Christian

should not always stand on the defensive, he should be offensive at times (II. Cor. x. 5).

4. **Persecution of faith** (verse 41-44). Faith is sure to be taunted with folly, and sneered at for its unreasonable action. Christ is *the* Man of Faith, and as He was "despised" (Is. liii. 3), "reviled" (I. Peter ii. 23), "hated" (John xv. 18), and scoffed at (Matt. xxvii. 43); so shall we be, for the servant is not above his Lord (John xiii. 16).

5. **Testimony of faith** (verse 45). Not in his own name, nor in his own strength did David come against Goliath, but, as he declared, in the name and strength of the Lord. In a like manner, the believer testifies that the power of the Lord, and the name of Jesus, are the potent forces by which spiritual results are achieved (Acts iii. 12, 13; I. Cor. ii. 4).

6. **Confidence of faith** (verse 46). David has no doubt as to the issue of the battle. Mark his confidence. "The Lord will deliver thee into mine hand, and I will smite thee." Faith's confidence is not born of self-assertion, but is begotten by the sure word of God. Since we have a "sure word" (II. Peter i. 19), we have every right to say "we are sure" (John vi. 69).

7. **Resource of faith** (verse 47). "The battle is the Lord's." Faith recognises that the battle is not its own but the Lord's, and what foe can stand against Him? The resource of faith is the Almighty God. The Power of faith lies in the Power which faith lays hold of.

8. **Victory of faith** (verses 49-51). When the man of faith takes the stone of Christ's victory over evil, and puts it in the sling of Divine utterance, and slings it in the strength of the Holy Ghost, it will bring down any foe. The Christian should never expect defeat, but always count upon the victorious Lord for complete and continual victory.

108. DAVID, KING OVER ISRAEL

II. SAMUEL V. 1-12

David as king over Israel. There is a sevenfold characteristic of David as king.

1. He was an **appointed** *king:* "The Lord said to thee" (ver. 2). He did not seek the office, but he was sought for the position (I. Samuel xvi. 11-13). The same is true of Christ. He was God-sent in His work (John iii. 17, 18), God-qualified for the work (Luke iv. 18), and God-honoured in the position He occupies (Psalm ii. 7). The blessed man of Psalm i. is the honoured man of Psalm ii.

2. David was a **kinsman** *king.* He was no foreigner imported for the place, but was one of the people. "We are thy bone and flesh" (verse 1). He was one of their race, and not a stranger. This was according to the righteous rule of Deut. xvii. 15. Christ also is one

of us. "He was one of us," was on a banner at the centenary of Stevenson. So we say of Christ, "He was one of us." He is our kinsman (Heb. ii. 14).

3. David was a **fitted** *king*. "Thou leddest out," &c. (verse 2). He had proved himself worthy of the position. "All through his past life, since the conflict with Goliath, David had showed generalship, wisdom, skill, forbearance, courage, knowledge of men, and trust in God." How much more so is Christ! He was fitted by His sufferings (Heb. ii. 10), and His whole life further demonstrates His fitness to be the Ruler of men. Psalm lxxii. is a prophetic statement of His reign in the days to come.

4. David was a **careful** *king*. "Thou shalt feed," &c. (verse 2). Literally, "Thou shalt *shepherd*." The metaphor expresses the care the ruler should have in reigning over his people. "The true king seeks not to obtain all he can from the people, but to do all he can for them; not to plunder the sheep, but to shepherd them." Psalm xxiii. is the expression of the shepherdly care of Christ for His people.

5. David was an **exemplary** *king*. "Thou shalt be a captain" (verse 2). Not only to lead Israel in time of war, but to be the leader in every good word and work. Christ is our Great Leader, and it is to Him we are to look (Heb. xii. 2, 3), of Him we are to learn (Matt. xi. 29), and after Him we are to follow (Mark viii. 34).

6. David was a **victorious** *king*. The Jebusites thought they were absolutely secure from the power of David, but they soon found out their mistake (verses 6-9). Christ is the Great Victor over all foes (Luke xi. 22; Heb. ii. 14; Col. ii. 15; Rom. xvi. 20).

7. David was the **accepted** *king*. Israel desired him to be their king, and anointed him as such. Christ is yet to be the acknowledged King on this earth (Isaiah xxxii. 1).

The kingship of David may not only be taken in a typical sense, as applicable to Christ; but as an illustration of the believer's conquering rule over himself (Proverbs xvi. 32), in the power of the Spirit (Phil. ii. 13).

109. DAVID'S THREEFOLD ANOINTING

David was three times anointed as king.

1. First among his brethren in secret by **Samuel**, at God's direction (I. Samuel xvi. 13).

2. Second, David was owned as king by **Judah** (II. Sam. ii. 4).

3. Third, he was anointed as king "over all **Israel**" (II. Sam. v. 3).

This threefold anointing of David as king, is typical of the threefold crowning of Christ. He is "crowned with glory and honour," as man now (Heb ii. 9). He will reign over the house of Israel, when He is acknowledged by Israel, and sits on David's throne (Luke i. 31-33); and He will yet be "King of kings, and Lord of lords" (Rev. xix. 16). All powers are to be under His power and to submit to His sway (I. Cor. xv. 24-28).

110. DAYS OF SCRIPTURE

1. **The Day of Jesus** (John viii. 56). The Day of Jesus is the *day of His humiliation*. It is of interest to note that the human name "Jesus" occurs twenty times in John viii. That day is *past*.

2. **The Day of Man** (I. Cor. iv. 3, R.V., margin). "Man's Day" is this present time, when man is acting after his own natural desire, and according to the god of this age (II. Cor. iv. 4, R.V. M.).

3. **The Day of Salvation.** "The Day of Salvation" (II. Cor. vi. 2) runs parallel with man's day, for it is the desire of God that those who will come out from the ranks of the world should be saved by faith in Christ.

4. **The Day of Christ.** "The Day of Christ" begins with Christ coming for His people, and ends with His coming with them (Phil. i. 6, 10; ii. 16; Eph. iv. 30).

5. **The Day of the Lord.** "The Day of the Lord" begins with the Lord's coming with His people, and extends to the end of the millennium. Mark the expressions in the Old Testament, "the day of the Lord"; "in that day."

6. **The Day of Judgment.** "The Day of Judgment" for the wicked dead is at the end of the millennium, as described in Rev. xx. 11-15. See Matt. x. 15; xi. 22, 24; xii. 36; Rom. ii. 5; Jude 6.

7. **The Day of God.** "The Day of God" is eternity (II. Peter iii. 12), when God will be all in all (I. Cor. xv. 28).

111. DEATH OF CHRIST

1. THE death of Christ is the *record* of the **greatest sin** that was ever committed (Acts ii. 23).

2. The *exhibition* of the **greatest love** that was ever seen (Rom. v. 8).

3. The *manifestation* of the **greatest victory** that was ever achieved (Heb. ii. 14).

4. The *introduction* of the **greatest force** that has ever operated (I. John iii. 16).

5. The *unlocking* of the **greatest problem** that has ever engaged man's attention (I. Peter. i. 11).

6. The *supply* of the **greatest incentive** that has ever been given (II. Cor. v. 14).

7. The *making known* of the **greatest example** we can ever imitate (Eph. v. 2).

112. DEATH OF CHRIST

THE cross of Calvary was ever casting its terrible shadow across the path of Christ. It is interesting and instructive to mark Christ's repeated reference to His death.

The death of Christ is—

1. The **testimony** to man's sin (Acts ii. 23).

2. The **triumph** of God's grace (Heb. ii. 9).

3. The **trysting place** where God and the sinner **can meet** (1. Timothy ii. 5, 6).

4. The **title** to eternal life (John xii. 24).

5. The **temple** for refuge (Heb. ix. 12-14).

6. The **teacher** for instruction (Tit. ii. 11, 12).

7. The **tether** for binding (Gal. ii. 20).

113. DEGREES OF FAITH

1. **No** faith. "How is it that ye have no faith?" (Mark iv. 40).

2. **Little** faith. "O ye of little faith" (Matt. xvi. 8).

3. **Great** faith. "O woman, great is thy faith" (Matt. xv. 28).

4. **So great** faith. "I have not found so great faith" (Matt. viii. 10).

5. **Full** of faith. "Full of faith and of the Holy Ghost" (Acts vi. 5).

6. **Weak** in faith. "And be ye not weak in faith" (Rom. iv. 19).

7. **Strong** in faith. "Was strong in faith, giving glory to God" (Romans iv. 20).

114. DEITY OF CHRIST

1. GOD the Father **affirmed** it. "This is My beloved Son, in whom I am well pleased" (Matt. iii. 17).

2. Christ **proclaimed** it. "Tell us whether Thou be the Christ, the Son of God." "Jesus saith unto him, Thou hast said" (Matt. xxvi. 63, 64; Mark xiv. 61, 62).

3. The angel **asserted** it to Mary. "That holy thing, which shall be born of thee, shall be called the Son of God" (Luke i. 35).

4. John the Baptist **announced** it. "And I saw, and bare record that this is the Son of God" (John i. 34).

5. A legion of demons **knew** it. "What have we to do with Thee, Jesus, Thou Son of God?" (Matt. viii. 29).

6. The disciples were **sure** of it. "Of a truth Thou art the Son of God" (Matt. xiv. 33).

7. The Roman centurion **avowed** it. "Truly this was the Son of God" (Matt. xxvii. 54).

8. The blind man by his action **owned** it. "He said, Lord, I believe" (John ix. 35-38).

9. Unclean spirits **acknowledged** it. "Thou art the Son of God" (Mark iii. 11).

10. The Eunuch **believed** it. "I believe that Jesus Christ is the Son of God" (Acts viii. 37).

11. Paul **preached** it. "He preached Christ in the synagogues, that He is the Son of God" (Acts ix. 20).

12. Peter **confessed** it. "Simon Peter answered and said, Thou art the Christ, the Son of the living God" (Matt. xvi. 16).

13. The Evangelists **declared** it. "The beginning of the Gospel of Jesus Christ, the Son of God" (Mark i. 1).

14. Nathaniel **professed** it. "Nathaniel answered and said unto Him, Rabbi, Thou art the Son of God" (John i. 49).

15. The apostle **wrote** of it. "These are written, that ye might believe that Jesus is the Christ, the Son of God" (John xx. 31).

16. The Holy Spirit **confirmed** it. "Declared to be the Son of God with power, according to the Spirit of Holiness" (Rom. i. 4).

115. DELIVERANCE

THE believer has a sevenfold deliverance for which he can praise God:—

1. Deliverance from the **curse** of a broken law (Gal. v. 1).
2. Deliverance from the **condemnation** of sin (Romans viii. 1-3).
3. Deliverance from the **servitude** of sin (Rom. vi. 18).
4. Deliverance from the **evil** in the world (Gal. i. 4).
5. Deliverance from the **power** of darkness (Col. i. 13).
6. Deliverance from the **fear** of death (Heb. ii. 15).
7. Deliverance from **self** in the death of Christ (Gal. ii. 20).

116. "DELIVER US FROM EVIL"

MATTHEW VI. 13

1. DELIVER us from an "**evil conscience**" (Heb. x. 22) by the application of the blood of Christ.

2. Deliver us from an "**evil heart of unbelief**" (Heb. iii. 12), by unwavering faith in God's Word.

3. Deliver us from "**this present evil world**" (Gal. i. 4), by living in the purpose Christ had, when He died for us.

4. Deliver us from "**evil speaking**" (Eph. iv. 31), by enabling us to speak the truth in love.

5. Deliver us from "**every evil work**" (II. Tim. iv. 18), by leading us in the Spirit to abound in every good work.

6. Deliver us from "**evil communications**" (I. Cor. xv. 33), by heart fellowship with Christ and those who are His.

7. Deliver us from "**all appearance of evil**" (I. Thess. v. 22), that Christ's honour may be unsullied.

117. DILIGENCE

EACH of the evangelists bears testimony to the diligence of the women in coming early to the sepulchre. Matthew says, "They came, at the end of the Sabbath, as it began to dawn toward the first day of the week." Luke, "They prepared their spices, and rested on the Sabbath, and came early the next day." John, "They came the first day of the week when it was yet dark" (Matt. xxviii. 1; Luke xxiv. 1; John xx. 1). It is only those who do things diligently and promptly that do things well.

See what the Lord says the Christian is to do diligently.

1. **Unity.** "*Endeavouring* to keep" (Eph. iv. 3).
2. **Study.** "*Study* to shew thyself," &c. (II. Tim. ii. 15).
3. **Rest.** "Let us *labour* to enter" (Heb. iv. 11).
4. **Calling.** "Give *diligence* to make," &c. (II. Peter i. 10).
5. **Watchfulness.** "Be *diligent* that ye may be found," &c. (II. Peter iii. 14).
6. **Business.** "Not slothful in *business*" (Rom. xii. 11).
7. **Consecration.** "Giving all *diligence*" (II. Peter i. 5).

The italicised words denote that they are one and the same in the Greek.

118. "DISCIPLE, WHOM JESUS LOVED"

WE will briefly refer to the Scriptures in John's Gospel where the "beloved disciple" so mentions himself, as illustrating the attitude and action of love in relation to our Beloved on whom we are leaning—not only upon His arm, but *Himself* (S. S. viii. 5).

1. **Rest** of love (xiii. 23).
2. **Confidence** of love (xiii. 25).
3. **Object** of love (xviii. 15).
4. **Unity** of love (xviii. 16).
5. **Contemplation** of love (xix. 26).
6. **Obedience** of love (xix. 27).
7. **Concern** of love (xx. 2).
8. **Companion** of love—zeal (xx. 3).
9. **Activity** of love (xx. 4).
10. **Belief** of love (xx. 8).
11. **Witness** of love (xx. 25).

12. **Sharp-sightedness** of love (xxi. 7).
13. **Close companionship** of love (xxi. 20).
14. **Wonderful** memory of love (xxi. 23).
15. **Testimony** of love (xxi. 24).

119. DOORS

An old writer has said, "The Holy Spirit rides in the chariot of His Word." If, therefore, we would have the Spirit of the Word, we must ponder the Word of the Spirit. The following references to some of the doors of Scripture present a complete ring of truth, in which are found seven precious gems.

1. **Sin.** Sin at the door.—"Sin lieth at the *door*" (Gen. iv. 7). To have sin call at the door like a beggar is bad enough, but to have it lying there like a wild beast is worse.

2. **Substitution.** Blood on the door.—"Take of the blood, and strike it on the two side posts, and on the upper *door* post of the houses" (Exodus xii. 7). "Christ our Passover sacrificed for us," proclaims Him, who has suffered in our stead, and who shelters us in consequence.

3. **Salvation.** Passing over the door.—"The Lord will pass over the *door*" (Exodus xii. 23). Lowth's translation is very suggestive, "The Lord will spring forward before the *door*." Since He stands between us and danger we are safe indeed.

4. **Security.** Preserved behind the door.—"The *door* of the ark . . . the Lord shut him in" (Gen. vi. 16; vii. 16). When the Lord shuts the door none can open it. It is significant that the first time the Hebrew word for atonement is translated, it is rendered "*pitch*" in connection with the ark (Gen. vi. 14). Christ is our Atonement to secure.

5. **Sanctification.** Nailed to the door.—"Bring him to the *door*" (Exodus xxi. 6). The freed slave out of love to his master has his ear bored with an awl to the door (see margin of Ps. xl. 6; and Isaiah l. 5).

6. **Sentry.** Sentinel before the door.—"Keep the *door* of my lips" (Psalm cxli. 3). If the Lord preserves the lips, no enemy shall open them to His dishonour, nor our shame.

7. **Station.** "Waiting at the posts of My *doors*" (Prov. viii. 34). The believer's attitude is that of prayerful expectancy, and faithful watching.

120. DOWN-GRADE-ISM OF ASA

II. Chronicles xvi

When anyone gets on the incline of backsliding, he soon finds himself in the road of departure from God. Thus it was with Asa; one step in the wrong direction prompted him to take another.

1. **Asa sought help in the wrong quarter** (verse 2). Instead of going to the King of Syria for help, he should have gone to the King of Heaven. The man who looks to man for assistance is cursed (Jer. xvii. 5), but he who looks to the Lord is helped indeed (Psalm cxxi. 2). The help of man, like water in a leaky vessel, is sure to run away, whereas the help of the Lord is like a mighty tornado, before which nothing can stand.

2. **Asa relied on the wrong person for aid** (verse 7). The king was but as a broken reed for Asa to lean upon; no wonder, therefore, that he came to the ground to his hurt. To rely on the Lord is to have the arm of the Living God to uphold us, as Asa had experienced when he trusted in the Lord on a previous occasion (verse 8). To trust in the Lord is the *secret* of a holy life (Gal. ii. 20); the *spur* to a separate life (Heb. xi. 8, 9); the *stimulus* to a useful life (Heb. xi. 7); the *stay* of a suffering life (Heb. xi. 24, 25); the *staple* to a tempted life (1. John v. 4); the *success* of a courageous life (Gideon: Heb. xi. 32); and the *safe-guard* of an active life (Paul: 1. Tim. iv. 10).

3. **Asa was angry with the wrong man** (verse 10). He should have been angry with himself; instead of that, he was wroth with the prophet. They that are wrong are the first to do wrong.

4. **Asa's oppression was in the wrong place** (verse 10). He should have oppressed himself by heartfelt penitence and confession; instead of that he acted the part of a tyrant in crushing some of the people.

5. **Asa consulted the wrong physician** (verse 12). "He sought not the Lord" is a sad sentence to have against one's name. It tells out a life of self-will and self-reliance.

121. EBED-MELECH

Jeremiah xxxviii. & xxxix

In the darkest page of history there is a gleam of sunshine, and in the chapters before us we have a bright illustration of the Gospel.

1. As the princes got Jeremiah put into the miry pit, so sin has placed us in the pit of iniquity and unbelief (Ps. xl. 2).

2. As Ebed-melech sought to rescue Jeremiah from the pit, and to save him from the death of starvation (Jeremiah xxxviii. 7-9), so Christ has died and acted for us, to deliver us from the wrath to come (1. Thess. i. 10).

3. As Ebed-melech acted according to the word of the king, so Christ has acted according to the word of God (John xvii. 4).

4. As Ebed-melech provided means to rescue Jeremiah (verse 11), so the Lord has decreed that those who are saved shall bear His message of salvation to others (John xx. 21).

5. As Jeremiah was saved from the miry pit by acting according

to the instructions that were given to him (verse 12), so we are saved by doing as the Lord directs (John v. 24).

6. As Jeremiah was assured by the king that he should not be put to death (Jer. xxxviii. 16), so the Lord assures us that we shall never perish (John x. 28, 29).

7. As Ebed-melech was rewarded because of his trust in the Lord (Jer. xxxix. 16-18), so all those who trust in Christ are rewarded with all spiritual blessings in Him (Eph. i. 3).

122. ENDURANCE

Believers are called to endure—

1. **Hardness.** As good soldiers. "*Endure* hardness as a good soldier of Jesus Christ" (II. Tim. ii. 3).

2. **Affliction.** As workers. "*Endure* afflictions, do the work of an evangelist" (II. Tim. iv. 5).

3. **Chastening.** As children. "If ye *endure* chastening, God dealeth with you as with sons" (Heb. xii. 7).

4. **Grief.** As Christians. "For this is thankworthy, if a man for conscience toward God *endure* grief" (I. Peter ii. 19).

5. **Contradiction.** Partners with Christ. "Consider Him that *endured* such contradiction of sinners against Himself" (Heb. xii. 3).

6. **Temptation.** Tried ones. "Blessed is the man that *endureth* temptation" (James i. 12).

7. **All things.** Elect's sake. "Therefore I *endure* all things for the elect's sake" (II. Tim. ii. 10).

123. ESAU

Genesis xxv. 27-32)

Esau represents a man of the world, and Jacob a man of God, although there are blemishes in his life.

As a man's countenance will often reveal the course of life he is leading, so the several sentences that speak of Esau indicate what kind of a character he was.

1. **The cunning hunter.** "Esau was a cunning hunter" (verse 27). He was no novice in the art of hunting, but he was an adept. By continually giving himself to this pleasure he had become an expert. This indicates at once, that he is a typical character of those who are wholly given over to the pursuits and pastimes of the pleasures of this evil age.

2. **The man of the field.** "A man of the field" (verse 27). From this we gather he was a man of wild and lawless habits, one who did not care to be under the restraint of home, but one who liked his own will and way.

3. **The thoughtful son.** "Isaac loved Esau, because he ate of his venison" (verse 28). From Gen. xxvii. 1, 2, we gather that Esau was willing to minister to his father's wants in obtaining venison for him. It has often been found that those who are not godly have kind and thoughtful traits in their character. It was kind of Esau to satisfy Isaac, whether it was wise for Isaac to want the venison, and thus to keep his son roaming.

4. **The fainting sportsman.** "Esau came from the field, and was faint" (ver. 29). Trapp well remarks upon Esau's faintness while in pursuit of pleasure: "Of carnal pleasures a man may break his neck sooner than his fast. Nor is it want of variety in them, but inward weakness, or the course of unsatisfyingness, that lies upon them. The creature is now as the husk without the grain, the shell without the kernel, full of nothing but emptiness; and so may faint us, but not fill us."

5. **The stamped individual.** "Esau said to Jacob, feed me, I pray thee, with that same red *pottage;* for I am faint: therefore his name was called Edom" (Margin, "red," ver. 30). Men have by their actions made their name to be identical with some special sin; hence to mention the name of some men is at once to bring up their sin. Judas is identified with covetousness, Eli with parental weakness, Jeroboam with idolatry, Simon Magus with simony, Korah with pride, and Esau with profanity (Heb. xii. 16).

6. **The thoughtless questioner.** "What profit shall this birthright do to me?" (ver. 32). Of what use can a birthright be to a man at the point of death? Esau says, in so many words, "I prefer present gratification to deferred privileges." Thus it was with the rich man mentioned in Luke xvi.; he lived for the present while on earth, and he lived to repent his folly in hell.

7. **The bad bargainer.** "Esau who for one morsel of meat sold his birthright" (Hebrews xii. 16). The birthright meant a double portion of his father's property (Deut. xxi. 17); it meant authority over his brethren (Genesis xxvii. 29; xlix. 3), and the right to the priestly office. The first-born of Israel were replaced by the Levites (Num. iii. 12). Esau did indeed despise the birthright by selling it for a mess of pottage. There are many to-day who are selling their eternal interests by living for self, living in sin, following the pleasure of the world and the desires of the flesh. What profit can these things give in this life? How will these things look on the death-bed, and in the coming eternity?

124. ESCAPE FROM

As the man-slayer had something to escape *from*, namely, the avenger, so the sinner has need to escape from—

1. The **curse** of a broken law (Gal. iii. 10).
2. The **justice** of God (Ex. xxxiv. 7).
3. The **consequences** of sin (Heb. x. 26, 27).

4. The **wrath** to come (I. Thess. i. 10).
5. The **guilt** of sin (Rom. iii. 19).
6. The **dominion** of sin (Rom. vi. 16).
7. The **love** of sin (John iii. 19).
8. The **power** of darkness (Col. i. 13).

125. ETERNAL BLESSINGS OF THE BELIEVER

1. We possess **eternal Life.** "Whosoever believeth in Him . . . have eternal life" (John iii. 15).

2. We are secured in an **eternal Covenant.** "Through the blood of the everlasting Covenant" (Heb. xiii. 20).

3. We are saved with an **eternal Salvation.** "He became the Author of eternal salvation" (Heb. v. 9).

4. We are liberated by an **eternal Redemption.** "Having obtained eternal redemption for us" (Heb. ix. 12).

5. We have an **eternal House.** "A house not made with hands, eternal in the heavens" (II. Cor. v. 1).

6. We are called to **eternal Glory.** "Who hath called us unto His eternal glory" (I. Peter v. 10).

7. We are kept for an **eternal Inheritance.** "Might receive the promise of an eternal inheritance" (Heb. ix. 15).

8. We are cheered by **eternal Comfort.** "Hath given us everlasting consolation" (II. Thess. ii. 16).

9. We know there is an **eternal Weight** of glory in the future. "Worketh for us a far more exceeding and eternal weight of glory" (II. Cor. iv. 17).

10. We shall dwell in **eternal Tabernacles.** "Receive you into everlasting habitations" (Luke xvi. 9).

11. We are aiming to have an abundant entrance into the **eternal Kingdom.** "An entrance shall be ministered unto you abundantly . . . . everlasting kingdom" (II. Peter. i. 11).

126. ETERNAL LIFE

1. God **is its Source.** "The Father hath life in Himself" (John v. 26).

2. **The risen Christ is its Channel.** "Who is made . . . after the power of an endless life" (Heb. vii. 16).

3. **The Holy Spirit is its Power.** "The Spirit of life in Christ Jesus hath made me free" (Rom. viii. 2).

4. **Faith is its Receiver.** "He that believeth on the Son hath everlasting life" (John iii. 36).

5. **Fruit is its Evidence.** "Ye have your fruit unto holiness, and the end everlasting life" (Rom. vi. 22).

6. **Christ Himself is its Embodiment.** "This is the true God and Eternal Life" (I. John v. 20).

7. **Glory is its Manifestation.** "When Christ, who is our Life, shall appear, then shall ye also appear with Him in glory" (Col. iii. 4).

8. **Eternity is its Duration.** "I give unto them eternal life, and they shall never perish" (John x. 28).

9. **Union with Christ is its Meaning.** "Except ye eat the flesh of the Son of Man and drink His blood ye have no life in you. Whoso eateth My flesh . . . hath eternal life" (John vi. 53, 54).

10. **Its Secret is knowing God and Christ.** "This is life eternal, that they might know Thee and Jesus Christ" (John xvii. 3).

127. "EVEN AS" IN EPHESIANS

1. **Even as, of sinnership.** "Children of wrath, *even as* others" (Eph. ii. 3).

2. **Even as, of calling.** "*Even as* ye are called in one hope of your calling" (Eph. iv. 4).

3. **Even as, of imitation.** "Forgiving one another, *even as* God for Christ's sake hath forgiven you" (Eph. iv. 32).

4. **Even as, of headship.** "Husband is the head of the wife, *even as* Christ is the head of the church" (Eph. v. 23).

5. **Even as, of love.** "Husbands love your wives, *even as* Christ also loved the church" (Eph. v. 25).

6. **Even as, of care.** "Nourisheth and cherisheth it, *even as* the Lord the church" (Eph. v. 29).

7. **Even as, of himself.** "Every one of you in particular, so love his wife *even as* himself" (Eph. v. 33).

128. EVERY "THOUGH" HAS ITS "YET"

1. **Confidence in God.** "*Though* He slay me, *yet* will I trust in Him" (Job. xiii. 15).

2. **Confidence in His power.** "*Though* after my skin worms destroy this body, *yet* in my flesh shall I see God" (Job xix. 26).

3. **Confidence in His care.** "*Although* the fig tree shall not blossom . . . . *yet* I will rejoice in the Lord" (Hab. iii. 17, 18).

4. **Confidence in His Word.** "*Although* my house be not so with God, *yet* He hath made with me an everlasting covenant" (II. Sam. xxiii. 5).

5. **Confidence in His purpose.** "*Although* I have scattered them among the countries, *yet* will I be to them as a little sanctuary" (Ezekiel xi. 16).

6. **Confidence in service.** "*Though* ye have ten thousand instructors in Christ, *yet* have ye not many fathers" (I. Cor. iv. 15).

7. **Confidence in His renewing.** "*Though* our outward man perish, *yet* the inward man is renewed day by day" (II. Cor. iv. 16).

8. **Confidence in the Lord.** *Though* we have known Christ after the flesh, *yet* now henceforth know we Him no more" (II. Cor. v. 16).

9. **Confidence in ministry.** "*Though* I be rude in speech, *yet* not in knowledge" (II. Cor. xi. 6).

10. **Confidence in His Resurrection.** "*Though* He was crucified through weakness, *yet* He liveth by the power of God" (II. Cor. xiii. 4).

11. **Confidence in His example.** *Though* He were the Son, *yet* learned He obedience" (Heb. v. 8, M.).

12. **Confidence in self.** "*Though* I should die with Thee, *yet* will I not deny Thee" (Matt. xxvi. 35).

129. EXAMPLE IN SERVICE

THE Servant—the Son of God. All God's servants are sons, and all God's sons are servants.

1. **Wise Servant.** "The people were astonished at His doctrine" (Matt. vii. 28).

2. **Obedient Servant.** "I delight to do Thy will, O My God" (Psalm xl. 8).

3. **Suffering Servant.** "Now is My soul troubled" (John xii. 27).

4. **Confident Servant.** "The word . . . . not Mine, but the Father's which sent Me" (John xiv. 24; xvi. 32).

5. **Persevering Servant.** "He stedfastly set His face" (Luke ix. 51).

6. **Accepted Servant.** "Whatsoever ye shall ask the Father in My name, He will give it you" (John xvi. 23).

7. **Victorious Servant.** "I have glorified Thee on the earth; I have finished the work" (John xvii. 4).

130. FACE OF JESUS

1. **Strong face.** "He stedfastly set His *face* to go to Jerusalem" (Luke ix. 51).

2. **Bowed face.** "And fell on His *face*" (Matt. xxvi. 39).

3. **An insulted face.** "Then did they spit in His *face*" (Matt. xxvi. 67).

4. **Covered face.** "And to cover His *face*" (Mark xiv. 65).

5. **Struck face.** "They struck Him on the *face*" (Luke xxii. 64).

6. **Shining face.** "His *face* did shine as the sun" (Matt. xvii. 2).

7. **Glorious face.** "Glory of God in the *face* of Jesus Christ" (II. Cor. iv. 6).

8. **Awe-inspiring face.** "Hide us from the *face* of Him" (Rev. vi. 16; xx. 11).

9. **Gladdening face.** "And they shall see His *face*" (Rev. xxii. 4).

131. FAINT NOT

1. **Prayer.** Faint not in prayer. "Pray and *not faint*" (Luke xviii. 1).

2. **Perseverance.** Faint not in confidence. "We *faint not*" (II. Cor. iv. 1).

3. **Preservation.** Faint not in hope. "For which cause we *faint not*" (II. Cor. iv. 16).

4. **Preparation.** Faint not in work, "Reap if we *faint not*" (Gal. vi. 9).

5. **Power.** Faint not in trusting. "I desire that ye *faint not*" (Eph. iii. 13).

6. **Practice.** Faint not in well doing. "*Faint not* in well doing" (II. Thess. iii. 13, margin).

7. **Patience.** Faint not under chastening. "*Nor faint* when thou art rebuked" (Heb. xii. 5).

132. FAITH

The eleventh of Hebrews might be called the Westminster Abbey of the Bible, for it is a series of memorials to the trials and triumphs of faith.

There is no mention of the failures of the Old Testament saints in Hebrews xi., for the simple reason that God had said, "Their sins and iniquities will I remember no more" (Heb. x. 17).

1. **Wisdom of faith** (verses 1, 2). Faith makes unseen things real, and future things present. Faith rests on facts, hence its wisdom. Presumption acts on its own authority, hence its folly. Newberry renders the words, "Evidence of things not seen," as follows: "conviction of facts not seen."

2. **Warrant of faith** (verse 3). The ground of faith's attitude and action is, "Thus saith the Lord." "Where the word of a king is, there is power" (authority).

3. **Worship of faith** (verse 4). The *ground* of worship is sacrifice (Heb. x. 19-22); the *object* of worship is God (Rev. xxii. 9); and the *power* of worship is the Holy Spirit (Eph. ii. 18).

4. **Walk of faith** (verses 5, 6). The walk of faith is illustrated by the three men who are said to have walked with God.

Fellowship with God—Enoch (Gen. v. 24).

Fidelity to God—Phinehas (Mal. ii. 6; Num. xxv. 12, 13).

Faith in God—Noah (Gen. vi. 9).

5. **Witness of faith** (verse 7). As unbelief and disobedience are synonymous terms, so are faith and obedience. It was because Noah was a man of faith that he obeyed God's direction, hence his witness.

6. **Wandering of faith** (verses 8-10). As a stranger and pilgrim, Abraham went forth at God's bidding. It was because he looked for a city that he dwelt in a tent.

7. **Waiting of faith** (verses 11, 12). Those who have the promise of God can afford to be patient before God. Waiting time is not wasted time. We must learn to "tarry" (Luke xxiv. 49; Acts i. 4), if we would triumph.

133. FAITH

HEBREWS xi. 13-22

1. **Trust of faith** (verse 13). The promises are received as bank notes, which are as good as cash. Mark the words, "received," "persuaded," "embraced," "confessed."

2. **Telescope of faith** (verse 13). Unbelief says, "Seeing is believing," but faith says, "Believing is seeing." The promises are "seen afar off," but they are *seen*.

3. **Testimony of faith** (verses 14-16). Faith declares by its actions what its aim is. "Came out" declares the separation of the man of faith; and the "wherefore" the consequent blessing.

4. **Trial of faith** (verses 17-19). Faith looks at God's presence and power, when tried. If the Lord does not deliver us *out* of the trial, He will be *with* us in it.

5. **Thoughtfulness of faith** (verse 20). Faith looks not on its own things, but looks out for others.

6. **Tact of faith** (verse 21). Faith's reverses are God's directions. Ponder the words "blessed" and "worshipped" in the light of Gen. xlviii. 17-21.

7. **Tranquility of faith** (verse 22). The thought of the future fills the man of unbelief with fear; but the man of faith can speak of the future with perfect calm.

134. FAITH

HEBREWS xi. 32

1. **Success of faith,** as illustrated in Gideon (Judges vi.).
2. **Song of faith,** as depicted in Barak (Judges v. 6, &c.).
3. **Strength of faith,** as seen in Samson (Judges xiii. 2, &c.).
4. **Sacrifice of faith,** as unfolded in Jephthah (Judges xi. 1, &c.).

5. **Supplication of faith,** as manifest in David (Psalms).

6. **Singleness of faith,** as made known in Samuel.

7. **Subject of faith,** as demonstrated in the prophets.

Ponder the "wherefore" of Heb. xii. 1, and observe how the Holy Spirit directs our gaze to the Man of Faith, for He is the Prince and Pattern of faith (not "*our*" faith, but of faith. The word "*our*" is in italics). Christ was the One who began, continued, and ended His life in simple confidence; hence we are bidden to look to Him as the Perfect Example of what faith in God accomplishes.

135. FAITH

"THE AIM AND ATTITUDE OF FAITH"

JOSHUA vi. 8-20

1. THE **place** of faith. "Before the Lord" (Josh. vi. 8; Phil. ii. 12).

2. The **testimony** of faith. "Blowing with the trumpets" (verse 9; I. Thess. i. 8).

3. The **attitude** of faith. "Until I bid you" (verse 10; Col. ii. 6).

4. The **rest** of faith. "Lodged in the camp" (verse 11; I. John ii. 28).

5. The **activity** of faith. "Rose early . . . . took up" (verse 12; Jas. ii. 22-26).

6. The **continuance** of faith. "Went on continually" (verses 13, 14; John viii. 31).

7. The **perfection** of faith. "Seven times" (verse 15; I. Thess. iii. 10).

8. The **boldness** of faith. "Shout" (verse 16; Acts iv. 13).

9. The **assurance** of faith. "The Lord hath given" (verse 16; I. John v. 10, 11).

10. **The recognition** of faith. "Devoted (margin) to the Lord" (verse 17; I. Pet. iii. 5).

11. The **separation** of faith. "Keep yourselves from the accursed thing" (verse 18; II. Cor. vii. 1).

12. The **service** of faith. To bring the consecrated things "into the treasury of the Lord" (ver. 19; I. Cor. vi. 20).

13. The **triumph** of faith. "The wall fell down flat" (verse 20; I. John v. 4, 5).

14. The **possession** of faith. "They took the city" (verse 20; Genesis xxii. 17).

Thus we have in miniature what faith is, what faith brings, and what faith does.

136. FAITH

HEBREWS xi. 23-31

1. **Courage of faith** (verse 23). The declarations of God are always to be regarded before the decrees of man.

2. **Choice of faith** (verses 24-26). Pleasures of sin are always renounced for the pleasures of God's right hand; and the treasures of earth are abandoned for the treasures of heaven.

3. **Calmness of faith** (verse 27). When we know what it is to look into the face of God, we shall never fear the frown of man.

4. **Covering of faith** (verse 29). The blood of atonement is faith's protection, and the presence of God is its confidence (Exodus xii. 13, 23).

5. **Confidence of faith** (verse 29). The Word of God was Israel's authority for crossing the Red Sea; hence the confidence they had.

6. **Conflict of faith** (verse 30). "The battle is the Lord's," is the war-cry of faith.

7. **Confession of faith** (verse 31). Rahab's action proclaims her faith.

137. FAITH

FAITH in God may be compared to many things.

1. Faith is the **hand** that receives the gift of God, and makes us rich (John i. 12).

2. Faith is the **eye** that looks into the unseen, and beholds things which are beyond human ken (Heb. xi. 1).

3. Faith is the **heart's response** to the call of the Lord (Rom. x. 10).

4. Faith is the **soul's reliance** on the Lord Jesus Christ (II. Timothy i. 12).

5. Faith is the **link** that connects with Christ and God (Heb. x. 22).

6. Faith is the **wire** along which the electricity of God's power runs and communicates itself to us (Gal. iii. 5).

7. Faith is the **operator** which causes the feet to run in glad and swift obedience, as is illustrated in Israel's marching round Jericho according to the Divine direction (Heb. xi. 30). Obedience is the proof of faith. Where there is no obedience there is no faith. Therefore if we would triumph, we must obey.

> "To trust and obey,
> There is no other way."

Or to put it more correctly,

> "To trust is to obey."

138. FAITHFUL SERVANT

1. A FAITHFUL servant of Christ is **holy in life.** "Be ye followers of me even as I also am of Christ" (I. Cor. xi. 1).

2. He has the **truth of God** as the authority of his utterance. "The truth of Christ is in me" (II. Cor. xi. 10).

3. The **unsearchable riches of Christ** are the theme of his preaching. "To preach . . . the unsearchable riches of Christ" (Eph. iii. 8).

4. The **love of Christ** is his constraining power. "The love of Christ constraineth us" (II. Cor. v. 14).

5. The **power of Christ** is his strength. "That the power of Christ may rest upon me" (II. Cor. xii. 9).

6. The **work of Christ** is his joy. "For the work of Christ he was nigh unto death" (Phil. ii. 30).

7. To **please Christ** in his ambition. "If I yet pleased men, I should not be the servant of Christ" (Gal. i. 10).

8. He recognises that he has to stand before the **judgment seat of Christ.** "We shall all stand before the judgment seat of Christ" (Rom. xiv. 10).

139. FAITHFULNESS OF GOD

1. HE is *faithful* that called us unto the fellowship of His Son. "God is faithful, by whom ye were called" (I. Cor. i. 9).

2. He is *faithful*, and will not suffer us to be tempted above what we are able to bear (I. Cor. x. 13).

3. The Lord is *faithful* to sanctify us wholly. "The very God of peace sanctify you wholly" (I. Thess. v. 23).

4. He is *faithful* to stablish and keep. "The Lord is faithful, who shall stablish you, and keep you from evil" (II. Thess. iii. 3).

5. His own character the ground of His faithfulness. "If we believe not, yet He abideth faithful; He cannot deny Himself" (II. Tim. ii. 13).

6. He is *faithful* to keep to His promises. "He is faithful that promised" (Heb. x. 23).

7. He is *faithful* to forgive, if we confess our sins. "If we confess our sins, He is faithful and just to forgive" (I. John i. 9).

140. FEASTS OF JEHOVAH

THERE are seven feasts mentioned in the twenty-third of Leviticus, all of which are typical, and especially shadow forth, in a brief way, the events from the cross to the glory.

1. The **Passover** is typical of Christ our Passover sacrificed for us (I. Cor. v. 7).

2. The **Unleavened Bread** of the holy life of the believer (I. Cor. v. 8).

3. The **Firstfruits,** of the resurrection of Christ (I. Cor. xv. 23).

4. **Pentecost,** of the coming of the Holy Spirit (Acts ii. 1-4).

5. The **Trumpets,** of the coming of Christ (I. Thess. iv. 16).

6. The **Day of Atonement,** of the time when the Jews shall see Christ as their Atonement (Zech. xii. 10).

7. The **Feast of Tabernacles,** of the rest and peace of the millennium (Isaiah xi.).

141. FEEDING THE FIVE THOUSAND

MARK vi. 30-44

CHRIST is the Pivot of Scripture. Take Christ away from the Scripture, and everything falls into confusion. See Christ in the Scripture, and the Key is found to unlock every difficulty, and solve every problem.

1. **Gathered to Jesus.** "The Apostles gathered themselves together unto Jesus" (verse 30). As Abraham came back to Bethel (The House of God, Gen. xiii. 3), and as Israel returned to Gilgal (The rolling away, Josh. v. 9), the place where the reproach of Egypt was rolled from them, after their battles with their enemies (Josh. x. 43), so the Apostles gathered to Christ. They could not leave Him (John vi. 68). He was the centre and circumference of their being.

2. **Speaking with Jesus.** "Told Him" (verse 30). To have the ear of Jesus to listen to our words, is to have the hand of Jesus to bless us in our work. Prayer is the *key* to open the storehouse of blessing (Matt. xv. 25-28), the *eye salve* to open the eyes (II. Kings vi. 17), the *harbinger* of peace (Phil. iv. 6, 7), the *swift messenger* in temptation (Eph. vi. 18), the *encourager* in persecution (Neh. iv. 9), the *dynamo* for power (Acts iv. 31-33), and the *succourer* of others (Acts xii. 5).

3. **Invited by Jesus.** "He said: Come," &c. (verse 31). The disciples were so busy that they had neither time to eat, nor leisure to commune with Christ. It is possible to be occupied with work for Christ, and lose sight of the Christ of the work. There should be the activity of Martha without her anxiety, blended with the attention of Mary and her restfulness; but the Mary character must precede the Martha. *We must go inside the veil to worship, before we go outside the camp to work.*

4. **Running after Jesus** (verse 33). The people were determined not to lose sight of Christ. So anxious were they to see and hear Him, that they "ran" after Him. O that every Christian was as desirous to keep Christ in view! Let the prayer of the bride be ours, namely, "Draw me, we will run after Thee" (Solomon's Song i. 4). If we are drawn we shall draw someone else, as is

indicated in the change of the singular pronoun "*me*" to the plural "*we*."

5. **Compassion of Jesus** (verse 34). Christ has the compassion of a *Shepherd* to find (Matt. ix. 36); the compassion of a *Provider* to supply (Matt. xv. 32); the compassion of a *Healer* to give sight (Matt. xx. 34); the compassion of a *Cleanser* to cleanse (Mark i. 41); the compassion of *Power* to deliver (Mark v. 19); the compassion of a *Deliverer* to emancipate (Mark ix. 22, 25); the compassion of a *Comforter* to console (Luke vii. 13); the compassion of a *Father* to love (Luke xv. 20); and the compassion of God to bless. Note the five times God is said to be "full of compassion" in Ps. lxxviii. 38; lxxxvi. 15; cxi. 4; cxii. 4; cxlv. 8.

6. **Instruction from Jesus.** "He began to teach them many things" (verse 34). We are not told what the "many things" were that Jesus taught the people. Doubtless He would teach them what they *were*, namely, sheep without a shepherd (Isa. liii. 6); and what He *was*, viz., the Good Shepherd seeking the wandering sheep (Luke xv.).

7. **Directed by Jesus** (verse 37). The Lord Jesus bids His disciples to give the multitude to eat. In like manner believers now are bidden to care for the hungry (Heb. xiii. 16), and, above all, to supply famishing beings with the Gospel of the Bread of Life.

8. **Questioned by Jesus.** "How many loaves have ye?" The Lord asks for what the disciples have got, and uses what they have to accomplish His purpose. "What is that in thine hand?" (Ex. iv. 2) was the question that the Lord put to Moses, and through that rod God did wondrous things. In like manner, if we only place ourselves and what we have at the disposal of the Lord, He can multiply and use them to His glory and others' good.

9. **Commanded by Jesus.** "He commanded them to make all sit down" (verses 39, 40). There must be quiet and order before Christ can meet the need of the people. In like manner there must be *quietness before the Lord* (Psalm lxii. 1, margin), and a *willingness to receive from the Lord* (John i. 12), before there can be *satisfaction in the Lord* (Psalm xvi. 2, R.V.).

10. **Look of Jesus.** "He looked up to heaven" (verse 41). That look of faith expresses His absolute dependence on His Father. What an Example for us! If we look to heaven before our actions, we shall be guided as to our actions, and in them.

11. **Blessing of Jesus** (verse 41). The blessing of Jesus made the bread to multiply to the satisfying of the need of the people. Verily the blessing of the Lord maketh rich (Proverbs x. 22). *The blessing of His grace* will make us rich unto salvation (Eph. ii. 6-8); *the blessing of His sanctification* will make us holy in life (1. Cor. i. 30); *the blessing of His strength* will make us strong to endure in the time of trial (11. Cor. xii. 9); and *the blessing of Himself will meet every need* (Col. ii. 10).

12. **Action of Jesus** (verse 41). Jesus "brake" the bread before He gave. In like manner His body was broken and bruised in death for us, before the blessing of His grace came to us.

13. **Gift of Jesus** (verse 41). As Christ gave the bread to the disciples to give to the multitude, so the Word of the Gospel is committed to believers to give to the unsaved (II. Cor. v. 19, 20).

14. **Divided by Jesus.** "Divided He among them all" (verse 41). The Lord saw that everyone got his portion. He overlooked none. He acts in the same way now. His desire is to bless, "whosoever" (John iii. 16)—"any man" (John x. 9).

142. FERVOUR OF THE HOLY SPIRIT

If we are all on fire with the fervour of the Holy Spirit, we shall kindle a flame in the souls of others. It is because there is so little fervour, that there is the great lack of moving power in the world. The late William Arnot used to tell of his being at a railway station, where he grew weary of waiting for the train to move. He inquired if the trouble was the want of water. "Plenty of water" was the prompt reply, "but it's no bilin'." That's the trouble in the Church, and with the individual Christian. What we want is—

1. **Fervency** in prayer (James v. 16).
2. **Enthusiasm** in service (Acts xvii. 6).
3. **Boldness** in testimony (Acts iv. 13).
4. **Constrainment** in work (II. Cor. v. 14).
5. **Spending** in toil (II. Cor. xii. 15).
6. **Graciousness** in life (Acts vi. 8, R.V.).
7. **Spirit-filledness** in heart (Eph. v. 18).

143. FIRE

What does fire represent?

1. **The presence of God.** "And Mount Sinai was altogether on a smoke, because the Lord descended upon it in fire" (Ex. xix. 18).

2. **Righteouness of God.** "From His right hand went a fiery law for them" (Deut. xxxiii. 2).

3. **Judgment of God.** The Lord shall trouble thee this day . . . . and burnt them with fire" (Josh. vii. 25).

4. **Favour of God.** "The fire came down from heaven and consumed the burnt offering" (II. Chron. vii. 1).

5. **Word of God.** "His word was in my heart as a burning fire" (Jer. xx. 9).

6. **Protection of God.** "For I, saith the Lord, will be unto her a wall of fire round about" (Zech. ii. 5).

7. **Searching of God.** "And I will bring the third part through the fire and will refine them as silver is refined" (Zech. xiii. 9).

144. FIRSTFRUITS

1. FIRSTFRUITS of **resurrection.** "Become the *firstfruits* of them that slept" (I. Cor. xv. 20).

2. Firstfruits of the **Spirit.** "Which have the *firstfruits* of the Spirit" (Rom. viii. 23).

3. Firstfruits of the **redeemed.** "We should be a kind of *firstfruits* of His creatures" (James i. 18).

4. Firstfruits of **Israel.** "If the *firstfruit* be holy," &c. (Rom. xi. 16).

5. Firstfruits of **Achaia.** "That it is the *firstfruits* of Achaia" (I. Cor. xvi. 15).

6. Firstfruits of **Asia.** "Who is the *firstfruits* of Achaia unto Christ" (Rom. xvi. 5).

7. Firstfruits unto **God** and the **Lamb.** "Being the *firstfruits* unto God and to the Lamb" (Rev. xiv. 4).

145. FIRST THINGS FIRST

WHAT the Lord says should be put first, should be followed, for He knows best.

1. **Seeking.** "Seek ye *first* the kingdom of God" (Matt. vi. 33).

2. **Cleansing.** "Cleanse *first* that which is within" (Matt. xxiii. 26).

3. **Reconciling.** "*First* be reconciled to thy brother (Matt. v. 24).

4. **Casting.** "*First* cast out the beam out of thine own eye" (Matthew vii. 5).

5. **Shewing.** "*First* to shew piety at home (I. Tim. v. 4).

6. **Partaking.** "Husbandman . . . *first* partaker of the fruits" (II. Tim. ii. 6).

7. **Delivering.** "I delivered unto you *first* of all," &c. (I. Cor. xv. 3).

146. FOLLOWING CHRIST

"FOLLOW Me" (John xii. 26) is Christ's command, after we have believed in Him. We should follow Him—

1. **Willingly,** as a sheep (John x. 27).

2. **Wholly,** as a servant (John xii. 26).

3. **Patiently,** as a sufferer (I. Peter ii. 21).
4. **Heartily,** as a saved one (Mark x. 52).
5. **Promptly,** as a disciple (Luke v. 11, 28).
6. **Constantly,** as a loving one (John xxi. 20).
7. **Imitatingly,** as a child of God (Eph. v. 1).

147. FOLLOWING THE LORD

1. *Whom* we are to follow (II. Thess. iii. 7; I. Peter ii. 21).
2. *Why* we are to follow (John viii. 12).
3. *How* we are to follow—

As believers, *fully*, like Caleb (Num. xiv. 24).
As children, *affectionately*, like Paul (Eph. v. 1; I. Cor. iv. 16).
As servants, *obediently* (John xii. 26).
As sheep, *attentively* (John x. 27).
As soldiers, *bravely*. David's mighty men (I. Chron. xi. 12).
As workers, *closely*, like Ruth (Ruth ii. 8).
As cross-bearers, *determinedly* (Matt. xvi. 24).
As worshippers, *rejoicingly* (Mark xi. 9).
As saved ones—*Jesus only*, like Bartimæus (Mark x. 52).
As His friends, *willingly* (Mark xv. 41).
As suffering ones, *consistently* (I. Peter ii. 21).
As loved ones, *lovingly* (I. Cor. xiv. 1).
As apprehended ones, *apprehendingly* (Phil. iii. 12).
As righteous ones, *righteously* (I. Tim. vi. 11).

148. FORGET NOT

1. **Person.** "*Forget not* the Lord" (Deut. viii. 11).

2. **Provocation.** Forget not past failure. "*Forget not* how thou provokedst the Lord thy God" (Deut. ix. 7).

3. **Prayer.** Forget not the poor. "*Forget not* the congregation of Thy poor for ever (Psalm lxxiv. 19).

4. **Punishment.** Forget not thine enemies. "*Forget not* the voice of Thine enemies" (Psalm lxxiv. 23).

5. **Praise.** Forget not benefits. "*Forget not* all His benefits" (Psalm ciii. 2).

6. **Practice.** Forget not commandments. "*Forget not* My law, but let thine heart keep My commandments" (Prov. iii. 1).

7. **Pleasing God.** Forget not to do good. "But to do good and to communicate *forget not*" (Heb. xiii. 16).

149. FORGIVENESS

1. **Unmerited** forgiveness. "When they had nothing to pay, He frankly *forgave* them both" (Luke vii. 42).

2. **Divine** forgiveness. "To the Lord our God belong mercy and *forgivenesses*" (Daniel ix. 9).

3. **Purchased** forgiveness. "In Whom we have redemption through His blood, the *forgiveness* of sins" (Eph. i. 7).

4. **Free** forgiveness. "That they may receive *forgiveness* of sins . . . . by faith that is in Me" (Acts xxvi. 18).

5. **Full** forgiveness. "Having *forgiven* you all trespasses" (Col. ii. 13).

6. **Practical** forgiveness. "*Forgive* us our debts, as we *forgive*" (Matthew vi. 12).

7. **Known** forgiveness. "Your sins are *forgiven* you for His name's sake" (I. John ii. 12).

150. FOR HIM

1. As the **Branches** to bear fruit for Him. "Herein is My Father glorified, that ye bear much fruit" (John xv. 8).

2. As **Lights** to shine for Him. "Let your light so shine before men" (Matt. v. 16).

3. As **Witnesses** to testify for Him. "Ye are witnesses of these things" (Luke xxiv. 48).

4. As **Servants** to serve for Him. "The servant is not greater than his Lord" (John xiii. 14-17).

5. As **Pilgrims** to abstain for Him. "As strangers and pilgrims, abstain from fleshly lusts" (I. Peter ii. 11).

6. As **Soldiers** to fight for Him. "Endure hardness, as a good soldier of Jesus Christ" (II. Tim. ii. 3).

7. As **Workmen** to work for Him. "Son, go work to-day in my vineyard" (Matt. xxi. 28).

151. FOUND

FOUND *by* Him a *sinner* (Matt. xiii. 44).
Found *in* Him a *saint* (Phil. iii. 9).
Found *of* Him a *servant* (II. Peter iii. 14).

1. **Found by Him a sinner.** This reminds us what we *were*, and what we *are* in ourselves. When He found us we were *guilty* (Lev. vi. 5, margin) because we had sinned; He found us as the woman did the piece of silver, *dead* and helpless (Luke xv. 9); He found us as the shepherd did the sheep, *far away from God*, and *unable* to get back (Luke xv. 4-6); He found us in a *desert place*, that is, in the *world* (Deut. xxxii. 10); He found us *asleep*, *unconscious* of the danger we were in (Matthew xxvi. 43); He found us like

the fig tree, when He looked for fruit, nothing but leaves (Matt. xxi. 19). But blessed be His name, *He found us* and brought us to Himself, and we are precious to Him, as the treasure was to the man who found it in the field.

2. **Found in Him a saint.** This reminds us of what we *are*, that is being in Christ, we *are* sanctified, accepted, and complete in Him; but it also reminds us that being in Him, as a stone in the building, as a member of His body, as a branch in the vine, the outward fact of this will be seen by the very life of Christ being manifested in our life.

3. **Found of Him a servant.** This reminds us of Him as the coming Lord (see Luke xix. 13) when He returns to reward His servants for work done for Him. How careful we should be as to the material we are building upon the foundation, and see to it that we are not building the wood of man's intellect, the hay of that which is pleasing to the imagination of the fleshly man, or the stubble of nothingness, giving no food to those to whom we go; but be careful that we are building on the foundation, the gold of divine righteousness, the silver of the atonement, and the precious stones of the glory, for our work will be tried as to its *quality*, not its *quantity*. If not successful, may we be faithful servants—faithful in walk and work—then we shall receive the Master's "Well done, good and faithful servant, enter thou into the joy of thy Lord."

152. FOUR GOOD WORKERS

"Borne of four" (Mark ii. 3).

Four men bringing one to Christ. We are not told who these men were, nor where they came from, but their action is recorded in the imperishable Word of God. These four men may be taken as an illustration of four things that are essential in seeking to bring others in contact with Christ: namely, prayer, faith, sympathy, and perseverance.

1. **Prayer.** Prayer is the hand that opens the door of heaven, and lets out the power of God. The prayer of faith, and the Spirit of God, are linked together like the yoked oxen that are ploughing in the field. "When they had prayed the place was shaken where they were assembled together; and they were all filled with the Holy Ghost" (Acts iv. 31). There is so little power in the Church, because there is so little prayer.

2. **Faith.** "When Christ saw their faith He said unto the sick," &c. (verse 5). If prayer is the hand that opens the door of blessing, faith is the hand that receives the blessing, and not for itself merely, but for others. This is not the only instance in the gospels where Christ blessed others for the faith's sake of the one pleading on their behalf. The Syro-Phenecian woman's daughter was healed for her mother's faith's sake (Matt. xv. 28), and the centurion and his servant is another case in point (Matt. viii. 10).

3. **Sympathy.** If the wind of declamation is blown upon any

soul, it but makes that one draw the cloak of indifference around him, but if the sun of Christian sympathy, the compassion of Christ, beams upon the unsaved one, he will soon throw off the cloak of indifference, and open up his mind to you (see Æsop's fable of the wind and the sun).

4. **Perseverance.** I saw a fishing-boat recently sailing up Loch Strivven in Scotland, but it had to tack as the wind was against it. So often in Christian work the unsaved will raise a wind of objections, let us not give up in consequence, but use the objections as helps, and thus perseveringly use our opponents to attain our desired end.

153. FOUR "IF SO BE'S"

1. **Indwelling.** "*If so be* that the Spirit of God dwell in you" (Rom. viii. 9). "If so be." Ah! here we have the secret, the test of the whole matter. If a man lives after the flesh, whatever colour it may assume, it is because he is self-centred, self-controlled, and self-aiming; but if a man lives after the spirit, in all the instincts of that holy nature, it is because the Spirit of God, in His consecrating love, controlling grace, and conforming power, lives in him.

2. **Resurrection.** The apostle, by the Holy Spirit, in speaking of the result if Christ is not raised from the dead, says, "We are found false witnesses of God; because we have testified of God that He raised up Christ, whom He raised not up, *if so be* that the dead rise not" (1. Cor. xv. 15). It is a proof that Christ is not raised from the dead if the dead rise not.

3. **Love for the Word.** Again, we find the words, "*if so be*" in relation to the Christian life. One result of Christ in the life is a love for the Word of God, and this love for the Word is an evidence that we know the Lord of the Word. As Peter says, "As new-born babes, desire the sincere milk of the Word . . . *if so be* ye have tasted that the Lord is gracious" (1. Peter ii. 2, 3).

4. **Suffering.** We read in Romans viii. 17: "And if children, then heirs, heirs of God, and joint heirs with Christ; *if so be* that we suffer with Him, that we also may be glorified together." The goal of glory is by the path of suffering, and there is no glory but by this path. From the use of the words it will be gathered that the secret of the believer being able to rise above the flesh is found in the indwelling presence of the Spirit of God; and if a professed believer does not walk according to the Spirit, it is because he has not the Holy Spirit; hence he does not belong to the Lord Jesus, however loud his profession may be.

154. FOURTEEN APPEARINGS OF CHRIST AFTER HIS RESURRECTION

THERE are no less than *fourteen* recorded appearings of Christ before Paul wrote to the Church of Corinth, and fifteen if we include Christ's manifestation to John in the Isle of Patmos. The fourteen appearings are as follows:—

1. To **Mary Magdalene** (John xx. 14; Mark xvi. 9).

2. To the other **women** (Matt. xxviii. 9).

3. To **Peter** (1. Cor. xv. 5; Luke xxiv. 34).

4. To the **two disciples** on their way to Emmaus (Mark xvi. 12, 13; Luke xxiv. 13-32).

5. The day He appeared to the **disciples,** in the absence of Thomas (John xx. 19-24).

6. To the **disciples** when Thomas was present (John xx. 24-29).

7. In Galilee, at the sea of Tiberias, to **Peter, John, Thomas, James, Nathanael,** and two **others** (John xxi. 1-14).

8. To the **disciples** on a mount in Galilee (Matt. xxviii. 16).

9. To more than **five hundred brethren** at once (1. Cor. xv. 6).

10. To **James** the apostle (1. Cor. xv. 7).

11. To all the **apostles** assembled together (1. Cor. xv. 7).

12. To all the **apostles** at His ascension (Luke xxiv. 50, 51; Acts i. 9, 10).

13. To **Stephen,** when he was being stoned to death (Acts vii. 56).

14. To **Paul** (1. Cor. xv. 8; Acts ix. 3-5; xxii. 6-10).

Such a mass of evidence attesting any given fact would be accepted as proof positive as to its validity in any court of justice.

155. FRUIT BEARING

THE evidence of union with Christ is fruit bearing (John xv.), and where there is no fruit there is no union, and no union means no life.

1. **Fruit of the Spirit.** Love. "The *fruit* of the Spirit is love" &c. (Gal. v. 22).

2. **Fruit of Righteousness.** Uprightness. "Filled with the *fruits* of righteousness, which are by Jesus Christ" (Phil. i. 11).

3. **Fruit of Holiness.** Separation to God. "Being made free from sin, and become servants unto God, ye have your *fruit* unto holiness" (Rom vi. 22).

4. **Fruit of our lips.** Thanksgiving. "Let us offer the sacrifice of praise to God continually, that is, the *fruit* of our lips" (Heb. xiii. 15).

5. **Fruit in Work.** Consistency. "Walk worthy of the Lord, being *fruitful* in every good work" (Col. i. 10).

6. **Fruit of Work.** Conversion and Consecration. "That I might have some *fruit* among you" (Rom. i. 13).

7. **Fruit of Generosity.** Ministering to others. "I desire *fruit* that may abound to your account" (Phil. iv. 17).

8. **Fruit unto God.** God's object in saving. "Bring forth *fruit* unto God" (Rom. vii. 4).

156. FRUIT OF THE SPIRIT

GAL. v. 22, 23

1. **Love** is the source of obedience. "If a man love Me, he will keep My words" (John xiv. 23).

2. **Joy** is the flower of holiness. "Righteousness, peace, and joy in the Holy Ghost" (Rom. xiv. 17).

3. **Peace** is the outcome of trustfulness. "Be careful for nothing . . . and the peace of God" (Phil. iv. 6, 7).

4. **Long-Suffering** is the wife of patience. "With long-suffering, forbearing one another in love" (Eph. iv. 2).

5. **Gentleness** is the daughter of love. "Gentle, shewing all meekness unto all men" (Titus iii. 2).

6. **Goodness** is the activity of grace. "To do good and to communicate forget not" (Heb. xiii. 16).

7. **Faith** is the faithfulness of courage. "This is the victory that overcometh the world, even our faith" (I. John v. 4).

8. **Meekness** is the lesson learned from Christ. "Learn of Me, for I am meek and lowly" (Matt. xi. 29).

9. **Temperance** is the mastery of faith. "Add to faith . . . . temperance" (II. Peter i. 5, 6).

157. FULNESS OF SUPPLY

WHEN Christ gave His disciples a draught of fishes He gave them such a supply that the boats were *filled* (Luke v. 6, 7). Christ never gives with a niggardly hand. There is sure to be an overplus when He gives. When He fed the people there were basketsful over.

1. He gives "*fulness* of **blessing**" to enrich us (Romans xv. 29).
2. *Fulness* of **Grace** to bless us (John i. 16).
3. *Fulness* of **Joy** to gladden us (John xv. 11).
4. *Fulness* of the **Spirit** to empower us (Eph. v. 18)
5. *Fulness* of **God** to sanctify us (Eph. iii. 19; Col. i. 19; ii. 9).
6. *Fulness* of **Faith** to assure us (Heb. x. 22).
7. *Fulness* of **Himself** to satisfy us (Eph. iv. 13).

158. GATHERED TOGETHER

THE "Gathered togethers" of Scripture are associated with the fellowship of God's saints.

1. Gathered together in **sorrow** (Luke xxiv. 33).
2. Gathered together for **worship** (Matt. xviii. 20).
3. Gathered together for **discipline** (I. Cor. v. 4).
4. Gathered together for **testimony** (Acts xiv. 27).

5. Gathered together in **service** (Ezra. iii. 1; Neh. viii. 1).

6. Gathered together for **prayer** (II. Chron. xx. 4; Acts xii. 12).

7. Gathered together in **glory** (Psalm l. 5; II. Thess. ii. 1).

159. "GAVE HIMSELF FOR"

THERE are seven places in the New Testament where the words "Gave Himself for," are distinctly associated with Christ's substitutionary work. In each case the Greek preposition, "*Huper*," translated "*for*," occurs. "*Huper*" means to act on behalf *of another, as acting in the stead of him*, in other words *a substitute.*

Why did Christ die?

1. To **pay** the ransom price. "*Gave Himself* a ransom *for* all" (I. Tim. ii. 6).

2. To **bear** our sins. "*Gave Himself for* our sins" (Gal. i. 4).

3. To **stand** in our place. "*Gave Himself for* me" (Gal. ii. 20).

4. To **have** us for Himself. "*Gave Himself for* it" (Eph. v. 25).

5. To **make** us acceptable to God. "*Given Himself for* us, an offering and a sacrifice to God for a sweet smelling savour" (Eph. v. 2).

6. To **redeem** us from all iniquity. "*Gave Himself for* us, that He might redeem us from all iniquity" (Titus ii. 14).

7. To **remind** us of our obligation to Him. "This is *My* body which is *given for* you" (Luke xxii. 19, 20).

160. GENESIS XXVIII. 15

1. **Presence in loneliness.** "I am with thee" (Matt. xxviii. 20).

2. **Preservation in danger.** "Will keep thee" (John xvii. 11, 12; I. Peter i. 5).

3. **Protection at all times.** "In all places" (John xiii. 1).

4. **Promise fulfilled.** "Will bring thee again into this land" (John xiv. 3).

5. **Perpetual companionship.** "I will not leave thee" (Heb. xiii. 5).

6. **Perseverance in blessing.** "Until I have done," &c. (Phil. i. 6).

161. GIFT OF THE HOLY SPIRIT

ACTS ii

THERE are four distinct gifts mentioned in the New Testament.

1. The *gift* of **Christ**, by God, to the world (John iii. 16).

2. The *gift* of the **Church**, by the Father, to Christ (John xvii. 6).

3. The *gift* by the **believer**, of himself, to God, for His occupation, use, and service (II. Cor. viii. 5).

4. The *gift* of the **Holy Spirit**, by Christ, to those who believe in Him (John i. 33; Acts ii. 38).

Let us note a few characteristics of the latter.

I. It was a Promised Gift. If we look back to the parting words of Christ, as recorded in John xiv. 16, we shall see that he spoke again and again of "The Comforter," whom He would send to take His place and carry on His work. It is well to remember that the Holy Spirit is *not* an influence, but a Person. His personality is most clearly taught by Christ, and also the diversity of His operation is most significant in the revelation of Christ concerning Him.

II. He is a Powerful Gift (Acts ii. 2-4, 37). The power of the Spirit is seen in the two similes used, "wind" and "fire"; and in the result produced, in that 3,000 were pricked to the heart and converted. The power of the Spirit is most marked in the change He made in the disciples. They were turned from cowardice to courage. Filled with the Spirit, there will be power to witness for Christ.

III. He is a Peculiar Gift (Acts ii. 5-13). The multitude could not understand what made the difference in the disciples, and as they heard them, there was one of two results. Some were "amazed," and others "mocked." *A man who is filled with the Holy Spirit will be a marked one.* The devil will seek to overthrow him, and men will scoff at him.

The peculiar features of the Holy Spirit are—He is *holy*, *loving*, *true*, and *righteous;* and those who possess Him are like Him; hence those who are not in possession of Him, do not like Him or His.

IV. He is a Prophetic Gift (Acts ii. 14-21). The Jews need not have wondered. We wonder that they should wonder, for they should have known their own Scripture, and have been expecting the fulfilment of its prophecies. Note the two "I wills" in verses 17, 18. The "I will" tells us of the certainty of the promise; and the "pouring out" of the sufficiency of the promise. The "pouring out" suggests another emblem of the Holy Spirit, viz., water.

The following five "**I will pour**" illustrate the above:—

Salvation (Prov. i. 23).

Satisfaction (Isaiah xliv. 3).

Speaking (Joel ii. 28).

Supplication (Zech. xii. 10).

Superabundance (Mal. iii. 10, margin).

V. Purchased Gift (Acts ii. 22-36). These verses describe the person and work of the Lord Jesus, and one of the consequences of His atoning work, namely, the gift of the Holy Spirit. It was Jesus in resurrection power who said to His disciples, "Receive ye the Holy Ghost" (John xx. 22).

VI. The preliminary to receiving the Gift (verse 38). Repentance towards God precedes the reception of the Holy Spirit. Repentance is taking God's side against one's self, as the publican did when he condemned himself in God's presence. Repentance is a change of mind wrought by the Holy Spirit, and shewn in the action. Repentance is opening the door to the Holy Spirit. Receiving the Spirit is to allow Him to come in and take possession of the house.

VII. Proclaimed Gift (verses 41-47). They proclaimed the gift in the following way:—

Confessing the Lord in baptism (verse 41).

Communing with the Lord's people. Note the words "fellowship," "together," "all," "one accord."

Continuing in the truth of God, and in oneness with each other (see verses 42-46).

Consecration of all to the Lord (verse 45).

Praising God (verse 47).

Additions to the Church of God (verse 47).

162. GLORIOUS PROTECTION

We may take the meaning of the names of the Cities of Refuge as illustrating the protection that Christ gives, and the kind of refuge Christ is (Num. xxxv.; Josh. xx., xxi.)

1. "**Kedesh.**" Kedesh means holy or separated. Christ is a Holy Refuge, and He is made such to His people (1. Cor. i. 30).

2. "**Shechem.**" Shechem means shoulder, or strength. Christ is a Strong Refuge. No shot of the enemy can pierce Him, He is impregnable (Ps. xviii. 2).

3. "**Hebron.**" Hebron means company, or fellowship. Christ is a Living Refuge, with whom we have been called to have fellowship (1. Cor. i. 9).

4. "**Bezer.**" Bezer means strong, or a stronghold. Christ is a Secure Refuge. Nothing can separate us from His love (Romans viii. 39), no one can condemn us (Romans viii. 34), and no one can take us from our hiding place (Col. iii. 3).

5. "**Ramoth.**" Ramoth means high, or high places. Christ is a High Refuge. We are made to sit with Him in heavenly places (Ephesians ii. 6).

6. "**Golan.**" Golan means a circle, or enclosed. Christ is a Perfect Refuge. The Lord has hedged His people in, on every side (Job i. 10).

163.—GLORY OF JESUS

1. The *glory* of His **Holiness** is seen in His life (Heb. vii. 26).

2. The *glory* of His **grace** is seen in His dealings with sinners (Luke vii. 47).

3. The *glory* of His **love** is seen in His Cross (Gal. ii. 20).

4. The *glory* of His **compassion** is seen in His weeping over Jerusalem (Luke xix. 41).

5. The *glory* of His **power** is seen in His miracles. Think of what He did. He raised the dead (Matt. ix. 25; Luke vii. 11-17; John xi. 44); He healed the sick (Matt. iv. 24); He opened the eyes of the blind (Matt. ix. 27-30); He unstopped deaf ears (Mark vii. 32); He unloosed stammering tongues (Matt. ix. 33); He fed five thousand and more from five barley loaves and two small fishes (John vi. 9, 10); He stilled the tempest (Mark iv. 39); He cast out demons (Mark v. 1-20); He cleansed the lepers (Matt. viii. 2-4); He straightened the crooked (Luke xiii. 11-13); He turned water into wine (John ii. 7-10); and He rose from the dead (II. Cor. v. 15).

164. "GO"

THERE are several commands that are associated with the monosyllable "*go*" which we may take to illustrate the commands of Christ.

1. **Power.** "*Go* in this thy might" (Judges vi. 14).

2. **Prayer.** "In Thy name we *go* against this multitude" (II. Chronicles xiv. 11).

3. **Progress.** "*Go* forward" (Exodus xiv. 15; Psalm lxxxiv. 7).

4. **Practice.** "*Go* and do thou likewise" (Luke x. 37).

5. **Proclamation.** "*Go* tell this people" (Isaiah vi. 9; Acts xxviii. 26).

6. **Perseverance.** "*Go* out into the highways," &c. (Luke xiv. 21-23; Matt. xxii. 9).

7. **Presence.** "My presence shall *go* with thee" (Ex. xxxiii. 14).

165. GOD'S CARE FOR HIS PEOPLE

1. He **watches** over them with His eyes (Psalm xxxiv. 15).
2. He **listens** to their prayers with His ears (I. Peter iii. 12).
3. He **instructs** them by His word (Deut. xxxiii. 3).
4. He **loves** them with His heart (I. John iii. 1).
5. He **supports** them by His hands (Hosea xi. 3).
6. He **kisses** them with His lips (Canticles i. 2).
7. He **leads** them by His Spirit (Romans viii. 14).
8. He **encourages** them by His promises (II. Peter i. 4).

166. GOD'S CHARGE TO ABRAM

GENESIS xvii. 1.

There are three reasons why the Lord charges Abram to walk before Him.

I. Because of past failure. For thirteen years it seems that Abram had been walking before Sarah in listening to her, and following her advice with reference to Hagar. When Ishmael was born, Abram was eighty-six years old (Gen. xvi. 16), and he was ninety-nine years old when the Lord appeared and gave him the charge to walk before Him. As A. Fuller says, "This admonition implies a serious reproof. It was like saying, 'Have no more recourse to unbelieving expedients; keep in the path of uprightness, and leave Me to fulfil My promise in the time and manner that seem good to come!'" What a lesson is here afforded us, never to use unlawful means under the pretence of being more useful, or promoting the cause of God. Our part is to walk before Him, and be upright, leaving Him to work out His own designs in His own way.

II. The Lord charges Abram to walk before Him, **because He commands it.** Where the word of a king is, there is authority. I know a little boy who, when he is told to do a certain thing, says to his father, "What for?" and the reply he receives is, "Because I tell you." It is quite sufficient when the Lord tells us to do anything, to do it without questioning.

III. The Lord bids Abram to walk before Him, **because of what He is.** "I am the Almighty God." The meaning of the words "*El Shaddai*," translated "Almighty God," is the Irresistible One, who is able to make and destroy. It is the name that expresses God's Almightiness, by which He was specially made known to the patriarchs (Exodus vi. 3). The title occurs six times in Genesis (xvii. 1; xxviii. 3; xxxv. 11; xliii. 14; xlviii. 3; xlix. 25), and thirty-one times in the book of Job. Some have derived *Shaddai* from Shad a nipple, because God feeds His children with sufficiency of all good things, as the loving mother doth the child with the milk of her breasts. Hence we might speak of God in His all-sufficiency as "The Many-Breasted God." There is no lack with Him, therefore we may well count upon supplies from Him. What does it mean to walk before God? (1) To live as in His sight, and under His inspection. (2) To realize at all times His presence and His providence. (3) To feel the dignity of the godly life. We are not to walk behind Him as if ashamed, but before Him, as conscious of the dignity of our high calling. (4) To feel the constant energy of spiritual life. The light of God's countenance is upon us, and in that we have life. We cannot fail with the Almighty power behind us. (5) To feel the love of God towards us. Unless there was redeeming love on God's part, it would be impossible for us to walk before Him. In *that* alone our souls can live and move. (6) To apprehend God's love by our faith. This is that power in the soul that lays hold of the Divine fulness. Hence "the just shall live by faith."

167. GOD'S COVENANT WITH ABRAM

GENESIS xvii. 2

"I WILL make my covenant" (verse 2). The covenant had already been given (Gen. xv. 18), but it is here ratified and enlarged. This covenant was unconditional. It has a threefold fulfilment as to the seed. (1) In Abram, being the father of many nations. "To the Jew, the Moslem, and the Christian alike, the prophet Abraham is a common ancestor. Trace these three forms of belief to their fountain-head, and they meet in the tent of that ancient confessor." (2) In Christ being the "Son of Abraham" (Matt. i. 1), for He was the promised "seed," as Paul says in speaking of the promise given by God to Abram, "He saith not, and to seeds, as of many; but as of one, and to thy seed, which is Christ" (Gal. iii. 16). (3) In the believer in Christ, for they who believe in Christ are said to be blessed with believing Abram, and to be his spiritual children. "If ye be Christ's, then are ye Abraham's seed" (Gal. iii. 29).

Notice the six "*I wills.*"

The "I will" of *Covenant* (verse 2).

The "I will" of *Fruitfulness* (verse 6).

The "I will" of *Creation* (verse 6).

The "I will" of *Establishing* (verse 7).

The "I will" of *Gift* (verse 8).

The "I will" of *Relationship* (verse 8).

168. GOD'S JUDGMENT ON SODOM

GENESIS xviii. 22-33

THE Holy Jehovah, the ministry of angels, the pleading of Abraham, the wrong position of Lot, the lingering wife of Lot, and filthy Sodom, are brought out in the following:—

I. The Lord answers the prayers of His people on behalf of others. One of the bright points in Abraham's life is his pleading on behalf of Sodom. His prayer is a model one. (1) It was the prayer of a man who was *right* with the Lord. Abraham "stood before the Lord" (verse 22). To stand before the Lord is to act as in His presence (Lev. xxiv. 4), and to be conscious of being right with Himself (I. Kings xvii. 1). (2) It was the prayer of a man who was in *intimate communion with the Lord*. "Abraham drew near" (verse 23). We must draw near to God in the full assurance of faith if we would have His ear (Heb. x. 22). (3) It was a *bold* prayer. Abraham begins to question the Lord (see verses 23, 24, 25). We may come "boldly" to the throne of grace (Heb. iv. 16), but we may not come rudely. (4) It was a *humble* prayer (verse 27). Cross out the words in italics—*am*, *but*. While he confesses that he is "dust and ashes," he is more than this, for he is an indestructible spirit, therefore to say he is "*but* dust and ashes" is not true, though to say he is "dust and ashes" is to express his utter abasement of himself. (5) The prayer was *persevering*. Abraham does not stop at one answer, but asks again and again. God's blessings, while they satisfy, create an appetite, and cause us to ask for more. (6) The prayer was *answered*. God gave Abraham all he asked. Abiding in Christ, we have a similar opportunity, for He says, "Whatsoever we ask," &c. (John xiv. 13; xv. 7). (7) The prayer was *limited*. Young says, "Ought not six gracious answers to have strengthened the faith of the suppliant rather than exhausted it. Who can tell whether, if he had asked that the cities should be spared even for Lot's sake, the request would not have been answered?" Trapp also remarks upon this—"Abraham hucked with the Lord so long, till he had brought Him down from fifty to ten; and mark that he left begging ere God left bating. Let us find praying hearts, and He will find a pitying heart."

II. God takes note of what is going on in the world. Sin has a voice which cries to God for vengeance, as when the blood of Abel spilt by Cain called for punishment (Gen. iv. 10), and as in the case of Sodom (Gen. xviii. 20). The sin of Sodom was *excessive* (Gen. xiii. 13); *grievous, great* (Gen. xviii. 20); *bitter* (Deut. xxxii. 32); *open* (Isaiah iii. 9; Gen. xix. 5); *hateful* (Jer. xxiii. 14); it was spoken of ever afterwards as being most abominable to the Lord, and called for severest measures upon those who were guilty of like iniquity (Deut. xxiii. 17; I. Kings xiv. 24; xv. 12; xxii. 46; Jude 7). There are some who seem to act as if God took no note of what they were doing, but He surely does. Not a single thing escapes His notice, for He not only notes the actions of men, but weighs them as well (I. Sam. ii. 3). Two children were playing in a room together. A plate of sweet cakes was brought in and laid upon the table. "Oh, I want one of those cakes!" cried the little boy, jumping up as soon as his mother left the room, and going on tip-toe towards the table. "No, no," said his sister, pulling him back, "You must not touch." "Mother won't know it; she did not count them," he cried, shaking her off, and stretching forth his hand. "If she didn't, God counted," answered the sister. Yes, God counts, as Job says, "Doth not He see my ways, and count all my steps?" (Job xxxi. 4).

III. God punishes sinners for their sins. The Dead Sea to-day is a silent and solemn witness to this fact, and the overthrow of Sodom is proverbial of God's righteous action against sin (Deut. xxix. 23; Is. xiii. 19; Jer. xlix. 18; l. 40; Amos iv. 11; Luke xvii. 29; II. Peter ii. 6; Jude 7). The French proverb on punishment is suggestive—"Punishment is the recoil of crime; and the strength of the backward stroke is in proportion to the original blow." "Whatsoever a man soweth, that shall he also reap" (Gal. vi. 7). If the farmer sows tares he does not expect wheat, neither can a sinner expect anything but punishment if he continues and dies in a course of sin.

169. GOD'S CREATIVE ACTS TYPICAL OF HIS NEW CREATION

1. **Darkness upon the Waters.** "Darkness was upon the face of the deep" (Gen. i. 2). This is typical of the state of the sinner in the darkness of sin, ignorance, and unbelief. The purpose of the Gospel, as Christ told Paul, is to "turn them from darkness to light" (Acts xxvi. 18).

2. **The Spirit moving upon the Waters.** "And the Spirit of God moved upon the face of the waters" (Gen. i. 2). This shadows forth the work of the Holy Spirit in regeneration; even as Peter, in reminding us of what the Lord has done for us, says, "Who hath called you out of darkness into His marvellous light" (I. Peter ii. 9).

3. **The Light shining forth.** "God said, Let there be light, and there was light" (Gen. i. 3). This reminds us of the light shining into the heart by the Holy Spirit, through the Word; in fact, the apostle uses it as an illustration of this truth, "God, who commanded the light to shine out of darkness, hath shined in our hearts, to give the light of the knowledge of the glory of God in the face of Jesus Christ" (II. Cor. iv. 6).

4. **Life and growth.** "Let the earth bring forth . . . . and the earth brought forth grass . . . herb . . . tree yielding fruit" (Gen. i. 11, 12). God said, and then life and fruit followed. So it is with us who have heard the voice of God. We have eternal life, and the evidence of it is growth in grace, for the command of Christ is very clear. "Let your light so shine before men, that they may see your good works, and glorify your Father which is in heaven" (Matthew v. 16).

5. **Blessing and fruit-bearing.** "And God blessed them, and God said unto them, Be fruitful," &c. (Gen. i. 28). In and by Him we are blessed; in Him is our fruit found, and by Him we are fruitful. This is the result of fellowship with Him, for "if we walk in the light, as He is in the light, we have fellowship one with another" (I. John i. 7), that is, with the Father and the Son.

6. **Union and power.** "God said, Let us make man in Our image, after Our likeness, and let them have dominion," &c. (Gen. i. 26). This was lost by sin, but, in a spiritual sense, is restored by accepting Christ; as Paul reminded the Ephesians, in telling them what they were, are, and should be, "Ye were sometimes darkness, but now are ye light in the Lord: walk as children of light" (Eph. v. 8).

7. **Sanctification** (Gen. ii. 3). As God set apart the seventh day as a day of rest, so He has set apart the believer in Christ for Himself; and because he is thus set apart, he is to separate from all that is, and those who are not the Lord's. "For what fellowship hath righteousness with unrighteousness? and what communion hath light with darkness?" (II. Cor. vi. 14).

170. GOD'S COVENANT WITH NOAH

GENESIS ix. 1-17

A COVENANT usually means a compact between two parties, delivered in solemn form, and requiring mutual engagements. As employed in Scripture, from the nature of the case, it must also be extended to mean God's *promise* by which He binds Himself to His creatures without terms, absolutely (Jer. xxxiii. 20; Ex. xxxiv. 10). Gesenius derives the term from the verb "to cut" (Isa. lvii. 8, margin), as it is a Hebrew phrase "to cut a covenant," and it was customary for the purpose of ratifying such, to divide an animal in parts (Gen. xv. 10, 17). Others derive it from the verb "to eat together," thus explaining the phrase "covenant of salt" (Num. xviii. 19; II. Chron. xiii. 5).

1. **Divine Covenant.** "I, behold, I," &c. (verse 9). The origin of the covenant is in God Himself. He also is the One who undertakes to fulfil all the conditions of the covenant. As illustrating this, notice how often the Lord uses the pronoun "*I*."

The "I" of *gift* (verse 3).

The "I" of *requirement* (verse 5).

The "I" of *establishment* (verses 9, 11).

The "I" of *making* (verse 12).

The "I" of *setting* (verse 13).

The "I" of *bringing* (verse 14).

The "I" of *remembering* (verses 15, 16).

The "I" of *looking* (verse 16).

The "I" of *assuring* (verse 17).

"Thou shalt" is a command, but no power to perform. "I will" is the Lord acting as we trust Him, and fulfilling His own word.

2. **Sure Covenant.** God assures Noah there shall not "any more" be a flood, &c. Note the "any more's" of verse 11, and the "no more" of verse 15. When the Lord says "no more" there is an end to the matter, and we may be sure that He will fully fulfil His word. When we have a "Thus saith the Lord" for anything we have a rock upon which we can build, and no storm can overthrow us. Notice three "no more's" of the New Testament as illustrating: *Atonement* (Heb. x. 18, 26). *Absolution* (Heb. x. 17; viii. 8). *Abiding* (John xv. 4).

3. **Ratified Covenant.** The bow in the cloud is God's sign and seal that He will surely keep to His covenant. God has set the bow of Christ's atonement in the dark cloud of our sin. He has set the bow of His consolation in the dark cloud of trial; the bow of His promise in the cloud of difficulty; and the bow of His coming again in the dark cloud of bereavement. Law says, "How can we render thanks enough for this superadded pearl in our diadem of encouragements! We are thus led to look for our bow on the cloud

of every threatening storm. In the world of nature it is not always visible; but in the world of grace it ever shines. When the darkest clouds thicken around us the Sun of Righteousness is neither set nor has eclipse, and His ready smile converts the drops into an arch of peace."

4. **Extent of the Covenant.** "Every living creature," &c. (verse 15). The covenant extends to "all flesh." The animal creation was destroyed, excepting those who were in the ark, but God says it shall not be so again. The animal creation has come under the curse of sin, but under Christ and in the Millennium it will be "delivered into the glorious liberty of the children of God" (Rom. viii. 19-23), and the scene depicted in Isaiah xi. shall be literally fulfilled.

5. **Perpetual Covenant.** "Everlasting covenant" (verse 16), that is, to last until it shall be needed no more. We cannot apply the adjective "everlasting" to nothing. As long as the covenant is needed it is in force. When the conditions that called forth the covenant no longer exist, then it can no longer apply. This, which would at first sight seem to be against "eternal punishment," is really an illustration of it, for the sinner can never cease to be; therefore the punishment (whatever it is) is always applied. How comforting it should be to the child of God that he is related to the eternal God, saved in an eternal salvation, quickened in an eternal life, comforted with eternal consolation, indwelt by the eternal Spirit, united to the eternal Saviour, kept for an eternal inheritance, and secured by an eternal covenant.

171. GOD'S DESIRE FOR THE WELFARE OF MEN

THE following seven facts speak for themselves, that the Lord desires the welfare of men:—

1. The **cross** of Christ declares it (John iii. 16).
2. The **nature** of God asserts it (I. John iv. 8, 9).
3. The **invitations** of Jesus affirm it (Mat. xi. 28).
4. The **word** of God reiterates it (John iii. 17, 18).
5. The **Spirit** of God repeats it (Rev. xxii. 17).
6. The **ambassadors** of the Gospel proclaim it (II. Cor. v. 20).
7. The **tears** of Christ confirm it (Luke xix. 41).

But if men will not have God's mercy in love, they must have His might in judgment. He is almighty in grace (Gen. xvii. 1), but He is also almighty to punish (Rev. xv. 3).

172. GOD'S DWELLING-PLACE (THE TABERNACLE)

GOD'S dwelling-place in the past eternity was in the high and holy place (Isa. lvii. 15). Speaking after the manner of men, God desired another dwelling-place, and so created man that He might have a companion to dwell and commune with. Sin came in and separated man from God. Notwithstanding this, God's heart went out towards him, for He says, "My delights were with the sons of men" (Prov. viii. 31), and He commanded Moses to make Him a sanctuary, that He might dwell among them (Ex. xxv. 8), which was but a shadow of Him who should come tabernacling among us (John i. 14, R.V., M.), and having by His own blood put away the hindrance—sin—and made a way even into the very presence of God, the sinner can now draw near to God, and God can *dwell in the believer*, on the ground of the finished work and living Person of our Lord Jesus Christ.

What was the Tabernacle made for?

God Himself gives the answer, "*that I may dwell among you*," but God comes nearer than that to us who believe in Him; "*I will dwell in them.*" This tells us that God dwells not now in any earthly temple of man's making, but in the *individual* believer in Christ (I. Cor. vi. 19), and also in the Church as a whole (II. Cor. vi. 16; Eph. ii. 22). This implies many truths. Among these we might notice—

1. **Regeneration by the Spirit of God through the truth.** He it was who quickened us from the death of sin, led us to Christ, begot in us a new nature, united us to, and made us one in, and with Christ, and He now *dwells in* every child of God as the One who witnesses to our acceptance, as God's mark upon us, as the Comforter to cheer, as the Teacher to instruct, and as the Indwelling Power, for us, in us, and by us to overcome our enemies, to glorify God, and to work in us mightily, thus to manifestly show that we are born again.

2. **Satisfaction in and with Christ.** He says, "He that eateth My flesh, and drinketh My blood, dwelleth in Me, and I *in him*" (John vi. 56). The thought here, is our union with Christ and His with us, and the satisfaction that flows to Him and to us, because we are in Him. What satisfaction it gives us as we remember that we are accepted in all the worthiness of the Person and work of Jesus, and also that He is in us the hope of glory!

3. **Relationship to God as our Father.** "I will *dwell* in them . . . . and I will be their God, and they shall be My people . . . . and will be a Father unto you, and ye shall be My sons and daughters, saith the Lord Almighty" (II. Cor. vi. 16-18). Here we have God's relationship to us—"Father"—He has sent forth His Spirit in our hearts, crying, Abba Father; and we have our relationship to Him—"sons and daughters." Thus the Spirit, Son, and Father *dwell* in us.

4. **Standing.** "Ye are not in the flesh, but in the Spirit, if so be that the Spirit of God *dwell* in you. Now if any man have not the Spirit of Christ, he is none of His" (Rom. viii. 9). We are no longer in the first Adam, but we stand accepted in the last Adam, the Lord from heaven; and the fact that this is so, is, that the Spirit of God dwelleth in us.

5. **Separation from the world.** "Be ye not unequally yoked together with unbelievers: for what fellowship hath righteousness with unrighteousness? and what communion hath light with darkness? and what concord hath Christ with Belial? or what part hath he that believeth with an infidel? and what agreement hath the temple of God with idols? for ye are the temple of the living God: as God hath said, I will *dwell* in them" (II. Cor. vi. 14-18). Notice a sevenfold contrast here—

1. Christian	and	Unbeliever.
2. Righteousness	and	Unrighteousness.
3. Light	and	Darkness.
4. Christ	and	Belial.
5. Believer	and	Infidel.
6. Temple of God	and	Idols.
7. Clean	and	Unclean.

Well may Paul ask, what agreement have these one with the other? None; therefore there is no other alternative for us but to be practically separated from the one to the other.

6. **Power.** "I will dwell and walk in them." This is our power. The Spirit is in us as our power to pray (Rom. viii. 26); He is in us as our power to keep (II. Tim. i. 14); He is in us as the source of fruit-bearing; He is in us as our power to enable us to walk in Christ; He is in us as our power to separate us from the world, and our power in work and testimony.

7. **Resurrection.** "If the Spirit of Him that raised up Jesus from the dead dwell in you, He that raised up Christ from among the dead shall also quicken your mortal bodies, because of His (margin) Spirit that dwelleth in you" (Rom. viii. 11). By His own almighty power shall He quicken our mortal bodies should we die; and if not, by His power shall we be caught up to meet Christ, and be changed in a moment, and be like Him.

173. GOD'S REMEMBRANCE

THERE are several things that God is said to remember.

1. He remembers **His people** (Isaiah xliv. 21; xlix. 15).
2. He remembers **we are dust** (Psalm ciii. 14).
3. He remembers **the sparrows** (Luke xii. 6).
4. He remembers **deeds of kindness** (Jer. ii. 2).
5. He remembers **our works** (Amos viii. 7).
6. He remembers **His mercy and truth** (Psalm xcviii. 3).
7. He remembers **His holy promise** (Psalm cv. 42).
8. He remembers **His covenant** (Lev. xxvi. 42, 45; Deut. iv. 31; Ezek. xvi. 60; Psalm cv. 8, cvi. 45).

Being God, He cannot forget, but knowing our frailty, He graciously speaks after the manner of men for our comfort and consolation.

174. GOD'S WORKMEN

"THERE were two men who had the oversight in making the tabernacle. The first was *Bezaleel*, the son of *Uri*, the son of *Hur*, of the tribe of *Judah;* and the second was *Aholiab*, the son of *Ahisamach*, of the tribe of *Dan* (Ex. xxxi. 1-6). We want to take these *seven* names and their meaning as illustrating the secret of success in Christian work in the divine sense of the word, and also the sort of workers God wants.

1. **Bezaleel,** which means *in the shadow of God.* If our work is to be God honouring, we must be dwelling in the secret place of God's presence.

2. **Uri,** which means *light of Jehovah.* Living in the light of Jehovah, in the light of His word and presence. And the result will be that our whole body will be full of light (Matt. vi. 22); thus the light that has shone into our hearts will shine out in our life in work for, and with the Lord (II. Cor. iv. 6, 7).

3. **Hur.** This name has a triple meaning—*free-born*, *noble*, *white*. *Free-born.* Only those that are born of the Spirit, by the Word and through faith in Christ, are made children of God; and as such, our Father says to us, "*Son*, go work to-day in My vineyard." *Noble.* As free-born ones our work must be noble, noble in its motive—the constraining love of Christ; noble in its object—the glory of God. *White.* As free-born noble ones our work must be white, no second motives, but pure, holy service to the Lord.

4. **Judah,** which means *praise.* Working Christians are joyful, praising ones. Believers who do not work for the Lord have plenty of time to listen to the doubts and fears the devil brings before them; but the working Christian is like the busy bee; as it passes from flower to flower getting the sweetness out of each, it seems to hum its song of praise as it goes buzzing along. So we shall find that as we speak to others of the love of Christ, that love will burn in our own hearts.

5. **Aholiab,** which means *tent of my father.* The tent is the symbol of separation from the world. As workers we are sent into the world, but we are no longer of the world, and no longer is the world in us, although we are in the world as a ship is in the water and the water not in the ship. If we would have power in service, there must be practical separation from all that is worldly, and a confession that we are pilgrims and strangers on the earth, and that "our citizenship is in heaven, from whence we look for the Saviour."

6. **Ahisamach,** which means *brotherly support.* The secret of manifest blessing from God in work done for Him is unity amongst the workers. "How can two walk together except they agree?" and this applies with equal force to work; there must be unity, brotherly support; no bickerings or jealousies, but a real interest in each other, and each other's work; remembering that it is the Lord's work, and that we should rejoice in whomsoever He uses.

7. **Dan**, which means *judgment*. As to our *persons*, we shall never be judged for our sin, because Jesus has borne the judgment for us. As *servants*, we shall be judged, that is, our *work*, of what sort it is. As *sons*, we are now to judge our *ways* by the Word of God; but we are also to judge what sort of work we are building on the foundation—which is Christ. If we are building on it the wood of vain-glory, loving to be seen of men; the hay of profession and the stubble of mixed motive, it will all be burnt up at the judgment seat of Christ. But if we build on the foundation, the gold of pure motive—the glory of God; the silver power of love, and the precious stones of prayerful faith, believing work and loving labour (I. Cor. iii. 11-15), these will stand the fire, and we shall receive the Master's "Well done, good and faithful servant, enter thou into the joy of thy Lord." Thus may we judge our work of what sort it is now, and be "stedfast, unmovable, always *abounding* in the work *of the Lord*, forasmuch as ye know that your labour is not in vain in the Lord" (I. Cor. xv. 58).

175. GOD'S WRITTEN WORD

Psalm cxix. 89-112

We give an acrostic on the title, as illustrating a few of the characteristics of the Word of God in it.

G Guiding Word (verse 105). It is a lamp unto our feet, to show how we should live; it is a light to our path, to reveal danger in the way; and it is a star that we shall find—as the wise men did—that leads to Christ. The Lord guides with His eye (Ps. xxxii. 8); with His counsel (Ps. lxxiii. 24); with His hands (Ps. lxxviii. 72); and with His Spirit (John xvi. 13). And all this is by His Word. There is no guidance apart from the truth.

O Overcoming Word (verse 98). We are wiser than our enemies, because we know their tactics through the Word. The way to overcome Satan is to meet him, as Christ did, with "It is written," and the secret of victory over the world is by letting the Word dwell in us (I. John ii. 14), and by simple faith in Christ.

D Delighting Word (verse 92). The Word enables us to delight in the Lord, as the Psalmist did (Ps. xxxiv. 2); to delight in the work of Christ, as the Samaritans did under the preaching of Philip (Acts viii. 8); it brings us joy, as the angels did to the shepherds (Luke ii. 10); and it gives us gladness.

S Strengthening Word (verse 112). The Word first inclines the heart, and then the heart is inclined to the Word. His Word puts strength of purpose in our hearts, so that we purpose to go in the strength of the Lord. He strengthens us by His Word for life's journey, as the angel did Elijah with the food (I. Kings xix. 7). He strengthens us for service, as Christ did the disciples with the promise of the enduement from on high (Luke xxiv. 49); and He empowers us for suffering, as He did Paul when He promised him sufficient grace (II. Cor. xii. 9).

W Winnowing Word (verse 102). We are very foolish, and the Lord has often to teach us by painful experience how weak and erring we are; but His purpose in all His dealings is, that the chaff may be winnowed away, and that we may the better serve Him.

R Rejoicing Word (verse 111). Jeremiah found rejoicing of heart, by eating the Word (Jer. xv. 16), and the Ethiopian found joy in the Lord by believing in Christ (Acts viii. 39). Search the Scriptures to be sure, believe them to be bright, practise them to be powerful, and rest in them to rejoice.

I Instructing Word (verse 95). Contemplation in the truth will enable us to confound our enemies. If we are instructed in the Word, and instructed by it, it will construct our character. Then we shall be like Abram's instructed servants (Gen. xiv. 14, margin), able to overcome our enemies in conflict.

T Testing Word (verse 96). We shall never be Pharisees boasting of our purity, if we go by the truth, and judge ourselves by the Word. The Word is a *light* to search out evil, a *hammer* to break down self, a *fire* to consume sin, and a *sword* to kill all that is not of God.

T Tried Word (verse 105). Christ is the Tried Stone (Isa. xxviii. 16). He is the Tried Stone in two senses. (1) Because He has been tried, and (2) because He tries. His Word is the same; it has come through the fire and stood the test; and as we try it, it tries us.

E Enduring Word (verse 89). God's Word is settled and more lasting than the heavens, for they shall pass away, but His truth remains. His Word is settled about sin and the sinner (Rom. iii. 10); the Saviour and His Work (Heb. x. 7); His servants and their message (Rom. x. 15); and about sanctification and the means of grace (Matt. iv. 4).

N Nerving Word (verse 107). Discouraged we are apt to be as Elijah was because of his enemies (I. Kings xix. 4); dismayed we may be as we think of the power of those we have to contend against, even as the companion of Elisha (II. Kings vi. 15); and disheartened as Israel was, because of the roughness of the way (Num. xxi. 4); but let us pray the Psalmist's prayer; then we shall have spiritual nerve to endure whatever comes.

W Wonderful Word (verse 103). It is the sweetest and dearest of all. There is no other like it, as David said of Goliath's sword (I. Sam. xxi. 9). It is sweeter than honey, more precious than gold, and lasting as God. It is wonderful because of its *Author;* because of its *contents;* and because of its construction.

O Omnipotent Word. The spirit that runs like an electric current through the words of the Psalmist is, that if anything is to be accomplished, it must be by and according to the Word.

R Refreshing Word (verse 103). When David's servants found the Egyptian in the field, he was almost dead; but they gave him food and his spirit came again, and he was refreshed and able to do David service (I. Sam. xxx. 12). Even so with the Word, it refreshes us, and with renewed vigour we go on our way.

D Delivering Word (verse 101). Goliath came against David in his own name, and was defeated. David went against Goliath in the name of the Lord, and according to His Word, and was delivered.

176. GRACE

1. THE grace that is in Christ Jesus is a **saving grace.** "By *grace* ye are saved" (Eph. ii. 5).

2. The grace that is in Christ Jesus is a **sufficient grace.** "My *grace* is sufficient for thee" (II. Cor. xii. 9).

3. The grace that is in Christ Jesus is a **stimulating grace.** "By the *grace* of God I am what I am" (I. Cor. xv. 10).

4. The grace that is in Christ Jesus is a **serving grace.** "Let us have *grace* whereby we may serve God acceptably" (Heb. xii. 28).

5. The grace that is in Christ Jesus is a **stablishing grace.** "It is a good thing that the heart be established with *grace*" (Hebrews xiii. 9).

6. The grace that is in Christ Jesus is a **sacrificing grace.** "Ye know the *grace* of our Lord Jesus Christ, that, though He was rich, yet for your sakes He became poor" (II. Cor. viii. 9).

7. The grace that is in Christ Jesus is a **supplying grace.** "Of His fulness have all we received, and *grace* for *grace*" (John i. 16).

177. GRACE

1. **Justified** by grace. "Justified freely by His *grace*" (Rom. iii. 24).

2. **Standing** in grace. "This *grace* wherein we stand" (Rom. v. 2).

3. **Saved** by grace. "By *grace* ye are saved" (Eph. ii. 5).

4. **Elected** by grace. "A remnant according to the election of *grace*" (Rom. xi. 5).

5. **Strengthened** by grace. "My *grace* is sufficient . . . . . . My strength is made perfect" (II. Cor. xii. 9).

6. **Working** by grace. "I laboured . . . . . . yet not I, but the *grace* of God" (I. Cor. xv. 10).

7. **Growing** in grace. "Grow in *grace*" (II. Peter iii. 18).

178. GRACIOUSNESS OF JESUS

WE do not wonder at the gracious words that fell from Christ's lips, for grace was poured into them (Ps. xlv. 2), the grace of God was upon Him (Luke ii. 40); yea, He was full of grace and truth

(John i. 14, 16). "His mouth is most sweet" (Song of Solomon v. 16). His mouth is sweet for many reasons.

1. Sweet, because **life-giving** (John vi. 63).

2. Sweet, because **supplying** (Song of Solomon i. 2).

3. Sweet, because **assuring** (Isaiah lviii. 14).

4. Sweet, because **sustaining** (Deut. viii. 3).

5. Sweet, because **comforting** (John xiv. 1).

6. Sweet, because **powerful** (Heb. iv. 12).

7. Sweet, because **searching** (Rev. i. 16).

The words of Christ are like oil upon the troubled waters, they bring calmness and comfort; they are like bread to the hungry man, they bring nourishment and nerve; they are like the warm spring, which causes nature to bud and blossom; they are like an unfailing spring, ever fresh and full; they are like a salve to a wound, healing and soothing; and they are like honey for sweetness and satisfaction.

179. GROANS

1. GROAN of the **captive.** "And God heard their groaning" (Ex. ii. 24; vi. 5; Acts vii. 34).

2. Groan of Christ on the **Cross.** "My groaning is not hid from Thee" (Ps. xxxviii. 9).

3. Groan of the **sympathising Saviour.** "He groaned in the spirit" (John xi. 33).

4. Groan of the **believer.** "We do groan, being burdened" (II. Cor. v. 2, 4; Rom. viii. 23).

5. Groan of the **Spirit.** "Maketh intercession for us with groanings," &c. (Rom. viii. 26).

6. Groan of the **afflicted soul.** "I am weary with my groaning" (Psalms vi. 6).

7. Groan of **creation.** "The whole creation groaneth" (Romans viii. 22).

180. HALF-HEARTEDNESS

II. CHRONICLES XXV. 1-16

MORE mischief is wrought in the camp of God's people from half-heartedness than from anything else.

1. **Half-heartedness is the weak spring in the life that will prevent our acting right firmly.** As the spring in the lock will not make the bolt act well if it is weak, so the half-heartedness of Amaziah caused him to act weakly in avenging the death of his his father (verse 4).

2. **Half-heartedness is the earthly gas that causes the heart to be inflated with worldly ambition.** Doubtless Amaziah

wanted to be big with his large army (verse 6). The balloon will ascend when filled with gas, but if any harm comes to it, the greater the damage when it falls; so those who rise through carnal ambition will have a greater fall when the evil day comes.

3. **Half-heartedness is the link that gives the ungodly the opportunity to couple themselves with the Lord's people.** Amaziah should not have been in association with Israel, as Israel was not in association with God (verse 7).

4. **Half-heartedness is the flaw that hinders the inflow of Divine power into the life.** Hence there is hesitation instead of promptitude, as in the case of Amaziah, when he vacillated after he had got the direct word from God through the prophet (verse 9).

5. **Half-heartedness is like a jaded horse which needs a great deal of spur and whip to make it go.** Amaziah did not act as before God; he needed the spur of the prophet's words to urge him to obedience (verses 7-10).

6. **Half-heartedness is like the sparrow which is caught in the trap in trying to get the crumbs.** Amaziah was caught by the idolatry of the people whom he had conquered (verse 14).

7. **Half-heartedness is the conductor that brings the lightning of God's punishment upon itself** (verses 15, 16). The rod of God's chastisement (Heb. xii. 5-11), and bodily death (I. Cor. xi. 30), are two ways by which God punishes His children.

181. "HALLELUJAH! WHAT A SAVIOUR"

Almighty Saviour to liberate us (Psalm cvi. 21).
Bruised Saviour to redeem us (Acts v. 30, 31).
Comely Saviour to adorn us (II. Peter i. 1).
Divine Saviour to bless us (Titus iii. 4).
Eternal Saviour to secure us (Jude 25).
Faithful Saviour to keep us (Phil. iii. 20).
Great Saviour to deliver us (Isaiah xix. 20).
Holy Saviour to sanctify us (Isaiah xliii. 3).
Indwelling Saviour to rule us (Isaiah xliii. 11).
Joyous Saviour to gladden us (Zeph. iii. 17).
Kind Saviour to crown us (Titus iii. 6).
Living Saviour to be with us (I. Tim. iv. 10).
Mighty Saviour to enable us (II. Peter iii. 18).
Near Saviour to guard us (Ex. xiv. 30).
Overcoming Saviour to defend us (Isaiah lxiii. 9).
Providing Saviour to enrich us (John iv. 42).

Quickening Saviour to change us (Eph. v. 23).
Righteous Saviour to clear us (Isaiah xlv. 21).
Strong Saviour to uphold us (Matt. xiv. 31).
Tried Saviour to befriend us (Heb. ii. 10).
Unlimited Saviour to save us (Heb. vii. 25).
Virtuous Saviour to purify us (Matt. i. 21).
Wise Saviour to teach us (James i. 21).
'Xcelsior Saviour—no other like Him (Acts iv. 12).
Yearning Saviour to sympathize with us (II. Timothy i. 9).
Zealous Saviour to serve us (I. Timothy i. 15).

182. HANDS OF CHRIST

1. **On His hands,** the privilege of believers (Isaiah xlix. 16).

2. **Under His hand,** or His hand upon us, the pavilion to hide (Ex. xxxiii. 22); I. Kings xviii. 46; Ezra vii. 6).

3. **His hand under us,** the position of benefit (Song of Solomon ii. 6; Isaiah xli. 10).

4. **In His hand the place of blessing** (Deut. xxxiii. 3).

183. HAND OF THE LORD

WHAT does this signify? Omnipotence.

1. **His power to carry out His purpose.** "To do whatsoever Thy *hand* and Thy counsel determined before to be done" (Acts iv. 28).

2. **His power to provide.** "Thou openest Thine *hand* and satisfiest the desire of every living thing" (Psalm cxlv. 16).

3. **His power to preserve.** "Neither shall any pluck them out of My *hand*" (John x. 28, 29).

4. **His power to protect.** "Thy right *hand*, O Lord, is become glorious in power" (Ex. xv. 6).

5. **The power of His presence.** "Behold an *hand* touched me which set me upon my knees and upon the palms of my hands" (Daniel x. 10).

6. **His power to perform His promise.** "The Lord thy God brought thee out thence through a mighty *hand*, and by a stretched out arm" (Deut. v. 15).

7. **His power to punish.** "David . . . . saw the angel of the Lord . . . . having a drawn sword in His *hand*" (I. Chron. xxi. 16).

184. HEAR

1. **Hear and believe.** "He that heareth My word, and believeth on Him that sent Me" (John v. 24).

2. **Hear and follow.** "The sheep hear His voice . . . . and follow Him" (John x. 3, 4).

3. **Hear to be.** "Whosoever heareth these sayings of Mine, and doeth them" (Matt. vii. 24).

4. **Hear and do.** "Ye are My friends if ye do whatsoever I command you" (John xv. 14).

5. **Hear and learn.** "She had a sister called Mary, which also sat at Jesus' feet and heard His word" (Luke x. 39).

6. **Hear and endure.** "If ye continue in My word, then," &c. (John viii. 31).

7. **Hear and love.** "While I was musing the fire burned" (Psalm xxxix. 3).

185. HEAVENLY PEOPLE

I. Cor. xv. 48

Israel is God's earthly people. The Church is God's heavenly people. They are—

1. **Born** with a heavenly birth (John i. 13).
2. **Seated** in heavenly places (Eph. ii. 6).
3. **Blessed** with heavenly blessings (Eph. i. 3).
4. **Called** with a heavenly calling (Heb. iii. 1).
5. **Kept** for a heavenly inheritance (I. Peter i. 4).
6. **Belonging** to a heavenly citizenship (Phil. iii. 20, R.V.)
7. **Represented** by a heavenly High Priest (Heb. ix. 24).

186. HELP OF THE LORD

II. Chron. xix. 9

If we can say "The Lord is my Helper," we can also declare, "I will not fear" (Heb. xiii. 6).

1. In **perplexity,** He is our Help to direct, as He did Eliezer (Genesis xxiv. 12, 42).

2. In **poverty,** He is our Help to provide, as He did Elijah (I. Kings xvii. 5, 6).

3. In **sickness,** He is our Help to strengthen, as He did Paul (II. Corinthians xii. 9).

4. In **bereavement,** He is our Help to console, as He did the sisters of Bethany (John xi. 25).

5. In **discouragement,** He is our Help to stimulate, as He did Joshua (Joshua i. 6-9).

6. In **disappointment,** He is our help to remind us that all things work together for good (Rom. viii. 28).

7. In **difficulty**, He is our Help to say to us, "Fear not . . . I will help thee" (Isaiah xli. 10).

187. HIDDEN

"Hid" (Hebrews xi. 23).

1. **Under the blood** we are hidden in safety from the judgment of God's wrath against sin, as Israel was in Egypt (Ex. xii. 13).

2. **In the Lord's hand** we are hidden from all danger (John x. 28, 29).

3. **In His tabernacle** we are hidden in secrecy for communion with Him (Psalm xxvii. 5; xci. 1).

4. **In His presence** we are hidden for protection from our enemies (Psalm xxxi. 20).

5. **Under His wings** we are hidden for comfort (Psalm lxi. 4)

6. **In His Word** we hide for victory and assurance (Ps. cxix. 114).

7. **In His quiver** we hide to be used (Isaiah xlix. 2).

The hiding of Moses was an act of faith, as we are told in Heb. xi. 23. The parents of Moses had confidence in God, and therefore hid their child in opposition to the king's commandment. If we would have the hiding that the Lord is able to give, we must put implicit confidence in Him at all times.

188. "HIM"

1. **Standing.** "*In* Him" (Ephesians i. 4).
2. **Trust.** "*Upon* Him" (1. Peter v. 7).
3. **Communion.** "*With* Him" (John i. 39).
4. **Safety.** "*By* Him" (Deut. xxxiii. 12).
5. **Praise and Prayer.** "*Through* Him" (Heb. xiii. 15, R.V.).
6. **Blessing.** "*From* Him" (Psalm lxii. 1).
7. **Service.** "*For* Him" (Luke ix. 52).

189. HIS LOVE

1. **Fellowship** of His love. Abram's love for Isaac (Gen. xxii. 2).
2. **Delight** of His love. Isaac's love for Rebekah (Gen. xxiv. 67).
3. **Desire** of His love. Isaac's love for Esau's venison (Gen. xxv. 28).
4. **Holiness** of His love. Rebekah's love for Jacob (Gen. xxv. 28).
5. **Service** of His love. Jacob's love for Rachel (Gen. xxix. 18).
6. **Bestowment** of His love. Jacob's love for Joseph (Genesis xxxvii. 3).
7. **Care** of His love. Jacob's love for Benjamin (Gen. xliv. 20).

190. "HIS NAME"

1. **Separated** to His Name. "To take out of them a people for *His Name*" (Acts xv. 14).

2. **Sonship** through faith in His Name. "Power to become the sons of God, even to them that believe on *His Name*" (John i. 12).

3. **Salvation** in His Name. "Thou shalt call *His Name* Jesus, for He shall save His people from their sins" (Matthew i. 21).

4. **Suffering** for His Name. "Rejoicing that they were counted worthy to suffer shame for *His Name*" (Acts v. 41).

5. **Separated** by His Name. "Let every one that nameth the *Name* of Christ depart from iniquity" (II. Tim. ii. 19).

6. **Submission** to His Name. "That the *Name* of our Lord Jesus Christ may be glorified in you" (II. Thess. i. 12).

7. **Service** in His Name. "For *My Name's* sake hast laboured" (Revelation ii. 3).

191. HIS PRESENCE

"THAT I MAY DWELL AMONG THEM" (Ex. xxv. 8).

1. **Power** of His presence. "Glory and honour are in His *presence*" (I. Chron. xvi. 27).

2. **Rest** of His presence. "My *presence* shall go with thee, and I will give thee rest" (Ex. xxxiii. 14, 15).

3. **Security** of His presence. "Thou shalt hide them in the secret of Thy *presence*" (Psalm xxxi. 20).

4. **Joy** of His presence. "In Thy *presence* is fulness of joy" (Psalm xvi. 11).

5. **Refreshing** of His presence. "Times of refreshing shall come from the *presence* of the Lord" (Acts iii. 19).

6. **Searching** of His presence. "The upright shall dwell in Thy *presence*" (Psalm cxl. 13).

7. **Good cheer** of His presence. "Be of good cheer; it is I; be not afraid" (Matthew xiv. 27).

192. HOLINESS

REASONS WHY THE BELIEVER SHOULD BE HOLY.

1. BECAUSE of what **God is.** "I am holy." Thomas Watson says, God is holy intrinsically. He is holy in His nature; His very being is made up of holiness, as light is the essence of the sun. He is holy in His Word. The Word bears a stamp of His holiness upon it, as the wax bears an impression of the seal. "Thy Word is very pure" (Psalm cxix. 140). It is compared to silver refined seven times (Psalm xii. 6). Every line in the Word breathes sanctity; it encourages nothing but holiness. God is holy in all His

operations. All He does is holy; He cannot act but like Himself; He can no more do an unrighteous action than the sun can darken. "The Lord is Holy in all His works" (Psalm cxlv. 17).

2. Because of what **He has done** (Lev. xi. 45). Because God brought Israel out of Egypt, and delivered them from Pharaoh, He had a claim upon their gratitude and obedience; even so has He upon us. We love, because He first loved us; we serve, because He has served us; we trust, because He has been true to us; we obey, because of His Word to us; and we walk in His ways because of what He has done for us.

3. Because **He commands it** (Lev. xix. 2). We are to be holy because the Lord tells us to be. He commands, and we must obey; for obedience is the life of holiness. It is not for us to compromise, or question as King Saul did in relation to Agag (1. Samuel xv. 20, 21), for to obey is better than sacrifice.

4. Because of **His relationship to us.** "Sanctify yourselves, therefore, and be ye holy, for I am the Lord your God" (Lev. xx. 7). Newberry, in the margin of his Bible, renders the title, "Lord," "Jehovah-Mekaddeshcem." Wherever we get the title Jehovah, it brings before us God in covenant relationship. There are ten different aspects in which God reveals Himself as Jehovah. He is Jehovah-Jireh, to provide for us; Jehovah-Ropheca, to heal us; Jehovah-Nissi, to enable us to conquer; Jehovah-Shalom, to calm us; Jehovah-Tsebahoth, to lead us; Jehovah-Rohi, to care for us; Jehovah-Heleyon, to lift us up; Jehovah Tsidkenu, to cover us; Jehovah-Shammah, who is with us; and Jehovah-Mekaddeshcem, to sanctify us.

5. Because of **His choice of us.** "And ye shall be holy unto Me, for I, the Lord, am holy, and have severed you from other people, that ye should be Mine" (Lev. xx. 26). Why has He chosen us? To save us from hell? Yes, but more than that; we are chosen in Christ that we should be holy, and without blame before Him in love. Talk not of election, if there is not the evidence of it in holiness of life. For, if we are like the Ephraimite, who said that he was not an Ephraimite, but when put to the test by the Gileadite, who told him to say "Shibboleth," betrayed that he was what he said he was not; in like manner our life will soon speak out what we are (Judges xii. 6).

6. Because of **our relationship to Him.** "They shall"—the priests—"be holy unto their God" (Lev. xxi. 6). Aaron and his sons were to be holy because they were priests. We are royal priests to shew forth the praises of Him, who has called us out of darkness into His marvellous light for that express purpose. How careful in demeanour, how courteous in manner, and constant in attendance the Queen's servants are. And why? Because they are the Queen's servants. We are servants of the King of kings, and that is the reason we are to be holy.

7. Because **He promises to do it.** "He shall be holy unto thee, for I, the Lord, which sanctify you, am holy" (Lev. xxi. 8). We may be sure of this, that when God tells us to be, to do, and to suffer, He will meet our need, even as in the case of Paul, who prayed thrice that the thorn might be removed, but the Lord answered by saying, "My grace is sufficient for thee."

193. HOLY SPIRIT AND CHRIST

If there is one thing more than another that is stated of the Lord Jesus, it is, that in His life and labours, as the Man and Servant of God, He was dependent upon the Holy Spirit. There are no less than *fifteen* direct references to the Holy Spirit and His action in relation to the Lord Jesus, and *vice versa.*

1. Christ was **born** of the Holy Spirit as to His human nature (Matthew i. 18).

2. The Holy Spirit was the Father's promised **gift** to Christ (Matthew xii. 18).

3. Christ was **sealed** with the Holy Spirit at His baptism (Mark i. 10).

4. The normal condition of Christ as to His life was, that He was **full** of the Holy Spirit (Luke iv. 1).

5. The Holy Spirit was the **sphere** in which Christ moved (Luke iv. 14).

6. Christ was **led** by the Holy Spirit (Matt. iv. 1).

7. The Holy Spirit was the **power** by which Christ exercised His ministry (Luke iv. 18).

8. The Holy Spirit was the **energy** in which Christ overcame the powers of Satan (Matt. xii. 28).

9. The Holy Spirit was the **secret** of Christ's joy (Luke x. 21).

10. The Holy Spirit was the **anointing** which enabled Christ to go about doing good (Acts x. 38).

11. The Holy Spirit was the **strength** which enabled Christ to offer Himself as a sacrifice to God on account of sin (Heb. ix. 14).

12. The Holy Spirit was the **might** by which Christ was raised from the dead (Romans viii. 11).

13. The Lord Jesus was the **Bestower** of the Holy Spirit to His disciples (John xx. 22).

14. The Holy Spirit was the **authority** by which Christ gave His commands (Acts i. 2).

15. The Holy Spirit was the **justifier** of Christ (1. Tim. iii. 16).

194. HONEY

1. **The manna** that fell in the wilderness tasted like honey. "The taste of it was like wafers made with *honey*" (Exodus xvi. 31).

2. **The land of Canaan,** which is typical of earthly blessing to the full, is said to be a land flowing with milk and honey. "I am come . . . to bring . . . unto a land flowing with milk and *honey*" (Exodus iii. 8).

3. **The abundance** of **God's favour and grace** is likened to honey. "He made him to suck *honey* out of the rock" (Deut. xxxii. 13).

4. **The preciousness and sweetness of God's Word** are—"Sweeter also than *honey* and the honeycomb" (Psalm xix. 10).

5. **Pleasant words** and sweetness of expression are compared to honey. "Pleasant words are as an honeycomb, sweet to the soul" (Proverbs xvi. 24).

6. **Christ's delight** in His people when they are bringing forth fruit is as a feast to Him. "I have eaten My honeycomb with My *honey*" (Solomon's Song v. 1).

7. **Pleasures of sin** and the lusts of the flesh are likened to honey. "For the lips of a strange woman drop as an honeycomb" (Proverbs v. 3).

195. HOUSE OF THE LORD

1. **House of Contemplation.** "One thing have I desired of the Lord, that will I seek after; that I may dwell in the *house of the Lord* all the days of my life, to behold the beauty of the Lord, and to enquire in His temple" (Psalm xxvii. 4).

2. **House of Satisfaction.** "They shall be abundantly satisfied with the fatness of Thy *house*; and Thou shalt make them drink of the river of Thy pleasures" (Psalm xxxvi. 8).

3. **House of Praise.** "Praise ye the Lord. Praise ye the Name of the Lord; praise Him, O ye servants of the Lord. Ye that stand in the *house of the Lord*, in the courts of the *house* of our God" (Psalm cxxxv. 1, 2).

4. **House of Fellowship.** "We took sweet counsel together and walked unto the *house* of God in company" (Psalm lv. 14).

5. **House of Offerings.** "I will go into Thy *house* with burnt offerings. I will pay Thee my vows" (Psalm lxvi. 13).

6. **House of Growth.** "Those that be planted in the *house of the Lord* shall flourish in the courts of our God" (Psalm xcii. 13).

7. **House of Holiness.** "Thy testimonies are very sure: holiness becometh Thine *house*, O Lord, for ever" (Psalm xciii. 5).

8. **House of Testimony.** "I will pay my vows unto the Lord now in the presence of all His people. In the courts of the Lord's

house, in the midst of thee, O Jerusalem. Praise ye the Lord" (Psalm cxvi. 18, 19).

9. **House of Blessing.** "Blessed be he that cometh in the Name of the Lord: we have blessed you out of the *house of the Lord*" (Psalm cxviii. 26).

10. **House of Constraint.** "I was glad when they said unto me, Let us go into the *house of the Lord*. Because of the *house of the Lord* our God I will seek thy good" (Psalm cxxii. 1, 9).

"Blessed is the man whom Thou choosest, and causest to approach unto Thee, that he may dwell in Thy courts: we shall be satisfied with the goodness of Thy *house*, even Thy holy temple" (Ps. lxv. 4).

196. HOW TO SERVE

"SERVE Him in sincerity and truth" (Joshua xxiv. 14). Sincerity and truth are the weights that keep the soul in balance.

Sincerity is the ring of the coin which tells out its genuineness; the straight line of rectitude, and the test of fidelity.

The term rendered "*sincerity*" is translated "*perfect*" in Gen. xvii. 1; "*without blemish*" in Lev. i. 3; "*full*" in Lev. xxv. 30; "*upright*" in Psalm xxxvii. 18; "*undefiled*" in Psalm cxix. 1; "*sound*" in Psalm cxix. 80; and "*whole*" in Proverbs i. 12. We should serve the Lord with—

Sincerity of purpose (Col. iii. 24).
Perfectness of walk (1. Thess. i. 9).
Unblemishedness of life (Acts xxvi. 7).
Thoroughness (Romans xii. 1).
Uprightness of heart (Romans xii. 2).
Undefiled conduct (Luke i. 74).
Soundness of motive (Romans vii. 6).
Wholeness of being (Hebrews xii. 28).

197. "I AM"

WHEN Moses wishes to know the name of the person who has sent him, that he may tell the children of Israel, he is told to say, "I Am hath sent me unto you" (Ex. iii. 14). When we have the "I Am" as our Commissioner, we have all He *is*, all He *has*, and all He can *do* at our back. It seems as if the Lord said, "Whatever you need, I, the great I Am, will supply it." The Jesus of the New Testament is the Jehovah of the Old Testament. Therefore the "I Am's" of the Gospel of John will illustrate this point. No less than eight times does Christ use the very words we have in relation to Himself.

Christ's word to the woman of Samaria. "*I* that speak unto thee *Am*" (John iv. 26). (The *He* is in italics in Revised Version, and should be left out).

Christ's word to the Jews. "Except ye believe that *I Am* (margin) ye shall die in your sins" (John viii. 24, R.V.) "Ye shall know that *I Am*" (John viii. 28, R.V., M.) "Before Abraham was *I Am*" (John viii. 58).

Christ's word to the disciples respecting His betrayal. "I tell you before it come to pass, that ye may believe that *I Am*" (John xiii. 19, R.V., M.)

Christ's word to Judas and the soldiers in response to their admission that they were seeking Him. "Jesus saith unto them, *I Am.*" No wonder they went back and fell to the ground when He said, "*I Am.*" Again, Christ asks them as to the One they are seeking, and in reply, "Jesus answered, I told you I Am" (John xviii. 5, 6, 8, R.V.) Leave out the "He" in each of the above verses. As in the former case, it is given in italics in R.V., and should be omitted. Thus the Great I Am is discovered in the lowly Jesus. What force and fulness this gives to Christ's titles!

Are we hungry? He says, "I Am the Bread of Life" (John vi. 35, 41, 48, 51).

Are we dark? He says, "I Am the Light of the world" (John viii. 12).

Do we need an open way to God? He says, "I Am the Way" (John xiv. 6).

Do we want an entrance into blessing? He says, "I Am the Door" (John x. 7, 9).

Do we need a substitute? He says, "I Am the Good Shepherd, who giveth His life for the sheep" (John x. 11, 14).

Do we need life? Christ says, "I Am the Life" (John xiv. 6).

Do we need truth? Christ says, "I am the Truth" (John xiv. 6).

Do we need fruitfulness? He says, "I Am the True Vine" (John xv. 1, 5).

Is it a question of raising our loved ones? He says, "I Am the Resurrection" (John xi. 25).

198. IGNORANCE

THE natural man is ignorant of the—

1. **Word of Christ.** "But they understood not that saying" (Mark ix. 32).

2. **Person of Christ.** "They knew Him not" (Acts xiii. 27; xvii. 23).

3. **Righteousness of God.** "Have not submitted themselves unto the righteousness of God" (Rom. x. 3).

4. **Goodness of God.** "Despisest thou the riches of His goodness" (Rom. ii. 4).

5. **Of the believer.** "As unknown" (II. Cor. vi. 9).

THINGS God would not have the believer ignorant of—

1. **Our standing.** "Know ye not that so many of us as were baptized into Jesus Christ, were baptized into His death" (Rom. vi. 3).

2. **His purpose towards Israel.** "Not . . . . . ignorant of this mystery" (Rom. xi. 25).

3. **The Old Testament.** "Not . . . . ignorant how that all our fathers" (I. Cor. x. 1).

4. **Gifts.** "Spiritual gifts . . . . I would not have you ignorant" (I. Cor. xii. 1).

5. **The Lord's coming.** "Ignorant . . . . concerning them which are asleep" (I. Thess. iv. 13).

Christ has compassion on the ignorant. "Who can have compassion on the ignorant" (Heb. v. 2).

Believer not ignorant of Satan's devices. "Not ignorant of his devices" (II. Cor. ii. 11).

199. "I KNOW'S" OF PAUL

1. "**I know** that in me, that is, in my flesh, dwelleth no good thing" (Rom. vii. 18).

2. "**I know** nothing by (against) myself" (I. Cor. iv. 4).

3. "**I know** in part; but then shall I know even as also I am known" (I. Cor. xiii. 12).

4. "**I know**" of all things working for good (Phil. i. 19).

5. "**I know** that I shall continue with you all" (Phil. i. 25).

6. "**I know** how to be abased, and I know how to abound" (Phil. iv. 12).

7. "**I know** whom I have believed" (II. Tim. i. 12).

200. INCLUSIVENESS OF "IN CHRIST"

"IN Christ" is an inclusive term, for it tells us that the believer is blessed with all spiritual blessings in Him.

1. In Christ we are **absolved** from all charges. "In (*en*, the preposition that is usually rendered *in*) Him all that believe are justified from all things" (Acts xiii. 39).

2. In Christ we have **bequeathed** to us untold bounty. "Freely bestowed on us in the Beloved" (Eph. i. 6, R.V.)

3. In Christ we are **chosen** in the holiness of His person. "Chosen us in Him . . . . that we should be holy" (Eph. i. 4).

4. In Christ we are **delivered** from all condemnation. "No condemnation to them which are in Christ Jesus" (Rom. viii. 1).

5. In Christ we have an **endowment** that is sufficient for all our need. "God shall fulfil every need of yours according to His riches in glory in Christ Jesus" (Phil. iv. 19, R.V.)

6. In Christ we are **filled** with the fulness of God. "In Him dwelleth the fulness of the Godhead bodily, and in Him ye are made full" (Col. ii. 9, 10, R.V.)

7. In Christ there is the **grace** that is impregnable in its protection. "Strong in the grace that is in Christ Jesus" (II. Tim. ii. 1).

8. In Christ there is a **happiness** that is satisfying in its nature. "Rejoice in Christ Jesus" (Phil. iii. 3).

9. In Christ there is an **inheritance** that is unchanging in its character. "In whom we have obtained an inheritance" (Eph. i. 11).

10. In Christ there is a **justification** that is irrevocable in its character. "Justified by faith in Christ" (Gal. ii. 16, R.V.)

11. In Christ there is a **keeping** that is certain in its security. "The peace of God . . . . shall guard your hearts and thoughts in Christ Jesus" (Phil. iv. 7, R.V.)

12. In Christ there is a **life** that is unending in its energy. "Gift of God is eternal life in Christ Jesus" (Rom. vi. 23, R.V.)

13. In Christ there is a **meetness** that is sufficient for God's presence. "Sanctified in Christ Jesus" (I. Cor. i. 2).

14. In Christ there is a **nearness** that is unequalled in its approach. "In Christ Jesus ye that once were far off are made nigh in the blood of Christ" (Eph. ii. 13, R.V.)

15. In Christ there is a **oneness** that is inseparable in its bond. "Ye are all one in Christ Jesus" (Gal. iii. 28).

16. In Christ we have a **position** that is unparalleled in its dignity. "Raised us up with Him and made us to sit with Him in the heavenly places in Christ Jesus" (Eph. ii. 6, R.V.)

17. In Christ we have a **redemption**, that is the channel of all blessing from God. "Justified freely by His grace through the redemption that is in Christ Jesus" (Rom. iii. 24).

18. In Christ we have a **salvation** that is mighty in its outcome. "Saved in (margin) His life" (Rom. v. 10, R.V.)

201. INCORRUPTIBLE THINGS

1. **Incorruptible God.** "Changed the glory of the incorruptible God" (Rom. i. 23; I. Tim. i. 17, R.V.)

2. **Incorruptible Blood.** "Not redeemed with corruptible things .... but with the precious blood of Christ" (I. Peter i. 18, 19).

3. **Incorruptible Word.** "Not of corruptible seed but of incorruptible, by the Word of God" (I. Peter i. 23).

4. **Incorruptible Inheritance.** "An inheritance incorruptible" (I. Peter i. 4).

5. **Incorruptible Apparel.** "The incorruptible apparel of a meek and quiet spirit" (I. Peter iii, 4, R.V.; Titus ii. 7; Eph. vi. 24).

6. **Incorruptible Crown.** "We an incorruptible" (I. Cor. ix. 25).

7. **Incorruptible Body.** "The dead shall be raised incorruptible" (I. Cor. xv. 52).

202. INCREASING

1. INCREASING in the **knowledge of God** as we walk worthy of Him, and are fruitful in every good work. "Being fruitful in every good work, and increasing in the knowledge of God" (Col. i. 10).

2. Increasing in the **knowledge of Christ** and becoming like Him in character, as we walk in fellowship with Him. "Learn of Me; for I am meek and lowly in heart" (Matt. xi. 29).

3. Increasing in the **knowledge of His will** by doing it. "That ye might be filled with the knowledge of His will" (Col. i. 9).

4. Increasing in the **knowledge of His love**, by being taken up with Him who loves us. "To know the love of Christ which passeth knowledge" (Eph. iii. 19).

5. Increasing in the **knowledge of His power** by trusting. "That I may know Him and the power of His resurrection" (Phil. iii. 10).

6. Increasing in the **knowledge of His glory** by looking to Him. "The light of the knowledge of the glory of God in the face of Jesus Christ" (II. Cor. iv. 6).

7. Increasing in the **knowledge of His purpose**, as we are taught by the Spirit through the Word. "When the Spirit of Truth is come, He will guide you into all truth" (John xvi. 13).

203. INDWELLING

What is the result or evidence of God dwelling in us, and we dwelling in God? We can but give a few of the Scriptures, reminding our readers that the Greek word *meno* is translated in our Testament by eight different words, viz., abide, continue, remain, tarry, be present, endure, stand, and dwell. The following are a few of the results or evidences.

Feeding upon Christ (John vi. 56).

Christ dwelling in our hearts by faith (Eph. iii. 17).
Keeping His commandments (I. John iii. 24).
Dwelling in love (I. John iv. 16).
Confessing Jesus as the Son of God (I. John iv. 15)
Abiding in the light (I. John ii. 10).
Not abiding in darkness (John xii. 46).
Abiding in Christ (John xv. 4-10).
Loving one another (I. John iii. 11).
Word of God abiding in us (I. John ii. 14).
Doing the will of God (I. John ii. 17).
Continuing in His Word (John viii. 31).
Continuing in love (John xv. 9).
Continuing in the Son (I. John ii. 24).
Continuing in the Father (I. John ii. 24).
His joy remaining in us (John xv. 11).
Walking as He walked (I. John ii. 6).
Continuing in the things we have heard (II. Tim. iii. 14).

204. "IN HIM"

1. **Faith** in Him (Colossians ii. 5). "Stedfastness of your faith in Christ."

2. **Redemption** in Him (Ephesians i. 7). "In whom we have redemption."

3. **Accepted** in Him (Eph. i. 6). "Accepted in the Beloved."

4. **Complete** in Him (Col. ii. 10). "Ye are complete in Him."

5. **Built up** in Him (Col. ii. 7). "Built up in Him."

6. **Rooted** in Him (Col. ii. 7). "Rooted in Him."

7. **Walking** in Him (Col. ii. 6). "Walk ye in Him."

205. IN LOVE

1. **Continue** in love. "Continue ye in My love" (John xv. 9; Hebrews xiii. 1).

2. **Increase** in love. "Make you to increase and abound in love" (I. Thess. iii. 12).

3. **Abound** in love. "Ye yourselves are taught of God to love one another . . . . that ye increase more and more" (I. Thess. iv. 9, 10).

4. **Walk** in love. "Walk in love, as Christ also hath loved us" (Ephesians v. 2).

5. **Be fervent** in love. "See that ye love one another with a pure heart fervently" (I. Peter i. 22; iv. 8).

6. **Unfeigned** in love. "By love unfeigned" (II. Cor. vi. 6; Romans xii. 9).

7. **Be perfected** in love. "Perfect love casteth out fear" (I. John iv. 18).

206. "IN ME"

WHAT manifold evidence there was in the life of Paul to the truth, that Christ lived in him. See the following Scriptures, noticing especially the words, "In me":—

1. **Salvation** by Him. "Revealed His Son *in me*" (Gal. i. 16).

2. **Shining** for Him. "They glorified God *in me*" (Gal. i. 24).

3. **Sanctification** by Him. "Seen *in me*" (Philippians iv. 9; I. Timothy i. 16).

4. **Service** with Him. "Christ speaking *in me*" (II. Cor. xiii. 3).

5. **Settled** confidence in Him. "Truth of Christ is *in me*" (II. Cor. xi. 10).

6. **Suffering** for Him. "Conflict *in me*" (Phil. i. 30).

7. **Spirit** manifested. "Mighty *in me*" (Gal. ii. 8; Col. i. 29).

207. "IN MY NAME"

1. **Surrendering.** Forsaking all for My Name sake. "Everyone that hath forsaken houses . . . . for *My Name's* sake" (Matt. xix. 29).

2. **Separation.** Gathered in My Name. "Gathered together in *My Name*" (Matt. xviii. 20).

3. **Suffering.** Hated for My Name's sake. "Ye shall be hated of all men for *My Name's* sake" (Matt. x. 22).

4. **Serving.** Working in My Name. "Whosoever shall give you a cup of water to drink in *My Name*" (Mark ix. 41).

5. **Supplicating.** Praying in My Name. "Whatsoever ye shall ask in *My Name*" (John xiv. 13).

6. **Sincerity.** Labouring for My Name's sake. "For *My Name's* sake hast laboured" (Rev. ii. 3).

7. **Strength.** Holding fast in My Name. "Thou holdest fast *My Name*" (Rev. ii. 13).

208. "IN NO WISE"

1. The "in no wise" of **fulfilment.** "*In no wise* pass from the law, till all be fulfilled" (Matt. v. 18).

2. The "in no wise" of **sinnership.** "No, *in no wise* . . . . all under sin" (Rom. iii. 9).

3. The "in no wise" of **helplessness.** "Could *in no wise* lift up herself" (Luke xiii. 11).

4. The "in no wise" of the **Work of Christ.** "A work which ye shall *in no wise* believe" (Acts xiii. 41).

5. The "in no wise" of **assurance.** "I will *in no wise* cast out" (John vi. 37).

6. The "in no wise" of **reward.** "He shall *in no wise* lose his reward" (Matt. x. 42).

7. The "in no wise" of **judgment.** "Shall *in no wise* enter therein" (Luke xviii. 17; Rev. xxi. 27).

209. INQUIRING—DIRECTED

To inquire of the Lord is to be directed by Him (II. Sam. ii. 1). The following seven links in the golden chain of the spiritual life are always connected, namely:—

1. **Faith** in the Lord (John iii. 16).
2. **Dependence** on the Lord (Psalm xxxvii. 7).
3. **Walking** with the Lord (Mal. ii. 6).
4. **Inquiry** of the Lord (Psalm xxvii. 14).
5. **Direction** by the Lord (Acts xiii. 2).
6. **Blessing** from the Lord (Deut. xxxiii. 20).
7. **Glory** to the Lord (I. Cor. x. 31).

The blessing of the Lord's guidance always comes along the lines of prayer and obedience. Self acts upon its own authority, and is discomfited, as was Balaam (Numbers xxii. 22-35), but faith goes at God's bidding, and is delivered (Exodus xiv. 15).

210. IN THE LIGHT

1. **Walking** in the light (I. John i. 7).
2. **Worshipping** in the light (I. Peter ii. 9).
3. **Warring** in the light (Rom. xiii. 12).
4. **Working** in the light (John iii. 21).
5. **Watching** in the light (John xi. 9).
6. **Witnessing** in the light (Phil. ii. 15).
7. **Waiting** for Christ in the light (Luke xii. 35-40).

211. IN THE LORD

1. **Unity.** Brethren in the Lord. "Many of the brethren *in the Lord*" (Phil. i. 14).

2. **Faith.** Trust in the Lord. "I trust *in the Lord*" (Phil. ii. 19, 24).

3. **Fellowship.** In the Lord. "Receive him, therefore, *in the Lord*" (Phil. ii. 29).

4. **Rejoicing.** Rejoice in the Lord. "Rejoice *in the Lord* alway" (Phil. iv. 4, 10).

5. **Stability.** Stand fast in the Lord. "Stand fast *in the Lord*" (Phil. iv. 1).

6. **Oneness.** Same mind in the Lord. "That they be of the same mind *in the Lord*" (Phil. iv. 2).

7. **Witness.** Example of rejoicing in the Lord. "I rejoiced *in the Lord* greatly" (Phil. iv. 10).

212. IN THE LORD'S HANDS

1. **The place of Blessing.** "All His saints are in Thy hand . . . every one shall receive of Thy words" (Deut. xxxiii. 3).

2. **The place of Chastisement.** "Let us fall now into the hand of the Lord" (II. Sam. xxiv. 14).

3. **The place of Creation.** "Thine hands have made me, and fashioned me together round about" (Job x. 8).

4. **The place of Life.** "In whose hand is the soul of every living thing and the breath of all mankind" (Job xii. 10).

5. **The place of Keeping.** "My times are in Thy hand" (Psalm xxxi. 15).

6. **The place of Supply.** "Thou openest Thine hand, they are filled with good" (Psalm civ. 28).

7. **The place of Disposal.** "The King's heart is in the hand of the Lord . . . . He turneth it whithersoever He will" (Prov. xxi. 1).

8. **The place of Hiding *a*nd Usefulness.** "In the shadow of His hand hath He hid me, and made me a polished shaft" (Is. xlix. 2).

9. **The place of Security.** "Neither shall any pluck them out of My hand" (John x. 28, 29).

213. IN THE MIDST

JESUS was the Centre of Attraction, as well as occupying a central position. It is of interest to mark how often we read of Christ being "*in the midst*."

"In the midst"—

1. As the **Centre of Attraction** (Matt. xviii. 20).
2. As the **Questioner** (Luke ii. 46).
3. As the **Servant** (Luke xxii. 27).*
4. As the **Living One** (Luke xxiv. 36).
5. As the **Unknown One** (John i. 26).*

* The word "*Mesos*" in these places is rendered "*among*."

6. As the **Sufferer** (John xix. 18).
7. As the **Peace-Giver** (John xx. 19).
8. As the **Revealer** (John xx. 26, 27).
9. As the **Inspirer** (Hebrews ii. 12).
10. As the **Glorified One** (Rev. i. 13).
11. As the **Searcher** (Rev. ii. 1).
12. As the **Lamb** (Rev. v. 6).
13. As the **Supplier** (Rev. vii. 17).

214. IN THE SPIRIT

1. As **Warriors.** Walk in the Spirit. "Walk in the Spirit, and ye shall not fulfil the lust of the flesh" (Gal. v. 16).

2. As **Redeemed Ones.** Continuing in the Spirit. "Having begun in the Spirit," &c. (Gal. iii. 3).

3. As **Suppliants.** Praying in the Spirit. "Praying always with all prayer and supplication in the Spirit" (Eph. vi. 18).

4. As **Worshippers.** Worship God in the Spirit. "Which worship God in the Spirit" (Phil. iii. 3).

5. As **Brethren.** Love in the Spirit. "Declared unto us your love in the Spirit" (Col. i. 8).

6. As **United Ones.** Access in the Spirit. "Have our access in one Spirit" (Eph. ii. 18, R.V.)

7. As **Obedient Ones.** Live in the Spirit. "If we live in the Spirit, let us," &c. (Gal. v. 25).

215. ISRAEL'S BONDAGE IN EGYPT

EXODUS i. 1-14

SIN is presented to us in various ways in the Word of God. Sin is a consuming disease which has destroyed the organs of man's spiritual sense. Sin is a huge barrier rising up like an impassable mountain, which keeps God from man and man from God. Sin is represented as a heavy burden, which oppresses the sinner with an awful weight when the conscience is awakened. Sin is as a lurking monster, which waits to pounce upon its unwary victim. Sin is a despotic master, who rules his subjects with an iron hand and a relentless will. Sin is stated to be such a master in Romans vi., and is illustrated in the Pharaoh who knew not Joseph.

1. **The cunningness of sin** (verse 10). "Let us deal *wisely* with them," was the conclusion the Egyptians came to, with regard to the Israelites; or, as the margin of Psalm lviii. 5 renders the term, "*cunning*," where the word occurs in relation to the charmer seeking to charm the serpent. Sin's policy is to present itself in as attractive a form as possible, and to hide its real purpose, which is

to get its victim entirely in its folds, and then to crush to death, as the serpent, which first fascinates its prey and then folds it in the grip of death.

2. **The reign of sin.** Pharaoh set taskmasters over the children of Israel (verse 11). The word here rendered "taskmaster" is one that is generally used for a "prince" or "ruler" (Ex. ii. 14; xviii. 21). But these rulers soon developed into oppressors, for when they are spoken of again (Ex. iii. 7; v. 6, 10, 13, 14) a stronger term is used, which means an "oppressor" (Job iii. 18). The same expression is used of the Anti-christ (Isaiah ix. 4; xiv. 4), when speaking of him as the "Exactor" (Dan. xi. 20, M.). Sin is a hard taskmaster, and those who are under its rule find it to be a greater despot than even the King of Babylon, who when his command was disobeyed, caused the three Hebrew young men to be cast into the fiery furnace.

3. **The affliction of sin** (verse 11). The meaning of the word "afflict" is to humble. The word is so rendered in Deut. viii. 2, 16. What an affliction it was to the Israelites to come from being specially honoured by the king and his prime minister, to be humbled to the position of serfs, and to the lash of the taskmasters. Sin's patronage may end in persecution. As the ruin of a stately castle will remind us of a glory passed away, so many an one who bears the humbling marks of iniquity, still carries with him a bearing which speaks of a position lost by sin. Anyone who has been in our common lodging houses will find many examples. Broken down clergymen, lawyers, and merchants are to be found in these places, like stranded vessels which are shipwrecked on the rocks, being broken to pieces by the waves as they dash against them.

4. **The burden of sin** (verse 11). The way they afflicted Israel was with burdens. There is a pleasure in sin, but there is also pain. Many a boy who has had pleasure in playing truant from school has found that it has led to the cane upon his back, or twenty-four hours extra in bed, much to his chafing. One cannot help being impressed with the fact that many a man will put himself to great trouble in seeking to achieve his sinful purpose. The sinner convicted by the Holy Spirit specially finds that sin is a terrible burden, as Bunyan pictures in his *Pilgrim's Progress*, when he depicts Christian with a heavy burden upon his back; and as the Psalmist confesses when he exclaims, "Mine iniquities are gone over mine head, as an heavy burden they are too heavy for me" (Ps. xxxviii. 4).

5. **The bitterness of sin** (verse 14). Sorrow is the child of sin and the bitter fruit of iniquity. At the bottom of every cup of iniquity there is a snake that bites the quaffer and leaves its poison in the veins to torment its victim. The young fellow who has weakened his body by his sinful ways, and is filled with remorse at the prospect of an untimely death, knows the bitterness of sin. The drunkard with his aching head, parched throat, and unsatisfied thirst, knows the sorrow of his evil way; and the one who is put into prison

because of his dishonest action, feels the misery of his evil ways as he is kept in durance vile and hard labour.

6. **The rigour of sin** (verses 13, 14). The Egyptians were really cruel to the Israelites, for so the term means as it is given in Ez. xxxiv. 4. By the sighs and cries which escaped the Israelites (Ex. ii. 23-24) this is evidenced. They were pressed and oppressed beyond measure, and groaned beneath their hard lot. Sin is more cruel than the taskmasters of Egypt. It sears the conscience (I. Tim. iv. 2), blinds the eyes of the understanding (Mark viii. 18), dulls the moral sense (Eph. iv. 19), kills kindly feeling (I. John ii. 9), deafens the ears of the soul (Mark viii. 18), binds the spirit with cords of iniquity (John viii. 34), and separates from God (Isa. lix. 2).

Jehovah graciously raised up a deliverer for Israel. In like manner the Lord has graciously sent a Saviour (John iii. 16-18) for us. To receive Him is to be saved by Him, and thus to be redeemed from the rigour of sin.

216. "I WILL"

NOTE the seven "I wills" in Exodus vi. 6-8, and see how they correspond to the blessings of the Gospel—

1. "I will" of **salvation.** "*I will* bring you," &c. (Eph. ii. 5).

2. The "I will" of **severance.** "*I will* rid you," &c. (Col. i. 13).

3. The "I will" of **power.** "*I will* redeem you," &c. (Eph. i. 19 to ii. 6).

4. The "I will" of **separation.** "*I will* take you to me," &c. (John xv. 16).

5. The "I will" of **relationship.** "*I will* be to you a God" (II. Cor. vi. 17, 18).

6. The "I will" of **leading.** "*I will* bring you," &c. (John xvii. 24).

7. The "I will" of **heritage.** "*I will* give," &c. (I. Peter i. 3, 4).

217. "I WILLS" IN PSALM CXXXII

1. The "I will" of **exaltation.** "*Will I* set upon thy throne" (verse 11).

2. The "I will" of **dwelling.** "Here *will I* dwell" (verse 14).

3. The "I will" of **blessing.** "*I will* abundantly bless" (ver. 15).

4. The "I will" of **satisfaction.** "*I will* satisfy her poor" (verse 15).

5. The "I will" of **clothing.** "*I will* also clothe her priests with salvation" (verse 16).

6. The "I will" of **growing.** "There *will I* make the horn of David to bud" (verse 17).

7. The "I will" of **degradation.** "His enemies *will I* clothe with shame (verse 18).

218. "I WILLS" OF GRACE

God's action in grace is seen in the Gospel. Under the law it was "Thou shalt," but under grace it is "I will." The following seven "I wills" of the New Testament illustrate the action of grace:—

1. The "I will" of **forgiveness** (Heb. x. 17).
2. The "I will" of **cleansing** (Mark i. 41).
3. The "I will" of **rest** (Matt. xi. 28).
4. The "I will" of **security** (John vi. 37).
5. The "I will" of **impression** (Heb. x. 16).
6. The "I will" of **service** (Matt. iv. 19).
7. The "I will" of **indwelling** (II. Cor. vi. 16).

219. "I WILLS" OF JOHN XIV

1. The "I will" of **hope.** "*I will* come again" (verse 3).

2. The "I will" of answered **prayer.** "If ye shall ask anything in My Name, *I will* do it" (verse 14).

3. The "I will" of **intercession.** "*I will* pray the Father" (verse 16).

4. The "I will" of **comfort.** "*I will* not leave you comfortless" (verse 18).

5. The "I will" of **presence.** "*I will* come to you" (verse 18).

6. The "I will" of **love.** "*I will* love him" (verse 21).

7. The "I will" of **silence.** "*I will* not talk much with you" (verse 30).

220. JACOB

GENESIS XXV. 27

In thinking of Jacob as a supplanter, we have not given him credit for many good things about him.

1. **The plain man.** "Jacob was a plain man." The margin of the Revised Version gives it that he was "quiet, or harmless, Heb. perfect." The Hebrew word is generally rendered elsewhere "perfect." It is thus given in speaking of the "perfect man" in Psalm xxxvii. 37; lxiv. 4. It is not always the most skilful or cunning that have the most character about them. Very often the quiet, studious boy who plods away at his lessons, and is called a

"muff," has the most character in him. A big drum makes plenty of noise when it is beaten, but it is empty for all that. So with many who make a loud noise as to acquirements. The fishermen that Christ chose to be His disciples were obscure and unlearned men, but filled with the Spirit of God, they were the men that God used to "turn the world upside down."

2. **The separate pilgrim.** "Dwelling in tents." The dwelling in tents was always the sign of a separated life (Heb. xi. 9). The patriarchs confessed that they had no city here, but that they looked for one. We show we are pilgrims and strangers on the earth, as we live a life separate from evil and walk in fellowship with God (1. Peter ii. 11, 12).

3. **The wily Jacob.** We certainly cannot justify the means by which Jacob obtained the birthright. To say the least, it was unkind and mean for Jacob to take advantage of his brother's hunger, even though he knew the Lord had said, "The elder shall serve the younger." Jacob's scheming is the blot upon his life, the spot in the sun of his character, and he had to reap what he sowed. He deceived Isaac, and Laban deceived him. It never pays to seek to hurry the hand of God. Men say, "the end justifies the means." That is a principle God never recognises. The end was the same when Moses disobeyed God in smiting the rock, but God did not justify the means, for he shut Moses out of the land for his disobedience.

221. JACOB'S BLESSING

GENESIS xxxii. 25-30

1. **Jacob received no blessing as long as he was struggling** (verse 25). Jacob was resisting the man who came to him, instead of submitting. Trusting in the Lord is the condition to be in to receive blessing, not striving against Him.

2. **Jacob's humiliation is the beginning of blessing** (v. 25). The angel touched the hollow of Jacob's thigh. His strength was gone, as his thigh is out of joint. The thigh out of joint humbled Jacob, and led him to see his weakness, and that brought him in joint with God.

3. **Jacob's clinging is the secret of his blessing** (verse 26). Jacob will not let the angel go till he blesses him; but mark, it is while he clings he is blessed, and not while he is striving. The resistance of unbelief and self-will will never receive blessing, but the tenacity of faith always does.

4. **Jacob's changed name an evidence of blessing** (verse 28). From Jacob, a supplanter, he is called "Israel," *i.e.*, a prince with God. In like manner they who believe in Christ have their name changed from children of wrath (Eph. ii. 3) to children of God (John i. 12); from sinners to saints.

222. JACOB'S ISOLATION

Jacob's isolation with God (Gen. xxxii. 24).—The very best thing for Jacob was to be alone with God. One has well said in speaking of this aloneness with God, "Jacob was left alone purposely for secret prayer, so the Church gets into 'the clefts of the rocks' (Cant. ii. 14); Isaac into the fields; Daniel to the river's side; Christ into the mount; Peter up to the house-top; that they may pour out their prayers and solace themselves with God in secret."

1. Alone with God we are stripped of self-righteousness, as in the case of Job (Job xlii. 6).

2. Alone with God we get to know our inward corruption and uncomeliness, as in the case of Daniel (Daniel x. 8).

3. Alone with Christ, He instructs in Divine things as He did His disciples (Mark iv. 34).

4. Alone with God we are led into greater blessing, as in the case of Jacob (verses 28, 29).

223. JACOB'S JOURNEY

GENESIS xxviii

JACOB on his way to Padan-aram, and his being met and encouraged by God, is one of the brightest features in his life.

1. **The Obedient Son.** "Jacob went out from Beersheba," &c. (verse 10). Jacob was not merely fleeing from Esau's ire in leaving home, but he was obeying his father (verse 7), in going to seek for a wife among his uncle's people. "Beersheba" means "the well of the oath" (Gen. xxi. 31); and "Haran" signifies "parched, dry." It will often be found that the path of obedience will lead us from some well of prosperity to a parched place of adversity and trial. But better be there with the Lord than in some pleasant way without Him.

> "Out of my stony griefs
> Bethel I'll raise."

2. **The Weary Man** (verse 11). Tired with his journey, he seeks a resting-place amid his not very inviting surroundings, for, as Stanley says in speaking of the place, "The track of the pilgrims winds through an uneven valley, covered, as with grave-stones, by large sheets of bare rock, some few here and there standing up like the cromlechs of Druidical monuments." Lonely, tired, home-sick, with the sky for his ceiling, and a stone for a pillow, he falls asleep, and finds that God gives to His beloved in sleep (Ps. cxxvii. 2, R.V., M).

3. **The Privileged Dreamer** (verse 12). Jacob sees in vision the way cast up from earth to heaven, thus connecting heaven and earth, and opening up communication between Jacob and God.

4. **The Enriched Descendant** (verse 13). God reveals Himself as the "God of Abraham and Isaac," and repeats the promise to

Jacob He gave to them, that he and his seed shall possess the land. Thus Jacob finds the blessedness of a godly ancestry. Grace does not run in the blood, but notwithstanding there are advantages in having godly parents.

5. **The Blessed Seed** (verse 14). Here again is a repeated promise. (See Gen. xii. 2, 3; xviii. 18; xxii. 18; xxvi. 4). After the flesh Israel has been a blessing to all nations (Rom. ix. 4, 5), and they are yet to be a greater blessing (Rom. xi. 12; Isaiah lx.)

6. **The Sustained Pilgrim** (verse 15). The presence of the Lord is to be the sustaining power of Jacob in all his wanderings. Mark what that meant to him, and what it also means to the believer in Christ.

7. **The Astonished Sleeper** (verse 16). Jacob little expected that the Lord would meet him where He did, but the unexpected often happens. When we little expect to find the Lord He finds us. Jacob is astonished as he recalls his dream, and is reminded that God has been speaking to him. Many who are spiritually asleep would do well to wake up to the fact that the Lord has spoken to them, and is still speaking (Eph. v. 14; Rom. xiii. 11-14).

8. **The Fearful Confessor** (verse 17). Jacob was not the only one who has been afraid in the conscious presence of God. Moses (Hebrews xii. 21), Job (Job xlii. 5, 6), Isaiah (Isaiah vi. 5), Peter (Luke v. 8), and John (Rev. i. 17, 18), were the same. A holy awe and a filial fear should ever characterise those who know the Lord (Phil. ii. 12).

9. **The Early Riser** (verse 18). Jacob was no laggard or lie-a-bed. He was up betimes. Sleepy heads never make wise heads, and sleepy hearts are never warm hearts. The early birds get the worms. The manna must be gathered in the morning, if there is to be the gathered manna.

10. **The Consecrating Remembrancer** (verses 18, 19). Jacob changes the name of the place from Luz to Bethel by anointing the pillar he had used as a pillow. "Luz" means "departure" or "perverseness;" and "Bethel" signifies the "house of God." Many a Luz has been made into a Bethel by the consecrating oil of God's grace, through faith in Him who died for sinners. On the 10th of May, 1869, at a place called Promontory Point, the junction was made completing the railway communication between the Atlantic and Pacific Oceans, in the United States of America. A silver spike was brought by the Governor of Arizona, another was contributed by the citizens of Nevada. They were driven home into a sleeper of Californian laurel with a silver mallet. As the last blow was struck the hammer was brought into contact with a telegraph wire, and the news was flashed and simultaneously saluted on the shores of two great oceans, and through the expanse of a vast continent, by the roar of cannon and the chiming of bells. When the awful abyss between God and man had to be bridged, the junction over the deepest chasm was made by the outstretched arms of the Son of God,

and as the spikes crushed through His opened palms, He cried, "It is finished," and swifter than electric current or lightning's flash the tidings were winged to the farthest bounds of three worlds. The stairway connecting earth with heaven is completed; the awful chasm is bridged. Luz is transformed into Bethel; Christ by dying has opened up the way to God.

224. JACOB'S PRAYER

GENESIS xxxii

THERE are six things we note about Jacob's prayer.

1. **Jacob's fear of his brother's anger was the prompter of his prayer** (verse 11). The cause of Jacob's fear of his brother was his mean conduct towards him; hence he is seen cringing before Esau like a guilty culprit supplicating for mercy; and acting like a coward in that he sends one company in front of the other, and sends a present to appease his brother's anger. Note that any punishment we unrighteously inflict upon others is sure to come back upon our own heads. But for all that the Lord listened to Jacob's cry. What a God of grace with whom we have to do!

2. **Jacob's relationship to God is his plea in prayer** (ver. 9). He pleads his relationship to God in the words, "O God of my father," &c. If we know God as our Father, the right way in speaking to Him is to call Him "Father" (see John i. 12, 13; Gal. iv. 6). But if we have not answered God's prayer (II. Cor. v. 20), how can we expect Him to answer ours? A father will often grant the request of his child while he refuses the plea of a stranger.

3. **God's promise is Jacob's argument in prayer** (ver. 9, 12). Jacob pleads two "I wills" of God. When we can pin our prayers to God's promise, we are sure He will perform His word. Mr. Spurgeon says, "Prayer should be pillared on promises, and pinnacled with praises."

4. **Jacob's prayer is mingled with confession** (ver. 10). All God's servants have ever confessed their unworthiness.

5. **Jacob's prayer is perfumed with praise** (verse 10). Jacob acknowledges the mercy he had received from God, and gives praise to God. A thank*ful* man is full of blessing, while a thank*less* man is full of complaint. If we bless God with our praises, He will bless us with His mercies.

6. **Jacob's prayer is definite, personal, and answered** (v. 11). "Deliver me," Jacob cries, and the sequel shows how graciously God granted his prayer. His prayer was short and to the point, and it brought a speedy answer.

225. JEHOSHAPHAT'S PRAYER

II. CHRONICLES XX. 1-13

IN the previous chapter we read of Jehoshaphat charging Judah to take heed and obey the Lord (verses 6, 7), and to walk before Him with a perfect heart (verse 9). At this time Judah seems to be in a fairly prosperous state, the surrounding nations are jealous of it, and join together to overthrow it. We find that the twentieth chapter opens with these words, "After this." Often we find that after great blessing comes trial. It was so in the case of Abraham. God gave him the promised seed, and then called upon him to offer up his son Isaac. After Israel had been brought out of Egypt, then they are confronted by the Red Sea. It was after Christ had been baptized, and acknowledged from heaven with the Spirit's anointing and the Father's voice, that He was led away into the wilderness to be tempted of the devil. "Every branch that beareth fruit, he purgeth it that it may bring forth more fruit." It is the fruitful branch that has the pruning.

1. **Preparation.** "Set himself to seek the Lord" (verse 3). If we would have power with God, we must have purity of heart. An uncondemning heart will surely bring abundant blessing. We do not expect the plant to grow while it is out of the ground, neither can we look for answers to our prayers unless we are in the conditions laid down in the Word.

2. **Proclamation.** "Proclaimed a fast" (verse 3). It is interesting to note a few of the fasts mentioned in the Word, and the reasons for them.

Direction (Ezra viii. 21), Idolatry (Jer. xxxvi. 9), Confession (Dan. ix. 3), Humiliation (Jonah iii. 5), To ask help (II. Chron. xx. 3).

3. **Consolidation.** "Gathered themselves together" (verse 4). Union in prayer means union of power. Get plenty of sticks and the fire will burn brightly.

4. **Solicitation.** "Ask help of the Lord" (verse 4). Jehoshaphat stands like a beggar knocking at the door, and will not go away until he is answered. The Lord encourages us to importunity in the parables of the importunate widow (Luke xviii. 1, &c.), and the importunate friend (Luke xi. 5, & c In Luke xi. 9 we have an acrostic on the word "Ask."

A "Ask, and it shall be given you."

S "Seek, and ye shall find."

K "Knock, and it shall be opened unto you."

5. **Supplication** (verses 6-13). Characteristics of Jehoshaphat's prayer.

His prayer was reverent (verse 6). He recognised God's power and pleasure, might, majesty, and holiness.

In his prayer he reminds God of what He has done in the past (verse 7). Past mercies lead us to hope for present ones. He who has blessed, will bless; He who has fed, will feed; He who has led, will lead.

He reminds God of the relationship He holds to him. "Our God." "God of our fathers" (verses 6, 7). A woman may forget her child, and a father neglect his offspring, but not so the Lord. He will remember to help us.

He pleads the promise of God (verse 9). See II. Chron. vi. 28-30. If we bring the cheque of God's promise, signed with the name of Jesus, He will surely keep to His word.

His prayer was pointed (verse 10). He did not ramble, but he knew what he wanted, and waited for what he asked.

His prayer was humble (verse 12). "We have no might." When we are weak, then are we strong, and when we are strong, then we are weak. Asa relied on himself and his physicians, and was distressed (II. Chron. xvi. 7, 12). Paul trusted in the Lord, and was strengthened (II. Cor. xii. 9).

His prayer was earnest (verse 12). "Neither know we what to do." Sore distress means sure deliverance. Man's extremity is God's opportunity.

His prayer was expectant. "Our eyes are upon Thee." "Judah stood" (verses 12, 13). Waiting in humble and believing expectation is sure to bring a hearty and bountiful blessing. Plead earnestly. Wait patiently. Trust fully. Shine brightly. Work expectantly. Behave wisely. Do manfully. Glorify God.

226. JEHOVAH IN PSALM XXVII

1. **Light**, to direct. "The Lord is my Light" (verse 1).

2. **Salvation,** to deliver. "And my Salvation" (verse 1).

3. **Strength,** to uphold. "The Lord is the Strength of my life" (verse 1).

4. **Object** of desire. "One thing have I desired of the Lord" (verse 4).

5. **House** of shelter. "That I may dwell in the house of the Lord" (verse 4).

6. **Beauty,** to admire. "The beauty of the Lord" (verse 4).

7. **Teacher,** to instruct. "To enquire in His temple" (verse 4).

8. **Protector,** to hide. "He shall hide me in His pavilion" (verse 5).

9. **Treasurer,** to keep. "In the secret of His tabernacle shall He hide me" (verse 5).

10. **Uplifter,** to save. "He shall set me up upon a rock" (ver. 5).

11. **Lord,** to worship. "I will sing praises unto the Lord" (verse 6).

12. **Hearer** of prayer. "Hear, O Lord, when I cry" (verse 7).

13. **Director** of saints. "Seek ye My face" (verse 8).

14. **God** of salvation. "O God of my salvation" (verse 9).

15. **Gatherer** of forsaken. "The Lord will take me up" (ver. 10).

16. **Leader,** to guide. "Lead me in a plain path" (verse 11).

17. **Goodness,** to bless. "The goodness of the Lord" (verse 13).

18. **Encourager,** to strengthen. "Be of good courage, and He shall strengthen thine heart" (verse 14).

227. JEHOVAH-JIREH

The Lord will provide for every emergency. When the knife was uplifted by Abraham and about to be plunged into the heart of Isaac, God stayed his hand and revealed Himself as Jehovah-Jireh in providing the ram, which was offered up in the stead of Isaac. How we are reminded by this of the Lord's provision for the sinner in the death of Christ. The believer in Christ can say, "He was offered up in the stead of me, even as the ram in the stead of Isaac." In temporal things as well as in spiritual matters the Lord is our Jehovah-Jireh. He will surely supply all our need. He will be our strength in weakness, our stay in sorrow, and our song in sadness. The following acrostic on Jehovah-Jireh illustrates in some measure what the Lord is to the believer :—

J **Justified** by His grace (Rom. iii. 24).
E **Equipped** by His armour (Eph. vi. 13).
H **Harboured** by His presence (Prov. xviii. 10).
O **Observed** by His eyes (Psalm xxxiv. 15).
V **Vitalized** by His life (Eph. ii. 5).
A **Assisted** by His strength (Isaiah xli. 10).
H **Honoured** by His name (I. John iii. 1).

J **Joined** to Himself by His Spirit (I. Cor. xii. 13).
I **Inspired** by His love (II. Cor. v. 14).
R **Raised** by His power (Eph. ii. 6).
E **Encouraged** by His Word (Deut. xxxi. 6, 8).
H **Helped** by His Spirit (Rom. viii. 26).

228. JEHOVAH'S PRESENCE

DEUTERONOMY i. 33

THE cloud was the symbol of the Lord's presence, and it was the secret of Israel's protection. Sometimes the cloud was *over* them;

sometimes *behind* them; and sometimes *before* them. Thus the Lord was over them to shield; behind them to defend; and before them to lead. So He is with us (Psalm lxxxiv. 11; Psalm xci. 4, 10; John x. 4). The Lord's presence is the—

1. **Salvation** from disquietude (Psalm xlii. 5, margin).
2. **Shield** from strife (Psalm xxxi. 20).
3. **Secret** of our gladness (Psalm xcv. 2).
4. **Secure** abode of the upright (Psalm cxl. 13).
5. **Source** of our joy (Psalm xvi. 11).
6. **Satisfier** of our need (Exodus xxxiii. 14).
7. **Supporter** of our life (Isa. lxiii. 9).
8. **Supply** of our desire (Acts iii. 19).

229. JESUS

THERE is no Gospel which brings out, in such a striking manner the humanity of Christ, as the one which presents in such a remarkable way the Deity of Jesus, namely, the Gospel according to John; and chapter xi. is an illustration of this fact. This may be gathered if the name "Jesus" is pondered over. It occurs no less than twenty-four times.

The **Attention** of Jesus (verse 4).
The **Love** of Jesus (verse 5).
The **Response** of Jesus (verse 9).
The **Word** of Jesus (verse 13).
The **Plainness** of Jesus (verse 14).
The **Coming** of Jesus (verse 17).
The **Approach** of Jesus (verse 20).
The **Lordship** of Jesus (verse 21).
The **Encouragement** of Jesus (verse 23).
The **Unfolding** of Jesus (verse 25).
The **Tarrying** of Jesus (verse 30).
The **Person** of Jesus (verse 32).
The **Eyes** of Jesus (verse 33).
The **Sympathy** of Jesus (verse 35).
The **Groaning** of Jesus (verse 38).
The **Command** of Jesus (verse 39).
The **Reminder** of Jesus (verse 40).
The **Faith** of Jesus (verse 41).
The **Direction** of Jesus (verse 44).
The **Work** of Jesus (verse 45).

The **Testimony** about Jesus (verse 46).
The **Atonement** of Jesus (verse 51).
The **Retirement** of Jesus (verse 54).
The **Hunting** of Jesus (verse 56).

230. JESUS

WHEN John Howard wanted to visit the prisons of Russia he sought an interview with the Czar. He explained his object, and the Czar gave him permission to visit any prison in his Empire. It was a long and weary journey; he knew how jealously the prisoners were guarded, and how averse the gaolers were to permit any one to visit them. But he set out in perfect confidence. When he arrived at a prison he would make his application, and was prepared for the refusal which invariably came. Then he produced the Czar's mandate, and the prison doors were immediately opened to him. He had faith in that name, and was justified by the results. In like manner, those who have faith in Him who bear the name of Jesus, find that there is in that name—

J **Justification** (Rom. iv. 24, 25).
E **Eternal Life** (John iv. 13, 14).
S **Salvation** (Matthew i. 21).
U **Union** (John xii. 24).
S **Satisfaction** (John vii. 37).

231. JESUS AND JOHN

WE note a sevenfold contrast between John and Jesus.

1. John was the **harbinger** of Christ. Christ was the **One announced.** John went before to prepare for Christ's coming.

2. John was the **voice.** Jesus was the **Word.** John was the voice that spake the word. Trapp says, "John was all voice . . . . his apparel, his diet, his conversation did preach holiness as well as his doctrine" (Mark vi. 20). John was a true voice, for he spake only of Jesus. He delighted to honour Him whom the Father honoureth. John is our example.

3. John was the **forerunner.** Jesus was the **Lord.** John went before to announce the coming of Christ. His special mission was to reprove men of their sins, and to get them to repent of them (Matt. iii. 6). Christ came to save men from their sins (Matt. i. 21).

4. John was the **herald.** Jesus was the **Person** spoken of. On the Day of Jubilee the priests blew the silver trumpets, and as their clarion notes rang out they told the people of redemption for the slave, rest for the weary, release for the debtor, and rejoicing for the sad (Lev. xxv.); so John comes to herald the approach of Him who was to give infinitely more than the Year of Jubilee gave to the Israelites.

5. John was the **testifier.** Jesus was the **Truth.** John's testimony was clear and pointed. He gave no uncertain sound. On one occasion he said, "Behold the Lamb of God, which taketh away the sin of the world" (John i. 29).

6. John was the **lamp.** Christ was the **Light.** Christ says of Himself, "I am the Light of the World" (John viii. 12), and of John He says, "He was a burning and shining *light*," or, as the Revised Version, "He was the *lamp* that burneth and shineth" (John v. 35). The word that Christ uses of Himself signifies light *underived*, as the light of the sun, hence that which shines by its own inherent power; but the word that Christ uses of John means the light of a lamp which is fed with oil, hence it is dependent upon something else for its being and shining. The lamp only burns as it is fed with oil. Could any two words describe in a more concise or clearer manner the truth that Christ is the Light dependent upon none, and that the servant of Christ can only be a light as he receives from Christ? Christ is essentially the Light of all knowledge, the Light of all holiness, the Light of all grace, the Light of all Love, the Light of all power, the Light of all joy, the Light of all truth, the Light of all compassion, and the Light of all righteousness; but we are in ourselves the very opposite to all that Christ is, and we can only resemble Him in any small degree as He ministers to us the oil of the grace of the Holy Spirit. He is the Minister who attends to the needs of His saints that they may shine for Him, even as the priest in the tabernacle continually supplied the lamps of the lampstand with oil that they might never go out (Lev. xxiv. 2, 4).

7. John was the baptizer in **water.** Jesus was and is the Baptizer in the **Holy Spirit** (John i. 33, R.V., M.).

232. JESUS AT THE GRAVE OF LAZARUS

1. **The Sympathy of Jesus** (John xi. 35). We might call this verse "Jesus wept," the shortest verse in the Bible with the greatest meaning. The heart of Jesus ever beats in sympathy with the need of humanity, as His hand is ever ready to meet the need He sees. Mr. Spurgeon has well called this verse "a unique verse," and said, "I have often felt vexed with the man, whoever he was, who chopped up the New Testament into verses. He seems to have let the hatchet drop indiscriminately here and there, but I forgive him a great deal of blundering for his wisdom in letting these two words make a verse for themselves, "Jesus wept." This is a diamond of the first water, and it cannot have another gem set with it, for it is unique. Shortest of verses in words, but where is there a longer one in sense? Let it stand in solitary sublimity and simplicity."

Three times we read of Jesus weeping. He wept tears of personal suffering (Heb. v. 7), tears of compassion (Luke xix. 41), and here tears of sympathy.

2. **The Command of Jesus** (verse 39). There was a work which those who were standing by the grave had to do, before Christ spoke the life-giving word that raised Lazarus from the dead, and that was to remove the stone which lay at the tomb's mouth. There are many stones that believers can roll away which keep the unsaved from hearing Christ's voice. Here are some stones to roll away:—

The rocky stone of ignorance.
The granite stone of unbelief.
The slaty stone of error.
The lime-stone of prejudice.
The hard stone of doubt.
The slippery stone of inconsistency.
The dazzling stone of fear.

3. **The power of Jesus** (verses 41-44). Disease, devils, and death had all to submit to Christ. The miracles of Christ in His earthly life are but illustrations of what He can do now in resurrection power by the Holy Spirit through the preaching of the Gospel. Those who are dead in ceremonialism (Rev. iii. 1) He can quicken; those who are buried in the pleasures of the world (1. Tim. v. 6) He can raise to delight in the pleasures that last for evermore (Psalm xvi. 11); those who are devoid of spiritual life and love, like the prodigal in the far country (Luke xv. 24), He can robe and rejoice (Luke xv. 22, 23); and those who, like the Ephesians, are ruled by the powers of darkness (Eph. ii. 1-3; Acts xix. 19) He can raise to the heavenly places (Eph. ii. 6), and make them fight against the powers that once held them in their grip (Eph. vi. 12).

233. JESUS BEFORE THE HIGH PRIEST

MARK xiv. 53-64

IF there is one thing more than another that impresses one in the life of Christ, it is the revealing power of His person, as He comes in contact with men. His presence was the searchlight to shew men in their real character.

There are seven characters in which Christ is seen in the portion of Scripture before us.

1. **The Passive Victim.** "They led Jesus away" (verse 53; Isaiah liii. 7, 8; Acts viii. 32). There is no resistance on the part of Christ, but meekly and humbly He allows Himself to be led away. What majesty there is in His passiveness! With a look He could have made His enemies fall back (John xviii. 6); with a word He could have called twelve legions of angels to His aid (Matt. xxvi. 53), and by His own power He could have escaped (Luke iv. 30), but He wills to allow Himself to be in the hands of wicked men, that the purpose of God may be accomplished (Acts ii. 23).

2. **The Neglected Lord** (verse 54). Where now is Peter's willingness to go even to death with Christ (verse 29)? Alas! Peter,

instead of following close to the Lord (Psalm lxiii. 8), is following "afar off." Christ is neglected by the man who professed so much. How true are the words of Cecil, "Our very virtues, left to themselves, bear us down, like weights to destruction."

3. **The Falsely Accused** (verses 55-59). There are three things about the false witnesses who spoke against Christ. They had to be sought or hired for the occasion; their witness was contradictory; and they told a lie in relation to the destruction of the Temple. If we compare John ii. 19 with Mark xiv. 58, it will be found that Christ did not say that *He* would destroy the Temple, but if the Jews destroyed it, He would build it again in three days.

4. **The Silent Saviour** (verses 60, 61). "He opened not His mouth" to vindicate Himself. He might have defended Himself from His false accusers. How truly was "silence golden" in the case of Christ, and herein the Holy Spirit points Him out to us as our Example (see 1. Peter ii. 21-23). Euripides was wont to say, "Silence was an answer to a wise man." What an answer we may see in the silence of Christ, if we are made wise by the Spirit of wisdom.

5. **The Blessed Christ** (verses 61, 62). Christ never hesitated to answer when the question touched His Deity. For Him not to answer then, would be to betray Himself. There is no hesitation in the reply of Christ when the High Priest asks Him if He is "The Christ." Like a clear trumpet blast, the answer comes: "I Am." Thus Christ says He is The Great I AM (Ex. iii. 14). It has often been said that Christians claim for Christ what He never claimed for Himself, namely, that He was God. But if the "I AM's" of Christ in the Gospel of John are studied, it will be seen that He claims to be God again and again.

6. **The coming Man** (verse 62). Christ proclaims that there is a day coming when He will be the Judge and not the judged; when Caiaphas will stand before Him, instead of Christ standing before Caiaphas; when the Prisoner will be the Potentate; when the Despised will be the Honoured One; and when the Weak One shall come in power.

There is no truth so prominent in the New Testament as the coming of the Lord Jesus, but of one thing we must be careful, and that is, to note the character in which He is coming. Here He says He will come as "The Son of Man," and hence in judgment (John v. 27), and not in grace, as when He comes as our Hope (1. John iii. 2, 3), and Saviour (Phil. iii. 20, 21).

7. **The Condemned Man** (verse 64). They condemned the Son of Man, and God the Son, as being guilty of blasphemy, and and therefore worthy of death. Can we not see beneath the hatred and cruelty of the authorities who condemned Christ to death, that He was delivered for our offences (Rom. iv. 25), that we might be freed from condemnation (Rom. viii. 1), and be able to say, "Who is he that condemneth" (Rom. viii. 34)?

234. JESUS CLEANSING THE TEMPLE

JOHN ii. 13-25

It was perfectly right for the people to get their money exchanged, and to buy and sell sheep, oxen, and doves, but it was wrong for these things to be done in the house of the Lord. The priests were also to blame in allowing these things to be within the precincts of the Temple.

1. **Desecration** is the first thought to which I direct attention. The Temple was set apart for God's worship and service, therefore to put it to a common use was to defile the house of God. Is not this an illustration of how sin has defiled man? God made man upright, like a beautiful temple, but by his inventions he has defiled the holy place of God. Our whole nature should be for the Lord. The outer court of the body with all its members, the inner court of the soul with all its affections, and the holy place of the spirit with all its capabilities. If we are *self-centred* we are desecrating the sacred shrine that has already been polluted by sin. If any one allows the idol of selfishness to be erected in his heart, he is a worse idolater than the heathen who bows down to blocks of wood and stone.

2. **Expulsion** (verse 15). "He drove them all out." When Christ comes into the hearts and lives of those who believe in Him, He turns out all that is opposed to His will, and will keep every unholy thing out, as we allow Him to be Governor of our being, by sanctifying Him as Lord in our hearts (1. Peter iii. 15, R.V.) A working man in the East End of London, in giving his experience, said, "When the Lord Jesus came into my heart, He turned out all the bad lodgers"; yes, and He will keep them out as well if we allow Him. We could not pray a better prayer than the little girl who said, "Please, Lord Jesus, come and live in my heart." Some time after she thanked the Lord for having come in, in the following words, "Lord Jesus, I thank Thee that Thou hast come to live in my heart. Now, Lord, please shut the door."

3. **Question** (verse 18). The Jews questioned Christ as to His authority for acting as He did. They were blinded by prejudice, for as Trapp remarks, "They might have seen sign enough, in His so powerfully ejecting those money-changers. The disciples call it zeal, the Jews rashness." The Jews were always asking for signs (Matt. xii. 38; xvi. 4), and this was the one thing that kept them out of the power and blessing of the Gospel (1. Cor. i. 22).

4. **Prediction** (verses 19-21). Christ predicts His resurrection in His reply to the Jews. Godet remarks, "This answer of Jesus is udden, like a flash of lightning. It springs from an immeasurable depth; it illuminates regions then completely unexplored by any other consciousness than His own. The words, 'Destroy this temple,' characterise the present and future conduct of the Jews in

its innermost significance, and the words, 'In three days I will raise it up,' display all the grandeur of the Person and of the future work of Jesus.

5. **Recollection** (verse 22). In the meantime they murmured not, much less opposed; we can do nothing against the truth, when at the worst, "but for the truth" (II. Cor. xiii. 8). "They laid up what they understood not; and as the waters cast up the dead, so did their memories that which seemed dead therein, by the help of the Holy Ghost," remarks Trapp. A good memory is a *blessing*, if we call to mind what the Lord has done (Deut. viii. 2), but it is a *bane* if it is the "Son, remember" to bring back to memory the evil things one has done, or the good things not done (Luke xvi. 25).

6. **Profession** (verse 23). These believers are only make-believes. They have got the King's head stamped on the coin of their profession, but the coin is made of base metal, therefore they are counterfeits. There was a great difference in the faith of the disciples mentioned in verse 11, and the mere faith of assent to Christ's power in these, as Godet remarks, "This faith had nothing inward and moral; it resulted solely from the impression of astonishment produced upon them by these wonders. *Signs* may, indeed, strengthen and develop true faith, where it is already formed, by displaying to it freely the riches of its object (verse 11). They may even, sometimes, excite attention, but not produce real faith. Faith is a moral act which attaches itself to the moral being of Jesus."

7. **Penetration** (verses 24, 25). The Holy Spirit seems to play upon the word "*believe*," as the word "*commit*" in verse 24, is the same as is translated "believe" in the other ninety-nine times in John's Gospel. Christ did not commit (believe in) Himself to them, as they did not commit themselves to Him. As Luthardt says, "As they did not give themselves morally to Him, neither did He give Himself morally to them."

In chapter i. we behold Christ discerning a man who was true in heart, and to whom Christ committed Himself (i. 48), but here He does not commit Himself because He knew that these disciples were not true to Him.

235. JESUS SAW

It would be of interest to look through the Bible and note how active the eyes of the Lord are (II. Chron. xvi. 9). I call attention to the seven times that we read "Jesus saw" in the Gospel by John.

1. He saw the **anxious enquirers**, and bade them come to and with Him (John i. 38).

2. He saw the **devout worshipper**, and commended him (John i. 47-50).

3. He saw the **impotent man**, and healed him (John v. 6).

4. He saw the **hungry multitude,** and supplied their need (John vi. 5).

5. He saw the **weeping mourners,** and was troubled for them (John xi. 33).

6. He saw the **distressed mother,** and cared for her (John xix.26).

7. He saw the **blind man,** and revealed Himself as "The Light of the world" (John ix. 1).

236. JESUS

The Name of Jesus in the Epistle to the Hebrews.

1. As **Son of Man.** "But we see *Jesus*, who was made a little lower than the angels for the suffering of death" (Heb. ii. 9).

2. As our **High Priest.** "We have a great High Priest, who is passed into the heavens, *Jesus*, the Son of God" (Heb. iv. 14, and vi. 20).

3. As our **Surety.** "By so much was Jesus made a Surety of a better testament" (Heb. vii. 22).

4. As the **Way** into the holiest. "Having therefore, brethren, boldness to enter into the holiest by the blood of Jesus" (Heb. x. 19).

5. As the **Author of faith.** "Looking unto *Jesus*, the Author and Finisher of our faith" (Heb. xii. 2).

6. As our **Mediator.** "And to *Jesus* the Mediator of the new covenant" (Heb. xii. 24).

7. As our **Sanctifier.** "Wherefore *Jesus* also, that He might sanctify the people with His own blood, suffered without the gate" (Hebrews xiii. 12).

237. JOHN AND HEROD

MARK vi. 14-29

LET us note a few contrasts between John and Herod.

1. **John was a faithful man; Herod was a faithless man.** The faithfulness of John is seen in that he rebuked Herod for living in sin (verses 17, 18). John was a man who had looked in the face of God; hence, he did not fear the frown of men. He who can speak with God in holy communion, will not fail in faithfulness to God, to tell men of their sins.

In contrast to John's faith*ful*ness we have Herod's faith*less*ness. In verse 20 we are told that Herod feared and observed John, heard him gladly, and did many things, but after all Herod was only a stony ground hearer (Mark iv. 16, 17). Spurgeon says of Herod, "Herod was a foxy man. We sometimes meet with these foxy people. They want to go to heaven, but they like the road to hell. They will sing a hymn to Jesus, but a good roaring song they like also. They will give a guinea to the Church, but how many guineas are spent on their own lust. They try and dodge between God and Satan. . . . . Herod was like a bird taken with lime-twigs; he wanted to fly; but, sad to say, he was willingly held, limed by his lust."

2. **John was a blessed man; Herod was a burdened man.** John was blessed in many ways. *John was a blessed man because of his character.* He was *pure* in heart, like a cleansed vessel, free from all contamination. He was *holy* in life, like the tabernacle, he was set apart for God's indwelling and use; and he was *righteous* in action like an even balance, he did that which was right between men and God, and men and men. *John was a blessed man because he suffered for the sake of truth.* Those who suffer for the sake of Christ are blessed, as He Himself says (Matt. v. 11, 12); their very shame is an occasion for rejoicing, as it is illustrated in the early Christians (Acts v. 41); and when any are called to seal their testimony with their death they are blessed indeed, for they receive the martyr's crown of life (Rev. ii. 10). *Herod was a burdened man.* Herod was burdened in many ways. *He was burdened with his sins.* He was living a shameful life and he knew it, but for all that he would not quit his sins. A load of guilt was upon him, and his iniquities hung about him like a mill-stone. *Herod was burdened with a troubled conscience.* When he heard of the miracles that Christ was doing, he thought that John had risen from the dead, and was troubled in consequence (verses 14-17). When a man's sins haunt him, he has a host of ghosts which make him afraid, and well they may. Joseph's brethren could not forget the sins they had committed against their brother. Twenty years after the memory of their action is still fresh (Gen. xlii. 21), yea, even later than that (Gen. l. 17). Shakespeare represents, in a striking manner, the accusation of a guilty conscience in his scene in "Macbeth," when he pictures Lady Macbeth trying to wash out the stain of blood from her hands. There is one stone in the floor of an old church in Scotland which stares out at you blood-red from the grey stones around it. The legend tells of a murder committed there, and of repeated fruitless attempts to cover the tell-tale colour of that stone. Morally the legend is true; every dead sin sends its ghosts to haunt the souls of the guilty. Committed sin is a *scar* that cannot be effaced, a *diamond-cut* that cannot be obliterated, a *mark* that cannot be rubbed out, a *stain* that cannot be washed out, an *impression* that is indelible, a *leak* that cannot be stopped, and a *burden* that cannot be removed—that is, from the human standpoint. All thing are possible with God, through faith in the atonement of Christ.

238. JONAH

The Book of Jonah is like an album in which we have many likenesses of Jonah.

1. A runaway **prophet** (i. 3).

2. A disobedient **servant** (i. 3).
3. A sleeping **saint** (i. 5).
4. A rebuked **believer** (i. 6).
5. A marked **man** (i. 7).
6. A **minister** of evil (i. 8).
7. A true **witness** (i. 9).
8. A conscious **offender** (i. 12).
9. A "down-grade" **Christian** (i. 15).
10. A **substitute** (i. 15).
11. A type of **Christ** (i. 17; Matt. xii. 40).
12. A **suppliant** (ii. 1).
13. A distressed **sinner** (ii. 2).
14. A prophetic **voice** (ii. 5; Psalm lxix. 1-4).
15. A bargaining **pleader** (ii. 9).
16. A restored **backslider** (ii. 10).
17. A dull **scholar** (iii. 1).
18. An obedient **servant** (iii. 3).
19. A faithful **messenger** (iii. 4).
20. A successful **evangelist** (iii. 5).
21. A displeased **servant** (iv. 1).
22. A discouraged **servant** (iv. 3).
23. A questioned **disciple** (iv. 4).
24. A watching **rebel** (iv. 5).
25. A shadowed **servant** (iv. 6).
26. A gladdened **servant** (iv. 6).
27. A chastened **child** (iv. 7).
28. A fainting **pilgrim** (iv. 8).

239. JOSEPH'S NAME

WHAT Joseph was *called*. Joseph's name was changed by Pharaoh to Zepthnath-paaneah. There are quite a number of meanings given to this name. In the Vulgate it is *Salvator Mundi*, which is *The Salvation* or *The Saviour of the World*. *Gesenius* gives it as *The Prince of the Life of the World*. *Brugsch*, *The Food of Life* or *The Food of the Living*. Others view the term as really an Egyptian word in Hebrew letters, and make it *The Governor of the abode of Him who lives*. According to the margin of our Bible, it signifies *A Revealer of Secrets*, or *The man to whom secrets are revealed*. The different meanings may well be summed up, "The discoverer of hidden things," or in the Egyptian tongue, "The Saviour of the World." Let us take up the different meanings given above as illustrating what Christ is.

1. **The Saviour of the World.** That Christ is the Saviour that God has appointed for the world, is stated again and again (John iii. 16; iv. 42).

2. **The Prince of the Life of the World.** "The Prince of Life" is one of Christ's titles. As such He was killed by His enemies (Acts iii. 15), and is now in resurrection power quickening those who are dead in trespasses and sins.

3. **The Food of Life.** "The Bread of Life" is another of Christ's titles (John vi. 35). Satisfaction is found in Christ as well as salvation.

4. **The Food of the Living.** Those who are alive from the death of sin find there is food provided for them. "Give her something to eat," were the words of Christ after He had given the young maiden life; and the Lord having given us life, provides nourishment for that life in Him who is "The Word of Life" through His written Word.

5. **The Governor of the Abode of Him who Lives.** As Pharaoh appointed Joseph to be governor over all His domain, so the Father has committed all power into the hands of Christ, as He Himself says "All power (authority) is given Me in heaven and on earth" (Matt. xxviii. 18). "The Father loveth the Son, and hath given all things into His hand" (John iii. 35).

6. **The Revealer of Secrets.** The Lord Jesus revealed to His disciples many things which had never been known before (Matt. xiii. 11, 17). He still reveals His secrets through His Spirit and Word to those who are spiritually minded (1. Cor. ii. 10), even as He made known His ways unto Moses (Psalm ciii. 7).

7. **The Man to whom secrets are revealed.** It was because the Father had given the words to Christ that He was able to speak them out to others (John xiv. 24).

There is a sense, in a limited degree, in which what we have said of Christ applies to the believer.

240. JOSEPH SOLD INTO EGYPT

GENESIS xxxvii. 28-36

WE look at Joseph as a type of Christ, and as an illustration of the believer. There is one point to which we draw attention, namely, the sufferings of Joseph.

Joseph being ill-treated by his brethren, is a type of the ill-treatment that Christ received at the hands of His brethren, and is an illustration of what we must expect from those who are not the Lord's.

There are seven things that Joseph's brethren did to him. They *hated* him (verses 4, 5, 8), they *envied* him (verse 11), they *conspired* against him (verse 18), they were going to *kill* him (verse 20), they *stripped* him (verse 23), they *cast him into a pit* (verse 24), and they *sold* him to the Ishmaelites (verse 28). All this is typical of the treatment that Christ received from His brethren according to the flesh.

1. **As Joseph was hated by his brethren, so was Christ, as He Himself says,** "They hated Me without a cause" (John xv. 25). Joseph was hated because he was the special object of regard to his father (verse 4), because of his words (verse 8), and because of his dreams, which predicted his future glory. In like manner the Jews hated Christ. They hated Him because of His special relationship to the Father, and would have stoned Him (John x. 30, 33). They hated him because of the faithful words He uttered, and would have cast Him down headlong (Luke iv. 28, 29); and they hated Him because He spoke of His coming glory, and spit in His face, smote Him with their hands, and condemned Him to death (Matt. xxvi. 64-67). We must not be surprised, therefore, if the world should hate us, for the Lord Himself has told us that this will be so (John xv. 18, 19), but this is our comfort that He telleth His Father and our Father about it (John xvii. 14).

2. **As Joseph was envied by his brethren** (Gen. xxxvii. 11), **even so was Christ.** The Roman ruler, Pilate, saw very plainly that the motive power which was actuating the chief priests and elders when they brought Christ before him was envy (Matt.xxvii.18; Mark xv. 10; John xi. 47, 48), even as Joseph was envied by his brethren, to which envy reference is made by the Holy Spirit (Acts vii. 9). Beware of envy, it is self-destructive. As Dr. Thomas once remarked, "I remember reading somewhere in a Grecian story of a man who killed himself through envy. His fellow-citizens had reared a statue to one of their number who was a celebrated victor in the public games. So strong was the feeling of envy which this incited in the breast of one of the hero's rivals that he went forth every night in order, if possible, to destroy that monument. After repeated efforts he moved it from its pedestal, and it fell, and in its fall crushed him. An unintentional symbolic act was this, showing the suicidal action of envy on the soul. It is ever an element of misery, a burning coal which comes hissing hot from hell."

3. **As Joseph was conspired against** (Gen. xxxvii. 18), **even so was Christ.** The chief priests were continually plotting against the Lord Jesus. His teaching was a bright light, which revealed the hollowness of their utterances, and the unreality of their pretences, hence the reason of their ire against the Lord's Anointed (Matt. xxi. 38; Mark xi. 18; xii. 12; Luke xix. 47; xx. 19). Judas was also used as a cat's-paw by the priests and scribes, that they might get Christ into their power (Matt. xxvi. 16; Mark xiv. 11); and they cared not what means they adopted to accomplish their diabolical purpose, for they even went the length of bribing false

witnesses against the Son of God (Matt. xxvi. 59; Mark xiv. 55). The servant is not above his Lord. As Christ was conspired against, even so was the Apostle Paul, as we read in the 23rd of the Acts. The same spirit is also manifested against God's people, although in a less malignant form, by the world, but the same fire of hate lies smouldering, although it does not burst forth into flame.

4. **As Joseph's brethren sought to kill him** (Gen. xxxvii. 20), **even so the Jews repeatedly sought the life of Christ.** The evil purpose of the Jews to murder Christ, runs through the Gospel of John, like the black line that is often seen running across the face of a piece of white marble. (See John v. 16, 18; vii. 1, 11, 19, 25, 30; viii. 37, 40; x. 39; xi. 8, 57). The pure, white, noble, holy life of Christ was in such striking contrast to the lives of the scribes and Pharisees that they hated Him in consequence. Thus also will the world hate the child of God who is true to the truth of Christ with that hatred which is murder in the bud (1. John iii. 15; Matt. v. 21,22).

5. **As Joseph was stripped of his clothes** (Gen. xvxvii. 23), **even so was Christ.** In the Judgment Hall He was stripped to have the scarlet robe put on Him in mockery, and at the Cross the soldiers parted His raiment among them (Matt. xxvii. 28,35). Verily, like the man in the parable of the Good Samaritan, He fell among thieves, and they stripped Him of His clothes. Oh! what a sight for angels to look upon, their Maker to be stripped, naked, bleeding, and dying upon a cross! Many a child of God has been stripped by the bloody Inquisition and put upon the rack, or else stripped by wild beasts in the arena at Rome.

6. **As Joseph was made a prisoner by being cast into the pit** (Gen. xxxvii. 24), **so Christ was bound and kept in durance vile** (Mark xv. 1). Wonder of wonders that Christ should condescend to be bound by man! That the creature should imprison the Creator! The Prophet Isaiah, in speaking in general terms of the sufferings of Christ, says "He was taken from prison and judgment" (Isaiah liii. 8). Many a servant of Christ has been cast into prison for the Gospel's sake, as Paul and Silas were at Philippi (Acts xvi.), and as John Bunyan at Bedford.

7. **As Joseph was sold for twenty pieces of silver** (Gen. xxxvii. 28), **even so was Christ for thirty pieces of silver sold by Judas who betrayed Him** (Matt. xxvii. 3). No one can prayerfully ponder the sufferings of Christ without being influenced. His patience under provocation, and His whole attitude while in the hands of wicked men are most majestic, and remind us of a noble lighthouse around which the angry waves beat and hiss in vain. He is truly an Example for those who believe in Him to act in a similar way when persecuted for His sake (1. Peter ii. 20-22). We must not forget that we are called to suffer for Christ, and with Him (Phil. i. 29; iii. 10), as well as to reign with Him; yea, the place of glory is only reached by the path of suffering (Rom. viii. 17).

241. JOSHUA AND SERVICE

JOSHUA xxiv. 13-25

THE keynote of this Bible reading is the word "serve." The children of Israel are reminded whom they did serve (verse 15), and whom they are to serve. The expression, "serve the Lord," or "serve Him," occurs nine times (verses 14, 15, 18, 19, 21, 22 and 24).

1. **Salvation is the ground of service.** Israel testifies what the Lord had saved them from, namely, from the bondage and bitterness of Egyptian tyranny, and from the enemies which surrounded their path as they were journeying to Canaan (verses 17, 18); and as a consequence they recognise that they ought to serve the Lord. This same principle is emphasized in relation to the believer in Christ. We do not serve to be saved, but we are saved to serve (Eph. ii. 8-10). We are not to do to be forgiven, but we are forgiven to do.

"Ah! nothing to do! for the sinner that's dead
Must needs have another to work in his stead;
And Jesus, in Calvary's terrible hour,
Redemption accomplished in marvellous power.

* * * *

"Not a tittle of work till we're saved from our sins,
For that's just the point where true service begins
When the conscience is purged, and the heart is made glad,
And the spirit set free that aforetime was sad."

2. **Separation is the forerunner of service.** The command of Joshua is clear and cutting: "Put away the gods" (verses 14, 23). The vessels which God uses must be clean (Isaiah lxvi. 20), and all who are associated with His service (Isaiah lii. 11). We also must put away the idols of the love of the world (I. John ii. 15), the pride of the flesh (III. John 9.), the worship of man (I. Cor. i. 12), the energy of human method for the Lord's work (I. Cor. ii. 13, 14), the love of money (I. Tim. vi. 10), the exclusive affection for earthly friends (Luke xiv. 26), and the applause of men (John v. 44). An idol is any object that comes in between us and the Lord, to the exclusion of Himself (I. John v. 21). The Lord cannot and will not use us in His service till we are wholly separated to Himself.

3. **Sincerity and truth are essentials in service** (verse 14). To serve the Lord "in sincerity and in truth" is to have two buttresses to the temple of our being, which give strength and beauty to it. There were two pillars to the Temple of Solomon, which were called Jachin and Boaz (I. Kings vii. 21). The meaning of these names is suggestive. Jachin signifies "He will establish," and Boaz means, "In Him is strength." If we have in our character sincerity and truth, we shall have what these pillars signify, namely, strength of heart and life, and establishment of soul (Heb. xiii. 9), and shall thus be able to resist the onslaughts of evil and error, for we shall be like a house founded on a rock (Matt. vii. 24).

4. **Singleness of aim the strength of service.** The word of Joshua plays upon this one theme again and again—"Serve the

Lord." The Lord demands our absolute service. He will not permit us to divide our actions between Himself and someone else. "Whatsoever ye do, do it heartily as to the Lord" (Col. iii. 23); "Whatsoever ye do, do all to the glory of God" (1. Cor. x. 31). "Do *all*" is the Divine call and claim. This reminds us that in our several relations we are privileged to serve the Lord, and that all we do we should do to Himself. The child in the home, in the school, and at play, the servant in the occupation, the mistress in the house, the master in the business, and the workman in the shop, are in their several duties to serve the Lord. How much better things would be done if in everything we did it as to, and for the Lord Himself!

5. **Supply the incentive to service.** If the "therefore" of verse 14 is pondered in its context, it will be seen that the reason why the Lord calls for the service is found in what He had given. "I have given you," &c.; "therefore fear the Lord and serve Him." The gracious love of God in giving Israel the good land which they did not deserve was the incentive which should compel them to give themselves in whole-hearted service to the Lord. In like manner God's love to us should constrain us to love Him; His faithfulness to us should be the magnetic force to cause us to be faithful to Him. Christ's death for us should be the moulding power to make us die to sin; and His life should be the elevator to lift us to the plain of walking as He walked.

242. JOY

1. Joy of **Salvation,** as we trust in Him. "Restore unto me the joy of Thy salvation" (Psalm li. 12).

2. Joy of **Union,** as we abide in Him. "That My joy might remain in you, and that your joy might be full" (John xv. 11).

3. Joy of **Communion,** as we talk to, and listen to Him. "Did not our heart burn within us, while He talked with us by the way" (Luke xxiv. 32).

4. Joy of **Service,** as we work for Him. "So that I might finish my course with joy" (Acts xx. 24).

5. Joy of His **Presence,** as we look to Him. "Then were the disciples glad when they saw the Lord" (John xx. 20).

6. Joy of His **Word,** as we feed upon and obey Him. "Thy word was unto me the joy and rejoicing of my heart" (Jer. xv. 16).

7. Joy of **Victory,** as we fight in Him. "Rejoice with great joy" (Neh. xii. 43).

8. Joy of **Suffering,** in fellowship with Him. "Rejoicing that they were counted worthy to suffer" (Acts v. 41).

9. Joy of **Glory.** "Ye rejoice with joy unspeakable and full of glory" (1. Peter i. 8).

243. JOY OF THE LORD

NEHEMIAH viii. 10

THE joy of the Lord, not our joy in Him, is our strength.

1. The joy of the Lord's **compassion** is our strength in testimony, as we remember we are saved by Him (Luke xv. 1-7).

2. The joy of the Lord's **treasure** (which is His people), is our strength in Christian life, as we recognise we are His property (Matt. xiii. 44).

3. The joy of the Lord's **Cross** is our strength in persecution, as we consider Him in prayerful meditation through His Word (Hebrews xii. 2, 3).

4. The joy of the Lord's **oneness** with us is our strength in fruit-bearing, as we abide in Him (John xv. 11).

5. The joy of His **presence** is our strength in our walk, as we look to Him in faith (Psalm cv. 43).

6. The joy of His **joy** is our strength in communion as we have fellowship with Him (Zeph. iii. 16, 17).

7. The joy of His **presentation** and commendation shall be our strength in glory to praise Him for all His grace given (Jude 24).

244. JOYFUL ONES

THERE are at least seven parties who rejoice at the repenting of a soul.

1. The Father (Zeph. iii. 17).
2. The Son (Luke xv. 6).
3. The Holy Spirit (Luke xv. 9).
4. The angels (Luke xv. 7).
5. Loved ones (Heb. xii. 23).
6. The Church (Acts xv. 3).
7. The one who repents (Luke xv. 24).

245. JUSTIFICATION

1. Self-judgment is its **fore-runner.** "This man went down to his house justified" (Luke xviii. 14).

2. God is its **Author.** "God that justifieth" (Rom. viii. 33).

3. Grace is its **Spring.** "Justified freely by His grace" (Romans iii. 24).

4. Blood of Christ is its **Purchaser.** "Justified by His blood" (Romans v. 9).

5. The resurrection is its **Proclaimer.** "Raised again for our justification" (Romans iv. 25).

6. Faith is its **Accepter.** "Being justified by faith" (Rom. v. 1).

7. Union is its **Confirmation.** "He that is dead is freed (margin, justified) from sin" (Rom. vi. 7).

8. The Holy Spirit is its **Effector.** "Justified . . . . by the Spirit" (I. Cor. vi. 11).

9. All things are in its **Scope.** "Justified from all things" (Acts xiii. 39).

10. Works are its **Evidence.** "By works a man is justified" (James ii. 24).

246. KEEP

1. Keep the **sayings** of Christ. "If a man *keep* My sayings, he shall never see death" (John viii. 51, 52).

2. Keep the **commandments** of Christ. "If ye love Me *keep* My commandments" (John xiv. 15).

3. Keep the **unity** of the Spirit. "Endeavouring to *keep* the unity of the Spirit" (Eph. iv. 3).

4. Keep **unspotted** from the world. "And to *keep* himself unspotted from the world" (James i. 27).

5. Keep in the **love** of God. "*Keep* yourselves in the love of God" (Jude 21).

6. Keep the **Faith.** "I have *kept* the faith" (II. Tim. iv. 7).

7. Keep **pure.** "*Keep* thyself pure" (I. Tim. v. 22).

247. KEEP

1. Keep yourselves in the **love of God.** "*Keep* yourselves in the love of God" (Jude 21).

2. Keep yourselves from **Idols.** "Little children, *keep* yourselves from idols" (I. John v. 21).

3. Keep unspotted from the **world.** "Pure religion . . . . . is this . . . . to *keep* himself unspotted from the world" (James i. 27).

4. Keep the **body** under. "But I *keep* under my body, and bring it into subjection" (I. Cor. ix. 27).

5. Keep the heart **diligently.** "*Keep* thy heart with all diligence; for out of it are the issues of life" (Prov. iv. 23).

6. Keep the Lord's **commandments.** "If ye love Me, ye wil *keep* My commandments" (John xiv. 15, R.V.).

7. Keep from the **paths of the destroyer.** "I have *kept* me from the paths of the destroyer" (Psalm xvii. 4).

248. KEEPING CHRIST'S WORDS

JOHN xiv. 15, 21, 23

To keep Christ's words is to evidence our love to Him. We should keep His words and commands and observe His directions—

1. **Faithfully,** as Adam was to keep the Garden of Eden (Genesis ii. 15).

2. **Constantly,** as the eyelid does the eye (Psalm xvii. 8).

3. **Wholly,** as the Levites kept the charge of the tabernacle (Numbers iii. 7; xxxi. 30, 47).

4. **Diligently,** as Jonathan did in looking out for David's enemies (1. Sam. xix. 2).

5. **Vigilantly,** as Saul's messengers watched for David (1. Samuel xix. 11).

6. **Attentively,** as we mark the example of a godly man and follow it (Psalm xxxvii. 37).

7. **Carefully,** as God did Israel in bringing them to Canaan (Joshua xxiv. 17).

249. KEEPING GOD'S WORD

THE good ground hearer, according to Luke, hears the Word God and keeps it, and brings forth fruit (Luke viii. 15). Thomas Watson, in his terse and telling way says, "If you would hear the Word aright, be not only attentive but retentive. Lay the Word up in your memories and hearts. The seed on the good ground are they who, having heard the Word, keep it." The Greek word for "keep" signifies "to hold the word fast, that it does not run away from us." If the seed be not kept in the ground, but is presently washed away, it is sown to little purpose; so, if the Word preached be not kept in our memories and in our hearts, it is preached in vain. Many people have memories like leaky vessels—the Word goes out as fast as it comes in: how, then, can it profit? If a treasure be put in a chest, and the chest be not locked, it may easily be taken away: a bad memory is like a chest without a lock—the devil can easily take out all the treasure.

1. Keep the Word carefully as a **treasure** locked in the heart of warm love, as Jeremiah did, when he said, "Thy words were found, and I did eat them, and Thy word was unto me the joy and rejoicing of mine heart" (Jer. xv. 16).

2. Keep the Word as a **preventative,** as when the housewife puts the camphor among the clothes to keep the moth away (Psalm cxix. 11).

3. Keep the Word as the **fire** is kept in the grate, then it will burn up the things not of God (Jer. xxiii. 29).

4. Keep the Word as the **miller** keeps the water running over the mill-wheel, then it shall keep us going (Isaiah xlviii. 18).

5. Keep the Word as the **mother** keeps the milk to nourish her child (I. Peter ii. 2).

6. Keep the Word as the **priest** kept the oil to make the lamps in the tabernacle burn (Lev. xxiv. 2).

7. Keep the Word as the **man** keeps the title-deeds to his house, for in the Word are found the title-deeds of our inheritance (I. Peter i. 3, 4).

250. KEPT

PETER was kept by sixteen soldiers (Acts xii.), but was not kept safely, but the four quaternion power of Christ that keeps us is—

I. His finished Work in its fourfold aspect.

1. *Godward.* God's claims met and God glorified. "I have glorified Thee on the earth, I have finished the work" (John xvii. 4).

2. *Satanward.* Powers of hell defeated. "That He might destroy the works of the devil" (I. John iii. 8).

3. *Worldward.* Separation from it. "Be not conformed to this world" (Rom. xii. 2).

4. *Selfward.* Crucified and dead. "I am crucified with Christ" (Galatians ii. 20).

II. His continual Work and Presence above.

1. He is our *Representative* in whom we are represented. "To appear in the presence of God for us" (Heb. ix. 24).

2. He is our *Intercessor* to plead on our behalf. "He ever liveth to make intercession for them" (Heb. vii. 25).

3. He is our *Advocate* to look after our interests. "We have an Advocate with the Father" (I. John ii. 1).

4. He is our *Saviour* to preserve to the end. "He is able also to save them to the uttermost" (Heb. vii. 25).

III. His Gifts and Grace.

1. His bestowed life. "Given to us eternal life, and this life is in His Son" (I. John v. 11).

2. His sufficient grace. "My grace is sufficient for thee" (II. Cor. xii. 9).

3. His mighty hand. "Kept by the power of God" (I. Peter i. 5).

4. His garrisoning peace. "And the peace of God . . . . shall keep your hearts and minds" (Phil iv. 7).

IV. His Promises.

1. To be with us to the end. "Lo I am with you alway, even unto the end of the world" (Matt. xxviii. 20).

2. To be with us by the Spirit. "By His Spirit that dwelleth in you" (Rom. viii. 11).

3. To be for us at all times. "If God be for us, who can be against us" (Rom. viii. 31).

4. To come again and receive us unto Himself. "I will come again and receive you unto Myself" (John xiv. 3).

251. KEPT AND KEEPING

WE do the trusting, and the Lord does the keeping. We hold Him, because He holds us. We cannot trust without Him, and yet, if we do not trust, it is our, not His fault. Ralph Erskine sweetly says on this point—

"Mine arms embrace my God, yet I
Had never arms to reach so high;
His alone me holds, yet lo!
I hold, and will not let Him go.

"I do according to His call;
And yet not I, but He does all:
But though He works to will and do,
I without force work freely too.

"I take hold of His cov'nant free;
But find it must take hold of me.
I'm bound to keep it, yet 'tis bail
And bound to keep me without fail."

1. **Purity and Preservation.** "*Keep* thy tongue from evil" (Psalm xxxiv. 13). "*Keep* the door of my lips" (Psalm cxli. 3). "All God's commands are God's enablings," and in the first Scripture we have a command in reference to the tongue; it is a *little* member, but it may do a great deal of mischief. It is the *little* foxes that spoil the vine. It is a *little* leaven, that leavens the whole lump. It is the little back-bitings and evil speakings that do harm to our own souls as well as to others. Let us by a definite act surrender our tongue to the Lord that He may keep the door of our lips, thus our speech will always be with grace.

2. **Patient and Possessed.** "*Keep* thy heart with all diligence" (Prov. iv. 23). "Thou wilt *keep* him in perfect peace, whose mind is stayed on Thee; because he trusteth in Thee" (Isaiah xxvi. 3). Keep the heart patiently stayed upon the Lord, and He will keep in perfect rest, for perfect trust in the perfect keeping power of Christ brings perfect peace.

3. **Prayer and Provision.** "O *keep* my soul" (Psalm xxv. 20). "He shall give His angels charge over thee, to *keep* thee in all thy ways" (Psalm xci. 11). We receive not because we ask not, and very often we ask and receive not, because we ask amiss; some known sin indulged in or unbelief will keep back the answer. There is provision for all our need in Christ. The soul has two hands, the empty hand of prayer, and the receiving hand of faith.

4. **Practice and Promise.** "I have *kept* the faith" (II. Tim. iv. 7). "Because thou hast *kept* the word of My patience, I also will *keep* thee from the hour of temptation" (Rev. iii. 10). Christ has given us

His word to keep, and we are to keep it at all costs; to keep it, and to be kept by it; to live it, and live by it; to preach it by life and lips; not to compromise or yield one iota. What God wants of us is faithfulness, even as a lady writing in the fly-leaf of a Bible given to an evangelist, said, "Do well, suffer for it, take it patiently, till you hear the Master's well done."

5. **Power and Power.** "*Keep* yourselves from idols" (I. John v. 21). "*Kept* by the power of God" (I. Peter i. 5). The first is the power of a separate walk. "What is self-surrender?" asked a young lady recently. "It is the surrender of self," was the reply, and it is only those who have surrendered themselves to Christ who know anything of His keeping, subduing, and sanctifying power.

6. **Protected and Protection.** "*Keep* My words" (John xiv. 23). "Peace of God, which passeth all understanding, shall *keep*," &c. (Phil. iv. 7). Obedience is the source of constant joy, implicit trust is the source of constant peace. If we would be protected from the wiles of the devil, and overcome him, we must keep the words of Christ, for Satan cannot stand before the charge, "It is written." And if we would have our hearts and minds guarded as with a military guard, and thus have thorough protection, we must be careful for nothing, prayerful about everything, and thankful for anything, then the peace of God shall garrison and keep our hearts and minds in Christ Jesus.

7. **Privilege and Perseverance.** "Able to *keep*" (II. Tim. i. 12). "That good thing which was committed unto thee, *keep* by the Holy Ghost" (II. Tim. i. 14). "*Keep* yourself in the love of God" (Jude 21). God's love has been perfected in our unworthiness, and His strength is perfected in our weakness. If we would know the power of God, we must trust Him; if we would know the guidance and power of the Spirit's presence, we must recognise Him; if we would realize the warmth of God's love, we must abide in Him.

Let us ever recognise the two sides of truth, for it is only as we keep ourselves in the power of God that we know His power to keep.

252. KEPT BY THE LORD

II. SAMUEL xxii. 44

THE king of Israel acknowledged that the Lord had kept him in the position he occupied as the head of the nations. God does not promise to keep the believer in earthly honour and position, but He is keeping us for Christ (Jude 1, R.V.), and the inheritance that shall never pass away (I. Peter i. 5).

1. He keeps us as a **garrison**, securely (Phil. iv. 7).
2. As a **gardener**, attentively (Isaiah xxvii. 3).
3. As a **treasurer**, carefully (I. Peter i. 5).
4. As a **parent**, lovingly (John xvii. 11).
5. As a **shepherd**, guardingly (I. Peter ii. 25).

6. As a **casket,** secretly (1. John v. 18, R.V.)
7. As the **eye-lid** the eye, instantly (Psalm xvii. 8).

253. LANDMARKS

ONE of the commands of Jehovah to Israel was, that they were not to remove the landmarks of their neighbour (Deut. xix. 14: xxvii. 17). Even more significant are the terse and telling terms which we find in Exodus xii., xiii., and xiv., as indicating the landmarks of God's grace to His people, and what He expects from them. There are seven terms which we may call the seven landmarks of Christian experience.

1. **The "Take" of Faith.** "*Take* . . a lamb." "*Take* of the blood" (Ex. xii. 3, 7). Faith takes the Pascal Lamb of God's appointing, and finds in His blood its blessing.

2. **The "Eat" of Satisfaction.** "*Eat* the flesh," &c. (Ex. xii. 8) Christ is the soul's Food as well as its Salvation (see John vi. 53-58).

3. **The "Shall not" of Assurance.** "The plague *shall not* be upon you (Ex. xii. 13). When we have God's "shall not" we are safe (John v. 24; Rom. vi. 14).

4. **The "Put away" of Separation.** "*Put away* leaven" (Ex. xii. 15). The leaven of wickedness must be entirely separated from the believer (1. Cor. v. 6-8).

5. **The "Sanctity" of Dedication.** "*Sanctify* unto Me" (Ex. xiii. 2). Separation to God Himself, to all He is, has, and desires, is the essence of consecration.

6. **The "Stand still" of Obedience.** "*Stand still* and see the salvation of the Lord" (Ex. xiv. 13). To obey the direction of the Lord is our highest service.

7. **The "Go-forward" of Progress.** "*Go forward*" (Ex. xiv. 15). To advance in the Divine life is the evidence of soul prosperity. Stagnation is a proof of death.

254. LEARN

1. Learn to **fear the Lord.** "That they may *learn* to fear Me" (Deuteronomy iv. 10).

2. Learn the **Word of God.** "That I might *learn* Thy statutes" (Psalm cxix. 71, 73).

3. Learn to **do well.** "*Learn* to do well" (Isaiah i. 17).

4. Learn to **maintain good works.** "And let ours also *learn* to maintain good works" (Titus iii. 14).

5. Learn to **be contented.** "For I have *learned* in whatsoever state I am, therewith to be content" (Phil. iv. 11).

6. Learn to **be obedient.** "Yet *learned* He obedience" (Heb. v. 8).

7. Learn of **Christ.** "*Learn* of Me" (Matt. xi. 29).

255. LEARN

L **Lovingly,** as Mary (Luke x. 39).
E **Earnestly,** as the Bereans (Acts xvii. 11).
A **Attentively,** as the people (Luke xix. 48).
R **Righteously,** as enjoined (Titus ii. 12).
N **Nobly,** as the disciples (John vi. 67-69).

256. LEARNING FROM CHRIST

"LEARN of Me" are the words of Christ as He bids us take His yoke upon us.

1. Learn to appreciate Christ's appreciation of others in His commendation of John (Luke vii. 28; John v. 35).

2. Learn the sufficiency of Christ's grace in supplying the five thousand (Mark vi. 42).

3. Learn to live upon Christ Himself as the Satisfier of the heart (John vi. 35).

4. Learn the mystery and majesty of Jesus as "The Christ" (Matt. xvi. 16).

5. Learn to know the glory of Christ's glory and kingdom (Luke ix. 29; II. Peter i. 16).

6. Learn to imitate the tenderness of Christ in His tenderness towards the children (Matt. xviii. 10).

7. Learn the practical power of Christ's teaching in relation to our conduct towards others (Luke x. 37).

8. Learn the might of Christ's power in His opening the blind man's eyes (John ix. 7).

9. Learn the power of Christ's life in raising Lazarus from the dead (John xi. 44).

10. Learn the searching character of Christ's teaching in His words to the young ruler (Luke x. 27, 28).

11. Learn the omniscience of Christ in His discovery of Zacchæus in the tree (Luke xix. 5).

257. LIBERTY

1. Freedom from the **slavery of sin.** "To set at liberty them that are bruised" (Luke iv. 18).

2. Freedom from **anxiety.** "And to let him have liberty" (Acts xxiv. 23).

3. Freedom **to be.** Hence to the right or authority. "To them gave He the right (M.) to become the sons of God" (John i. 12).

4. Freedom of **approach.** "Boldness (M., liberty), to enter into the holiest" (Heb. x. 19).

5. Freedom to **go where one will.** "Where the Spirit of the Lord is, there is liberty" (II. Cor. iii. 17; James i. 25).

258. "LIBERTY"

1. **The purpose of Christ.** He came "to set at *liberty*" (Luke iv. 18).

2. **We are called to liberty.** "Ye have been called unto *liberty*" (Galatians v. 13).

3. **We have the Spirit of liberty.** "Where the Spirit of the Lord is, there is *liberty*" (II. Cor. iii. 17).

4. **We have liberty into the presence of God.** "Having therefore, brethren, *liberty* to enter into the holiest by the blood of Jesus" (Heb. x. 19, mar.)

5. **We have the law of liberty,** which we are to look into. "Whoso looketh into the perfect law of *liberty* and continueth therein . . . . this man shall be blessed" (James i. 25).

6. **We are to stand fast in the liberty.** "Stand fast therefore in the *liberty* wherewith Christ hath made us free" (Gal. v. 1).

7. **We are waiting for the glorious liberty.** "Delivered from the bondage of corruption into the glorious *liberty* of the children of God" (Rom. viii. 21).

259. LISTENING TO CHRIST

1. Listening to Him as our **Teacher,** we shall be instructed by Him (Luke x. 39).

2. Listening to Him as our **Captain,** we shall have victory through Him (I. Timothy vi. 12).

3. Listening to Him as our **Guide,** we shall be led safely by Him (Matt. xxviii. 19, 20).

4. Listening to Him as our **Lover,** we shall be jealous for Him (John xiv. 15).

5. Listening to Him as our **Lord,** we shall render service to Him (John xiii. 13-15).

6. Listening to Him as our **Helper,** we shall be upheld by Him (Isaiah xli. 10).

7. Listening to Him as our **Shepherd,** we shall follow Him (John x. 27).

260. LIVING WATER

CHRIST as the Living Water may be viewed in relation to other things to which He is likened, as being its complement.

1. The Son of the Living God is its **personification** (Matthew xvi. 16; John vi. 69).

2. The Living Bread is its **nourishment** (John vi. 51).
3. The Living Christ is its **security** (John xiv. 19).
4. The Living Word is its **assurance** (Heb. iv. 12; I. Pet. i. 23).
5. The Living High Priest is its **joy** (Heb. vii. 25).
6. The Living Stone is its **foundation** (I. Pet. ii. 4).
7. The Living Way is its **privilege** (Heb. x. 20).
8. The Living Hope is its **glory** (I. Pet. i. 3, R.V.).

261. LOOK BACK

As the Lord reminded Israel what they were (Deut. xv. 15), and from what He had saved them (Deut. viii. 14); so He bids us not to forget what we were, and from what He has saved us.

1. It is well for us to remember the **pit** from which we have been rescued (Psalm xl. 2).
2. The **rock** from whence we have been hewn (Isaiah li. 1).
3. The **darkness** from which we have been brought (Col. i. 13).
4. The **pollution** from which we have been cleansed (I. Cor. vi. 9-11).
5. The **wrath** from which we are delivered (John iii. 36).
6. The **death** from which we have passed (John v. 24).
7. The **desolation** from which we have been taken (Eph. ii. 12).

262. LOOKS OF CHRIST

1. THE look of **anger and grief,** because of unbelief. "*Looked* round about on them with anger, being grieved for the hardness of their hearts" (Mark iii. 5).
2. Look of **recognition and oneness.** "*Looked* round about on them which sat about Him" (Mark iii. 34).
3. Look of **enquiry and encouragement.** "He *looked* round about to see her that had done this thing" (Mark v. 32).
4. Look of **rebuke.** "When He had turned about and *looked* on His disciples, He rebuked Peter" (Mark viii. 33).
5. Look of **discouragement.** "Jesus *looked* round about, and saith unto His disciples" (Mark x. 23).
6. The look of **stimulus.** "Jesus, *looking* upon them, saith, ... with God all things are possible" (Mark x. 27).
7. Look of **inspection.** "When He had *looked* round about upon all things" (Mark xi. 11).
8. The look of **reproach.** "The Lord turned, and *looked* upon Peter" (Luke xxii. 61).

263. LOVE

"God is Love" (I. John iv. 8, 16).

We have the—

1. **God** of love (II. Cor. xiii. 11). Source of love.
2. **Love** of God (Rom. v. 5). Love overflowing to us.
3. Love of the **Father** (I. John iii. 1). Manner of His love.
4. **Love** of Christ (Rom. viii. 35). Manifestation of His love.
5. **Spirit** of love (II. Tim. i. 7). Power of His love.
6. **Comfort** of love (Phil. ii. 1). Consolation of His love.
7. **Labour** of love (Heb. vi. 10). His love constraining.

264. LOVE

1. **Love is the evidence of faith in Christ.** "We *love* Him, because He first loved us" (I. John iv. 19).

2. **Love is the proof of life in Christ.** "We know that we have passed from death unto life, because we *love* the brethren" (I. John iii. 14).

3. **Love is the stamp of genuineness.** "Though I have all faith . . . . and have not *charity* (love) I am nothing" (I. Cor. xiii. 2).

4. **Love is the motive power in service.** "The *love* of Christ constraineth us" (II. Cor. v. 14).

5. **Love is careful to obey.** "If ye *love* Me, ye will keep My commandments" (John xiv. 15, R.V.)

6. **Love is the fruit of the Spirit.** "The fruit of the Spirit is *love*" (Galatians v. 22).

7. **Love is the queen of graces.** "Now abideth faith . . . . greatest of these is *charity* (I. Cor. xiii. 13).

265. LOVE

Love is a *debt* we owe to all, and a payment ever to be rendered. Love is a *duty*. The highest form of duty (Rom. xiii. 8, 9, 10). He that loves not, believes not; and he that believes not, loves not.

1. Love is the **Divine mark** that we are born again (I. John iv. 16, 17).

2. Love is the **unanswerable testimony** of allegiance to Christ (John xiv. 15).

3. Love is the **legible seal** that we know the love of God (I. John iv. 17).

4. Love is the **unmistakable evidence** that we are taught of God (I. John iv. 9).

5. Love is the **beautiful livery** of heaven (Col. iii. 14).

6. Love is the **royal badge** of discipleship (John xiii. 35).

7. Love is the **plain assurance** of having passed from death unto life (1. John iii. 14).

266. LOVE OF GOD

NOTE the following seven points in relation to the forgiving love of God:—

1. **Unmerited** in its bestowment (Col. i. 12-14).
2. **Divine,** in its source (Psalm cxxx. 4).
3. **Costly,** in its purchase (Eph. i. 7).
4. **Free,** in its manner (Rom. iii. 24, 25).
5. **Full,** in its extent (Psalm ciii. 3).
6. **Practical,** in its outcome (Luke vii. 42).
7. **Known,** in the experience (1. John ii. 12).

267. LOVE OF GOD—ITS CHARACTER

1. UNMERITED in its Object (1. John iv. 10).
2. Unsought in its Action (Rom. v. 8).
3. Universal in its Offer (John iii. 16).
4. Unbounded in its Work (Eph. ii. 4).
5. Unknown in its Nature (Eph. iii. 19).
6. Unbroken in its Ministry (Rom. viii. 39).
7. Unending in its Character (Jer. xxxi. 3).

268. LOVE OF JESUS

1. **The Definiteness of Love.** "Jesus loved Martha and her sister and Lazarus" (John xi. 5).

2. **Perpetuity of Love.** "Having loved His own which were in the world, He loved them unto the end" (John xiii. 1).

3. **Favour of Love.** "Leaning on Jesus' bosom one of His disciples, whom Jesus loved" (John xiii. 23).

4. **Example of Love.** "Love one another, as I have loved you" (John xiii. 34).

5. **Record of Love.** "That disciple whom Jesus loved saith unto Peter, It is the Lord" (John xxi. 7).

6. **Attractiveness of Love.** "Peter, seeth the disciple whom Jesus loved" (John xxi. 20).

7. **Commission of Love.** "Jesus saw the disciple whom He loved" (John xix. 26).

269. LOVE'S CHARACTER

THE character of His love—

1. Great (Eph. ii. 4).
2. Inexpressible (John iii. 16).
3. Free (Hosea xiv. 4).
4. Inconceivable (Eph. iii. 19).
5. Unselfish (I. John iv. 10).
6. Unchanging (John xiii. 1).
7. Inseparable (Rom. viii. 35-39).
8. Everlasting (Jer. xxxi. 3).
9. Unquenchable (Song of Solomon viii. 7).
10. Strong (stronger) as death (Song of Solomon viii. 6).
11. Perfect (I. John iv. 18).

270. LOVE'S PICTURE

WE have in I. Cor. xiii. a picture of the character of the love of God as manifested in Christ, also showing what should be the character of our love to Him.

1. **His suffering love.** "Love suffereth long" (Luke xxii. 44).
2. **His compassionate love.** "Is kind" (Luke x. 33).
3. **His contented love.** "Envieth not" (Luke xxii. 42).
4. **His self-abasing love.** "Vaunteth not itself" (John iv. 34).
5. **His humbling love.** "Not puffed up" (Phil. ii. 7, 8).
6. **His wise love.** "Doth not behave unseemly" (John vii. 46).
7. **His unselfish love.** "Seeketh not her own" (John xvii. 22).
8. **His patient love.** "Not easily provoked" (John xxi. 15-17).
9. **His unsuspicious love.** "Thinketh no evil" (Luke vii. 39).
10. **His holy love.** "Rejoiceth not in iniquity" (John ii. 15).
11. **His truthful love.** "Rejoiceth in the truth" (Luke xxiv. 26).
12. **His bearing love.** "Beareth all things" (Gen. xlv. 1).
13. **His expecting love.** "Hopeth all things" (Acts vii. 56).
14. **His trusting love.** "Believeth all things"(John xvii. 18).
15. **His enduring love.** "Endureth all things" (Heb. xii. 2).
16. **His unchanging love.** "Never faileth" (John xiii. 1).

271. LOVE'S SEVENFOLD CORD

THERE is a sevenfold cord of love between the Father and the Son, mentioned in the Gospel according to John.

1. **Committal of Love.** "The Father *loveth* the Son, and hath given all things into His hand" (John iii. 35).

2. **Complacency of Love.** "Therefore doth My Father *love* Me, because I lay down My life" (John x. 17).

3. **Communion of Love.** "As the Father hath *loved* Me, so have I loved you" (John xv. 9).

4. **Co-equality of Love.** "Thou . . . . . hast *loved* them, as Thou hast loved Me" (John xvii. 23).

5. **Character of Love.** Eternal. "Thou *lovedst* Me before the foundation of the world" (John xvii. 24).

6. **Constrainment of Love.** "The *love* wherewith thou hast loved Me may be in them" (John xvii. 26).

7. **Communication of Love.** "The Father *loveth* the Son and sheweth Him all things that Himself doeth" (John v. 20).

272. MADE IN CHRIST

THERE are many things the believer is said to be "made" in Christ. Sin had *un*made us, but grace *re*makes us.

1. "**Made nigh.**" Nearness. "*Made* nigh by the blood of Christ" (Eph. ii. 13).

2. "**Made righteous.**" Righteousness. "*Made* the righteousness of God in Him" (II. Cor. v. 21).

3. "**Made white.**" Purity or Holiness. "Washed their robes and *made* them white in the blood of the Lamb" (Rev. vii. 14).

4. "**Made accepted.**" Favoured. "*Made* us accepted in the Beloved" (Eph. i. 6). The word "accepted" only occurs in one other place in the New Testament, and that is in Luke i. 28, where it is rendered "*highly favoured*," or as the margin, "*graciously accepted, or much graced.*"

5. "**Made meet.**" Sufficiency. "*Made* us meet to be partakers of the inheritance of the saints in light" (Col. i. 12). The term "*meet*" is rendered in II. Cor. iii. 6, "*hath made able*," or sufficient.

6. "**Made heirs.**" Heirship. "Being justified by His grace, we should be *made* heirs" (Titus iii. 7).

7. "**Made kings and priests.**" Nobility. "*Made* us kings and priests unto God and His Father" (Rev. i. 6).

273. MAN FULL OF GRACE

ACTS vi. 8, R.V.

THOSE who are full of grace are—

1. **Responsive to grace.** "Helped them much, which had believed through *grace*" (Acts xviii. 27).

2. **Built up by grace.** "I commend you to God, and to the word of His *grace*, which is able to build you up" (Acts xx. 32).

3. **Testify of grace.** "To testify the Gospel of the *grace* of God" (Acts xx. 24).

4. **Dependent upon grace.** "We believe that through the *grace* of the Lord Jesus Christ, we shall be saved" (Acts xv. 11).

5. **Holy through grace.** "Great *grace* was upon them all" (Acts iv. 33).

6. **Continue in grace.** "Persuaded them to continue in the *grace* of God" (Acts xiii. 43).

7. **Evidenced by grace.** "When he had seen the *grace* of God, was glad" (Acts xi. 23).

274. MAN OF FAITH

Acts vi. 5

Faith is the root grace that unites the soul to the soil of God's love and power, and causes all the other graces to flourish, hence a "man full of faith" is a—

1. **Man of Prayer,** as Elijah was. "Elias was a man . . . . he prayed earnestly" (James v. 17).

2. **Man of Work,** as Noah was. "By faith Noah . . . . prepared an ark" (Heb. xi. 7).

3. **Man of obedience,** as Abram was. "Abraham, when he was called . . . . went out not knowing whither he went" (Heb. xi. 8).

4. **Man of Communion,** as Enoch was. "By faith Enoch . . . pleased God" (Heb. xi. 5, 6).

5. **Man of Separation,** as Moses was. "By faith he forsook Egypt," &c. (Heb. xi. 25-28).

6. **Man of Victory,** as David was. "I come to thee in the Name of the Lord of Hosts, the God of the armies of Israel, whom thou hast defied" (I. Sam. xvii. 45).

7. **Man of Faithfulness,** as Samuel was. "Samuel said unto him, the Lord hath rent the kingdom of Israel from thee this day" (I. Samuel xv. 28, 33).

275. MANIFESTATIONS OF THE LORD

The Lord Jesus has told us that if we keep His words He will manifest Himself to us (John xiv. 21). There are certain conditions which must be observed by us if we would have manifestations of, and from the Lord.

1. The manifestation of His **power** is conditional upon our waiting on the Lord in prayer (Acts i. 8, 14 ; ii. 4).

2. The manifestation of His **joy** is conditional upon our abiding in Christ (John xv. 10, 11).

3. The manifestation of His **peace** is conditional upon carefulness for nothing, prayerfulness in everything, and thankfulness for anything (Phil. iv. 6, 7).

4. The manifestation of His **knowledge** is conditional upon doing God's will (John vii. 17).

5. The manifestation of His **purpose** is conditional upon walking with the Lord (Psalm ciii. 7).

6. The manifestation of His **love** is based upon dwelling in God (1. John iv. 16).

7. The manifestation of His **glory** is given to those who are taught by the Holy Spirit (1. Cor. ii. 9, 10).

276. MANNER OF GOD'S LOVE

1. John iii. 1

The manner of His love—

1. He loves as a Father (1. John iii. 1). Heartily.
2. ,, ,, Mother (Gen. xxv. 28). Tenderly.
3. ,, ,, Bridegroom (Gen. xxiv. 67). Earnestly.
4. ,, ,, Brother (John xv. 9). Affectionately.
5. ,, ,, Shepherd (Luke xv. 4-6). Perseveringly.
6. ,, ,, Husband (Eph. v. 25). Devotedly.
7. ,, ,, Sister (John xi. 32). Sincerely.
8. ,, ,, Friend (Prov. xvii. 17). Constantly.

277. MELCHISEDEK

There is a difference between atonement and priesthood—

1. Atonement is a thing of death, and priesthood a thing of life.

2. Atonement is once for all, finished; priesthood is continuous.

3. Atonement was accomplished on earth, priesthood is carried on in heaven.

4. Atonement is for the sinner, and priesthood for the saint.

Christ is a priest after the order of Melchisedek. Melchisedek was without father or mother in a priestly sense, *i.e.*, his priesthood was of a different order from Aaron's, which depended on descent and genealogy, and lasted for a definite period. Christ is the Eternal One. His priesthood begins and ends with Himself.

It is interesting to note the three things that Melchisedek did when he met Abraham (Gen. xiv. 18-20).

I. **He brought forth bread and wine to him.** Bread is strengthening and wine is symbolical of joy. Our High Priest ministers to us His own word and joy.

II. **He blessed him.** We are blessed in our High Priest. We read that when Christ was about to ascend to heaven, He led His disciples as far as Bethany, and there, with uplifted hands, He blessed them (Luke xxiv. 50). We never read that those hands were put down.

III. **He received from Abraham a tenth** of what he had taken. Our High Priest waits for our gifts and offerings. There are four we can give—

1. Our **bodies** (Romans xii. 1).
2. Our **service** (Phil. ii. 17; Heb. xiii. 16).
3. Our **money** (Phil. iv. 18).
4. Our **praise** (Heb. xiii. 15).

278. THE MERCY OF THE LORD

As God had mercy on Nineveh, so He has had mercy upon us. It is for us to believe in, and accept His mercy, by accepting Christ.

Think of the character of His mercy.

1. **His mercy is great** (Num. xiv. 18; Psalm ciii. 11; cxlv. 8). It is great, because the Father is the Source of it; it is great, because of the price it cost before it could reach us, for sin had blocked up the way. The cost was the blood of Christ.

2. **His mercy is enduring** (I. Chron. xvi. 34, 41; II. Chron. v. 13; vii. 3, 6; xx. 21; Ezra iii. 11; Psalm cvi. 1; cvii. 1; cxviii. 1; cxxxvi. 1 to the end; and Jer. xxxiii. 11). Having put His hand to the plough, He never looks back.

3. **His mercy is plenteous** (Psalm lxxxvi. 5, 15; ciii. 8). He does not dole it out grudgingly, but showers it upon us abundantly.

4. **His mercy is tender** (Luke i. 78). He has mercy upon us, not as a judge, but as a Father.

5. **His mercy is rich,** or He is rich in mercy (Eph. ii. 4). He keeps not the riches of His mercy to Himself, but, like Joseph, who gave of his abundance to his brethren, even so the Lord gives us of His fulness.

6. **His mercy is saving** (Titus iii. 5). We should never have been saved if our salvation had depended upon ourselves; but He held out the sceptre of mercy to us, as Ahasuerus did to Esther.

7. **His mercy is abundant** (I. Peter i. 3). It is not like a brook that dries up in the summer, but like the sea, which is unlimited. His mercy shall be as an attendant to accompany us (Psalm xxiii. 6), and as an army to encompass us (Psalm xxxii. 10).

279. MIGHTY GOD

ISAIAH ix. 6

HE is mighty in many ways. His mighty acts declare His power.

1. He is mighty to **save** (Isaiah lxiii. 1).
2. He is mighty to **deliver** (Deut. iii. 24 : vii. 8, 19).
3. He is mighty to **conquer** (Joshua iv. 24 ; II. Cor. x. 4).
4. He is mighty to **strengthen** (Gen. xlix. 24).
5. He is mighty to **use** in His **service** (Col. i. 29).
6. He is mighty in **word** (Luke xxiv. 19).
7. He is mighty in **work** (Mark vi. 2).

280. MIND OF CHRIST

1. **Stedfast** mind, and Christ the **Power.** "That ye stand fast in one spirit with one *mind*" (Phil. i. 27).

2. **Loving** mind, and Christ the **Principle.** "Like-*minded*, having the same love" (Phil. ii. 2).

3. **Humble** mind, and Christ the **Pattern.** "Let this *mind* be in you, which was also in Christ Jesus" (Phil. ii. 5).

4. **Unselfish** mind, and Christ the **Passion.** "Like-*minded* . . . . . all seek their own, not the things that are Jesus Christ's" (Phil. ii. 20, 21).

5. **Developed** mind, and Christ the **Progress.** "If ye be otherwise *minded*, God shall reveal even this unto you" (Phil. iii. 15).

6. **Guarded** mind, and Christ the **Peace.** "The peace of God . . . . keep your hearts and *minds*" (Phil. iv. 7).

7. **Musing** mind, and Christ the **Pathway.** "Whatsoever things are true . . . . *think* on these things" (Phil. iv. 8, R.V.).

281. MINISTRY OF ANGELS

THERE are many things the Lord does through the ministry of angels. The following are a few out of the many—

1. Angels **guide in difficulty,** as seen in Eleazer's mission. "He shall send His angel before thee" (Gen. xxiv. 7, 40).

2. Angels **deliver from evil,** as Jacob testifies. "The Angel which redeemed me from all evil" (Gen. xlviii. 16).

3. Angels **commission in work,** as is evidenced in Gideon. "There came an angel of the Lord" (Judges vi. 11, 22).

4. Angels **encourage in despondency,** as we gather from Elijah when under the juniper tree. "As he lay and slept under a juniper tree, behold then an angel touched him, and said unto him, Arise and eat" (I. Kings xix. 5, 7).

5. Angels **shield from harm** by their presence, as David assures us. "The angel of the Lord encampeth round about them that fear Him, and delivereth them" (Psalm xxxiv. 7).

6. Angels **defeat our adversaries,** as we have illustrated in Hezekiah's deliverance from Sennacherib. "Then the angel of the Lord went forth and smote in the camp of the Assyrians," &c. (Isaiah xxxvii. 36).

7. Angels **preserve in the midst of danger,** as we have demonstrated in the cases of the three Hebrew young men and Daniel. "Who hath sent His angel and delivered His servants" (Daniel iii. 28; vi. 22).

282. MORIAH

THERE are many typical characters in the Book of Genesis. *Adam*, typical of Him who is the last Adam, the Lord from Heaven. *Melchisedek*, typical of our High Priest. *Joseph*, typical of Christ as the Ruler and Provider. *Isaac*, typical of Christ as the Obedient One, even unto death.

I. **Moriah, the typical place.** (Genesis xxii.; John iii. 16). There are many truths we might gather, but we point out this one.

1. *The love of Abraham for Isaac* (verse 2). The first time the word "lovest" occurs in the Bible, is here, and it is typical of the love the Father has for Christ.

2. *The obedience of Isaac.* He did not hesitate, but went at once. This is typical of Christ, who was obedient unto death (Phil. ii. 8).

3. *The unity between Abraham and Isaac.* "They went both of them together" (verse 6). This is typical of the unity there was between the Father and Christ. He finished the work the Father gave Him to do, and it was with, and by the Father He did the work.

4. *The burden of Isaac* (verse 6). In Bagster's Bible, the reference is John xix. 17. It is significant. There we are told that Christ bare His cross, just as Isaac bore the wood. The cross is what Christ endured at the hands of man; but, as Peter said on the day of Pentecost, they were only carrying out the purpose of God.

5. *Isaac upon the Altar.* He is in figure offered up, but Christ was in reality. "Hath given Himself for us, an Offering and a Sacrifice to God, for a sweet smelling savour" (Eph. v. 2).

6. *Isaac is in figure received from the dead* (Heb. xi. 19). Christ was raised from the dead in reality.

7. *The ram offered in the stead of Isaac* (verse 13). Here we have substitution. Christ has died instead of every believer, and they shall never die for their sins. Distinguish between provision and substitution. Christ has made provision for all, by His death, but it is only those who receive Him that get the benefit of His work.

II. **Moriah, the place of sin, judgment, and mercy** (I. Chron. xxi.) David's sin was in numbering the people without the atonement money. The Lord was displeased with David for numbering the people, and sent a pestilence that destroyed 70,000 of them. Why did God thus deal with His servant? Was David wrong in numbering the people? We think not. Where was the evil? In this. In Exodus xxx. 12, it says, "When thou takest the sum of the children of Israel, after their *number*, then shall they give every man a ransom for his soul unto the Lord, when thou *numberest* them; that there be no plague among them, when thou *numberest* them." Now the sin of David was, that he did not call for the atonement money, and hence he broke a distinct command of God, and the consequent plague followed. What a rebuke to those who, to-day, are scouting the atonement, and pooh-poohing the blood-theology! As surely as the judgment fell upon Israel for their disobedience, so surely will it fall upon all those who scout the blood of Christ; for verily they trample beneath their feet the blood of God's dear Son, and God shall treat them likewise. When David found out how he had sinned, he went up to the threshing-floor of Ornan, and there offered burnt and peace offerings; and then, and not till then, the angel put up his sword, and the plague ceased. The offering comes in between the offended and the offender, and the fire coming down upon the offering tells that the offended is satisfied and the offender is accepted.

III. **Moriah, the place of purchase** (I. Chron. xxi. 24, 25; Eph. i. 7-14). David bought the threshing-floor of Ornan, and the oxen for fifty shekels of silver (II. Sam. xxiv. 24); and the site of the Temple for six hundred shekels of gold (I. Chron. xxi. 25). David buying the site for the Temple reminds us of Christ, who has redeemed us, who believe in Him, not with corruptible things as silver and gold, but with His own precious blood. And as Moriah was purchased to erect a dwelling for God, so the believer is redeemed to be indwelt by the Holy Spirit.

IV. **Place of progress** (I. Kings vi. 7; Eph. ii. 19-22). The building of the Temple is an illustration of the growth of the believer in Christ, and also the progress of the Church as a whole. Every sinner saved is another stone in the holy building.

In II. Peter i. 5-7, we have the building up of the character of the believer. Faith is the first stone on the foundation, and love is the top-stone. We might call these so many stones of faith:—

Virtue is faith undaunted.
Knowledge is faith apprehending.
Temperance is faith overcoming.
Patience is faith untiring.
Godliness is faith imitating.
Brotherly kindness is faith in practice.
Love is faith at work.

283. MUST

THIS word speaks the necessity of the truth declared.

1. **The must of worship Him.** "They that worship Him *must* worship Him in spirit and in truth" (John iv. 24).

2. **The must of work.** "I *must* work the works" (John ix. 4).

3. **The must of purpose.** "Them also I *must* bring" (John x. 16).

4. **The must of regeneration.** "Ye *must* be born again" (John iii. 7).

5. **The must of sacrifice.** "Even so *must* the Son of Man be lifted up" (John iii. 14; xii. 34).

6. **The must of resurrection.** "He *must* rise again from the dead" (John xx. 9).

7. **The must of increase.** "He *must* increase, but I must decrease" (John iii. 30).

284. NAMES OF BELIEVERS

IT is a most profitable study to note the names that are given to believers, for as the names of God denote His character and claims, so the names of believers denote their calling in Christ and what their character should be before Him.

A **Ambassadors** to represent God in the world. "We are ambassadors for Christ" (II. Cor. v. 20).

B **Branches** in Christ, the Vine, for the Spirit of God to manifest His fruitfulness through them. "I am the Vine, ye are the branches" (John xv. 5).

C **Citizens** of heaven in a strange land, which they are travelling through. "Fellow-citizens with the saints and of the household of God" (Eph. ii. 19).

D **Disciples** following Christ, their Master, and listening to Christ, their Teacher. "Whosoever doth not bear his cross, and come after Me, cannot be My disciple" (Luke xiv. 27).

E **Elect** ones of God for His use and glory. "Elect of God, holy and beloved" (Col. iii. 12).

F **Friends** of Christ, to have fellowship with Him and lovingly to do as He bids. "Ye are My friends if ye do whatsoever I command you" (John xv. 14).

G **Garden** enclosed as His own property for His delight and satisfaction. "A garden enclosed is My sister, My spouse" (Song of Solomon iv. 12).

H **Heirs** of God, joint heirs with Christ, to enjoy what they have with Him. "Heirs of God and joint heirs with Christ . . . . that we may be also glorified together" (Rom. viii. 17).

I Instruments to be fitted and used at His disposal. "Sanctified and meet for the Master's use" (II. Tim ii. 21).

J Jewels that are precious and priceless to Him. "They shall be Mine, saith the Lord of Hosts, in that day when I make up My jewels" (Mal. iii. 17).

K Kings. Made so by His grace to reign with Christ in His kingdom. "Made us kings and priests unto God and His Father" (Revelation i. 6).

L Lights to reprove sin by their holiness, to represent Christ by their harmony with His will and Word. "Ye are the light of the world. Let your light so shine," &c. (Matt. v. 14, 16).

M Members of Christ's body as to their union with Him, and hence members one of another. "For we are members of His body" (Eph. v. 30). "We are members one of another" (Eph. iv. 25).

N New Creatures in Christ Jesus, as reminding them of the new position they enjoy in Him, and the new practice they are to exemplify by Him. "If any man be in Christ he is a new creature" (II. Cor. v. 17).

O Offerers to Him of themselves—spirit, soul, and body; their praise and prayers. "That ye present your bodies a living sacrifice, holy, acceptable unto God, which is your reasonable service" (Romans xii. 1).

P Pilgrims and strangers, hence they have nothing in common with the world, nor wish to. "I beseech you as strangers and pilgrims abstain from fleshly lusts" (I. Peter ii. 11).

R Redeemed ones, as those who have been purchased and liberated. "Ye were not redeemed with corruptible things . . . . but with the precious blood of Christ" (I. Peter i. 18).

S Stewards, in their responsibility to God. "Occupy till I come" (Luke xix. 13).

T Temple of God, being indwelt by the Holy Spirit. "Know ye not that ye are the temple of God, and that the Spirit of God dwelleth in you?" (I. Cor. iii. 16).

U Undefiled as to what the Lord calls them, because He sees them in Christ (Song of Solomon iv. 7).

V Vessels of mercy, as partakers of His grace. "That He might make known the riches of His glory on the vessels of mercy" (Romans ix. 23).

W Worshippers, as to their adoration and admiration of the Lord in His greatness and goodness. "O that men would praise the Lord for His goodness" (Psalm cvii. 8).

285. NINE "NOTS"

ROMANS XIII. 8-14

1. THE "not" of **uncleanness.** "Thou shalt *not* commit adultery" (Matt. v. 27, 28).

2. The "not" of **murder.** "Thou shalt *not* kill" (Matt. v. 21, 22; I. John iii. 15).

3. The "not" of **stealing.** "Thou shalt *not* steal" (Mal. iii. 8-10).

4. The "not" of **false witness.** "Thou shalt *not* bear false witness" (Col. iii. 9).

5. The "not" of **coveting.** "Thou shalt *not* covet" (Col. iii. 5).

6. The "not" of **rioting and drunkenness.** "*Not* in rioting and drunkenness" (Eph. v. 18).

7. The "not" of **chambering and wantonness.** "*Not* in wantonness and chambering" (Eph. iv. 29).

8. The "not" of **strife and envying.** "*Not* in strife and envying" (I. Peter ii. 1, 2).

9. The "not" of the **flesh.** "Make *not* provision for the flesh," &c. (Gal. v. 24).

286. OBEDIENCE

1. OBEDIENCE of **faith.** "A great company of the priests were *obedient* to the faith" (Acts vi. 7).

2. Obedience of **love.** "If ye love Me *keep* My commandments" (John xiv. 15).

3. Obedience to **death.** "Became *obedient* unto death" (Phil. ii. 8).

4. Obedience to **Christ.** "Bringing into captivity every thought to the *obedience* of Christ" (II. Cor. x. 5).

5. Obedience unto **righteousness.** "Of *obedience* unto righteousness" (Rom. vi. 16).

6. Obedience is **remembered.** "He remembereth the *obedience* of you all" (II. Cor. vii. 15).

7. Obedience is **spoken of.** "Your *obedience* is come abroad unto all men" (Rom. xvi. 19).

287. OBEDIENCE

1. OBEDIENCE is the **recognition** of the claims of God (Acts v. 29).

2. The **mark** of conversion to the authority of Christ (Rom. vi. 16).

3. The **evidence** of our relationship to God the Father as His children (I. Peter i. 14).

4. The **characteristic** of faith, for faith always responds to the Word of God (Heb. xi. 8).

5. The **proof** of our love to Christ (John xiv. 15, R.V.)

6. The **condition** of receiving the Spirit's power (Acts v. 32).

7. The **indicator** of the Spirit's working (Phil. ii. 12, 13).

288. "ONCE"

ONE of the key-words of Hebrews ix. and x. is the term "once," which occurs seven times.

1. **The once of limitation** (ix. 7). The High Priest could only enter the Holiest of all, one day in the year, though he went in several times on that one day.

2. **The once of completion** (ix. 12). The Revised Version says that Christ has entered into the Holiest "*once for all*," therefore His atoning work is complete. Mark also the contrast—Christ entered in with His own blood.

3. **The once of manifestation** (ix. 26, R.V.) Christ was hidden behind the veil of His Godhead before His incarnation, but He is God manifest in the flesh. Ponder the purpose of His appearing; it was to "put away sin," which sin kept man from God, and God from man.

4. **The once of condemnation** (ix. 27). Death on account of sin, and judgment for sin, are the common heritage "laid up" (R.V., margin), for the natural man.

5. **The once of substitution** (ix. 28). Those that believe in Christ, and know Him personally as their Saviour and Lord, are not looking for death or judgment, but for His second coming, because Christ has stood in their place and borne the judgment for them. Mark the "*as*" and "*so*" of ix. 27, 28.

6. **The once of purification** (x. 2). The sacrifices under the Levitical economy were only effectual in atoning for the sins of the past year, and even then could not give a cleansed conscience; but Christ has, once and for ever, dealt with the question of sin in its penal aspect. Hence the believer is no longer a condemned criminal at the bar of justice, but a child in the family of God, with a perfect conscience, because freed from guilt by the blood of Christ.

7. **The once of sanctification** (x. 10). The blood of Christ, which is the purchase price of our salvation, is also the means of our separation to God. As those who are sanctified in Christ to God, which is our privilege, we are responsible to be separate in heart and life to the Lord in all things. We do not seek to be saintly to become saints, but as saints we are to do those things that are consistent with our calling (1. Cor. i. 2—the words "*to be*" are in italics; Eph. v. 3).

289. ONENESS OF BELIEVERS

Believers are members of Christ's body, hence members one of another. As illustrating this, we will take the word "*together*" as showing our oneness with Christ and one another.

1. **Oneness in death.** "Planted *together* in the likeness of His death" (Romans vi. 5).

2. **Oneness in resurrection.** "Quickened . . . and raised up *together*" (Eph. ii. 5, 6).

3. **Oneness in position.** "Made us sit *together* in heavenly places" (Eph. ii. 6).

4. **Oneness in suffering and glory.** "If we suffer with Him . . . . glorified *together*" (Rom. viii. 17).

5. **Oneness by possession.** "Builded *together* . . . . . habitation of God" (Eph. ii. 22). Not only purchased and pardoned, but possessed by the Holy Spirit, who will fill us, as God of old filled the tabernacle and Temple with His presence.

6. **Oneness in fitness.** "Fitly framed *together*" (Eph. ii. 21). As the coverings of the tabernacle were coupled together, as the stones in Solomon's Temple (each one was put in its own place), so each believer is first made fit, then fitly framed, then fitly framed together—thus fit to live and serve in the place he occupies.

7. **Oneness in place at the coming of Christ.** "Live *together*" (I. Thess. v. 10); "heirs *together*" (I. Peter iii. 7); caught up *together* to meet Christ in the air (I. Thess. iv. 17). Different positions in glory, but all with Him.

8. **Oneness in fellowship.** We read of the disciples who were on the way to Emmaus, that they "*talked together*;" and "how can two walk *together* except they are agreed?" These two were talking of the Lord, and He of whom they were conversing drew near and spoke to them; the secret of true fellowship one with another is communion with the Lord Himself.

9. **Oneness in sympathy.** "Comfort yourselves *together*" (I. Thessalonians v. 11).

10. **Oneness in prayer.** "Peter and John went up *together* into the Temple at the hour of prayer" (Acts iii. 1). The secret of Judah's victory over Ammon and Moab was, "that they gathered themselves *together*" to ask help of the Lord (II. Chron. xx. 4).

11. **Oneness in work.** Sower and reaper working and receiving the joy of service now, and at the great harvest *together* (John iv. 36).

12. **Oneness in worship.** "They sang *together* by course in praising and giving thanks unto the Lord" (Ezra iii. 11).

13. **Oneness in thought.** "Perfectly joined *together* in the same mind" (I. Cor. i. 10).

14. **Oneness in conflict.** "Children of Israel went out . . . gathered *together* as one man" (Judges xx. 1).

15. **Oneness in love.** "Knit *together* in love" (Col. ii. 2).

16. **Oneness in labour.** "Striving *together* for the faith of the Gospel" (Phil. i. 27). In all the above Scriptures we see the union there is from God's standpoint amongst all those who are His; and if we would have manifest unity among the Church of God, there

must be—and it will only come in this way—the recognition of our oneness in Christ, hence our oneness one with the other.

Christians, remember there are many children in the family. They may call themselves by different names, but there is only one family—one Father; many members in the body, but only one body—one Head; many stones in the building, but only one house—one Foundation; many branches in the Vine, but only one Vine; many sheep in the flock, but only one flock—one Shepherd; many priests, but only one order—one High Priest; many crumbs, but only one Loaf; many citizens, but only one city.

290. ONLY

THE first commandment is God's claim to have the *absolute* place in the heart and life (Ex. xx. 3). Jehovah will not share with another. Christ repeats this same truth when Satan would have Him to worship himself (Matt. iv. 10). The following Scriptures where the word "only" occurs will illustrate the absoluteness of God's claim:

1. **Saved** by the Lord only (II. Kings xix. 19; Isaiah xxxvii. 20).
2. **Separated** only unto the Lord (I. Sam. vii. 3, 4).
3. **Sacrificing** only to the Lord (Ex. xxii. 20).
4. **Serving** only the Lord (Matt. iv. 10).
5. **Speaking** only the word of the Lord (Numbers xxii. 35).
6. **Seeing** only the Lord (Matt. xvii. 8).
7. **Singing** only of the Lord (Romans xvi. 27).

291. OPEN THINGS

THE open tomb of Jesus (Mark xvi. 4) proclaims—

1. An opened **Fountain** for sin (Zech. xiii. 1).
2. An opened **Heaven** for blessing (Mark i. 10).
3. An opened **heart** for Christ (Acts xvi. 14).
4. An opened **understanding** for Christ (Luke xxiv. 45).
5. An opened **Bible** for comfort (Luke xxiv. 32).
6. An opened **mouth** for testimony (Eph. vi. 19).
7. An open **face** for privilege (II. Cor iii. 18).
8. An open **door** for revelation (Rev. iii. 8).

292. OUGHTNESS OF THE CHRISTIAN LIFE

ALL God's children feel there are many things we ought to do, but we do not always rise to the occasion.

1. **The oughtness of Prayer.** "Men *ought* always to pray" (Luke xviii. 1).

2. **The oughtness of Ministry.** "*Ought* to wash one another's feet" (John xiii. 14).

3. **The oughtness of Obedience.** "*Ought* to obey God" (Acts v. 29).

4. **The oughtness of God-pleasing.** "*Ought* to walk and to please God" (I. Thess. iv. 1).

5. **The oughtness of Walking.** "*Ought* himself also to walk, even as He walked" (I. John ii. 6).

6. **The oughtness of Love.** "We *ought* also to love one another" (I. John iv. 11).

7. **The oughtness of Obligation.** "We *ought* to lay down our lives for the brethren" (I. John iii. 16).

293. "OUR GOD"

1. THE God of **Truth** to sanctify. "A God of truth and without iniquity" (Deut. xxxii. 4).

2. God of all **Grace** to establish. "But the God of all grace . . makey ou perfect, stablish, strengthen, settle you" (I. Peter v. 10).

3. The God of **Peace** to calm. "The God of peace shall be with you" (Phil. iv. 9).

4. The God of **Love** to enrich. "Be perfect, be of good comfort, be of one mind, live in peace, and the God of love and peace shall be with you" (II. Cor. xiii. 11).

5. The God of all **Comfort** to console. "The God of all comfort, who comforteth us in all our tribulations" (II. Cor. i. 3, 4).

6. The God of **Patience** to enable. "Now the God of patience and consolation grant you to be like-minded one toward another, according to Christ Jesus" (Rom. xv. 5).

7. The God of **Hope** to cheer. "Now the God of hope fill you with all joy and peace in believing" (Rom. xv. 13).

8. The God of **Glory** to attract. "The God of glory appeared unto our father Abraham" (Acts vii. 2).

9. The God of **Judgment** to search. "The Lord is a God of judgment" (Isa. xxx. 18).

10. The Father of **Mercies** to bless. "Blessed be God . . . . the Father of mercies" (II. Cor. i. 3).

294. OUR SPEECH

THE Lord tells us in Ephesians what we are to do with our speech:

1. **Testimony.** "Speaking the truth in love" (iv. 15).

2. **Test of conversion.** "Put off . . . . former conversation" (iv. 22).

3. **Thinking of others.** "Speak every man truth with his neighbour" (iv. 25).

4. **Thoroughness.** "No corrupt communication proceed out of your mouth" (iv. 29).

5. **Tattling to be done with.** "Evil speaking be put away" (iv. 31).

6. **Trifling to be put away.** "Foolish talking . . . . not to be named" (v. 4).

7. **Thankfulness.** "Speaking . . . . psalms," &c. (v. 19).

295. PATHS

1. **Path of life.** "Thou wilt show me the *path* of life" (Ps. xvi. 11).

2. **Plain path.** "Teach me Thy way, O Lord, and lead me in a plain *path*" (Psalm xxvii. 11).

3. **Path of uprightness.** "Who leave the *paths* of uprightness to walk in the ways of darkness" (Prov. ii. 13).

4. **Path of the just.** "The *path* of the just is as the shining light" (Prov. iv. 18).

5. **Paths of righteousness.** "He leadeth me in the *paths* of righteousness for His Name's sake" (Psalm xxiii. 3).

6. **Paths of peace.** "Her ways are ways of pleasantness, and all her *paths* are peace" (Prov. iii. 17).

7. **Straight paths.** "And make straight *paths* for your feet, lest that which is lame be turned out of the way" (Heb. xii. 13).

296. PAST AND PRESENT WALK OF THE ONE WHO NOW BELIEVES IN CHRIST

1. **Once walking away from God, as Adam.** "And Adam . . . hid from the presence of the Lord" (Gen. iii. 8).

Now walking with God, as Enoch. "And Enoch walked with God" (Gen. v. 22).

2. **Once walking in our own way, as Balaam.** "Balaam rose up in the morning . . . . God's anger was kindled because he went" (Num. xxii. 21, 22).

Now walking in the truth, as the elect lady and her children. "Walking in truth" (II. John 4).

3. **Once walking after the world, as Demas.** "Demas hath forsaken me, having loved this present evil world" (II. Tim. iv. 10).

Now walking after the world to come, as Abram. "He looked for a city . . . whose builder and maker is God" (Heb. xi. 10).

4. **Once walking in unbelief, as Israel.** "Because of unbelief they were broken off" (Rom. xi. 20).

Now walking in faith, as Moses. "By faith he forsook Egypt" (Heb. xi. 27).

5. **Once walking in darkness, as Judas.** "Went immediately out; and it was night" (John xiii. 30).

Now walking in the light, as John. "If we walk in the light" (1. John i. 7).

6. **Once walking in hatred, as Saul of Tarsus.** "Saul yet breathing out threatenings" (Acts ix. 1).

Now walking in love, as Paul. "Because ye were dear unto us" (1. Thess. ii. 8).

7. **Once walking in sin, as the Ephesians.** "Ye walked according to the course of this world" (Eph. ii. 2).

Now walking in Christ, as the early Church. "Walking in the fear of the Lord" (Acts ix. 31).

297. WISDOM'S START AND SEPARATION

Proverbs i. 1-15

Proverbs i. brings out in vivid contrast the wisdom of the wise and the folly of the foolish. The one is under the power of God, and therefore has His authority, and the other is under the will of self, and in consequence ends his career in dismay and destruction.

1. **Wisdom's start.** "The fear of the Lord is the beginning of knowledge" (verse 7). Gladstone said some time since, "The older I grow the more confirmed I am in my faith and religion. I have been in public life fifty-eight years, and forty-seven in the Cabinet of the British Government, and during these forty-seven years I have been associated with sixty of the master minds of the country, and all but five of the sixty were Christians." The above gives colouring to the statement that the men were what they were because they were Christians.

What a difference there is between the fear of the Lord and the fear of man. The latter brings "a snare" (Proverbs xxix. 25), while the former is:—

Departing from evil (Proverbs iii. 7).

Hating all evil (Proverbs viii. 13).

Prolonging of days (Proverbs x. 27).

Inspirer of confidence (Proverbs xiv. 26).

Fountain of life (Proverbs xiv. 27).

Minister of contentment (Proverbs xv. 16).

Instructor of wisdom (Proverbs xv. 33).

Satisfier of soul (Proverbs xix. 23).

Harbinger of true riches (Proverbs xxii. 4).

Keeper of the heart (Proverbs xxiii. 17).

Steadier of the soul (Proverbs xxiv. 21).

The fear of the Lord means to *reverence* Him humbly, to *submit* to Him gladly, to *trust* in Him wholly, to *obey* Him continually, to *love* Him supremely, to *follow* Him fully, and to *walk* with Him confidingly.

2. **Wisdom's separation.** The three "*nots*" are pointed in their bearing and practical in their application. They are "Forsake thou not" (verse 8), "Consent not" (verse 10), and "Walk not" (verse 15).

"*Forsake thou not.*" The law of the mother which the son is exhorted not to forsake, is the law of God which the mother had made hers by her faith and obedience, just as Paul speaks of the Gospel of God as "My Gospel" (II. Tim. ii. 8). Sherman says, "'Wanted—a boy who obeys his mother.' So advertised one employer. Thousands of such boys are wanted. I never yet knew a lad prosper in the world who did not love his mother." The mother's apron strings, if fastened on by the Lord, are cables to keep the soul steady on the sea of life.

"*Consent not*" (verse 10). "This is the defence, a blunt, peremptory 'No.' The method of defence must be different from the enemy's mode of attack. His strength lies in making gradual approaches; ours in a resistance, sudden, resolute, total." As a good man said of temptation, "I cannot help an ill bird flying over my head, but I can prevent him from making a nest in my hair." Whoever hesitates and argues when a known sin is presented before him, is already half lost.

"*Walk not*" (verse 15). Separation from sin and sinners is the Christian's safety. If we walk with the ungodly we shall be contaminated by them, even as a canary if put with a sparrow, will begin to chirrup like it. Abraham (Gen. xii. 10), Lot (Gen. xix. 17), Jehoshaphat (II. Chron. xviii. 1), Peter (Luke xxii. 55), got into bondage of spirit, bitterness of soul, and lost the blessing of the Lord's approval, through fellowship of the ungodly.

298. PAUL'S EXPERIENCE

Acts xxvi. 5-26

1. **Conversion of Paul.** The Apostle tells Agrippa what he *was* when in his natural state; namely, a self-righteous Pharisee (verse 5), an opponent to Jesus (verse 9), a persecutor of the saints (verse 10), a misguided man in obeying the priests (verse 10), an inflicter of punishment upon God's people (verse 11), an instrument in the hands of Satan in causing some of the disciples of Christ to blaspheme (verse 11), and a fanatic, in that he was "exceedingly mad" in his unholy service (verse 11); but a vision of Christ in His holiness caused him to see his sinfulness. It was Paul's *obedience*

to the heavenly vision that was the pivot upon which the persecutor became the pleader with God and men (verse 19).

2. **Commission of Paul.** Being *saved* through Christ he was next *sent* by Christ to preach the Gospel. We are saved to serve, we do not serve to be saved. Paul was sent to accomplish a five-fold purpose in the power of the Holy Spirit (verse 18).

Revelation. "Open their eyes."

Repentance. "Turn from darkness to light."

Release. "From the power of Satan unto God."

Remission. "Receive forgiveness of sins."

Riches. "Inheritance."

All these blessings are bestowed upon those who have faith in Christ.

3. **Consecration of Paul.** "I was not disobedient," &c. (ver. 19). Obedience is the law of the Kingdom of Grace.

4. **Continuance of Paul** (verse 22). The Apostle tells us the secret of his continuance: it was because he obtained (not attained) help from God. *Obtainment* is the secret of *attainment*. Mark that the Apostle obtained help for a specific object, viz., that he might witness to and of the things in the Scriptures.

5. **Creed of Paul** (verse 23). He believed in the sufferings of Christ for the sins of man, and in the resurrection of Christ for the justification of the believer (Rom. iv. 25).

6. **Calmness of Paul** (verse 25). Festus thinks that Paul is mad as he listens to the earnest and burning words which fall from his lips, and tells him so; but, as the Apostle says, he is perfectly cool and calm, and speaks forth "the words of truth and soberness."

7. **Courage of Paul** (verse 26). The Apostle does not hesitate to tell King Agrippa that he knew what he was speaking about, and then begins to put pointed questions to him. Courage is one of the fruits of the filling of the Holy Spirit (Acts iv. 31).

299. PEACE

1. Peace is of **heavenly origin** as to its source. "God is not the author of confusion, but of peace" (I. Cor. xiv. 33).

2. Peace is a **fruit of the Spirit** as to its impartation. "The fruit of the Spirit is . . . peace" (Gal. v. 22).

3. Peace is a **product of the Cross** as to its channel. "So making peace . . . . by the Cross" (Eph. ii. 15, 16).

4. Peace is a **plant of obedience** as to its condition. "If ye walk in My statutes, and keep My commandments, I will give peace" (Leviticus xxvi. 3, 6).

5. Peace is a **variegated plant** as to its fulness. "Peace I leave with you, My peace I give unto you" (John xiv. 27).

300. PEACE

GRACE, mercy, and peace are the trio of Gospel blessings. Grace is love planning to bless, mercy is love acting, and peace is love enjoyed.

P Purchased Peace. There are many who talk about "making their peace with God." This is an impossibility. Man can never make his peace with God; but there is something better, and that is, that Christ has made peace by the blood of His Cross. The purchase price of the peace of the Gospel is the blood of Christ (Col. i. 20).

E Embodied Peace. "He is our Peace." It is not merely something from Christ, but Christ Himself, who is the believer's peace (Eph. ii. 14). I remember an aged saint exclaiming to me once, "Oh, I wish I had peace!" I asked her, "Have you Christ?" "Oh, yes!" she replied. "Then you have got peace, because you have Christ, for 'He is our Peace.'" If we sever blessing from Christ we shall never enjoy blessing, but if we see that we have every blessing in Christ (Eph. i. 3), and that Christ is every blessing, then we have blessing.

A Abiding Peace. "My peace I give unto you" (John xiv. 27) is Christ's gift to His people. Whatever Christ gives must be like Himself, enduring and unfailing, for He is "the same yesterday, to-day, and for ever" (Heb. xiii. 8). The things of this world pass away (1. John ii. 17), but the things of the world to come are like the words of Christ (Matt. xxiv. 35), they never pass away.

C Complete Peace. The peace of God is perfect in its nature and perfect in its keeping (Isa. xxvi. 3). Like a circle, it is complete in its character, and encircling in its embrace. To be complete in Christ (Col. ii. 10) is to have a complete peace, because we are in a complete Saviour.

E Ennobling Peace. When the Lord Jesus has said peace to the sin-sick soul (Luke vii. 50), and when the peace of God rules in the heart (Col. iii. 15), through being anxious for nothing, prayerful in everything, and thankful for anything (Phil. iv. 6, 7), then in the quietness and calmness which are begotten by the Holy Spirit (Rom. xv. 13) the life shall be calm as a river (Isa. lxvi. 12), and the peace of God shall play upon the face (Acts vi. 15).

301. PEACE IN ISAIAH

1. **Prince of Peace.** "And His Name shall be called . . . . the Prince of Peace" (ix. 6).

2. **Perpetuity of Peace.** "Of the increase of His government and peace, there shall be no end" (ix. 7).

3. **Perfection of Peace.** "Thou shalt keep him in perfect peace" (xxvi. 3).

4. **Power of Peace.** "Lord, Thou wilt ordain peace for us" (xxvi. 12).

5. **Possessor of Peace.** "And He shall make peace with Me" (xxvii. 5).

6. **Parent of Peace.** "And the work of righteousness shall be peace" (xxxii. 17).

7. **Promise of Peace.** "He said . . . . there shall be peace and truth in my days" (xxxix. 8).

8. **Protection of Peace.** "He pursued them and passed in peace" (xli. 3, M.)

9. **Provider of Peace.** "I make peace" (xlv. 7).

10. **Partner of Peace.** "Then had thy peace been as a river" (xlviii. 18).

11. **Publisher of Peace.** "That publisheth peace" (lii. 7).

12. **Permanence of Peace.** "Neither shall the covenant of My peace be removed" (liv. 10).

13. **Price of Peace.** "The chastisement of our peace was upon Him" (liii. 5).

14. **Preciousness of Peace.** "Great shall be the peace of thy children" (liv. 13).

15. **Progress of Peace.** "And be led forth with peace" (lv. 12).

16. **Prospect of Peace.** "He shall enter into peace" (lvii. 2).

17. **Proclamation of Peace.** "Peace, peace to him that is far off" (lvii. 19).

18. **Picture of Peace.** "I will extend peace to her like a river" (lxvi. 12).

302. PEOPLE OF GOD

BALAAM's words about God's people (Numbers xxiv. 5-9, 17-19; Deut. xxxiii. 29), illustrate what God does for them.

1. **God's people are a goodly people** (verse 5). Goodly because partakers of the goodness of God. The valleys, with their fruitfulness and flowers, are an illustration of the goodly fruits and fragrance that are produced in the lives of those who are possessed by, and are under the power of Him.

2. **God's people are a supplied people** (verse 7). Water poured out of buckets is but a simile of His continual supply and His all-sufficient grace to meet our every need.

3. **God's people are an exalted people.** "His people shall be higher than Agag" (verse 7). Our King is Christ; He is exalted to the right hand of God (Phil. ii. 9), and we are exalted with Him (Ephesians ii. 6).

4. **God's people are a delivered people.** We are delivered from the wrath to come (I. Thess. i. 10); from the second death (II. Cor. i. 10); from our enemies (Luke i. 74); and from this present evil world (Galatians i. 4).

5. **God's people are an honoured people** (verses 17-19). Israel was honoured because Christ came from them, and was of them.

6. **God's people are a happy people** (Deut. xxxiii. 29). Happy because their sins are forgiven (Psalm xxxii. 1, 2); because chosen by Him (Psalm xxxiii. 12); because trusting in Him (Psalm xxxiv. 8). because occupied with Him (Psalm xl. 4); because ministering to others for Him (Psalm xli. 1); because abiding in Him (Psalm lxv. 4; lxxxiv. 4); because strengthened by Him (Psalm lxxxiv. 5). The word "blessed" in the Psalms is the same word that is rendered "happy" in Deuteronomy xxxiii. 29).

7. **God's people are a saved people.** Saved by the death of Christ as to the means of salvation (John x. 9-11); saved by the Holy Spirit as to the effectual cause of salvation (Titus iii. 5); saved by faith as to the reception of salvation (Luke vii. 50); saved by the Gospel as to the knowledge of salvation (I. Cor. xv. 2); saved by the risen living Christ as to being kept from sinning (Rom. v. 10); and saved by hope as to the completeness of our salvation (Rom. viii. 24).

303. PERSONALITY OF THE HOLY SPIRIT

THE Personal **Comforter** for fellowship (John xiv. 16).

The Personal **Companion** to cheer. "*He* dwelleth with you" (John xiv. 17).

The Personal **Teacher** to instruct. "*He* shall teach" (John xiv. 26).

The Personal **Witness** to testify. "*He* shall testify of Me" (John xv. 26).

The Personal **Ambassador** to represent (John xvi. 7).

The Personal **One** manifested. "*He* is come" (John xvi. 8).

The Personal **Reprover** convicting. "*He* will convict" (John xvi. 8, R.V.).

The Personal **Title-giver.** "*He*, the Spirit of Truth" (John xvi. 13).

The Personal **Guide** directing. "*He* will guide" (John xvi. 13).

The Personal **Servant** listening. "*He* shall not speak from Himself" (John xvi. 13, R.V.).

The Personal **Hearer** speaking. "*He* shall hear" (John xvi. 13).

The Personal **Speaker** declaring. "That shall *He* speak" (John xvi. 13).

The Personal **Revealer** unfolding. "*He* will show" (John xvi. 13).

The Personal **Work** accomplished. "*He* shall glorify Me" (John xvi. 14).

The Personal **Receiver** making known. "*He* shall receive of Mine" (John xvi. 14).

304. PLACES OF BLESSING

1. **On His shoulders.** The place of strength. "He layeth it on His shoulders" (Luke xv. 5).

2. **On His bosom.** The place of confidence. "He then lying on Jesus' breast, saith unto Him, Lord, who is it?" (John xiii. 25).

3. **On His heart.** The place of affection. "And they shall be upon Aaron's heart" (Ex. xxviii. 15-30).

4. **On His hands.** The place of remembrance. "I have graven thee upon the palms of My hands" (Isaiah xlix. 16).

5. **On His forehead.** The place of thought. "And it shall be upon Aaron's forehead" (Ex. xxviii. 38).

6. **On His wings.** The place of power. "They shall mount up with wings as eagles" (Isaiah xl. 31).

7. **In His arms.** The place of support. "Underneath are the everlasting arms" (Deut. xxxiii. 27).

8. **At His feet.** The place of blessing. "Mary, which also sat at Jesus' feet, and heard His word" (Luke x. 39).

9. **In His hand.** The place of use. "I the Lord thy God will hold thy right hand saying unto thee, fear not . . thou shalt thresh the mountains" (Isa. xli. 13-15).

305. PLEASING THE LORD

THERE are several ways by which we, as believers in Christ, may please the Lord.

1. By **not pleasing ourselves** (Romans xv. 1).
2. By **walking worthy of the Lord** (Col. i. 10).
3. By **suffering wrongfully** (1. Peter ii. 19, 20).
4. By **walking with God** (Heb. xi. 5).
5. By **believing in God** (Heb. xi. 6).
6. By **ministering to the need** of others (Heb. xiii. 16).

306. POSITION OF CHRIST

The Position of Christ. "Sit Thou on My right hand." He sits at the right hand of God—

1. As our **Intercessor** to plead for us (Romans viii. 34).
2. As the **Honoured One** for us (Mark xvi. 19).

3. As the **Channel** of blessing to us (Acts ii. 33).
4. As the **Waiting One** to receive us (Acts vii. 56).
5. As **Head** of the body, to minister to us (Eph. i. 20-22).
6. As the **Object** to attract us (Col. iii. 1).
7. As the **Sin-purger** who has cleared us (Heb. i. 3).
8. As the **Glorified One** who is to reign (Heb. i. 13).
9. As our **Representative** (Heb. viii. 1).
10. As the **Accomplisher** of His work (Heb. x. 12).
11. As the **Conqueror** over His foes (Heb. xii. 2).
12. As the **Almighty One** (I. Peter iii. 22).
13. As the **Expecting One** (Psalm cx. 1).

307. POWER

"GIVE me a fulcrum and a lever and I will move the world," said one. Christ is the Lever of Power, and a believing (obedient) heart is the fulcrum.

1. The **power of Christ's Resurrection** will raise us above an earthly and selfish life (Phil. iii. 10).

2. The **power of Christ's Grace** will enable us to glory in infirmity (II. Cor. xii. 9).

3. The **power of Christ's Spirit** will make Him a reality in our experience (Eph. iii. 16).

4. The **power of His Keeping** will preserve us to the heavenly inheritance (I. Peter i. 4, 5).

5. The **power of His Love** will give us to enjoy the "all things" that pertain to life and godliness (II. Peter i. 3).

6. The **power of Christ's Ministry** will operate through us as we allow Him (Acts i. 8; iii. 12; iv. 33).

7. The **power of His Favour** will urge us to be faithful to Him (II. Tim. ii. 1).

308. POWER

1. **Spirit sanctifying** power as seen in Stephen. "And Stephen, full of faith and power, did great wonders and miracles among the people" (Acts vi. 8).

2. **Doing good** power, as illustrated in Christ. "Who went about doing good" (Acts x. 38).

3. **Bodily healing** power, as demonstrated in the healing of the lame man. "As though by our own power or holiness we had made this man to walk" (Acts iii. 12).

4. **Grace begetting** power. "That ye may abound in hope, through the power of the Holy Ghost" (Rom. xv. 13).

5. **Christ endearing** power. "To be strengthened with might by His Spirit in the inner man" (Eph. iii. 16).

6. **Service enabling** power. "Wherefore I also labour, striving according to His working, which worketh in me mightily (Col. i. 29).

7. **Glorifying in infirmity** power, as made known in Paul. "Most gladly, therefore, will I rather glory in my infirmities, that the power of Christ may rest upon me" (II. Cor. xii. 9).

8. **Patience giving** power. "Strengthened with all might, according to His glorious power, unto all patience" (Col. i. 11).

9. **Soul keeping** power. "Who are kept by the power of God through faith unto salvation" (I. Peter i. 5).

309. POWER OF DARKNESS

DARKNESS represents that which is evil, hence men love darkness, &c. There is the darkness of ignorance, the darkness of misery, and the darkness of sin.

1. **Subtle power.** "Now the serpent was more subtle than any beast" (Gen. iii. 1).

2. **Blighting power.** "Behold all that he hath is in thy power" (Job i. 12). "Satan smote Job with sore boils" (Job ii. 7).

3. **Accusing power.** "Doth Job fear God for nought?" (Job i. 9).

4. **Resisting power.** "Satan standing at his right hand to resist him" (Zechariah iii. 1).

5. **Constraining power.** "Satan provoked David to number Israel" (I. Chron. xxi. 1).

6. **Opposing power.** "Get thee behind Me, Satan" (Mark viii. 33).

7. **Binding power.** "Satan hath bound these eighteen years" (Luke xiii. 16).

8. **Sifting power.** "Satan hath desired to have you, that he may sift you as wheat" (Luke xxii. 31).

9. **Robbing power.** "Then cometh the devil, and taketh away the word out of their hearts" (Luke viii. 12).

10. **Lying power.** "Why hath Satan filled thine heart to lie to the Holy Ghost?" (Acts v. 3).

11. **Hindering power.** "We would have come . . . . Satan hindered us" (I. Thess. ii. 18).

12. **Persecuting power.** "The messenger of Satan to buffet me" (II. Cor. xii. 7).

13. **Destructive power.** "Then entered Satan into Judas" (Luke xxii. 3).

310. PRACTICAL POWER OF CHRIST'S RESURRECTION

1. The resurrection of Jesus in its practical power is associated with our blessing (Acts iii. 26).

2. Our conduct towards others (Rom. xiv. 9, 10).

3. Our object in life (II. Cor. v. 15).

4. Our walk in newness of life (Rom. vi. 4).

5. Our stay in service (II. Tim. ii. 8).

6. Our fruit-bearing (Rom. vii. 4).

7. Our power for every emergency (Eph. i. 19, 20).

311. PRAYER

"They tell Him of her" (Mark i. 30).

"They tell Him of her." How simple and yet how striking the words! In them are found the essential and essence of prayer. Emphasize each word.

"*They* tell Him of her." The men who are in touch with Christ have the ear of Christ. Holy John, zealous Peter, discriminating James, and faithful Andrew, are the men who are in touch with Christ. These men in their several characteristics may be taken as illustrating four essentials in prayer, namely, holiness, zeal, discrimination and faithfulness.

1. **Holiness** of heart and life are the **foundation of prayer.** It is no use lifting up our hands if they are not holy (I. Tim. ii. 8); nor must we approach the golden altar of incense to offer praise before we have washed away the filthiness of flesh and spirit at the laver of God's truth by confession (II. Cor. vii. 1).

2. **Fervency** of spirit is the **prevailer in prayer.** It was the importunate widow who got her plea granted (Luke xviii. 5); it was the persistent friend who got his need supplied (Luke xi. 8).; and it was the incessant knocking of Peter which caused the inmates to let him into the house (Acts xii. 16).

3. **Discrimination** is the **wisdom of prayer.** There are some things for which God's people ask, that they have already got in Christ; others are praying when they should be acting, asking God to do things which they can do themselves; and others are praying in a wrong spirit. To discriminate in prayer is to observe the conditions for prevailing in prayer.

4. **Faithfulness** is the **backbone of prayer.** Faithfulness may be read two ways. First, consistency or fidelity to the Word of God in whole-hearted obedience; and second, fulness of faith, that is, an unhesitating and unceasing confidence and trust in God.

"They *tell* Him of her." What is prayer? It is illustrated here. Speaking to Christ is prayer. Prayer is not getting on to the stilts of wordism, nor floating in the balloon of honeyed phrases by the aid of the gas of human eloquence, inflating the mind with self-conceit; but it is simply telling the Lord the heart's need, or speaking to Him in a natural manner as we ask favours for others.

Telling Him the *trouble*, as the disciples of John, when they went and informed Christ that their teacher was beheaded (Matt. xiv. 12).

Telling Him the *sorrow*, as when Mary went to Christ about her dead brother Lazarus (John xi. 32).

Telling Him the *pain*, as when Paul prayed about the thorn in the flesh (II. Cor. xii. 8).

Telling Him the *grief*, as when the Syrophenician woman cried to Christ about her daughter (Matt. xv. 22).

Telling Him the *joy*, as when the disciples spoke of the demons they had cast out in His name (Luke x. 17).

Telling Him the *difficulty*, as when the disciples asked to be taught how to pray (Luke xi. 1).

Telling Him the *sickness*, as in the present case.

"They tell *Him* of her." There is no need to mention *His* name, we have only to put a capital H to the pronoun for it to be recognised that we speak of Christ. He has made it possible for us to tell Him, for He has died for us; hence we can come boldly to the throne of grace through the consecrated way of His atonement, and speak to Him face to face. He has told us to come to Him, for He has said "Whatsoever we shall ask in prayer, believing, we shall receive." His promise is our plea and introduction in speaking to Him. We remember who He is, and as we do so we are drawn towards Him, as the needle is drawn to the loadstone.

He is the *Shepherd* who tends us, and ever looks after our interests.

He is the *Priest* who represents us, and succours us in the hour of temptation.

He is the *Friend* who thinks of us, and always sympathises with us.

He is the *Brother* who cares for us, and is ever ready to aid us.

He is the *Saviour* who delivered us, and will always keep us.

He is the *God* who has blessed us, and will never leave us.

He is the *Lover* who loves us, and will never be unfaithful.

Tell Him, for He *cares*. Tell Him, for He *knows*. Tell Him, for He *loves*. Tell Him, for He is *listening*. Tell Him *all*. Tell Him *often*. Tell Him *always*. Tell Him *now*.

"They tell Him *of her*." They were very definite in their petition and pointed in their plea. They did not vacillate or hesitate, but they went right to the mark and hit it. And methinks as they saw the once fevered patient calm and cool, as she waited upon them, they rejoiced; and if they had wanted a new name for Simon's wife's mother, they might have called her Answered-Prayer.

312. PRAYER OF FAITH

1. **Confession** of sin. "To seek by prayer and supplications" (Daniel ix. 3-20).

2. **Cleansing** from sin. "Thy sin purged" (Isaiah vi. 7).

3. **Consecration** to the Saviour. "Behold, he prayeth" (Acts ix. 11-20).

4. **Confidence** in the Saviour. "Said unto the Lord, increase our faith" (Luke xvii. 5).

5. **Courage** from the Saviour. "They lifted up their voice to God with one accord" (Acts iv. 24-33).

6. **Calmness** in the Saviour. "The peace of God . . . . shall keep your hearts and minds" (Phil. iv. 6, 7).

7. **Communion** with the Saviour. "Did not our heart burn . . while He talked with us" (Luke xxiv. 32).

313. PREPARATION

REHOBOAM is condemned because he did not prepare "his heart to seek the Lord" (II. Chron. xii. 14), while Jehoshaphat is commended for seeking Him (II. Chron. xix. 3). If we would bring upon us a like commendation, then let us carry out the following points in the acrostic on preparation.

P Praying in the name of Jesus (John xiv. 14).

R Regarding the merit of Jesus (Heb. x. 19).

E Expecting an answer for the sake of Jesus (John xv. 16).

P Purity of heart (Psalm lxvi. 18).

A Abiding in Christ (John xv. 7).

R Righteousness of life (I. Tim. ii. 8).

A Asking according to God's will (I. John v. 14).

T Trusting wholly in the Lord (Heb. xi. 6).

I Importunity, "Ask--Seek—Knock" (Matt vii. 7).

O Obeying the word of the Lord (John xv. 7).

N Nothing in our hearts condemning us (I. John iii. 21, 22).

314. PRESENCE OF CHRIST

THE presence of Christ is **protection**, as the three Hebrew young men found (Daniel iii. 25, 27).

The presence of Christ is **preservation**, as Peter experienced (Matthew xiv. 30, 31).

The presence of Christ is **power**, as Paul knew (II. Cor. xii. 9).

The presence of Christ is **peace**, as the disciples were made to know (John xx. 21, 26).

The presence of Christ is **progress,** as we see from John x. 27, for the sheep follow Him.

The presence of Christ is **paradise,** as John found in the Isle of Patmos (Rev. i. 13-18).

The presence of Christ is **provision,** as we see in His feeding the multitude (John vi. 11).

315. PRESENCE OF GOD WITH DAVID

"The Lord was with David" (I. Sam. xviii. 12, 14, 28). All that David had achieved, and all that He was, were due to the presence of the Lord. The secret of David's greatness (II. Sam. v. 10), the cause of his victories (II. Sam. xxii. 30), the source of his overcoming Goliath (I. Sam. xvii. 45), the reason of his wise behaviour (I. Sam. xviii. 14), and the strength of his comfort (Psalm xxiii. 4), were all found in the Lord's presence with him. To recognise God's presence with us means:—

1. **Rest** in walk (Ex. xxxiii. 14).
2. **Refreshment** in trial (Heb. xiii. 5, 6).
3. **Rejoicing** in trouble (Acts xxvii. 23).
4. **Renewal** in weakness (Isaiah xl. 31).
5. **Resource** in service (Matt. xxviii. 20).
6. **Reflection** in life (II. Cor. iii. 18).
7. **Reward** in persecution (II. Tim. iv. 17).

316. PRESENCE OF THE LORD

The presence of the Lord to His people means:—

1. **Light in trouble.** "Lord, lift Thou up the *light* of Thy *countenance* upon us" (Psalm iv. 6).

2. **Joy in sorrow.** "In Thy *presence* is fulness of *joy*" (Psalm xvi. 11).

3. **Hiding in persecution.** "Thou shalt *hide* them in the secret of Thy *presence*" (Psalm xxxi. 20).

4. **Help in discouragement.** "I shall yet praise Him for the *help* of His *countenance*" (Psalm xlii. 5).

5. **Health in disquietude.** "Who is the *health* of my *countenance* and my God" (Psalm xlii. 11).

6. **Encouragement in life.** "His *countenance* doth behold the upright" (Psalm xi. 7).

7. **Gladness in responsibility.** "Thou hast made him exceeding *glad* with Thy *countenance*" (Psalm xxi. 6).

317. PRESERVATION

"THOU SHALT PRESERVE" (Psalm xxxii. 7).

JEHOVAH will preserve His people:—

1. **Securely**, as a strong city. "We have a strong city" (Is. xxvi. 1).

2. **Continually**, as a watchman. "The Lord shall preserve thy going out" (Psalm cxxi. 8).

3. **Immediately**, as the eye-lid does the eye. "He kept him as the apple of His eye" (Deut. xxxii. 10; Psalm xvii. 8).

4. **Calmly**, as the strong man keeps the weaker one. "Thou (Jehovah) wilt keep him" &c. (Isaiah xxvi. 3-6).

5. **Carefully**, as the gardener keeps the garden. "I, the Lord, do keep it; I will water it every moment" (Isaiah xxvii. 3).

6. **Affectionately**, as the parent keeps the child. "I will hold thine hand, and will keep thee" (Isaiah xlii. 6).

7. **Powerfully**, as a garrison keeps the camp. "Kept by the power of God" (1. Peter i. 5).

318. PREVAILING PRAYER

GENESIS xxxii

1. **Prevailing prayer pleads the promises** (verse 9). Trapp says:—"Promises must be prayed over. God loves to be burdened with, and to be importuned in His own words; to be sued upon His own bond. Prayer is putting the promises into suit. Such prayers will be nigh the Lord day and night (1. Kings viii. 59). He can as little deny them as deny Himself."

2. **Prevailing prayer confesses its unworthiness** (verse 10). We do not receive blessing because of our confession, but we are not blest without it.

3. **Prevailing prayer asks definitely** (verse 11). Jacob knew what he wanted, and prayed accordingly. He had offended and robbed his brother, and now he seeks deliverance from his righteous anger. The Lord often over-rules our blunders to our benefit and His own glory. Jacob not only prays for himself, but also for those who are near and dear to him.

4. **Prevailing prayer is to be alone with God** (verse 24). The words of Christ are "Pray in secret" (Matt. vi. 6). Christ is our Example in this, for He went to the mountain to pray (Matt. xiv. 23). Praying in secret we shall get revelations of His glory, as Daniel did at the riverside (Dan. viii. 16); we shall have the consciousness of the presence of Christ, as John had on the Isle of Patmos (Rev. i.); we shall be commissioned, as Peter was, when he was on the house-top at Joppa (Acts x. 9); we shall meet the Rebekahs of blessing, as Isaac did, when meditating in the field (Gen. xxiv. 63); and we shall receive blessing, as Jacob did.

5. **Prevailing prayer is intensely earnest.** Trapp well remarks, in speaking of the angel wrestling with Jacob: "There wrestled a man with him; in a proper combat, by might and sleight; to the raising of dust and causing of sweat, as the word importeth. This strife was not only corporeal, but spiritual; as well as by the force of his faith, as strength of body. 'He prevaileth,' saith the prophet (Hosea xii. 4), by prayers and tears. Our Saviour also prayed Himself into 'an agony' (Luke xxii. 44); and we are bidden to 'strive in prayer' (Rom. xv. 30); Nehemiah prayed himself pale (Neh. ii. 2); Daniel prayed himself 'sick' (Dan. viii. 27). Hannah prayed, striving with such an unusual motion of her lips, that old Eli, looking upon her, thought her drunk (1. Sam. i. 13). Elijah puts his head betwixt his knees, as straining every spring of heart in prayer (1. Kings xviii. 42). Every sound is not music, so neither is every uttering of petitions to God a prayer. It is not the labour of the lips, but the travail of the heart. Common beggary is the easiest and poorest trade; but this beggary, as it is the richest so it is the hardest."

6. **Prevailing prayer is seen in a clinging faith** (verse 26). Jacob got no blessing while wrestling, but the wrestling led to the blessing. The angel touched his thigh, and then he could wrestle no more, but he held on the tighter, and would not let the angel go till he received a blessing from him. Three boys each gave a definition of faith, which definitions illustrate the tenacity of faith. The first boy said, "It was taking hold of Christ;" the second, "keeping hold;" and the third, "not letting go."

7. **Prevailing prayer is rewarded** (verses 28-30). 1. He got his name changed from Jacob, the supplanter, to Israel, the prince of God. 2. He received definite blessing from God. 3. He was a testimony for God ever afterwards in his halting gait.

319. PRIDE

1. Kings xx. 1-30.

In the attitude and action of the King of Syria we have an illustration of the course and consequence of pride (verse 10).

1. **The demand of pride** (verses 1-6). Pride is always over-reaching in its claims, selfish in its requests, and cruel in its commands.

2. **The boast of pride** (verse 10). Pride never uses a small i, but always the capital I. What a lot of "I" there was in the Pharisee's prayer!

3. **The recklessness of pride** (verse 12). Pride ever seeks to "enjoy itself," although danger may be near. Nero played his fiddle while Rome was burning.

4. **The enemy of pride** (verses 13-15). God hates pride; it is an abomination to Him.

5. **The pastime of pride** (verse 16). Ben-hadad was drinking when he should have been on the alert. What an illustration of

those who are drunken with self-conceit and arrogance. "This one thing I do," is their cry: "I seek to find satisfaction in what the world offers."

6. **The assumption of pride** (verse 18). The King of Syria took it for granted that he would take captive those who had come out from Israel; so the sinner thinks his plans will be sure to succeed, till they are exploded; then he discovers his folly.

7. **The overthrow of pride** (verses 19-21). Destruction is the result of pride (Prov. xvi. 18). Pride is the forerunner of destruction. It was so in the case of Korah, when he in his pride coveted the priesthood (Numbers xvi).

8. **The persistence of pride** (verses 22-27). Although defeated, Ben-hadad returns to his former course. How like one, who, although he has had to smart for his action, still seeks to follow his former course of conduct.

9. **The punishment of pride** (verses 27-30). The sinner can no more escape the punishment that his sin deserves, than the moth can escape being burnt by coming in contact with the lighted candle.

320. PRIDE

EXAMPLE OF PRIDE—UZZIAH (II. Chron. xxvi. 16-23).

As Lot's wife was a standing testimony to the judgment of God, so is Uzziah. The king wilfully went against the command of God in offering incense, which the priests alone were authorised to do (Num. xviii. 7). Note the steps of his pride—

1. A **description** of pride. "His heart was lifted up" (verse 16).
2. The **outcome** of pride. "Transgressed" (verse 16).
3. The **presumption** of pride. "Went in" &c. (verse 16).
4. The **anger** of pride. "Wroth" (verse 19).
5. The **smiting** of pride. "Smitten" (verse 20).
6. The **shame** of pride. "Hasted also" (verse 20).
7. The **separation** of pride. "Cut off" (verse 21).
8. The **isolation** of pride. "A leper" (verse 23).

321. PRIESTHOOD OF CHRIST

CHRIST, as our Saviour, speaks of His saving grace. Christ, as our High Priest, tells out His sustaining grace. Christ, as our High Priest, is seen in the Epistle to the Hebrews, as the—

1. **Deliverer,** to assure (ii. 15).
2. **Succourer,** to sustain (ii. 18).
3. **Sympathizer,** to comfort (iv. 15).
4. **Forerunner,** to supply (vi. 20).

5. **Saviour,** to preserve (vii. 25).
6. **Watcher,** to care (x. 21).
7. **Shepherd,** to sanctify (xiii. 20).

322. PROVISION OF THE GOSPEL

WHEN we call to mind the ample provision God has provided in the death and person of His Son, we discover an ocean of grace. The following alphabet will illustrate in some small degree the fulness of the Gospel. In the Gospel we find—

Acceptance for the unworthy (Eph. i. 6).
Blessing for the cursed (Gal. iii. 13).
Cleansing for the polluted (I. John i. 7).
Deliverance for the captive (II. Cor. i. 10).
Enrichment for the poor (II. Cor. viii. 9).
Fulness of pardon for the guilty (Luke vii. 42).
Grace for the prodigal (Luke xv. 22).
Heaven for the hell-deserving (Col. i. 13).
Inheritance for the beggar (I. Peter i. 3-5).
Joy for the miserable (Luke ii. 10).
Kiss of welcome for the wanderer (Luke xv. 20).
Life for the dead (John v. 25).
Might for the feeble (Rom. v. 6).
Nearness for those who are afar off (Eph. ii. 13).
Open door for the undeserving (John x. 9).
Peace for the enemy (Col. i. 20).
Quietness for the troubled (Luke vii. 50).
Righteousness for the unrighteous (II. Cor. v. 21).
Salvation for the lost (Eph. ii. 5).
Truth for the untrue (John xiv. 6).
Union for the severed (Rom. xi. 17).
Virtue for the depraved (I. Cor. vi. 11).
Welcome for all (Rev. xxii. 17).

323. "PUT ON"

1. PUT Him on as **Jesus,** to save from and to the uttermost. "Jesus . . able also to save them to the uttermost" (Heb.vii. 22-25).

2. Put Him on as **Lord,** to rule and regulate the actions. "*Put* ye *on* the Lord Jesus Christ" (Rom. xiii. 14).

3. Put Him on as **Christ,** to transform the life like His. "As many of you as have been baptised into Christ, have *put on* Christ" (Galatians iii. 27).

4. Put Him on as **Holiness,** to manifest Himself. "*Put on* the new man . . . . . . created in righteousness and true holiness" (Eph. iv. 24; Col. iii. 10).

5. Put Him on as **Armour,** to protect in all offensive and defensive warfare. "*Put on* the whole armour of God" (Eph. vi. 11).

6. Put Him on as **Power,** to act through in service. "Until ye be *endued*" (same word as "*put on*") "with power from on high" (Luke xxiv. 49).

7. Put Him on as **Light,** that He may be seen. "Let us *put on* the armour of Light" (Rom. xiii. 12).

324. REDEMPTION

1. **God is its Author.** "Who of God is made unto us Redemption" (1. Cor. i. 30).

2. **The blood of Christ is its purchase price.** "In Whom we have redemption through His blood" (Eph. i. 7).

3. **Christ Himself is its Personification.** "But of Him are ye in Christ Jesus . . . . redemption" (1. Cor. i. 30).

4. **The Lord Jesus is its depository.** "The redemption that is in Christ Jesus" (Rom. iii. 24; Col. i. 14).

5. **Deliverance is its meaning.** The word "deliverance" in Hebrews xi. 35, is the same as rendered "redemption" in other Scriptures.

6. **Christ's coming is its completion.** "Waiting for the adoption, to wit, the redemption of our body" (Rom. viii. 23).

7. **The indwelling Spirit of God is its security.** "The Spirit of God, whereby ye are sealed unto the day of redemption" (Eph. iv. 30; i. 14).

325. RELATION OF CHRIST TO THE FATHER

1. **He is begotten by the Father.** "The glory as of the only Begotten of the Father" (John i. 14).

2. **He dwells in the bosom of the Father.** "The only begotten Son, which is in the bosom of the Father" (John i. 18).

3. **He did the will of the Father.** "I seek not Mine own will, but the will of the Father which hath sent Me" (John v. 30).

4. **He lives by the Father.** "As the living Father hath sent Me, and I live by the Father" (John vi. 57).

5. **He did the works of the Father.** "If I do not the works of My Father, believe me not" (John x. 37).

6. **He spake of the Father.** "As the Father said unto Me, so I speak" (John xii. 50).

7. **He glorified the Father.** "I have glorified Thee on the earth" (John xvii. 4).

8. **He is the Way to the Father.** "No man cometh unto the Father, but by Me" (John xiv. 6).

326. RESPONSIBILITY REGARDING THE WORD OF GOD

DEUTERONOMY vi. 3-15

THERE are seven things Israel were to do with the statutes and commands of Jehovah, which are indicated in the following points:—

1. "**Observe**" (verse 3). The Hebrew word rendered "observe" means to hedge about, to guard, to protect. No less than twenty times in Deuteronomy is the same word translated "observe," namely, Deut. v. 32; vi. 3, 25; viii. 1; xi. 32; xii. 1, 28, 32; xv. 5; xvi. 1, 12, 13; xvii. 10; xxiv. 8; xxviii. 1, 13, 15, 58; xxxi. 12; xxxii. 46. The term is of frequent occurrence, and variously translated. To observe the word of the Lord is a comprehensive duty. This may be seen by reference to passages of Scripture where the Hebrew word "*Shamar*" occurs. In Gen. ii. 15, and Psalm xvii. 8, the word is rendered "*keep;*" in Num. xxxi. 30, 47, "*kept;*" in 1. Sam. xix. 2, "*take heed;*" in 1. Sam. xix. 11, "*watch;*" in Psalm xxxvii. 37, "*mark;*" and in Josh. xxiv. 17, "*preserved.*" The incidents in which the words occur afford illustrations as to how we are to observe the commands of Jehovah.

2. "**In thine heart**" (verse 6). R.V., "Upon thine heart." We generally speak of the head as the seat of intelligence, and the heart as the seat of the affections. We may grasp truth intelligently, and yet not lay hold of it with the heart. The wee fellow who said that faith was "grasping Jesus with the heart" had the key to the situation. If the fountain of the heart be clean, the stream of the life will correspond.

3. "**Teach**" (verse 7). The margin says, "Whet or sharpen." Dr. Young remarks, "The original verb generally signifies to whet or sharpen. I prefer deriving it from a root signifying to repeat, to do a thing a second time." The Hebrew word is rendered "*whet*" in Deut. xxxii. 41; "*sharp*" in Psalm xlv. 5; and "*pricked*" in Psalm lxxiii. 21. From the meaning and the usage of the word it will be seen that no light or listless teaching is meant, but a diligent teaching which is as a sharp sword to cut, an arrow to stick, and an instrument to pierce.

4. "**Talk**" (verse 7). The children of Israel were not to talk occasionally about the law of the Lord, but sitting and walking, however engaged, lying down and when rising up, that is, early and late this was to be the theme of their conversation. To talk of the

Word of the Lord, is to have the Lord of the Word (Luke xxiv. 32); and to impart that Word to others, is to have the comfort and cleansing of the truth, even as the pipe is cleansed which is the medium of conveying water to those who desire it.

5. "**Bind**" (verse 8). The statutes of the Lord were to be bound on the hands of the Israelites. The law of the Lord was to be bound on the hand as a sign that it must be righteous in all its actions. Nothing mean or unrighteous was to be performed by the people of God, but the rule of heaven was to be knit to their being, that they might do the right thing always. The word translated "*bind*" is given "*knit*" in I. Sam. xviii. 1, in speaking of Jonathan being knit to David in love; and "*joined together*" in stating that the wall of Jerusalem was completed under Nehemiah (Neh. iv. 6). The command of love should be knit to our nature as Jonathan's heart was bound to David; and the whole life should be complete in righteous action. No flaw in our dealings with each other.

6. "**Frontlets**" (verse 8; Exodus xiii. 16; Deut. xi. 18). The Word of the Lord was to be as "frontlets between the eyes," that is, their thought and sight were to be ruled by the truth of God. What a difference it would make in the life, if the Word of the Lord dwelt in us richly (Col. iii. 16), it would then be held forth more effectively (Philippians ii. 16). We need the tongue of the taught to teach (Isaiah l. 4, R.V.).

7. "**Write**" (verse 9). Written on the posts and gates of the house, that all who come to the house may see and observe.

"All this is perfectly beautiful. The Word of God written in the heart; flowing out in loving instruction to the children in the bosom of the family; shining out in all the activities of the daily life, so that all who came inside the gates or entered the house might see that the Word of the Lord was the standard for each, for all, and in everything."

327. REST

1. **Rest of Salvation.** "Stand still, and see the salvation of the Lord" (Ex. xiv. 13).

2. **Rest of Conscience** about our sins. "I will give you rest" (Matthew xi. 28).

3. **Rest from the fear of Judgment.** "There is, therefore, now no condemnation" (Rom. viii. 1; John v. 24).

4. **Rest from fear of death.** "Though I walk through the valley of the shadow of death, I will fear no evil" (Psalm xxiii. 4).

5. **Rest from the power of sin.** "Because we have sought the Lord . . . He hath given us rest" (II. Chron. xiv. 7).

6. **Rest of heart** in fellowship with Christ. "Take My yoke . . ye shall find rest" (Matt. xi. 29).

7. **Rest in Service** from doubt and anxiety. "We which have believed do enter into rest" (Heb. iv. 3).

8. **Rest from the presence of sin** in glory. "There remaineth therefore a rest to the people of God" (Heb. iv. 9).

328. RESULTS OF ABIDING IN CHRIST

1. **Walking as Christ walked.** "So to walk, even as He walked" (I. John ii. 6).

2. **Loving the brethren.** "He that loveth his brother abideth in the light" (I. John ii. 10).

3. **Not ashamed at Christ's coming.** "And not be ashamed before Him at His coming" (I. John ii. 28).

4. **Sinning not.** "Whosoever abideth in Him, sinneth not" (I. John iii. 6).

5. **The witness of the Spirit.** "We know He abideth in us, by the Spirit" (I. John iii. 24).

6. **Possessing the Father and Son.** "He that abideth . . . he hath both the Father and Son" (II. John 9).

7. **Prayers answered.** "If ye abide in Me . . . . ye shall ask what ye will" (John xv. 7).

8. **Fruit-bearing.** "He that abideth . . . bringeth forth much fruit" (John xv. 5).

329. RESURRECTION OF CHRIST

THE resurrection of Christ is the *heart* of Christianity, which makes it pulsate with the life of God; it is the *keystone* to the arch of truth, which holds all the faith of the Gospel together; it is the *foundation* of the Church; it is the *mainspring* of Christian activity; it is the *lever* of power which shall move the world; and it is the *link* that unites all believers.

The death of Christ tells us of the *love* of *God*, and the resurrection of Christ tells us of the *power* of *God*, and of the following seven facts:—

1. That God is satisfied and glorified (Romans viii. 33, 34).
2. That our sins are gone (Eph. i. 7).
3. That we are accepted in Christ (Eph. i. 6).
4. That we are united to Christ (Col. ii. 12; iii. 1).
5. That every foe is vanquished (Col. ii. 15).
6. That we shall for ever live with Him (John xiv. 19).
7. That the Spirit is given to the believer (John vii. 39).

Further, the resurrection of Christ was announced in the Scriptures. The death, burial, and resurrection of Christ, were "according to the

Scriptures." Mainly the Old Testament is meant when the New Testament speaks of "the Scriptures." Where, in the Old Testament is the resurrection of Christ mentioned? Peter, on the Day of Pentecost, by the Holy Spirit, says in the "sixteenth Psalm" (Psalm xvi. 8-11; Acts ii. 24-32); and Paul at Antioch says in the "second Psalm" Psalm ii. 7; Acts xiii. 32-37). The God-breathed Scriptures (II. Tim. iii. 16) were the basis and the authority of the utterance of the apostles, therefore they had an authority above all question, for "where the word of a king is, there is power" (Eccles. viii. 4); and the hearers who received their message had a solid rock upon which to rest, which could never be moved (I. Corinthians xv. 1-4).

330. SACRIFICE OF CHRIST

1. **Necessary Sacrifice.** "What the law could not do, in that it was weak through the flesh, God, sending His own Son in the likeness of sinful flesh, and by a *sacrifice* for sin (margin), condemned sin in the flesh" (Rom. viii. 3).

2. **Offered Sacrifice.** "Who needeth not daily to offer up *sacrifice* . . . . He offered up Himself" (Heb. vii. 27).

3. **Removing Sacrifice.** "Put away sin by the *sacrifice* of Himself" (Heb. ix. 26).

4. **Perfect Sacrifice.** "Offered one *sacrifice* for sins for ever" (Hebrews x. 12).

5. **Accepted Sacrifice.** "Christ . . . . hath given Himself for us, an offering and a *sacrifice* to God for a sweet smelling savour" (Ephesians v. 2).

5. **Substitutionary Sacrifice.** "Christ, our Passover, is *sacrificed* for us (I. Cor. v. 7).

7. **Remembered Sacrifice.** "Gather My saints together unto Me, those that have made a covenant with Me by *sacrifice*" (Psalm l. 5).

331. SACRIFICE, THE GROUND OF BLESSING

SACRIFICE is the ground of all God's bestowments and blessings. There is one principle which runs through the Scriptures from end to end, like the lead in a pencil, and that is, that all God's approaches to man, and all man's approaches to Him, are on the ground of sacrifice.

1. **Acceptance.** Abel's acceptance with the Lord (Heb. xi. 4).

2. **Regeneration.** Noah's looking out on a new world in covenant promise (Gen. viii. 20, 21).

3. **Preservation.** Israel's protection in Egypt (Ex. xii. 13).

4. **Access.** Entrance into the holiest of all in the tabernacle (Leviticus xvi. 14).

5. **Cleansing.** Cleansing of the leper (Lev. xiv. 6).

6. **Consecration.** Consecration of the temple (1. Kings viii. 5).

7. **Bestowment.** The bestowment of a kingdom (1. Sam. xvi. 1-5).

All the above blessings and many more, are grounded upon sacrifice.

332. SAFEGUARDS.

The safeguards are connected with the word "lest" in the Epistle to the Hebrews.

1. **Hearing.** "Give the more earnest heed to the things which we have heard, *lest* at any time we should let them slip" (Heb. ii. 1).

2. **Heeding.** "Take heed, brethren, *lest* there be in any of you an evil heart of unbelief" (Hebrews iii. 12).

3. **Exhorting.** "Exhort one another daily, ... *lest* any of you be hardened through the deceitfulness of sin" (Heb. iii. 13).

4. **Labouring.** "Labour, therefore, to enter into that rest, *lest* any man fall after the same example of disobedience" (Heb. iv. 11, M.).

5. **Considering.** "Consider Him . . . . *lest* ye be wearied and faint" (Heb. xii. 3).

6. **Making.** "Make straight paths for your feet, *lest* that which is lame be turned out of the way" (Heb. xii. 13).

7. **Looking.** "Looking diligently, *lest* any man fail of the grace of God: *lest* any root of bitterness springing up trouble you, and thereby many be defiled" (Heb. xii. 15).

333. SAFETY

The following is a sevenfold illustration of the Christian's safety as found in the Old Testament.

1. **Jehovah's name.** The safety of the name of Jehovah is as a **tower** to befriend in the time of need (Proverbs xviii. 10).

2. **Jehovah's presence.** The safety of God's presence is a **covering** to protect in danger (Deut. xxxiii. 12).

3. **Jehovah's promise.** The safety of God's promise is a **refuge** from the snare of fear (Proverbs xxix. 25).

4. **Jehovah's power.** The safety of God's power is an **uplifter** to put us out of the enemy's reach (Psalm xii. 5).

5. **Jehovah's arm.** The safety of God's arm is a **strengthener** to sustain at all times (Psalm cxix. 117).

6. **Jehovah's leading.** The safety of God's leading is a **safeguard** in all difficulty (Psalm lxxviii. 53).

7. **Jehovah's keeping.** The safety of God's keeping is a **minister** of calm repose (Psalm iv. 8).

334. SALVATION

SALVATION, like God, is a trinity. It has a past, present, and future aspect to the believer in Christ.

1. **Past salvation.** Those who are Christ's are saved from what they deserve as sinners, because Christ has died for them and borne in His body the curse that sin merits (Gal. iii. 13; II. Cor. v. 21; I. Thess. i. 10; Eph. ii. 8; II. Tim. i. 9).

2. **Present salvation.** Believers are being saved from the despotism of sin as they abide in Christ and look to Him who lives in the power of an endless life (Rom. v. 9; Heb. vii. 25), and who, by the Holy Spirit, is able to work in us mightily, so that we can work out our own salvation with fear and trembling (Phil. ii. 12).

3. **Future Salvation.** The Lord's children will be saved from the disgrace of sin when Christ returns; hence we wait for Him as a Saviour (Phil. iii. 20); for this we are kept (I. Peter i. 5), and for this Christ will return (Heb. ix. 28). It is this aspect of salvation of which the Lord says, "It is nearer" (Rom. xiii. 11).

335. SALVATION

WHAT is comprehended in the most comprehensive word "salvation"? The following acrostic will indicate, in some small degree, Salvation

	From		*To*
S	Sin (Matt. i. 21).	S	Sanctification (Heb. x. 10, 14).
A	Alienation (Eph. ii. 12).	A	Adoption (Eph. i. 5).
L	Lifelessness (Eph. ii. 1).	L	Life eternal (John v. 24).
V	Vileness (Psalm li. 5).	V	Virtue (II. Peter i. 3).
A	Aversion (Romans viii. 7).	A	Acceptance (Eph. i. 6).
T	Thoughtlessness (Isaiah i. 3).	T	Thoughtfulness (Phil. iv. 8).
I	Independence (Psalm xiv. 1).	I	In-ness (II. Cor. v. 17).
O	Obstinacy (Isaiah xlviii. 4).	O	Obedience (John x. 27).
N	Neglectfulness (Prov. xiii. 4).	N	Nobleness (Acts xvii. 11).

336. SAMENESS OF CHRIST

CHRIST is the Ever-living, Immutable, and Unchanging One.

1. **Christ's eternal relationship with God.** "The *same* was in the beginning with God" (John i. 2).

2. **Christ's identity known by what He did.** "The *same* is He who baptizeth with the Holy Ghost" (John i. 33).

3. **Christ's exaltation because of His faithful work.** "God hath made that *same* Jesus . . . . Lord and Christ" (Acts ii. 36).

4. **Christ's return.** "This *same* Jesus, which is taken up from you into heaven, shall so come" (Acts i. 11).

5. **Christ's immutability.** "Thou are the *same* and Thy years shall not fail" (Heb. i. 12).

6. **The Holy Spirit's Testimony.** "Jesus Christ the *same* yesterday, and to-day, and for ever" (Heb. xiii. 8).

337. SAMSON, A TYPE OF CHRIST

1. **An angel foretold his birth.** "Angel . . . . said . . . . lo, thou shall conceive, and bear a son" (Judges xiii. 3 to 5). So it was in the case of Christ. "Angel said . . . thou shall conceive . . . and bring forth a Son" (Luke i. 30, 31).

2. **He was separated unto God.** "No razor shall come on his head: for the child shall be a Nazarite unto God from the womb" (Judges xiii. 5). Even so it was with Christ. "He shall be called a Nazarene" (Matt. ii. 23).

3. **He acted in the power of the Holy Spirit.** "The Spirit of the Lord began to move him" (Judges xiii. 25). "The Spirit of the Lord came mightily upon him" (Judges xiv. 6; xv. 14). The same was true of Christ. "Holy Ghost descended upon Him"; "Jesus, being full of the Holy Ghost . . . . led by the Spirit"; "returned in the power of the Spirit"; "the Spirit of the Lord is upon Me" (Luke iii. 22; iv. 1, 14, 18).

4. **He was mighty to overcome his enemies.** "He found a new jaw-bone of an ass, and put forth his hand and took it and slew a thousand men therewith" (Judges xv. 15). As Samson used a dead jaw-bone as the instrument to overcome his enemies, even so Christ, by His own death, has destroyed him that had the power of death, that is the devil (Heb. ii. 14).

5. **He was treated unkindly by his own people.** "Her father said, I verily thought that thou hadst utterly hated her (his wife), therefore I gave her to thy companion" (Judges xv. 2). As Samson's wife was given to another by her father—thus they rejected him—so the Jews, by their sin and unbelief, rejected Christ and gave themselves into the power of Satan, for Christ came to His own, but they received Him not (John i. 11).

6. **He was misused and mocked.** "She began to afflict him . . . . put out his eyes . . . . bound him with fetters of brass, and he did grind in the prison house . . . . . he made them sport" (Judges xvi. 19, 21, 25). As Samson was ill-used, even so was Christ. He was "despised and rejected of men, a Man of Sorrows, and acquainted with grief" (Isaiah liii. 3).

7. **He destroyed more enemies by his death than he ever did in his life.** "So the dead which he slew at his death were more than they which he slew in his life" (Judges xvi. 30). Even

so with Christ. By His death He has been the death of death; He has robbed death of its sting, the grave of its terrors, sin of its power, and Satan of his authority.

338. SANCTIFICATION OF THE LEVITES

THE Levites were set apart from their brethren for the service of the tabernacle. Notice the points of similarity between the Levites and believers:—

1. **Choice.** "Take the Levites" (Num. viii. 6). "As many as Thou hast given Him" (John xvii. 2).

2. **Cleansing.** "Cleanse them" (Num. viii. 6). "Now ye are clean" (John xv. 3).

3. **Supplication.** "Offer the Levites" (Num. viii. 11). "I pray for them" (John xvii. 9).

4. **Claiming.** "The Levites shall be Mine" (Num. viii. 14). "They are Thine" (John xvii. 9).

5. **Service.** "To do the service" (Num. viii. 15). "Even so have I also sent them into the world" (John xvii. 18).

6. **Given** to Aaron (Num. viii. 19). "Thou gavest them Me" (John xvii. 6).

7. **Separation.** "Separate the Levites" (Num. viii. 14). "Sanctify them" (John xvii. 17).

339. "SANCTIFY YOURSELVES"

JOSHUA iii. 5

How can we sanctify ourselves (II. Cor. vii. 1)? In the following sevenfold manner:—

1. By the mortification of the old sinful nature within us (Col. iii. 5; Rom. viii. 12, 13).

2. By the expulsion from our life of all evil habits (Col. iii. 9; Galatians v. 24).

3. By the denial of self itself, in ignoring its existence (Luke ix. 23, 24).

4. By the enthronement of Christ in the heart by the Spirit (Eph. iii. 17; I. Peter iii. 15, R.V.).

5. By being satisfied with Christ through heart fellowship with Him (Matt. xi. 29; Psalm lxxiii. 25).

6. By delighting in God's will and control (Ps. xl. 8; I. Thess. v. 18).

7. By making it our aim to do all things to the glory of God (I. Corinthians x. 31).

340. SATAN, A SERPENT

GENESIS iii. 1-15

THERE are five things we notice in relation to Satan—

1. **Those who are down themselves will often seek to drag others to the same level.** We read of the serpent, the devil, and as suggestive of his character, that it "*was more subtle*," (ver. 1). The question naturally arises, how had the serpent become more subtle? It seems to suggest that Satan had become subtle through sin, for the words "was more subtle" would be more correctly translated, "had become more subtle." Having sinned, Satan seeks to lead others to act in a like manner.

2. **Satan often uses the creatures of God to carry out his own purpose.** He used the *hands* of Achan to take the wedge of gold (Joshua vii. 1), the *lips* of Ananias and his wife to lie to the Holy Spirit (Acts v. 3), the *mind* of Judas to conceive the betrayal of Christ (John xiii. 27), the *eyes* of Lot to look towards Sodom (Gen. xiii. 10, 12), the *feet* of Abram to go down into Egypt (Gen. xii. 10), the *words* of Peter to deny Christ (Luke xxii. 57), and the serpent to deceive Eve.

3. **Satan's policy is to get men to doubt the truth of God's word.** Notice Satan's question in verse 1, as suggesting a doubt; and then ponder his boldness as seen in his words in verse 4, contrasting his words with God's plain command in Gen. ii. 17, as understood according to the woman's statement in verse 3; and the wicked, lying imputation of Satan upon God's goodness in verse 5.

4. **Satan's character is symbolized in the serpent.** The serpent is crooked (Isaiah xxvii. 1), poisonous (Psalm lviii. 4), bites (Prov. xxiii. 32; Eccles. x. 8, 11; Amos v. 19; ix. 3); has a divided tongue (Psalm cxl. 3), has a gliding motion (Prov. xxx. 19), conceals itself (Ecclesiastes x. 8; Amos v. 19), and its sound is threatening (Jeremiah xlvi. 22). That "old serpent" is one of the devil's names (Revelation xx. 2).

5. **Satan and the serpent are both punished.** The former by having his head bruised (verse 15), and the latter by crawling upon the ground, and eating dust (verse 14). As the receiver of stolen goods is punished as well as he that stole them, so the one who allows himself to be led into sin by Satan, is punished as well as he who leads into sin.

341. SAVED

1. **Saved by grace** as to the source of salvation. "By grace ye are saved" (Eph. ii. 5).

2. **Saved by Christ** as to the means of salvation. "By Me if any man enter in, he shall be saved" (John x. 9).

3. **Saved by the Holy Spirit** as to the regeneration and

renewal of salvation. "Regeneration, and renewing of ,the Holy Ghost" (Titus iii. 5).

4. **Saved by faith** as to the reception of salvation. "Thy faith hath saved thee" (Luke vii. 50).

5. **Saved by the Gospel** as to the knowledge of salvation. "By which also ye are saved . . . . I preached unto you" (I. Cor. xv. 2).

6. **Saved by the risen life of Christ** as to the keeping of salvation. "We shall be saved by His life" (Rom. v. 10).

7. **Saved by abiding in Christ** as to the fruitfulness of salvation "Except these abide in the ship, ye cannot be saved" (Acts xxvii. 31).

8. **Saved by baptism** as to the confession of salvation. "Baptism doth also now save us" (I. Peter iii. 21).

9. **Saved by hope** as to the prospect of salvation. "We are saved by hope" (Rom. viii. 24).

10. **Saved by endurance** as to the reality of salvation. "He that endureth to the end shall be saved" (Matt. x. 22).

11. **Saved by fire** as to service. "He himself shall be saved, yet so as by fire" (I. Cor. iii. 15).

342. SAVIOUR

THE BIRTH OF CHRIST (LUKE ii. 8-20).

THE Incarnation of Christ is one of the pillars to the temple of truth, for as the kinsman only could redeem the lost inheritance of an Israelite (Lev. xxv. 25; Ruth iv. 10), so Christ had to become our Kinsman, to have the *right* to redeem us (Heb. ii. 14).

I shall take the title "Saviour" and give an acrostic upon it, as illustrating the purpose for which Christ was born, and as indicating the scope of His work.

S Suitable Saviour.

A Almighty Saviour.

V Vicarious Saviour.

I Immutable Saviour.

O Only Saviour.

U Universal Saviour.

R Royal Saviour.

S Suitable Saviour (I. Tim. i. 15). As the key fits the lock and turns the wards of it, so Christ suits the sinner, in that He can turn him from darkness to light. As the medicine which is effective in its operation overcomes the disease and banishes it from the system of the patient, so Christ is the medicine for the soul, for in His blood there is cleansing, in His life there is quickening, in His death there is reconciliation, and in Himself there is every spiritual blessing. We may say with the litttle boy who put out one of his hands and, pointing to each finger with the forefinger of the other hand, made an acrostic on the name "Jesus."

Jesus Exactly Suits Us Sinners

A Almighty Saviour (Acts v. 31). All authority belongs to Christ (Matt. xxviii. 18), and all strength is His (II. Cor. xii. 9). As the huge crane can lift up the heavy goods, so Christ can lift up the sinner from the horrible pit (Psalm xl. 2). As the engine can draw the heavy train, so Christ makes us go along the lines of God's truth in glad obedience to His will. As the quickening word of Christ brought Lazarus from the grave (John xi. 43, 44); so He can quicken those who are dead in trespasses and sins (Eph. ii. 1).

V Vicarious Saviour (Matt. xxvii. 42). The title "*vicar*" means one who supplies the place of another; hence, speaking of Christ being a "vicarious Saviour" refers to the fact that He was a Substitute for those who believe in Him when He died upon the cross (II. Cor. v. 21). Think of the many times it is said, "Christ died for us." As the ram was offered up in the stead of Isaac (Gen. xxii. 13), so Christ was offered instead of us (Eph. v. 2).

I Immutable Saviour (Heb. vii. 24). He is the unchanging One. The same yesterday, to-day, and for ever (Heb. xiii. 8). The yesterday of the Cross, the to-day at the right hand of God, and the for ever in the glory, find Him unchanging in the intensity of His love, in the preciousness of His promises, in the strength of His power, in the tenderness of His sympathy, in the sufficiency of His grace, and in the longing of His heart. His heart ever beats in love towards us. His hand is ever ready to aid us.

O Only Saviour (Acts iv. 12). There is no other than the Lord Jesus who can meet our need and satisfy the claims of God. As He alone could span over the great gulf which sin had made, by His atoning death, so He alone can bring us from the land of darkness and death into His life, light, and liberty. As the door of the house is the way by which entrance is obtained to it, so Christ is the door through which we enter into the blessing of salvation (John x. 9; xiv. 6).

U Universal Saviour (John x. 9). Christ is not a universal Saviour in the sense of saving everybody whether they will or not, but He offers to save "any man"—"whosoever" will accept Him. There is a tradesman in the West-end of London who calls himself "The Universal Provider." It does not mean that he provides for everyone, but he is willing to do so. In a like manner Christ offers Himself as a Saviour to all, but it is only those who receive Him who know Him as their Saviour.

R Royal Saviour (Luke ii. 11). The Saviour is "Christ the Lord." He is no mere man; He is Lord of lords, King of kings—very God. He is royal in name, royal in office, royal in nature, royal in speech, royal in action, royal in death, royal in resurrection, royal in ascension, royal in His word, and royal in glory.

343. SAVIOUR OF LIFE OR DEATH

II. CORINTHIANS ii. 16

Christ is one of two things to all. He is either the Stone on which we are broken in penitence and to salvation, or He is the Stone to grind in pieces unto punishment and condemnation (Luke xx. 18). This is brought out in the following sevenfold contrasts :

1. The pillar of cloud was **light** to Israel, and **darkness** to the Egyptians (Ex. xiv. 20).

2. The ways of the Lord are to walk in for our **blessing,** or ways to stumble in to our **hurt** (Hosea xiv. 9).

3. God is a **consuming fire** to **purify** His people (Mal. iii. 3), and a **burning fire** to **scorch** His enemies (Mal. iv. 1).

4. Christ is **life** to those who receive Him (John iii. 36), while He is **wrath** to those who reject Him (Rev. vi. 16).

5. Christ is the **Chief Corner-stone** to those who rest on Him in faith for salvation (I. Peter ii. 6), while He is a **Stone** of **Stumbling** to those who will not have Him (I. Peter ii. 8).

6. Christ is **precious** to those who believe (I. Peter ii. 7), while He is **despised** by those who neglect Him (Isaiah liii. 3).

7. When Christ comes He brings **eternal rest** for His people, but He gives **eternal destruction** to those who have not obeyed the Gospel (II. Thess. i. 6, 7).

344. SEEING

" HE . . . . came seeing" (John ix. 7), so it is said of the blind man. The believer sees the following seven things :—

1. **Sin in his members.** " I *see* another law in my members" (Romans vii. 23).

2. **Jesus crowned with glory.** " We *see* Jesus" (Heb. ii. 9).

3. **The calling of grace.** " Ye *see* your calling, brethren" (I. Cor. i. 26).

4. **An open heaven.** " Hereafter ye shall *see* heaven open" (John i. 51).

5. **God, as he is pure in heart.** " Blessed are the pure in heart, for they shall *see* God" (Matt. v. 8).

6. **The evil of unbelief.** " We *see* that they could not enter in because of unbelief" (Heb. iii. 19).

7. **The day of the Lord approaching.** " Ye *see* the day approaching" (Heb. x. 25).

345. SEEING THE LORD

1. **Seeing the Lord brings conviction.** "I have heard of Thee by the hearing of the ear; but now mine eye *seeth* Thee" (Job xlii. 5; Isaiah vi. 1).

2. **Seeing the Lord brings salvation.** "Fear ye not, stand still, and *see* the salvation of the Lord, which He will shew to you to-day" (Ex. xiv. 13).

3. **Seeing the Lord as the Object of faith.** "But we *see* Jesus, who was made a little lower than the angels, for the suffering of death crowned with glory" (Heb. ii. 9).

4. **Seeing the Lord brings deliverance.** "But when he *saw* Jesus afar off, he ran and worshipped Him" (Mark v. 6).

5. **Seeing the Lord brings joy.** "Then were the disciples glad, when they *saw* the Lord" (John xx. 20).

6. **Seeing the Lord is attraction.** "And looking upon Jesus as He walked, he saith, *Behold* the Lamb of God" (John i. 36).

7. **Seeing the Lord will be likeness.** "When He shall appear, we shall be like Him; for we shall *see* Him as He is" (I. John iii. 2).

346. SELF-CONFIDENCE

II. Chronicles xxv. 17-28

One of the saddest things that can be witnessed, is, when a person has known the Lord and goes away from Him (II. Chron. xxv. 2, 27; Gal. v. 7). Self-confidence is the child of half-heartedness.

1. **Self-confidence looks earthward instead of heavenward.** The king of Judah "took advice" (verse 17), not from God but from men.

2. **Self-confidence acts in its own strength.** Amaziah "sent," and said (verse 17). He who sides with self takes sides against God, and runs on a rock to his own destruction.

3. **Self-confidence is fostered by wrong.** Idolatry was the hot-bed that caused the self-confidence of Amaziah to flourish (verse 20).

4. **Self-confidence is the forerunner of defeat.** "Put to the worse" (verse 22) is ever the summary of the life of the child of the flesh.

5. **Self-confidence meets with bondage, damage, and loss.** The king of Israel "took" the king of Judah and "brake" the wall of Jerusalem (verse 23). Brokenness of spirit (Luke xxii. 62), and bondage of heart are ever the outcome of self's action (Gal. v. 1).

6. **Self-confidence reaps what it sows.** Amaziah had conspired against God in his self-action, and now he is paid back in his own coin in being conspired against (verse 27).

7. **Self-confidence meets with death** (verse 27). "Boast,"

"Would not hear," "Put to the worse," "Brought," "Brake," "Turn away," "Fled," "Slain," are the words that sum up the downgradeism of the king of Judah.

347. SELF-WILL

1. **Self-will turned Paradise into a desert.** It has been well said, "My will and not Thine be done, turned Paradise into a desert. Thy will and not Mine be done, turned the desert into a Paradise" (Romans v. 19).

2. **Self-will is the mother of sin.** This is illustrated in Cain, when he in self-will came to God in his own way instead of God's way, and was jealous because Abel's sacrifice was accepted and his was rejected, which jealousy led him on to kill his brother (Jude 11).

3. **Self-will is the forerunner of disaster.** Lot chose the well-watered plain of Sodom, and then soon after was found in Sodom, but he lost all he had in Sodom, and only escaped with his life (Gen xiii. 10).

4. **Self-will shuts out from blessing.** Moses struck the rock twice when God told him to speak to it, and was shut out of the promised land in consequence (Num. xx. 11, 12).

5. **Self-will brings punishment.** King Saul lost his kingdom and the Holy Spirit through consulting his own will in opposition to God's word, when the latter told him to destroy all the Amalekites (I. Samuel xv. 23).

6. **Self-will brings injury to others.** Peter acted on his own authority when he cut off the ear of the servant of the high priest (Luke xxii. 50).

7. **Self-will means loss of blessing.** The prodigal son found the difference between the swine troughs and the father's table, and between the far country and the old homestead (Luke xv. 16, 17).

348. SENT FORTH

MATTHEW X. 1-16

THE ones who are sent forth are those whom Christ has chosen, called, ordained and empowered (verse 1; Mark iii. 13-15; Luke vi. 13). As it was with the Apostles, so it is with believers to-day. Those who are chosen in Christ (Eph. i. 4), called by Christ (Rom. viii. 30), ordained by Him (John xv. 16), and empowered by Him (Acts i. 8), are set apart to work with Him (II. Cor. vi. 1).

Let us look at the directions that Christ gave to His disciples.

1. They were to be **generous**: "Freely ye have received, freely give" (verse 8). The Lord had not stinted them, in giving them blessing, neither were they to hold back the blessing from others. When Samson found the honey in the carcase of the lion, he took

some home to his parents (Judges xiv. 9); when the four lepers came upon the spoil of the Syrians, they kept not the good things to themselves, they went and informed the inhabitants of the city of Samaria (II. Kings vii. 8-10); even so, those who have received the grace of God, should pass it on to others.

2. The disciples were to be **careless as to their comfort** (verses 9, 10). They were not to carry a large portmanteau, nor to have a bag of gold with them. In the East it was customary to give hospitality to those who asked for it. Customs are not the same with us in the West, although all who are the Lord's should ever be willing to extend hospitality to the servants of Christ. Those who have the love of souls will not be careful of their own ease and comfort (I. Thess. ii. 8, 9).

3. The disciples were to be **courteous.** When they came to a house they were to "salute" it (verse 12). Their salutation "Peace be to this house," or "Peace be unto you," would be the benediction of God. A Christian should always be a walking blessing, shedding forth the fragrance of Christ wherever he goes, and this shall be so, as Christ dwells in the heart; for as scent in the clothes will betray itself, so Christ will be known when He lives in the soul.

4. The disciples were to be **independent** (verse 14). If the people to whom they went would not receive them nor their message, then they were not to force themselves upon these unwilling persons, but to shake the dust off their feet, as indicating that they would not take the dust of their floors from them; as Trapp says, "In token that you sought not theirs but them, and that you will not carry away so much as any of their dust."

5. The disciples were to be **patient.** They were to be as "sheep" (verse 16). No one can read the history of the Church without being impressed with the correctness of the Saviour's simile in comparing the disciples of Christ to sheep in the midst of wolves. Mr. Fox relates how the Christians in Calabria, in 1560, were thrust into one house as in a sheepfold, and how the executioner came and fetched them out one by one and butchered them all, to the number of eighty-eight.

6. The disciples were to be **wise** (verse 16). Matthew Henry remarks: "Wise—not as foxes, whose cunning is to deceive others—but as serpents, whose policy is to defend themselves, and to shift for their own safety."

7. The disciples were to be "**harmless** as doves" (verse 16). It is related of Francis Xavier, that as he was preaching in one of the cities of Japan, a man went up to him, pretending that he had something to communicate in private. Upon his approach, Xavier leaned his head to hear what he had to say. The scorner thus gained his object, which was to spit freely upon the face of the devoted missionary, and thus to insult him in the most public manner. Xavier, without speaking a word or showing any sign of

annoyance, took out his pocket handkerchief, wiped his face, and went on with his sermon, as if nothing had happened to interrupt him. By such an heroic control of his passions, the scorn of the audience was turned into admiration. The most learned doctor of the city, who happened to be present, said to himself, that a law which taught men such virtue, inspired them with such courage, and gave them such complete mastery over themselves, could not but be from God. Afterwards he desired baptism, and his example was followed by others. So effectually did the meekness of the missionary promote the success of the work.

349. SEPARATION

God divided the light from the darkness; the waters from the waters, and the day from the night (Genesis i. 4, 7, 14, 18). As in the beginning, so is it now with the Christian and the world. We have several illustrations of this in the Books of Moses. We shall take seven, and give the corresponding truths from the New Testament.

1. **Separation.** Division between light and darkness. "What communion hath light with darkness" (II. Cor. vi. 14).

2. **Manifestation.** "I will put a division between My people and thy people" (Ex. viii. 23). "In this" (sinning and not sinning, see I. John iii. 8-9) "the children of God are manifest, and the children of the devil" (I. John iii. 10).

3. **Conversation.** "Ye shall therefore put difference between clean beasts and unclean, &c." (Lev. xx. 25). "As He which hath called you is holy, so be ye holy in all manner of living" (I. Peter i. 13-16, R.V.).

4. **Dedication.** "All the days of his separation he is holy unto the Lord" (Num. vi. 8). "Be ye separate" (II. Cor. vi. 17).

5. **Isolation.** "The people shall dwell alone" (Num. xxiii. 9). 'Be not conformed to this world" (Rom. xii. 2).

6. **Sanctification.** "Thou shalt not plow with an ox and ass together" (Deut. xxii. 10). "Be ye not unequally yoked together with unbelievers" (II. Cor. vi. 14).

7. **Consecration.** "Thou shalt not wear a garment of divers sorts" (Deut. xxii. 11). "Put off the old man with his deeds" (Col. iii. 9). "Put ye on the Lord Jesus" (Rom. xiii. 14).

350. SERVICE

S Sent one to witness.
E Epistle to be read.
R Representative to manifest forth.
V Voice to speak.
I Instrument to be used.
C Child to obey.
E Endowed one with power.

S Sent one to witness. "Christ" means the Anointed or Sent One. Forty-three times in John's Gospel alone, do we find Him saying that His Father sent Him. The authority of Jesus as the Sent One was, that His Father sent Him; the evidence that He was the Sent One was, that He did the will of the Father (John iv. 34), that He honoured the Father, and that His works were a witness that He was sent by the Father (John v. 36); and His confidence was, that He was speaking His Father's word in His Father's Name (John vii. 16, and xiv. 24). And as the Father sent Jesus, so Christ has sent us (John xx. 21), and our authority and confidence are, that Christ has sent us in His Name, with His Word, to do His will, that we may bring honour to His Name by our life and testimony bearing witness to Him.

E Epistle to be read (II. Cor. iii. 3). Paul in this passage seems to say, "We do not need any letter of commendation of ourself to you; for you, who were blessed under our ministry, are our epistle, known and read of all men." "Forasmuch as ye are manifestly declared to be the epistle of Christ ministered by us, written not with ink, but by the Spirit of the living God; not in tables of stone, but in fleshy tables of the heart." That is, the work of the Holy Spirit through the preaching of the Word is manifestly seen by the life that we are now living, and the world sees the work of God by its manifestation in our godly walk. It has often been said, and said truly, that while the world will not read the Word of God, they will read the Christian, and can Christ be glorified in us more, than when they take knowledge of us that Christ is manifestly seen in our walk?

R Representative to manifest forth (I. John ii. 8). When Christ was here, He represented the Father. "He that hath seen Me hath seen the Father." Christ represented us on the cross by taking our sin, and now, as our great High Priest, He represents us at God's right-hand. The Spirit having quickened us, the light of the glorious Gospel having shone into our hearts, and chased the darkness of sin and unbelief away, we are to let our light shine. As John says, "Which thing is true in Him" (Christ), "and in you: because the darkness is past, and the true light now shineth." That is, when Jesus was here, He was the Light of the world; but now we are the light of the world (a very poor light at the best), and we are responsible to shine as such, holding forth the Word of Life.

V Voice to speak. John the Baptist said that he was the voice of one crying in the wilderness; and we are to speak for Christ. How many souls, humanly speaking, are lost for want of a word! We should speak out boldly, like Peter on the day of Pentecost (Acts ii. 14); lovingly, like Stephen when praying for his enemies (Acts vii. 60); earnestly, like Paul when he said to the jailor, "Do thyself no harm" (Acts xvi. 28).

I Instrument to be used. There are different kinds of instruments mentioned in the Word, which may be taken as illustrating what the Christian is and should be. An instrument is something that is taken up and used by another.

C Child to obey. "A son honoureth his father, and a servant his master" (Mal. i. 6). And how do they do this but by obedience to them? Even so we obey the Lord.

E Endowed one with power. Service with Him as Christ. As we have already said, "Christ" not only means the Sent One, but the Anointed One. He was anointed with the Holy Spirit, and we as Christians are therefore anointed ones. We have the indwelling presence of the Holy Spirit, and He is our power in service; therefore, let us be subject to Him, and thus will the "Name of our Lord Jesus Christ be glorified in us."

351. SEVEN "I HAVE'S" OF PAUL TO TIMOTHY

1. **Remembrance.** "*I have* remembrance of thee" (II. Tim. i. 3). Remembering others at the throne of grace, brings blessing upon ourselves, as well as upon them.

2. **Faith.** "*I have* believed" (II. Timothy i. 12). The man who has believed in Christ, knows it, and can speak accordingly.

3. **Committal.** "*I have* committed unto Him" (II. Timothy i. 12). To trust ourselves to the Lord's keeping is to be safe, sure, and happy.

4. **Conflict.** "*I have* fought a good fight" (II. Timothy iv. 7). To fight for right and truth, is to fight a good fight.

5. **Completion.** "*I have* finished my course" (II. Tim. iv. 7). To look back and see that what we attempted has been accomplished, brings content.

6. **Fidelity.** "*I have* kept the faith" (II. Timothy iv. 7). To be faithful, means the "well done" for a reward.

7. **Commission.** "Tychicus *I have* sent to Ephesus" (II. Tim. iv. 12). If we cannot go on an errand of mercy, let us send another in our place.

352. SEVEN L'S IN RELATION TO THE HOME IN BETHANY

1. **Loved by Christ.** "Jesus loved Martha, and her sister, and Lazarus" (John xi. 5).

2. **Listening to Christ.** "Sat at Jesus' feet, and heard His word" (Luke x. 39).

3. **Labouring for Christ.** "Martha . . . serving" (Luke x. 40).

4. **Longing for Christ.** "His sisters sent unto Him" (John xi. 3).

5. **Light through Christ.** "Take ye away the stone" (John xi. 39).

6. **Life in Christ.** "Lazarus, come forth" (John xi. 43).

7. **Liberty by Christ.** "Loose him, and let him go" (John xi. 44).

353. SEVEN LOOKS

1. **Outward look of salvation.** "*Look* unto Me, and be ye saved" (Isaiah xlv. 22).

2. **Outward look in service.** "*Look* on the fields" (John iv. 35).

3. **Upward look of faith.** "Will I direct my prayer unto Thee, and will *look* up" (Psalm v. 3).

4. **Inward look of enquiry.** "Whoso *looketh* into the perfect law of liberty" (James i. 25).

5. **Inward look of examination.** "*Look* to yourselves" (II. John 8).

6. **Onward look of perseverance.** "Let thine eyes *look* right on" (Proverbs iv. 25). "*Looking* unto Jesus" (Heb. xii. 2).

7. **Onward look of expectancy.** "We *look* for the Saviour" (Philippians iii. 20).

354. SEVEN POSITIONS THE LORD HOLDS FOR HIS PEOPLE

1. **Within us**—Power. "Christ liveth in me" (Gal. ii. 20).

2. **Before us**—Example. "When He putteth forth His own sheep, He goeth before them" (John x. 4).

3. **Above us**—Representative. "To appear in the presence of God for us" (Hebrews ix. 24).

4. **Beneath us**—Sustainer. "Underneath are the everlasting arms" (Deuteronomy xxxiii. 27).

5. **Beside us**—Guide. "He is at my right hand, I shall not be moved" (Psalm xvi. 8).

6. **Around us**—Deliverer. "The Angel of the Lord encampeth round about them that fear Him" (Psalm xxxiv. 7).

7. **Behind us**—Protector. "The God of Israel will be your Rereward" (Isaiah lii. 12).

355. SEVEN "IT IS ENOUGHS"

THE principal thought in connection with the words "It is enough," is, that a requirement has been met, or satisfaction has been given.

1. **Pharaoh's cry of fear.** "Entreat the Lord (for *it is enough*) that there be no more mighty thunderings" (Exodus ix. 28). When the sinner sees that his sin calls forth the judgment of God, it makes him cry out with dread.

2. **The Saviour's word of resignation.** "*It is enough*, the hour is come" (Mark xiv. 41). Christ knew it was inevitable that He should be delivered into the hands of wicked men, and be crucified, that the purpose of God might be fulfilled (Acts ii. 23).

3. **Jehovah's word of satisfaction.** "*It is enough:* stay now thine hand" (II. Sam. xxiv. 16; I. Chron. xxi. 15), were the words of Jehovah to the destroying angel as He punished Israel for David's sin. The sacrifices offered up stayed the hand of God in judgment (II. Sam. xxiv. 25; Eph. v. 2).

4. **Jacob's cry of assurance.** "They told him all the words of Joseph," &c. "Israel said, *it is enough*" (Gen. xlv. 27, 28). The words of our Divine Joseph assure us of our interest in Him (John iii. 36; v. 24); and of His joy in us (Neh. viii. 10).

5. **Christ's word of fellowship.** "*It is enough* for the disciple that he be as his Master" (Matt. x. 25). It should be a joy to the disciples of Christ, that they are privileged to suffer for Him (Acts v. 41), and with Him (Phil. iii. 10).

6. **The Lord's word of approbation.** "Here are two swords. And He said, *It is enough*" (Luke xxii. 38). The Lord often allows His people to have things for Him, which He does not need. He looks at the heart's desire more than the blundering hand.

7. **Elijah's cry of discouragement.** "He requested for himself that he might die; and said, *It is enough*" (I. Kings xix. 4). What a mercy it is that the Lord does not do as we wish, but that He answers our prayers as He knows best for our good!

356. SEVEN MEN IN A HURRY

THERE is a hurry which is loose and disorderly, and there is a haste which is deliberate and commendable (compare Isaiah xxviii. 16, with Luke xix. 5, 6).

1. **A worshipping demoniac.** "When he saw Jesus afar off, he *ran* and worshipped Him" (Mark v. 6). The demons, and the man whom they possessed, did homage to Christ. Christ is the Object of believers' worship.

2. **An enthusiastic questioner.** "There came one *running*, and kneeled to Him, and asked Him, Good Master, what shall I do that I may inherit eternal life?" (Mark x. 17). Enthusiasm that is born of self-righteousness is worthless. It can ask questions, but it does not fulfil directions.

3. **An earnest seeker.** "He *ran* before, and climbed up into a sycamore tree to see Him" (Luke xix. 4). A seeking sinner will always be discovered by the all-seeing Saviour. Mark the words, "to see Him," and "Jesus saw him."

4. **A considerate man.** "One *ran* and filled a sponge full of vinegar" (Mark xv. 36). When this man heard the Saviour cry, he sought to relieve Him by moistening His lips with the sour wine (Matt. xxvii. 48; Mark xv. 36; John xix. 29). Christ will remember the kindly action, as He remembers every cup of cold water given to Him and to His.

5. **The loving father.** "When he was yet a great way off, his father saw him, and had compassion, and *ran*," &c. (Luke xv. 20). This is the only time in the Bible that we read of God being in haste. "He said," and it was done, in creation. "He *ran*" and welcomed the prodigal, in redemption.

6. **The curious disciples.** "They *ran* both together" (John xx. 4). Mary Magdalene proclaims that the tomb is empty, in which the body of Christ was laid. Peter and John cannot believe their ears, so they run to the sepulchre to see. Curiosity may lead to enquiry, enquiry to faith, faith to love, and love to work.

7. **A diligent servant.** "Philip *ran* thither to him" (Acts viii. 30). With an intensity born of the Holy Spirit, Philip hurried forward to point the eunuch to Christ the Sin-bearer.

357. SEVEN MOMENTS

THE smallest fraction of time is of importance with the Lord, and where God speaks of "moments," it either indicates the constancy of His care, or the quickness of an action.

1. **Forsaking.** "For a small *moment* have I forsaken thee" . . . . . "In a little wrath I hid My face from thee for a *moment*" (Isaiah liv. 7, 8). When the Lord forsakes His people, there is some cause in them for His so doing, but He cannot forsake them for long.

2. **Protecting.** "Hide thyself as it were for a little *moment*, until the indignation be over-past" (Isaiah xxvi. 20). God ever protects His people first, before He acts in judgment to the world. Noah must be in the ark before the flood comes; and Israel must be protected by the blood of the Pascal Lamb, before the angel of Jehovah smites the first-born.

3. **Keeping.** "I, the Lord, do keep it. I will water it every *moment*" (Isaiah xxvii. 3). He will keep the vineyard from all evil, and keep it to all good.

4. **Trying.** "Try him every *moment*" (Job vii. 18). The Lord never allows the rust of worldliness to remain on His people. He brightens them by His word, and sharpens them by His grace.

5. **Tempting.** "The devil . . . . . shewed unto Him all the kingdoms of the world in a *moment* of time" (Luke iv. 5). We have little conception of the power which Satan possesses, but, when he can, in a moment of time, bring before one the kingdoms of the world, his power must be enormous.

6. **Affliction.** "Our light affliction, which is but for a *moment*" (II. Cor. iv. 17). The "affliction" is "light," and only for a "moment"; but the "glory" is weighty and "eternal."

7. **Transformation.** "We shall all be changed, in a *moment*" (I. Cor. xv. 51, 52). The change will be so rapid that there will be no time to think about it.

358. STRANGE THINGS

"We have seen strange things to-day" (Luke v. 26); so said the people, after they had seen the working of Christ's power in the healing of the palsied man. We shall find many strange things mentioned in the Bible.

1. **Idolatry.** Strange gods. "Put away the *strange* gods" (Gen. xxxv. 2). Before there can be communion with God at Bethel, there must be separation from idols. There is a Tree where we can bury idols, namely, Christ, the Tree of Life, for death with Him is separation from things that are strange to Him (ii. Corinthians v. 14, R.V.).

2. **Sacrifice.** Strange fire. "Nadab and Abihu offered *strange* fire before the Lord" (Lev. x. 1). To offer strange fire was to take fire that had not fed upon a sacrifice, as the Lord had commanded (Ex. xxx. 9; Lev. xvi. 12).

3. **Degeneration.** Strange vine. "How art thou turned into the degenerate plant of a *strange* vine unto Me?" (Jeremiah ii. 21). Disobedience is the mother of degeneration.

4. **Disturbers.** Strange doctrines. "Be not carried about with *strange* doctrines" (Heb. xiii. 9). Strange doctrines are the teachings of men, which are contrary to the Word of Truth. These are as a strong wind which carries the vessel on to the rocks.

5. **Opposition.** Strange thinking. "They think it *strange* that ye run not with them" (i. Peter iv. 4). Because the believer will not go with the world, the world therefore opposes him.

6. **Trial.** Trials seemingly strange. "Beloved, think it not *strange* concerning the fiery trial" (i. Peter iv. 12). Trials are like nuts with hard shells. They may be hard like the shells, but they have within them the kernels of blessing.

7. **Judgment.** Strange work. "The Lord shall rise up . . . and do His *strange* work" (Isaiah xxviii. 21). The Lord would much rather exercise His mercy in grace than exhibit His might in wrath.

359. SEVEN RESURRECTIONS

1. The **persons** whom Christ raised as shewing forth His power (Matthew xi. 5).

2. **Christ's** resurrection as manifesting His pre-eminence (i. Corinthians xv. 20).

3. **Believer's** resurrection with Christ, declaring our oneness with Him (Eph. ii. 6).

4. **Israel's** national resurrection, or God's purpose accomplished concerning them (Ez. xxxvii. 11, 12).

5. The resurrection of **Anti-Christ,** or the person that Satan shall raise (Rev. xvii. 8).

6. The resurrection of the **bodies of believers** who have died (Jude 9; Matt. xxvii. 53; 1. Thess. iv. 16; Rev. vi. 9-12; xx. 4).

7. Resurrection of the **unsaved** (Rev. xx. 5, 11-13).

360. "SEVEN SPIRITS"

REVELATION iv. 5

WE have a sevenfold description of the power of the Holy Spirit in Isaiah xi. 2, 3.

1. "**The Spirit of Jehovah**" is the Holy Spirit in relation to God the Father, in His immutability and power resting upon Christ, to enable Him, as Man, to fulfil the offices of Prophet, Priest, and King. Thus, we have in this verse the three Persons of the Godhead.

2. "**The Spirit of wisdom**" reminds us of the power that will enable Christ to act in a becoming *manner*, as when He rested upon the makers of the tabernacle, and directed them *how* to make the tabernacle (Exodus xxxi. 3; xxviii. 3; xxxv. 30 to xxxvi. 2). Wisdom is the right application of knowledge.

3. "**The Spirit of understanding.**" The Hebrew word translated here "understanding," really means "Power to distinguish, so as to separate between good and evil." The Holy Spirit had to chide the Hebrews because they were but children in the spiritual life, when they should have been full-grown (Heb. v. 14).

4. "**The Spirit of counsel.**" That is, Christ has power to impart counsel, as well as being the Counselled One, for His name is "Counsellor" (Isaiah ix. 6), and this, because as Man, the Holy Spirit counselled Him. Does He not intend to convey this truth to us in the words of John x. 15: "As the Father knoweth Me, even so know I the Father, and I lay down My life for the sheep?" He thus acquaints His hearers with the fact that His knowledge of His Father's holiness, justice, demands, love, grace, mercy, was a perfect knowledge; that He knew precisely what man needed, and He therefore "laid down His life for the sheep." How very comforting and assuring to know this!

5. "**The Spirit of might.**" Power characterized Christ's words and work. His word was with authority (Luke iv. 32), and His work was in power (Luke iv. 36), even the power of the Holy Spirit, as He Himself confessed (Matt xii. 28).

6. "**The Spirit of knowledge.**" We have abundant evidence of Christ's all-knowledge. He saw Nathaniel under the fig tree worshipping; and He knew the shallowness and unreality of certain who professed to believe on Him (John i. 48; ii. 24, 25).

7. "**The Spirit of the fear of the Lord.**" "He was heard in that He feared" (Heb. v. 7), is the comment of the Holy Spirit, in relation to Christ's action and attitude as Man in relation to God.

361. SEVEN SUPPERS

1. **Sinners' supper of pleasure.** "Herod . . . made a supper to his lords" (Mark vi. 21).

2. **Gospel supper.** "A certain man made a great supper" (Luke xiv. 16).

3. **Entertaining the Master, the supper of communion.** "There they made Him a supper, and Martha served" (John xii. 2).

4. **Supper of love.** "When thou makest a supper" (Luke xiv. 12).

5. **Marriage supper of the Lamb.** "Blessed are they which are called unto the marriage supper of the Lamb" (Rev. xix. 9).

6. **Supper of the Great God.** "Unto the supper of the Great God" (Rev. xix. 17).

7. **Supper of remembrance.** "To eat the Lord's supper" (1. Corinthians xi. 20).

362. SEVEN TABLES

1. **Table of shittim wood.** "Thou shalt also make a table of shittim wood" (Ex. xxv. 23).

2. **Anointed table.** "Thou shalt anoint . . . . . . the table" (Exodus xxx. 26).

3. **Holy table.** "Upon the pure table before the Lord" (Leviticus xxiv. 6).

4. **Provided table.** "He shall set it in order before the Lord" (Leviticus xxiv. 8).

5. **Prepared table.** "Thou preparest a table before me" (Psalm xxiii. 5).

6. **The King's table.** "While the King sitteth at His table" (Song of Solomon i. 12).

7. **The Lord's table.** "Be partakers of the Lord's table" (1. Corinthians x. 21).

363. SEVEN THATS

1. **The that of encouragement.** "I desire *that* ye faint not" (Ephesians iii. 13).

2. **The that of strengthening.** "*That* He would grant you . . to be strengthened with might" (Eph. iii. 16).

3. **The that of indwelling.** "*That* Christ may dwell in your hearts" (Eph. iii. 17).

4. **The that of stability.** "*That* ye, being rooted and grounded in love" (Eph. iii. 17).

5. **The that of fulness.** "*That* ye might be filled with all the fulness of God" (Eph. iii. 19).

6. **The that of ability.** "Now unto Him *that* is able to do" (Ephesians iii. 20).

7. **The that of almightiness.** "Exceeding abundantly above all *that* we ask or think" (Eph. iii. 20).

364. SEVEN THINGS IT PLEASED GOD TO DO

1. **To bruise His Son.** "It *pleased* the Lord to bruise Him" (Isaiah liii. 10).

2. **To make all fulness to dwell in Him.** "It *pleased* the Father that in Him should all fulness dwell" (Col. i. 19).

3. **To save them that believe.** "It *pleased* God . . . to save them that believe" (1. Cor. i. 21).

4. **To reveal His Son in the saved ones.** "It *pleased* God . . . . to reveal His Son in me" (Gal. i. 15, 16).

5. **To make us His people.** "It hath *pleased* the Lord to make you His people" (1. Sam. xii. 22).

6. **To make us one in Christ.** "Set the members every one of them in the Body as it hath *pleased* Him" (1. Cor. xii. 18).

7. **To give us a resurrection body.** "God giveth it a body as it hath *pleased* Him" (1. Cor. xv. 38).

365. SEVEN THINGS THE LORD DOES FOR THE BELIEVER IN PSALM XXIII

1. **A sheep fed.** "I shall not want" (verse 1).

2. **A child led.** "He leadeth me beside the still waters" (verse 2).

3. **A backslider restored.** "He restoreth my soul" (verse 3).

4. **A friend comforted.** "Thy rod and Thy staff they comfort me" (verse 4).

5. **A warrior feasted.** "Thou preparest a table before me" (verse 5).

6. **A priest anointed.** "Thou anointest my head" (verse 5).

7. **A pilgrim housed.** "I will dwell in the house of the Lord for ever" (verse 6).

366. SEVEN THINGS THE WORD OF GOD DOES IN PSALM XIX

1. **Restores the soul.** "Converting the soul" (verse 7).

2. **Instructs the mind.** "Making wise the simple" (verse 7).

3. **Gladdens the heart.** "Rejoicing the heart" (verse 8).

4. **Enlightens the understanding.** "Enlightening the eyes" (verse 8).

5. **Squares the life.** "True and righteous altogether" (verse 9).

6. **Purifies the spirit.** "The fear of the Lord is clean" (verse 9).

7. **Satisfies the nature.** "More to be desired . . . than gold" (verse 10).

367. SEVEN TIMES THE WORDS, "IN THE LORD," OCCUR IN EPHESIANS

1. **Faith in the Lord Jesus.** "Faith *in the Lord* Jesus" (i. 15).

2. **Holy temple in the Lord.** "Holy temple *in the Lord*" (ii. 21).

3. **Testifying in the Lord.** "Testify *in the Lord*" (iv. 17).

4. **Light in the Lord.** "Light *in the Lord*" (v. 8).

5. **Children to obey their parents in the Lord.** "Children obey your parents *in the Lord*" (vi. 1).

6. **Strong in the Lord.** "Be strong *in the Lord*, and in the power of His might" (vi. 10).

7. **Faithful in the Lord.** "Faithful minister *in the Lord*" (vi. 21).

368. SEVEN TIMES CHRIST IS SAID TO SPEAK TO HIS FATHER

1. **When men were rejecting Him.** "I thank Thee, O Father . . . . even so, Father" (Matt. xi. 25, 26).

2. **At the raising of Lazarus.** "Father, I thank Thee that Thou hast heard Me" (John xi. 41).

3. **When the Cross loomed before Him.** "Father, save Me from this hour" (John xii. 27, 28).

4. **In the upper room.** "Father, the hour is come" (John xvii. 1, 5, 11, 21, 24, 25).

5. **In the Garden of Gethsemane.** "Father, if it be possible" (Matt. xxvi. 39, 42).

6. **On behalf of His enemies.** "Father, forgive them" (Luke xxiii. 34).

7. **His last act.** "Father, into Thy hands I commend My spirit" (Luke xxiii. 46).

369. SEVEN "THOU HASTS" IN PSALM XXX

1. **Salvation.** "*Thou hast* lifted me up" (verse 1).

2. **Sanctification.** "*Thou hast* healed me" (verse 2).

3. **Resurrection.** "*Thou hast* brought up my soul from the grave" (verse 3).

4. **Preservation.** "*Thou hast* kept me alive" (verse 3).

5. **Established.** "*Thou hast* made my mountain to stand strong" (verse 7).

6. **Exultation.** "*Thou hast* turned for me my mourning into dancing" (verse 11).

7. **Separation and gladness.** "*Thou hast* put off my sackcloth and girded me with gladness" (verse 11).

370. SHADOW

"I sat down under His shadow" (Cant. ii. 3).

The shadow, when used in connection with God, represents what He is to His people.

1. **Place of protection.** "Hide me under the *shadow* of Thy wings" (Psalm xvii. 8).

2. **Place of confidence.** "The children of men put their trust under the *shadow* of Thy wings" (Psalm xxxvi. 7).

3. **Place of refuge.** "In the *shadow* of Thy wings will I make my refuge" (Psalm lvii. 1).

4. **Place of rejoicing.** "In the *shadow* of Thy wings will I rejoice" (Psalm lxiii. 7).

5. **Place of power.** "The *shadow* of the Almighty" (Psalm xci. 1).

6. **Place of communion.** "I sat down under His *shadow* with great delight" (Canticles ii. 3).

7. **Place of shelter.** "A *shadow* in the daytime from the heat" (Isaiah iv. 6).

8. **Place of rest.** "The *shadow* of a great rock in a weary land" (Isaiah xxxii. 2).

9. **Place of security.** "In the *shadow* of His hand hath He hid me" (Isaiah xlix. 2).

10. **Place of covering.** "I have covered thee in the *shadow* of Mine hand" (Isaiah li. 16).

371. SIN

1. **Within us is an operating principle.** "I know that in me . . . dwelleth no good thing" (Rom. vii. 18).

2. **Upon us is a burdensome weight.** "As a heavy burden they are too heavy for me" (Psalm xxxviii. 4).

3. **Over us is a tyrannical master.** "Ye were the servants of sin" (Rom. vi. 17).

4. **Before us is a lurking monster.** "Sin lieth at the door" (Genesis iv. 7).

5. **Beside us is a sure detective.** "Be sure your sin will find you out" (Num. xxxii. 23).

6. **Beyond us is an accusing witness.** "Some men's sins . . . . going before to judgment" (1. Tim. v. 24).

7. **Behind is as a pursuing foe.** "Some men's sins . . . . . follow after" (1. Tim. v. 24).

372. SIN

It is an axiom in science, that for every effect there must be an adequate cause. Thus sins committed, have their cause in heart corruption. The heart is diseased, therefore the life is wrong (Matt. xv. 19). The fountain is foul, therefore the stream is impure (James iii. 11). Insanity is enthroned in the mind, therefore madness rules the man's actions (Eccles. ix. 3). As a bad liver paints its owner's face with a yellow hue, so sin within, is the cause of the black colour in the life of man (Rom. iii. 12). As the engine moves the screw which moves the steamer, so sin is the moving cause of all the sinful acts in the life (Rom. vii. 15). As when the regulator in the watch is wrongly set, the watch will be wrong; so long as the heart is wrong, the man is wrong (Jer. xvii. 9). As everything in nature brings forth "after his kind" (Gen. i. 12), so sin, being within (Rom. vii. 18), like a smouldering fire, it will burst forth into flame in the life. Heart corruption is the cause of all corruption. As salt in meat, or leaven in meal, will permeate the whole; so sin in the heart gives a heart to sin, which makes it beat in wickedness and rebellion against God.

1. **Sin inherited.** As the heir in an entailed estate inherits the estate after the decease of his parent, so we have inherited the estate of sinfulness which Adam acquired by his disobedience (Rom. v. 12).

2. **Sin colouring.** As the negro inherits his black skin from his parents, so we have inherited the black nature of sin (John iii. 6; Jeremiah xiii. 23).

3. **Sin transmitted.** As the law of heredity proves that the parent's sin can be transmitted to the child, so the Scriptures declare Adam has passed on to us the evil of sin (Rom. v. 12).

4. **Sin tainting.** As the insane person owes, very often, his insanity to his ancestors, from whom he received the taint of madness, so the madness of sin has been bequeathed to us (Psalm xiv. 3).

5. **Sin embittering.** As it is the nature of a crab-apple tree to transmit its sourness to its fruit, so the sourness of iniquity is an inherited quality (Psalm li. 5).

6. **Sin stinging.** As it is the nature of a nettle to sting, because it is the fac-simile of its parent, so it is the nature of a sinner to sin (Rom. viii. 7)

7. **Sin reproducing.** As the child is like its parents in the face, so we show our relationship to Adam by our sins (Eph. ii. 3).

373. SIN

Leprosy illustrates the loathsomeness of sin, consumption the deceitfulness of sin, palsy shows the helplessness of the sinner when in the power of sin.

1. **Blindness.** Sin has blinded the eyes of man's understanding so that he cannot see the danger he is in (II. Cor. iv. 4), nor the beauty there is in Christ (Isaiah liii. 2).

2. **Deafness.** Sin has deafened man's hearing, so that he cannot hear God calling him (Mark viii. 18).

3. **Defilement.** Sin has defiled man's mind and polluted his imagination, so that he cannot appreciate Divine things (Gen. vi. 5).

4. **Corrupting.** Sin has corrupted man's heart, so that he has no love for God, and no desire for the things of God (Gen. vi. 12).

5. **Paralysis.** Sin has paralysed man's will, so that he has no power to raise himself from the helpless position he is in, and no moral force to enable him to walk in the ways of God (Rom. v. 6).

6. **Separation.** Sin has separated man's soul from God (Isaiah lix. 2), so that he is dead in sins" (Eph. ii. 1).

7. **Rebellion.** Sin has filled man's mind with rebellion, so that he is said to be "carnal" and "enmity against God" (Rom. viii. 7).

374. SIN

Genesis iii

As the River Forth can be seen winding its way towards Edinburgh from Stirling, so we see the course of sin in the chapter before us.

1. **Sin is often a pleasant thing in contemplation** (verse 6). Sodom apples are pleasant to look upon, but a mouthful of dust is the outcome of tasting. The bait is caught at, as a desirable morsel by the fish, but the hook is there as well. The food in the trap is tempting to the bird, but the prison-cage comes afterwards.

2. **Sin is disobedience** (Rom. v. 19). There is no mention of Eve taking an apple, as is often said. The sin was disobedience to God's command. The meaning of the word transgression is "to go beyond the command of God," as the schoolboy, who goes beyond the boundary prescribed by the schoolmaster.

3. **Sin is prolific.** One sin leads to another. As the one thistle will produce many thistle seeds, so one sin begets many others. Eve was led to lust with her eyes, and following in the train came the lust of the flesh and the pride of life.

4. **Sin is the knowledge of evil** (verse 5). Knowledge is good when it leads us to know God, for to know Him is to trust Him (Psalm ix. 10), but knowledge is evil when it enables the sinner to

sin in a more clever way, and when it is purchased at the price of punishment, as the boy found when he was sent to gaol for stealing the apples, although he only wanted to know how they tasted.

5. **Sin is contagious.** "And gave" (verse 6). As the fever-stricken patient will communicate the disease by shaking the hand of another, so the sinner spreads a pestilence by his actions.

6. **Sin is optional.** Satan did not force Eve to sin; she was enticed by him (I. Tim. ii. 14), and she in turn enticed Adam, and "he did eat" (verse 6), but in each case it was a voluntary action.

7. **Sin involves others** (Rom. v. 12; I. Cor. xv. 22). No one lives to himself, everyone is exerting an influence either for good or evil. Many a man owes his taste for the drink to his drinking father or mother.

8. **Sin brings shame** (verse 7). Moral nakedness (Rev. iii. 17) and a conscious unfitness for God's presence is the cause of shame. A naked soul is a Christless soul, for He alone is the garment of salvation (Isaiah lxi. 10).

9. **Sin brings fear** (verse 10). Conscience makes cowards of us all. But how did man obtain a conscience? By sin. It is consciousness of coming judgment that fills the sinner with dread, even as the terrified animals flee before the prairie fire.

10. **Sin brings punishment** (verses 14-19). By the very necessity of His own nature God must punish sin. He can by no means clear the guilty. No man can break the law of nature without being punished; even so with the law of God, and the command to repent and believe in Christ.

375. SIN AND GRACE

II. CHRONICLES XV. 1-10

THE glowing bow of God's grace is seen in the dark cloud of the people's sin.

1. **A gracious message** (verses 1, 2). The message promises that if the people will side with the Lord, the Lord will side with them (see Luke ix. 50).

2. **A grievous case** (verse 3). It was sad to be without God, without law, and without instruction; but the unsaved are in a worse plight. They have

No God (Ephesians ii. 12).
No Christ (Ephesians ii. 12).
No light (Ephesians iv. 18; v. 8).
No life (I. John v. 12).
No peace (Isaiah lvii. 21).
No liberty (Colossians i. 13).
No hope (Ephesians ii. 12).

3. **A good find** (verse 4). To find the Lord is to find all good, as the prodigal found when he came home to his father. To find the Lord is to be found of the Lord (Luke xv. 5-7, 8-10).

4. **A gloomy country** (verses 5, 6). When men get wrong with God, they are sure to fall out with each other. Gloom is the daughter of godlessness.

5. **A grand promise** (verse 7). An honest heart is the one essential for the seed of God's truth to bring forth fruit (Matt. xiii. 23), and diligence is the forerunner of blessing. Work and reward go together.

6. **A genuine revival** (verse 8). There are always two sides to a genuine revival, namely the *negative* side—the "putting away" (1. Peter ii. 1, R.V.), and the *positive* side—renewing "the altar of the Lord" (verse 8).

7. **A gathered host** (verses 9, 10). When men get near to God, they get near to each other. The true basis of union is found in gathering around the True Centre—Christ (1. Cor. xii. 12).

376. SIN—ITS EXTENT AND NATURE

SIN cannot be estimated by our consciousness (Num. xv. 27-30). "Though he wist it not, yet is he guilty" (Lev. v. 17).

What is sin? The Holy Spirit has given us a sevenfold answer to the question.

1. "**Sin is lawlessness,**" namely, self-will (1. John iii. 4, R.V.). King Saul is an example (1. Sam. xv. 23).

2. "**All unrighteousness is sin**" (1. John v. 17). Unrighteousness is crookedness. Balaam is an illustration (Jude 11).

3. "**Whatsoever is not of faith is sin**" (Rom. xiv. 23). Cain illustrates this (Heb xi. 4, 6).

4. "**The thought**" (**device**) "**of foolishness is sin**" (Prov. xxiv. 9). Korah is an example (Num. xvi. 1-3).

5. "**The plowing of the wicked is sin**" (Prov. xxi. 4). Sin sums up the whole life of the godless man.

6. "**To him that knoweth to do good, and doeth it not, to him it is sin**" (James iv. 17). Failure to do right is as much sin as doing wrong. Eli (1. Sam. iii. 13).

7. "**Of sin because they believe not on Me**" (John xvi. 9). Unbelief is the mother of all sin. Eve believed the devil's lie, and thus disbelieved God, and fell in consequence (Gen. iii. 1-6).

Man naturally, is the embodiment of sin, hence he cannot please God (Rom. viii. 8), therefore all he does while in the state of nature is sin in the sight of God. Man may not believe this of himself, but it is none the less true, although not known. Job thought he was fairly good till he came into the clear shining of the Lord's presence, then he saw himself, and turned with loathing from the sight (Job xlii. 5, 6).

377. SNARES

THERE are two things the child of God ever needs to remember, and these are, that he has a wise Keeper, and that he has a wily enemy, and this wily enemy is always on the look-out to entangle us in the meshes of his snares.

1. **The snare of pride.** "The *snare* of the devil" (I. Tim. iii. 7). The snare in which Satan entangled himself to his own downfall was pride (Ezekiel xxviii. 1-9). Beware of this gin. It has many colours and shapes.

2. **The snare of riches.** "They that will be rich fall into temptation, and a *snare*" (I. Tim. vi. 9). Glittering gold is a snare that has fascinated many to their overthrow and destruction (Acts v. 1-9).

3. **The snare of sleepiness.** "Awake (margin) themselves out of the *snare* of the devil" (II. Tim. ii. 26). Strife will stir up the old man, but it will put the better man to sleep.

4. **The snare of idolatry.** "Gideon made an ephod . . . . . which thing became a *snare* unto Gideon, and to his house" (Judges viii. 27). Idolatry is committed when anything or anyone is put in the place of God.

5. **The snare of faltering.** "Thine eye shall have no pity upon them, neither shalt thou serve their gods, for that will be a *snare* unto thee" (Deut. vii. 16).

6. **The snare of fear.** "The fear of man bringeth a *snare*" (Prov. xxix. 25). If we fear God, we need fear no one else, be he man or devil.

7. **The snare of evil companionship.** "They shall be *snares* and traps unto you" (Joshua xxiii. 13). The breath of the world will tarnish and infect us in our spiritual life.

378. SONGS OF DEGREES

PSALMS cxx. to cxxxiv

THE heading for each Psalm being an idex of its contents.

Psalm cxx. **Distress**, or crying unto the Lord.

,, cxxi. **Divine** aid, or kept by the Lord.

,, cxxii. **Dwelling**, or the house of the Lord.

,, cxxiii. **Direction**, or guided by the Lord.

,, cxxiv. **Deliverance**, or saved by the Lord.

Psalm cxxv. **Defence,** or shielded in the Lord.
,, cxxvi. **Delight,** or rejoicing in the Lord.
,, cxxvii. **Protection,** or blest by the Lord.
,, cxxviii. **Promise,** or fearing the Lord.
,, cxxix. **Persecution,** or suffering with the Lord.
,, cxxx. **Prayer,** or waiting upon the Lord.
,, cxxxi. **Practical** sanctification, or humble before the Lord.
,, cxxxii. **Perseverance,** or communion with the Lord.
,, cxxxiii. **Power,** or anointed by the Lord.
,, cxxxiv. **Praise,** or glorifying the Lord.

379. SPARROWS

1. **Sad Sparrow.** "I watch, and am as a sparrow alone upon a house-top" (Psalm cii. 7).

2. **Protected sparrow.** "Every bird of every sort" (Gen. vii. 14).

3. **Abiding sparrow.** "Yea, the sparrow hath found a house" (Psalm lxxxiv. 3).

4. **Remembered sparrow.** "Not one of them is forgotten before God" (Luke xii. 6).

5. **Reckless sparrow.** "As a bird hasteth to the snare" (Proverbs vii. 23).

6. **Offered sparrow.** "And the priest shall command that one of the birds be killed" (Lev. xiv. 5).

7. **Working sparrow.** "Where the birds make their nests" (Psalm civ. 17).

380. STATE OF THE SINNER

THE state of the natural man is deplorable in the sight of God (Psalm xiv.). The following are a few of the characteristics of the one who lacks the life of God.

1. **Carnal state.** "The carnal mind is enmity against God" (Romans viii. 7).

2. **Deceitful state.** "The heart is deceitful" (Jer. xvii. 9).

3. **Unrighteous state.** "None righteous" (Rom. iii. 10).

4. **Lifeless state.** "Dead in trespasses and sins" (Eph. ii. 1).

5. **Godless state.** "Without God" (Eph. ii. 12).

6. **Christless state.** "Without Christ" (Eph. ii. 12).

7. **Darkened state.** "Darkness" (Eph. iv. 18; v. 8).

8. **Enslaved state.** "Servants of sin" (Rom. vi. 17).

9. **Hopeless state.** "Having no hope" (Eph. ii. 12).
10. **Helpless state.** "Without strength" (Rom. v. 6).
11. **Cursed state.** "Cursed is every one" (Gal. iii. 10).
12. **Guilty state.** "Guilty before God" (Rom. iii. 19).
13. **Condemned state.** "Condemned already" (John iii. 18).

381. STARS

STARS may be taken to represent believers. In the following passages of Holy Writ a resemblance will be found between the two.

1. **Made.** "He made the stars also" (Gen. i. 16). "Created in Christ Jesus" (Eph. ii. 10).

2. **Sealed.** "Sealeth up the stars" (Job ix. 7). "Sealed with that Holy Spirit of promise" (Eph. i. 13).

3. **Exalted.** "Behold the height of the stars" (Job xxii. 12). "Made us sit together in heavenly places in Christ Jesus" (Eph. ii. 6).

4. **Not pure.** "The stars are not pure in His sight" (Job xxv. 5). "If we say that we have no sin, we deceive ourselves" (I. John i. 8).

5. **Ordained.** "The stars, which Thou hast ordained" (Ps. viii. 3). "I have chosen you, and ordained you," &c. (John xv. 16).

6. **To rule.** "The stars to rule by night" (Psalm cxxxvi. 9). "He that overcometh . . . will I give power over the nations, and he shall rule them with a rod of iron" (Rev. ii. 26, 27).

7. **Numbered.** "He telleth the number of the stars" (Ps. cxlvii. 4). "The Lord knoweth them that are His" (II. Tim. ii. 19).

8. **Called.** "He calleth them all by their names" (Ps. cxlvii. 4). "He calleth His own sheep by name" (John x. 3).

9. **Praising.** "Praise Him, all ye stars of light" (Ps. cxlviii. 3). "To the praise of the glory of His grace" (Eph. i. 6).

10. **Light-givers.** "The stars for a light by night" (Jer. xxxi. 35). "Ye are the light of the world" (Matt. v. 14).

11. **Differing.** "One star differeth from another star in glory" (I. Corinthians xv. 41). "Diversities of gifts, but the same Spirit" (I. Corinthians xii. 4).

12. **Held.** "He had in His right hand seven stars" (Rev. i. 16). "My sheep . . . . shall never perish, neither shall any man pluck them out of My hand" (John x. 27, 28).

382. STEPS IN THE CHRISTIAN LIFE

THERE are some terms that relate to the Christian life which are of pressing importance, because of the issues involved in relation to them. The following seven words indicate a few aspects of the Christian's life, namely, "Believe," "Pray," "Abide," "Walk," "Take," "Stand," "Watch."

1. **To believe on Christ** is the **secret** of the Christian life (Galatians ii. 20).

2. **To pray to Christ** is the **stay** of the Christian life (Phil. iv. 6).

3. **To abide in Christ** is the **strength** of the Christian life (John xv. 4).

4. **To walk as Christ** is the **shining out** of the Christian life (1. Peter ii. 21).

5. **To take from Christ** is the **supply** of the Christian life (Isaiah xxvii. 5).

6. **To stand with Christ** is the **staple** of the Christian life (Ephesians vi. 14).

7. **To watch for Christ** is the **standing order** of the Christian life (Mark xiii. 33). The term watchfulness is a comprehensive one. It signifies far more than merely holding the truth of the Lord's coming. It covers the whole trend of the spiritual life in the variety of its traits.

383. STEPS IN TRUE CONSECRATION

II. CHRONICLES XVII

THE right attitude of the soul to the Lord is the secret of true consecration.

1. **Companioning with the Lord** (verse 3). The Lord was with Jehoshaphat, because he was with the Lord by obedience to His word. To be is to have.

2. **Directing to the Lord** (verse 4). As the ship will be kept on its right course as the helmsman is guided by the compass, so the believer will be right in life as he directs his way by the written word of the living God.

3. **Blessing from the Lord** (verse 5). The way of Jehoshaphat was stablished, because he was stedfast, for the time being, in the way of the Lord. If we are faithful to the Lord by obeying His word, He will be faithful to us in giving us His blessing.

4. **Encouraged in the Lord** (verse 6). The king was encouraged (margin) in the ways of the Lord by the Lord's blessing. There is no fear of the Lord's blessing; the only fear is, lest we should fail to fear the Lord who blesses.

5. **Word of the Lord** (verse 9). To teach the Word of the Lord is to impart the greatest blessing upon mankind. See Ps. xix. 7-11 as to what the Word of God is and does.

6. **Power through the Lord** (verse 10). The greatest influence that any man can exert, is the influence that comes from the presence of God with him.

7. **Offering unto the Lord** (verse 16). To give ourselves to the Lord, and to allow ourselves to remain in His hands, is the very essence of consecration (Rom. vi. 13; xii. 1).

384. STEPS OF FAITH

GENESIS xii. 1-9

1. **The Beginning of Faith.** "The Lord had said" (verse 1). Faith has no existence apart from revelation. *Nature* is a revelation of God's handiwork. *Christ* is God manifest in the flesh. The *Written Word* is the unfolding of Christ the Living Word; and by that Word, heard as the voice of God, faith is begotten in the soul, for faith cometh by hearing, and hearing by the Word of God (Romans x. 17).

2. **The Call of Faith.** "Get thee out," &c. (verse 1). Abram is called to separate himself from his country and kindred. It was no light task, but faith is always obedient (Hebrews xi. 8). The same principle applies to the believer in Christ. Christ says we must be willing to leave all to follow Him, and no earthly relation must hinder. See the three "*Cannots*" in Luke xiv. 26-33.

3. **The Promise of Faith.** See the four "*I wills*" in verses 1, 2, and 3. When the Lord says, "I will," it means that He gives the power to perform. His "I will" is the name to the cheque that is honoured at Heaven's bank. The "Thou shalt" of the Law only brought consternation and condemnation, but the "I will" of grace always brings consecration and consolation to faith.

4. **The Blessing of Faith.** "Be thou a blessing" (ver. 2, R.V.). Faith having received the promise of God, and thus being blessed by God, is now responsible to be a blessing. Notice the Revised Version gives the more correct reading. Every blessing and privilege of grace brings a corresponding responsibility. Having received, we are to give (John vi. 11). Having heard, we are to tell (John iv. 29; I. John i. 3). Having found, we are to find (John i. 45).

5. **The Obedience of Faith.** "Abram departed, as the Lord had spoken" (verse 4). It was enough for Abram that he had God's command to leave his kin and country; so to faith it is sufficient that the Lord speaks for it to act. From reason's standpoint it was a foolish thing for Abram to leave home not knowing where he was going (Heb. xi. 8), but it was enough for him that God had said, "I will shew thee" (Gen. xii. 1). Surely it is better to walk with God in the dark than go by ourselves in the light? Faith says, "Yes," and acts accordingly.

6. **The Concern of Faith.** "Abram took," &c. (verse 5). Abram did not leave his family behind him, but took them with him. Faith is ever concerned about the welfare of others. It is never content to be blessed alone. "Go home to thy friends, and tell them how great things the Lord hath done for thee" (Mark v. 19) is the Lord's word to faith—faith never hesitates to respond, for the evidence of faith in Christ is seen in its concern for the welfare of others, as illustrated in the case of the saints at Thessalonica, who, having "turned to God," were "ensamples" to others, and who,

having "received the Word," "sounded the word out" to their neighbours (1. Thess. i. 9, 7, 6, 8).

7. **The Enemy of Faith.** "The Canaanite was then in the land" (verse 6). The Canaanite would probably dispute Abram's right to be in the land; and there are those who question the believer's walk of faith. Self says, "I would not." Unbelief says, "I cannot." Reason says, "I will not." The world says, "It pays not." Satan says, "Do not." But faith says, "Why not?" By faith, God is my Father, Christ is my Saviour, the Holy Spirit is my Comforter, Holiness is my walk, Truth is my regulator, Saints are my companions, and Heaven is my home.

8. **The Revelation of Faith.** "The Lord appeared unto Abram" (verse 7). This was for Abram's encouragement and strength. Trapp well says, "The sight of those wicked Canaanites might discourage him and unsettle his faith." But then the sight of God relieved him; and the promise, "Unto thy seed will I give this land," could not but put spirit into him, and make his good old heart to dance in his bosom. When the poor soul sinks sometimes at the sight of those Canaanites, and despairs almost of a conquest, God lets in a beam of His own light, and comforts it with some cordial promise, which is as Boaz was to Naomi, "A restorer of thy life, and a nourisher of thine old age" (Ruth iv. 15).

9. **The Worship of Faith.** "There builded he an altar" (verse 7). The altar speaks of four things, namely, confession, atonement, communion, and worship. Three of the four things are related to worship. *Confession* of sin is the *prelude* to worship, for there can be no worship if there is sin on the conscience. *Atonement* is the *basis* of worship, for we can only worship God through the sacrifice of Christ (Heb. x. 19, 22; Eph. ii. 18). *Communion* is *essential* to worship, for we can only worship the Lord as we have all things in common with Him; and worship itself is the heart boiling over with gratitude to Him for His love and mercy to us (Psalm ciii. 1, 2).

10. **The Dwelling of Faith.** "His tent" (verse 8). The tent is the symbol of pilgrim life (Heb. xi. 9), and a confession that Abram was looking for an abiding city (Heb. xi. 10). In like manner the believer in Christ is a stranger and pilgrim (1. Peter ii. 11). As a "stranger" he has no home in the world; that is, the world cannot satisfy him; and as a "pilgrim" he is passing through the world, that is, his aim and object are to please God in having no fellowship with the evil things in the world (1. John ii. 16), as Bunyan's pilgrims—Christian and Faithful—would not have anything to do with Vanity Fair, its goods or its occupants, and were persecuted in consequence.

385. STRENGTH OF THE LORD

THE Lord gives a sevenfold strengthening to His people as they trust Him.

1. **The strength of His grace to empower.** "My grace is sufficient for thee, for My strength is made perfect in weakness" (II. Cor. xii. 9).

2. **The strength of His arm to sustain.** "Fear thou not, for I am with thee: be not dismayed, for I am thy God, I will strengthen thee" (Isaiah xli. 10).

3. **The strength of His love to inspire.** "The love of Christ constraineth us" (II. Cor. v. 14).

4. **The strength of His armour to protect.** "Be strong in the Lord, and in the power of His might. Put on the whole armour of God" (Eph. vi. 10, 11).

5. **The strength of His joy to gladden.** "The joy of the Lord is your strength" (Neh. viii. 10).

6. **The strength of His Word to comfort.** "This is my comfort in my affliction, for Thy Word hath quickened me" (Psalm cxix. 50).

7. **The strength of His power to qualify.** "Ye shall receive power, after that the Holy Ghost is come upon you, and ye shall be witnesses unto Me" (Acts i. 8).

386. STRONG DRINK

Isaiah v. 11-14

There are seven things which are said in relation to "strong drink" and the man who swallows it.

1. **Strong drink fascinates.** Strong drink is the first thing in the morning and the last thing at night that the man follows who is under its spell. As when one is fascinated by a deadly serpent and is spell-bound to destruction, so those who are under the attraction of the demon drink find themselves enchanted to their destruction.

2. **Strong drink inflames.** "Till wine inflame them" (Isa. v. 11). As a fever will inflame the body, causing the pulse to throb with unnatural rapidity, and the temperature to rise till it seems that the body will be consumed, so the drink will create a burning which eats out the very life of its victim.

3. **Strong drink obliterates.** "They regard not" (verse 12). As the continual use of a coin will in time efface the image of the sovereign upon it, so drink dulls and deadens the sensibility of the soul, till it becomes utterly indifferent to the claims and Being of God, and obliterates all desire for Him.

4. **Strong drink dissipates.** "Neither consider the operation of His hands" (verse 12). As the sharp instrument plunged into the eye destroys the sight, so the drink eats away the optic nerve of the man's inner nature till he cannot see the work and the working of God.

5. **Strong drink captivates.** "Therefore My people are gone into captivity" (verse 13). As the spider will coil its web round the struggling fly till it has it completely in its power, so the drink will bind its victim till he is mastered, and the man is a helpless slave. Colonel Gardiner relates, that when he was considered by his military companions to be one of the most handsome and highly favoured of his day, he has seen a dog enter the mess-room, prowling for food, and looked at the creature with envy, inwardly groaning and exclaiming, "Oh that I were that dog." Many a helpless slave of drink has had a similar desire.

6. **Strong drink enervates.** "Their honourable men are famished, and their multitude dried up with thirst" (verse 13). Instead of plenty there is famine. Instead of satisfaction there is thirst. As consumption wastes the sufferer till he becomes enervated, so drink spoils the powers of the drinker. The mind becomes enfeebled, the brain becomes muddled, the body becomes weak, the hand becomes shaky, the face becomes bleared, the home becomes wretched, and the pocket becomes empty. Adams well says, "The drunkard drowns all his substance at the ale-house, and though he devours much is the leaner every way. Drunkenness is a costly sin. It is like gunpowder—many a man is blown up by it. He throws his house so long out at windows till at last his house throws him out of doors."

7. **Strong drink compensates.** As the farmer expects to reap the same kind of corn that he sows, and more than he sows; so the drunkard shall reap what he sows (Gal. vi. 8), and more than he sows (verse 14). Baxter says, "Oh, what a sight it is to see a man go merry and laughing to damnation, and make a jest of his own undoing, to see him at the brink of hell and will not believe it, like a madman boasting of his wit, or a drunken man boasting of his sobriety, or as the swine is delighted when the butcher is shaving his throat to cut it, or as the fatted lambs are skipping in their pasture that to-morrow must be killed and eaten, or as the bird sits singing when the gun is levelled to kill him, or as the greedy fish run, striving which shall catch the bait, that must presently be snatched out of their element and lie dying on the bank."

387. SUBSTITUTION OF CHRIST

The Apostle Paul, in writing to the Church at Corinth, said, "I will very gladly spend and be spent for you" (II. Cor. xii. 15). The preposition "huper," translated "for," is the one Paul uses, and is applied to Christ as the One who was not only willing, but who did "spend" and was "spent out" (II. Cor. xii. 15, R.V., M.), in acting on our behalf.* The meaning of the word is bending over to protect, as a mother bird will cover her young at the sacrifice of

* "*Huper*" is rendered "*On behalf*" in II. Cor. i. 11; v. 12; viii. 24; Phil. i. 29. In II. Cor. v. 20 it is "*stead*," and in Philemon 13.

her own life; or service rendered on behalf of another, thus acting in his stead, as when the priest offered "sacrifices *for* sins" on behalf of another (Heb. v. 1). The following will illustrate how faithfully and fully Christ acted on behalf of those who believe in Him. The preposition "*huper*" occurs in each case, and is rendered "*for*."

Christ as Giver. "Given *for* you" (Luke xxii. 19; I. Cor. xi. 24).

Christ as Atoner. "Shed *for* you" (Luke xxii. 20).

Christ as the Bread. "Bread . . . *for* the life of the world" (John vi. 51).

Christ as the Good Shepherd. "Good Shepherd giveth His life *for* the sheep (John x. 11).

Christ as the Volunteer. "I lay down My life *for* the sheep" (John x. 15).

Christ as the Provision for ungodly ones and sinners. "Christ died *for* the ungodly" (Rom. v. 6); "Christ died *for* us" (Romans v. 8).

Christ as the Passover. "Christ our Passover, sacrificed *for* us" (I. Cor. v. 7).

Christ as the Fulfiller of Scripture. "Christ died *for* our sins according to the Scriptures" (I. Cor. xv. 3).

Christ as the Sin-bearer. "He hath made Him to be sin *for* us" (II. Corinthians v. 21).

Christ as the Deliverer. "Gave Himself *for* our sins, that He might deliver" (Gal. i. 4).

Christ as the Substitute. "Gave Himself *for* me" (Gal. ii. 20).

Christ as the Curse-bearer. "Made a curse *for* us" (Gal. iii. 13).

Christ as the Burnt-offering. "Himself *for* us, an offering and a sacrifice to God for a sweet-smelling savour" (Eph. v. 2).

Christ as the Lover. "Loved . . . . gave Himself *for* it" (Ephesians v. 25).

Christ as the Saviour. "Salvation through our Lord Jesus Christ, who died *for* us" (I. Thess. v. 10, R.V.).

Christ as the Ransom. "A Ransom *for* all" (I. Tim. ii. 6).

Christ as the Redeemer. "Gave Himself *for* us, that He might redeem us," &c. (Titus ii. 14).

Christ as the Kinsman. "Taste death *for* every man" (Hebrews ii. 9).

Christ as the Sacrifice. "Sacrifice *for* sins" (Heb. x. 12).

Christ as the Sufferer. "Suffered *for* us" (I. Peter ii. 21).

Christ as the Reconciler. "Just *for* the unjust, that He might bring us to God" (I. Peter iii. 18).

Christ as the Example. "Christ hath suffered *for* us . . . . likewise," &c. (I. Peter iv. 1).

Christ as the Inspirer. "He laid down His life *for* us, and we ought," &c. (I. John iii. 16).

We have thus given in detail the principal Scriptures that speak of Christ's vicarious action, as it is of essential importance to be clear upon this main fact, for to be wrong here is to be wrong at every point.

388. TAKE

1. **Salvation.** "*Take* the cup of salvation" (Psalm cxvi. 13).
2. **Service.** "*Take* My yoke" (Matt. xi. 29).
3. **Separation.** "*Take* ye away the stone" (John xi. 39).
4. **Suffering.** "*Take* up His cross" (Matt. xvi. 24).
5. **Sufficiency.** "*Take* hold of My strength" (Isaiah xxvii. 5).
6. **Supplication.** "*Take* with you words" (Hosea xiv. 2).
7. **Submission.** "*Take* no thought for your life" (Matt. vi. 25).

389. TAKE HEED

A HEEDLESS person is thoughtless, but a heeding person is wide-awake.

The following seven "take heeds" show how the Christian should ever be on the alert:—

1. **Hearing.** "*Take heed* what ye hear" (Mark iv. 24; Luke viii. 18).
2. **Watching.** "*Take ye heed*, watch and pray" (Mark xiii. 33).
3. **Working.** "*Take heed* how he buildeth" (I. Cor. iii. 10).
4. **Heart.** "*Take heed*, brethren, lest there . . . an evil heart of unbelief" (Hebrews iii. 12).
5. **Standing.** "*Take heed* lest he fall" (I. Cor. x. 12).
6. **Covetousness.** "*Take heed* and beware of covetousness" (Luke xii. 15).
7. **Oneself.** "*Take heed* unto thyself" (I. Tim. iv. 16).

390. TACTICS OF SATAN

SIN was in the world before man. Satan is the originator of sin. (Ezekiel xxviii. 11-19, under the name of the King of Tyre, describes what Satan was before he fell, and what he became by his iniquity.

Satan's method and manner of working are displayed in the following seven instances:—

1. He puts evil into the hearts of men, as illustrated in the case of Ananias (Acts v. 3).

2. He endeavours to keep men from that which is of God, as seen in the instance of Joshua (Zech. iii. 1).

3. He catches away the seed of God's truth, lest man should be benefited (Matt. xiii. 19).

4. He blinds men to their true condition and the beauty of Christ (II. Corinthians iv. 4).

5. He hinders the servants of Christ in the work of the Gospel (I. Thess. ii. 18).

6. He tries to lead men into sin, as is portrayed in the temptation of Christ (Matt. iv. 1-11).

7. His aim is to get men to discredit the word of God, as may be gathered from the temptation of Eve (Gen. iii. 1-5).

391. TEN MEN WITH ONE CRY

THERE are ten men in the Scriptures who have one cry. The cry is, "I have sinned." But how differently they utter this confession.

1. **The cry of hardened Pharaoh,** as he is smarting unde the judgment of God, but yet goes on in his rebellious way (Exodus ix. 27; x. 16).

2. **The cry of covetous Baalam,** as he confesses to the angel (Num. xxii. 34), but still clings to the wages of unrighteousness.

3. **The cry of discovered and deceitful Achan,** as he confesses his iniquity to Joshua (Jos. vii. 20), but who would not have said anything if he had not been found out.

4. **The cry of reckless and rebellious King Saul,** as he finds His sin is discovered (I. Sam. xv. 24, 30).

5. **The cry of convicted David,** when his sin is revealed to him by Nathan (II. Sam. xii. 13).

6. **The cry of persecuting but penitent Shimei,** as he acknowledges his wrong-doing to David (II. Sam. xix. 20).

7. **The cry of chastened and yet chafing Job,** as he is smarting under his affliction (Job vii. 20).

8. **The cry of humbled Micah,** as he judges himself before the Lord (Micah vii. 9).

9. **The cry of traitorous Judas,** as he beholds the result of his unholy act (Matthew xxvii. 4).

10. **The cry of the convicted and comfortless prodigal,** as he returns to his father's house (Luke xv. 21).

392. THE AGONY IN GETHSEMANE

MARK xiv. 32-42

"IT has been said by a great poet that great characters and great souls are like mountains—they always attract storms; upon their heads break the thunders, and around their bare tops flash the lightnings and the seeming wrath of God. Nevertheless, they form a shelter for the plains beneath them. This marvellous saying finds an illustration in the lowliest, saddest soul the world has ever had living in it—the Lord Jesus Christ. Higher than all men, around His head seemed to beat the very storms of sin; yet beneath the shelter of His great, consoling, sustaining spirit, what lowly people, what humble souls, what poor babes as to wisdom, what sucklings as to the world's truth, have gained their life in this world and eternal rest in God." It is because Christ has passed through the valley of the shadow of death and the vale of suffering that He is able to succour and comfort His own in similar circumstances (Psalm xxiii. 4; Heb. ii. 10). There are some spots on earth which are memorable because of the scenes that have been enacted upon them, or because of some personal association with them. Bethel was a place that was dear to Jacob, for it was there that God revealed Himself to him. In like manner Gethsemane is a spot that is ever green in the memory of the child of God, for there the Saviour poured out His soul in strong crying and tears (Heb. v. 7), and sweat, in intense agony, great drops of blood (Luke xxii. 44).

1. **The Praying Man** (verse 32). One aspect of the life of Christ is, that His life was a life of prayer. From His first appearance in public at His baptism (Luke iii. 21) till the end of His career on the cross (Luke xxiii. 46) He was a Man of Prayer. It is a profitable study to mark in the Gospel according to Luke how often Christ is found in the act of praying.

2. **The Amazed Redeemer** (verse 33). Mark alone tells us that Christ was "sore amazed." The same term is rendered "greatly amazed" in referring to the people who came running to Christ when He came down from the mount of transfiguration (Mark ix. 15), and the word is translated "affrighted" in speaking of the women's fright at the sepulchre when they saw the young man in a white garment inside (Mark xvi. 5, 6). What was the sight that affrighted Christ? Could it be that He had a sight of the evil of sin, the baseness of iniquity, and the awful punishment man's disobedience merited? Or did He see the "*cup*" He was to drink (Psalm lxxv. 8), the "*sin*" that He was to be made (II. Cor. v. 21), the "*curse*" He was to be accounted (Gal. iii. 13), the "*sword*" that was to pierce Him (Zech. xiii. 7), the "*horrible pit*" into which He was to be cast (Psalm xl. 2), the "*iniquities*" which were to be laid upon Him (Isaiah liii. 6), and the "*stripes*" He was to receive? (Isaiah liii. 5).

3. **The Sorrowful Christ** (verse 34). Matthew says, He "began to be sorrowful" (Matt. xxvi. 37); Luke says He was in "an agony" (Luke xxii. 44); and Mark says He was "sore amazed," "very heavy," and "exceeding sorrowful unto death." The pangs of hell got hold of Him, and the sorrows of death compassed Him.

4. **The Persistent Pleader** (verses 35-39). Christ used the "same words" in His importunate pleading. It was no mere repetition with Him, but a holy clinging to His Father to be released, if possible, from the fiery ordeal through which He was about to pass.

5. **The Acquiescing Son** (verse 36). "Not what I will" was the key-note of the life of Christ (John iv. 34).

If we would please God, and have untold and uninterrupted blessings, like Christ, we must acquiesce in the will of God. Payson was asked, when under great bodily suffering, if he could see any particular reason for the dispensation. "No," he replied, "but I am as well satisfied as if I could see ten thousand; God's will is the very perfection of all reason." Young McCall, of the Livingstone Congo Mission, when struck down in the midst of his work, said, as his last words, "Lord, I gave myself to Thee, body, mind, and soul. I consecrated my whole life and being to Thy service; and now, if it please Thee to take myself, instead of the work which I would do for Thee, what is that to me? 'Thy will be done.'"

393. THE ARK

GENESIS vi

THERE are three thoughts in connection with the ark; salvation, security, and supply.

1. **Salvation.** The ark being made of wood is a type of the humanity of Christ (Heb. ii. 7). The pitch with which the ark was covered is a type of the atonement of Christ. The ark would not have been able to keep out the waters of judgment, if it had not been pitched with pitch, so neither would the humanity of Christ save—He must die for us.

We are safe indeed, sheltered by the atonement of Christ. Here is an alphabet as to what the atonement of Christ does for those that believe in Him. It is the Anchor that will hold us eternally secure; the Balm that heals our wounded spirit; the Covering that makes us lovely in God's sight; the Day-star to illuminate our soul; the Entrance into untold blessing; the Food that satisfies our longings; the Guarantee of eternal glory; the Harbour of Refuge for quietness; the Invincible argument against Satan to overcome him; the Joy-bringer of gladness and happiness; the Key to unlock the mysteries of heaven; the Liberator from all bondage; the Mainspring of a holy life; the Nutriment of our life; the Obliterator of our sins; the Pillow to rest on now, in death, and for ever; the Quickener to all that is of God; the Rest-giver to the conscience; the Saviour of our souls; the Tower that shelters; the Unburdener from all our cares; the Voice that prevails with God; the Warrant to heaven; and the Yoke that binds us for ever to Him.

2. **Security.** "The Lord shut him in" (Gen. vii. 16). In the ark was safety and security. How safe are we who are in Christ? As safe as Christ is. As the ark surrounded Noah and his family, so the Lord surrounds us.

3. **Supply.** There was plenty of food in the ark (Gen. vi. 21). Christ satisfies as well as saves.

394. THE BELIEVER IN RELATION TO THE FLESH

1. **The flesh has been judged in Christ.** "Knowing this, that our old man is crucified with Him" (Rom. vi. 6).

2. **We have died to the flesh.** "They that are Christ's have crucified the flesh" (Gal. v. 24).

3. **We are not in the flesh.** "But ye are not in the flesh, but in the Spirit" (Rom. viii. 9).

4. **The flesh is in us.** "I know that in me (that is in my flesh) dwelleth no good thing" (Rom. vii. 18).

5. **The flesh is opposed to the new life.** "The flesh lusteth against the Spirit" (Gal. v. 17).

6. **Make no provision for the flesh.** "Make not provision for the flesh, to fulfil the lusts thereof" (Rom. xiii. 14).

7. **Put no confidence in the flesh.** "Have no confidence in the flesh" (Phil. iii. 3).

395. THE BOOK OF GENESIS

A BOOK OF ABSOLUTE FACTS.

GENESIS means beginning. This book has been well called "the seed plot of the Bible," from the fact, that nearly every truth in the Word of God is foreshadowed here.

There is no uncertain sound or hesitating manner in the language of this book; we may say of it, as the people said of the Lord Jesus, "This teaches with authority, not as others." We can only notice a few of the facts, and we would remind our readers that these notes are rather suggestive than exhaustive.

First fact—"That God was before everything else." "When did God have a beginning?" asked a bright-faced little fellow of his Sunday-school teacher one day. The teacher was lost for a minute or two for a reply, when he suddenly exclaimed: "There must have been someone without a beginning to make a beginning." There are men who tell us that God evolved from something, and began to be, but we ask who made the something? We are content to believe in Jehovah, the One who always was, who always is, and who always will be.

Second fact—"That God created—caused to be—all things." The heavens with their glory; the earth with its beauty; the sea in its majesty; the animals in their variety; the birds with their song; the flowers in their splendour; the fish in their plentitude; and man with his intellect and powers.

Third fact—"That God made man in innocence." There is a difference between an innocent and a holy man. The innocent man is not conscious of evil; the holy man is, and overcomes it. Our first parents were innocent and pure. Without sin, but not beyond the possibility of sinning.

Fourth fact—"Sin was introduced into this world by Satan." Then sin was before our first parents fell? Yes. But it was through their disobedience that we participate in it.

Fifth fact—"Sin has separated man from God." The moment man sinned he became dead Godward—that is, separated from God; and the whole human family being represented in Adam, fell with him (Rom. v. 12, margin).

Sixth fact—"A Deliverer was foretold." "The Seed of the woman shall bruise his head." This is not a promise given, but a fact stated.

Seventh fact—"That sin always brings punishment." Look at our first parents being driven out of the garden, the avenging waters of the deluge, and the smoking ruins of Sodom, in confirmation of this. We must be punished for our sins, or accept Him who has made perfect satisfaction to God.

396. THE BOOK OF GENESIS

A Book of Typical Persons.

What one has said of the whole Bible may well be applied to this book.

"This Book contains:—The mind of God, the state of man, the way of salvation, the doom of sinners, and the happiness of believers. Its doctrines are holy, its precepts are binding, its stories are true, and its decisions are immutable. Read it to be wise, believe it to be safe, and practice it to be holy. It contains light to direct you, food to support you, and comfort to cheer you. It is the traveller's map, the pilgrim's staff, the pilot's compass, the soldier's sword, and the Christian's charter. Here Paradise is restored, heaven opened, and the gates of hell disclosed.

Christ is the Grand Object.

Our good its design, and the glory of God its end. It should fill the memory, rule the heart, and guide the feet. Read it slowly, frequently, prayerfully. It is a mine of wealth, a Paradise of glory, a river of pleasure. It is given you in life, will be opened at the judgment, and be remembered for ever. It involves the highest responsibility, will reward the labourer, and condemn all who trifle with its contents."

But to come to the point before us. There are at least *nine* persons who typify Christ in this book. *Adam*, the representative of the whole human race, typical of Him who is the last Adam, the Lord from heaven. *Abel*, the one who was accepted of God, typical of Him who offered Himself to God, and glorified Him in His life and death, and in whom the Father delighted. *Noah*, the obedient one, typical of Him whose meat it was to do the will of Him who sent Him. *Enoch*, the pleasing one, typical of Him of whom the Father said, "This is My beloved Son, in whom I am well pleased." *Melchizedek*, the priestly king, typical of Him who, like Melchizedek as to His priesthood, has no beginning and no end, the ever-loving One. *Abraham*, the faithful one, typical of Him who is the faithful and true One. *Isaac*, the peaceful one, typical of Him who is the Prince of Peace, who has made peace by the blood of His Cross, and who is now the Embodiment of peace—"He is our Peace." *Jacob*, the working one, typical of Him who laboured to secure His own, and this at the sacrifice of Himself. *Joseph*, the royal one, typical of Him who is yet to sit on His own throne. Although rejected now, He must reign in spite of the malice and hatred of men, and the craft and subtlety of the devil.

Further, there are seven persons who typify the believer—1, *Eve*, or union with Christ; 2, *Seth*, or relationship to Him; 3, *Enoch*, or walking with Him; 4, *Abram*, or obedience to Him; 5, *Lot*, or backsliding from Him; 6, *Rebekah*, or loved by Him; 7, *Rachel*, or all to Him.

Again, there are seven sets of persons:—

1. Adam and Eve, or Christ and the Church.
2. Cain and Abel, or faith and unbelief.
3. Two Enochs, or worldliness and walking with God.
4. Abram and Lot, or faithfulness and unfaithfulness.
5. Sarah and Hagar, or the two covenants.
6. Ishmael and Isaac, or the two natures.
7. Jacob and Esau, or cunning and carelessness.

397. THE BOOK OF THE REVELATION

1. **It is a book of stupendous facts.**

Facts referring to the Church, the Jew, Israel, the Gentiles, Satan, the beast, the false prophet, heaven, hell, time, and eternity.

2. **It is a book of symbols.** Seals. Bowls. Trumpets.
3. **It is a book telling of present and future judgment.**

Present judgment as brought out by Christ being in the midst of the churches, in the character in which He is seen; and future in relation to the world, antichrist, Satan, Rome, and corrupt Christianity.

4. **It is a book of precious realities.**

"See the "*I knows*," and the "*I wills*" of Christ to the seven churches. Also the "*No mores*."

5. **It is a book full of Old Testament allusions.**

There are from 200 to 300 references and allusions to the Old Testament in this book. More than in any one Gospel or Epistle.

6. **It is a peculiar book, if we contrast it with the Gospel and the Epistle of John.**

In the Gospel of John, we have Christ as the One in whom we believe; in the Epistle, the One whom we love; and in the Revelation, as the One we are waiting for.

In the Gospel we see Christ as the Apostle, *i.e.*, the sent One; in the Epistle, as our Advocate; and in the Revelation, as the King.

In the Gospel, it is His work on the Cross for us; in the Epistle, it is His work for us in heaven; in the Revelation, His work as Judge.

In the Gospel, we see Christ as the Word of God in creation and grace for us; in the Epistle, as the Word of Life manifested to us; and in the Revelation, as the Word of God in judgment.

7. **It is a Book revealing Christ.**

We see Christ as the great High Priest judging the evil in the churches; as the Lamb on the Throne; as the Object of worship in heaven; as the Man of war overthrowing His enemies; as the Judge judging the wicked; as the Bridegroom of His church; and as the King reigning in righteousness.

"Revelation of Jesus Christ"—not of John. Revelation—the unfolding or unveiling the Lord and His purpose. Where did Christ get the Revelation? "From His Father." What is its purpose? "To *show* unto His servants," &c. To whom are these things made known? "His servants," or, more correctly, His bond-slaves. It is the same word as in Rev. vi. 15. "*Bondman*."

When are these things to take place? "*Shortly*," or speedily, same word as in Luke xviii. 8—"speedily."

398. THE BRIDGE OF SIGHS

The Bridge of Sighs is the bridge which connects the Palace of the Doge with the State prisons of Venice. Over this bridge the State prisoners were conveyed from the judgment-hall to the place of execution.

"I stood in Venice, on the Bridge of Sighs,
A palace and a prison on each hand."

May we not say that the earthly life of the Lord Jesus was a Bridge of Sighs, over which He passed, from the palace of the Father, to the death of the cross? Verily it was. Three times in the New Testament we read of the Lord Jesus sighing or groaning.

1. **Christ sighed as He looked up to heaven in healing the deaf and dumb man** (Mark vii. 34). He was grieved in heart, and groaned in spirit as He saw how sin had caused men to be deprived of their faculties. The term "*sighed*" is rendered "*groan*" in Romans viii. 23, and II. Cor. v. 2, 4; "*grief*" in Hebrews xiii. 17; and "*grudge*" (margin "*groan*") in James v. 9. The meaning of the word "*stenazo*" is to sigh in sympathy, or to groan in distress. How this reminds us of the sympathy of Christ with suffering humanity.

2. **Christ sighed deeply when the Pharisees in unbelief came and asked Him for a sign** (Mark viii. 12). The expression that is used is even more forcible than the previous one, for it is the word "*stenazo*" with the prefix "*ana*," which, together, means to fetch up a deep drawn sigh. Christ was greatly moved at the unbelief of the Jews. It made Him to be in bitterness of soul.

3. **Christ groaned intensely when He saw Mary weeping after the death of Lazarus,** and as He listened to the questioning of the Jews respecting His power (John xi. 33, 38). The margin of the Revised Version says, "He was moved with indignation in Himself." The classical use of the expression is applied to the snort of a warhorse. Christ may have been moved with indignation when He saw the unbelief of the Jews, and as He listened to their questions; or He may have been deeply moved and agitated when He saw the ravages of sin, and longed to accomplish that death on the ground of which God should ultimately banish death (Rev. xx. 14), and kill sorrow.

The groans of Christ in His life were but the forerunners of His deeply-moving cry, when He cried out in heart anguish on the cross, "My God, My God, why hast Thou forsaken Me?" Verily the sighs of Christ were many on our account. We hear Him saying, "My sighs are many, and My heart is faint" (Lam. i. 22).

399. THE CITIES OF REFUGE

HEBREWS vi. 18 makes a distinct allusion to the Cities of Refuge, and the man fleeing there for safety, as a type of Christ the Shelter for the sinner. Let us look at the kind of Refuge which Christ is.

1. Christ is a **Protecting Refuge.** Jehovah is said to be in Isaiah xxv. 4, "A Refuge from the storm;" and in Psalm lix. 16 the Psalmist says, "Thou hast been my Defence and Refuge in the day of my trouble." As the man who had killed another inadvertently, found protection from the avenger of blood in the City of

Refuge, so those who flee to Christ find protection from the wrath to come (I. Thess. i. 10), from the curse of a broken law (Gal. iii. 10), from the justice of God (Exodus xxxiv. 7), from the consequence of sin (Heb. ix. 26), from the power of darkness (Col. i. 13), from the love of the world (Gal. i. 4), and from the dominion of sin (Rom. vi. 16), and find safety in the day of trouble.

2. Christ is a **Pleasant Refuge.** In Joel iii. 16 we read, "The Lord will be the Hope of His people," or, as the margin gives it, "The place of repair, or harbour." The Hebrew word rendered "*hope*" is the same as in the two previous passages of Scripture, where it is translated "*refuge*." The marginal reading of "*harbour*" is suggestive of a pleasant harbour of refuge, such as is being built at the present at Peterhead and Sunderland. They are being built at great cost, to provide havens of rest for the storm-tossed mariners, where they can be in safety and calm. We can quite understand a sailor who has known the protection of one of these harbours regarding it as a pleasant place. But what is this in comparison with what Christ is? He is the Altogether Lovely (Cant. v. 16). Rest of conscience (Matthew xi. 28), joy of heart (John xv. 11), satisfaction of soul (Psalm xxxvi. 8), brightness of hope (I. Peter i. 3), gladness of spirit (John xx. 20), preciousness of promise (II. Peter i. 3), and pleasantness of peace (Prov. iii. 17), are found in Him.

3. Christ is a **Permanent Refuge.** "The Eternal God is thy refuge" (Deut. xxxiii. 27). The word "*refuge*" might be, and perhaps better, rendered "*habitation*." The Lord is the Home of those who have fled to Him. The refugee was not to go out of his place of safety until the death of the high priest (Josh. xx. 6). Our High Priest will never die, therefore with Him we shall live in the power of His endless life. It is in this sense that He "saves evermore" (Heb. vii. 25, margin). Those whom the Lord takes up He never gives up (John x. 28, 29). For "ever with the Lord" (I. Thess. iv. 17), is the lock that shuts us into the glory and gladness of His presence for ever. Among the precious "no mores" of the Book of the Revelation is this one, "He shall go no more out" (Rev. iii. 12).

4. Christ is a **Personal Refuge.** More than once the Psalmist chants the words, "The Lord, He is my Refuge" (Psalm xci. 2, 9). Well for us if we can sing—

> "Jesus, my heart's dear Refuge;
> Jesus has died for me."

It is not enough to know that Christ is the Saviour we need, the essential thing is to make personal application to Him, and each to receive Him for oneself. The testimony of Go'ds saints is one on this point. Dr. Doddridge on his dying bed said, "I have no hope in what I have been or done, yet I am full of confidence, and this is my confidence, there is a Hope set before me. I have fled, I still fly for refuge to that Hope. In Him I trust, in Him I have strong consolation, and shall assuredly be accepted in this Beloved of my soul." Having fled to Christ as the hiding place, the next thing is to make Him our abiding place, for as there is no safety out of Christ, neither is there joy if we are not abiding in Him by obedience to His Word; as Hewetson said, "I never have a moment's peace when I return in the slightest degree to conformity with the world; but I always have great peace when my soul returns home to its City of Refuge, the Lord Jesus Christ. Communion with Christ is the only source of satisfaction, the only source of lasting enjoyment."

"Son of God, Thy Father's treasure,
He yet gives Thee all to me;
Angels vainly toil to measure
What I have in having Thee.
Grace so vast bewilders Heaven;
God to me His Christ has given."

400. THE CRIES OF CHRIST

1. **The cry of the Witness.** "Jesus *cried* and said, He that believeth on Me believeth not on Me, but on Him that sent Me" (John xii. 44). Faithful in its testimony and full in its promise.

2. **The cry of the Teacher.** "He *cried*, He that hath ears to hear, let him hear" (Luke viii. 8). Powerful in utterance and practical in outcome.

3. **The cry of the Life-giver.** "He *cried* with a loud voice, Lazarus, come forth" (John xi. 43). Quickening and liberating.

4. **The cry of the Satisfier.** "Jesus stood and *cried*, saying, If any man thirst let him come unto Me and drink" (John vii. 37). Sure, lasting, refreshing and free.

5. **The cry of the Rebuker.** "Then *cried* Jesus in the Temple as He taught, saying, ye both know Me," &c. (John vii. 28). Searching and mouth-stopping.

6. **The cry of the Surrenderer.** "Jesus *crying* with a loud voice, said, Father into Thy hands," &c. (Luke xxiii. 46, R.V., M.). Patient and passive.

7. **The cry of the Sufferer.** "Jesus *cried* with a loud voice saying, My God! My God! why hast Thou forsaken Me?" (Matt. xxvii. 46). Cry of Cries.

401. THE DEATH OF CHRIST

THE pith and power of the Gospel are the death and resurrection of Christ. The former is its pith, and the latter is its power. The death of Christ is—

1. **Real as to its Occurrence.** "Christ that *died*" (Rom. viii. 34). "Christ *died*" (Rom. xiv. 15; I. Cor. viii. 11). Towering o'er the wrecks of time, there is one fact that shines out in unmistakable reality, and that is, the death of Christ.

2. **Substitutionary in its Character.** "Christ *died* for the ungodly," "Christ *died* for us" (Rom. v. 6-8). Christ was acting on our behalf that He might protect us from the consequence of sin in dying in our stead.

3. **Definite in its Work.** "He *died* unto sin once" (Rom. vi. 10). "Christ *died* for our sins" (I. Cor. xv. 3). His death had distinct relation to our sin. He died to bear away our *sins*, and to be judged for our *sin*.

4. **Freeing in its Aim.** "He *died* for all, that they which live should not henceforth live unto themselves, but unto Him who *died* for them and rose again" (II. Cor. v. 15). In the death of Christ we have the magnet which draws us from self to Himself.

5. **Practical in its Purpose.** "To this end Christ both *died*, and rose, and revived, that He might be Lord both of the dead and living" (Rom. xiv. 9). He died that He might gain us, and now we are His absolute property.

6. **Assurance of Future Glory.** "Who *died* for us, that, whether we wake or sleep, we should live together with Him" (I. Thess. v. 10). The blood-red mark of Christ's cross is stamped on every certificate of heaven.

7. **Guarantee that our loved ones, who have fallen asleep, shall be with us in Christ's coming glory.** "If we believe that Jesus *died* and rose again, even so them also which sleep in Jesus will God bring with Him" (I. Thess. iv. 14). There is one ray that shall make the golden glory of Christ's splendour bear a rosy tint, and that is the red light of Calvary.

402. THE DIVINE HELPER

"THE Lord is my Helper" (Heb. xiii. 6).

1. **Past Helper.** "Thou hast been my *Help*" (Psalm lxiii. 7).

2. **Present Helper.** "A very present *Help* in trouble" (Psalm xlvi. 1).

3. **Powerful Helper.** "I have laid *help* upon One that is mighty" (Psalm lxxxix. 19).

4. **Protecting Helper.** "The Lord God will *help* me" (Isaiah l. 7, 9).

5. **Precious Helper.** "I will *help* thee" (Isaiah xli. 10, 13, 14).

6. **Providing Helper.** "The *Helper* of the fatherless" (Psalm x. 14).

7. **Perpetual Helper.** "The God of Jeshurun, who rideth upon the heaven, in thy *help*" (Deut. xxxiii. 26).

403. THE EYES OF THE LORD

1. **Seeing, to strengthen.** "The eyes of the Lord run to and fro throughout the whole earth, to show Himself strong" (II. Chron. xvi. 9).

2. **Seeing, to encourage.** "Before that Philip called thee, when thou wast under the fig-tree, I saw thee" (John i. 47, 48).

3. **Seeing, to direct.** "I will guide thee with Mine eye" (Psalm xxxii. 8).

4. **Seeing, to deliver.** "Behold, the eye of the Lord is upon them that fear Him . . . to deliver" (Psalm xxxiii. 18, 19).

5. **Seeing, to protect.** "The eyes of the Lord are upon the righteous" (Psalm xxxiv. 15).

6. **Seeing, to discover.** "The eyes of the Lord are in every place, beholding the evil and the good" (Prov. xv. 3).

7. **Seeing, to preserve.** "The eyes of the Lord preserve him that hath knowledge" (Prov. xxii. 12, R.V.).

8. **Seeing, to heal.** "He saw his wife's mother laid . . . He touched her hand and the fever left her" (Matt. viii. 14, 15).

9. **Seeing, to provide.** "When He saw the multitudes, He was moved with compassion on them" (Matt. ix. 36).

10. **Seeing, to comfort.** "When the Lord saw her, He had compassion on her" (Luke vii. 13; John xi. 33, and xix. 26).

11. **Seeing, to commend.** "He saw also a certain poor widow casting in thither two mites" (Luke xxi. 1, 2).

12. **Seeing, to lament.** "When He was come near, He beheld the city, and wept over it" (Luke xix. 41).

404. THE EXCLUSIVENESS OF "IN CHRIST"

"In Christ" is an exclusive expression, for a "man in Christ" is the opposite to a man in the flesh. The apostle Paul, in an incidental way, gives us the key to the cause of the difference in his life when he refers to himself as a "man in Christ." For one to be in the nation of Israel meant, that he occupied a peculiar and separate position. Israel as a people dwelt alone, and were not reckoned among the nations.

1. **They were excluded from eating what they would.** "And these ye shall have in abomination," &c. (Lev. xi. 13-47). In like manner the believer in Christ is excluded from feeding upon the garbage of worldly novels, and the cunning treatises of men, who in the form of a story, propagate error. We have to feed upon the pure, unadulterated Word of God, and then we shall grow in the knowledge and grace of God.

2. **They were excluded from wearing apparel of a mixed texture.** "Neither shall a garment mingled of linen and woollen

come upon thee" (Lev. xix. 19; Num. xv. 38). The believer in Christ is to put off all old habits formed in sin, and make no provision for the flesh to fulfil the desires thereof.

3. **They were excluded from sowing their land with mixed seed.** "Thou shalt not sow thy vineyard with divers seeds" (Deut. xxii. 9). Likewise in a spiritual sense the believer in Christ is excluded from mixing with the pure seed of the Word of God, the deductions and opinions of men, or the experiences that are in opposition to truth.

4. **They were excluded from yoking clean and unclean animals in agricultural labour.** "Thou shalt not plough with an ox and an ass together" (Deut. xxii. 10). The believer in Christ must not yoke worldly methods with Divine principles. The popular theory among many of God's people is, that the end justifies the means. The Lord did not think so when He shut Moses out of the land for striking the rock twice instead of speaking to it.

5. **They were excluded from marrying any but Israelites.** "Neither shalt thou make marriages with them" (Deut. vii. 3). The believer in Christ is strictly enjoined to "marry in the Lord," and not to be "unequally yoked together with unbelievers" (I. Cor. vii. 39; II. Cor. vi. 14).

6. **They were excluded from fellowship with the surrounding nations.** "I am the Lord your God, which have separated you from other people" (Lev. xx. 24). The believer in Christ is separated to God as sanctified in Christ, and as saints, *i.e.*, God's separated ones, we are to keep ourselves sacred to God.

7. **They were excluded from acting in any way as they would.** "Therefore shall ye observe all My statutes, and all My judgments, and do them. I am the Lord" (Lev. xix. 37). The believer in Christ right gladly does the will of Christ, for to be in the yoke of His will is to find rest and refreshment to the soul. It will be apprehended at once that to be in Christ means, that we are therefore excluded from the old sphere of sin and the world, and that we live a heavenly life, because we are a heavenly people. When Venice was in the hands of the Austrians, those alien tyrants swarmed in every quarter, but the Venetians hated them to the last degree, and showed their enmity upon all occasions. After this fashion will every true Christian treat his inbred sins; he will not be happy under their power, nor tolerate their dominion, nor show them favour. If he cannot expel them, he will not indulge them.

405. THE FATHER'S SEVENFOLD GIFT TO CHRIST

"Thou gavest Me."

1. **Completion.** "I have finished the work which *Thou gavest Me* to do" (John xvii. 4).

2. **Manifestation.** "I have manifested Thy name unto the men which *Thou gavest Me* out of the world" (John xvii. 6).

3. **Possession.** "Thine they were, and *Thou gavest* them *Me*" (John xvii. 6).

4. **Revelation.** "I have given unto them the words which *Thou gavest Me*" (John xvii. 8).

5. **Preservation.** "Those that *Thou gavest Me* I have kept" (John xvii. 12).

6. **Identification.** "The glory which *Thou gavest Me* I have given them" (John xvii. 22).

7. **Perfection.** "Of them which *Thou gavest Me* have I lost none" (John xviii. 9).

406. THE GOOD SAMARITAN'S ACTION IN REGARD TO THE MAN WHO FELL AMONG THIEVES

THERE are many thoughts which are suggested if we take the Good Samaritan as a type of Christ (Luke x. 30-37).

I. **Condescension of the Good Samaritan.** "He came where he was" (verse 33), unlike those who passed by on the other side. In like manner Christ came where we were. He came to our *humanity*, and took it upon Him (Heb. ii. 14). He came to our *sorrow*, and became acquainted with it (Isaiah liii. 4); He came to our *death*, and died it (I. Peter iii. 18); He came to our *sin*, and bore it (II. Cor. v. 21); He came to our *curse*, and passed through it (Gal. iii. 13); He came to our *woe*, and endured it (Heb. xii. 2); and He came to our *lowness*, to lift us out of it (Phil. ii. 8).

II. **Compassion of the Good Samaritan.** "He had compassion on him" (verse 33). Repeatedly we read of Christ being moved with compassion in His life, but the compassion of His compassion was, when He took pity upon us, as He saw us in our sin (Ezek. xvi. 8), and died on our account (Rom. v. 6, 8), for as David had compassion on Mephibosheth, and brought him to his own house (II. Sam. ix.), so Christ has had compassion upon us, in dying to meet our need.

III. **Care of the Good Samaritan.** There are seven things the Good Samaritan did for the man.

1. He "*went to him.*" He did not send a deputy to do his work. So with Christ. He saves (II. Tim. i. 9). He gives (John xiv. 27). He sustains (Isaiah xli. 10). He accompanies (Ex. xxxiii. 14), and He keeps (Jude 24).

2. He "*bound up his wounds.*" So with Christ. He heals by His stripes (Isaiah liii. 5), and comforts by His grace (II. Cor. xii. 9).

3. He "*poured in oil and wine.*" So with Christ. He gives unction of His Spirit (I. John ii. 27; II. Cor. i. 21), and the wine of His joy (Psalm civ. 15).

4. He "*set him on his own beast.*" In like manner, Christ gives us to sit in the place where He had been (Eph. ii. 6).

5. He "*brought him to an inn.*" So Christ brings us to a place of safety (Isaiah xxxii. 2), and into the banqueting house of His fellowship (Song of Solomon ii. 4).

6. He "*took care of him.*" So with Christ. Those who are taken up by Him are not given up. They are in His mighty grip (John x. 28), and cared for (I. Peter v. 7).

7. *He left supplies for the man.* "He took out two pence." What a supply we have in Christ (Eph. i. 3; Phil. iv. 19).

407. THE GOSPEL

1. **Divine Gospel.** "Separated unto the Gospel of God" (Romans i. 1).

2. **Gracious Gospel.** "To testify the Gospel of the grace of God" (Acts xx. 24).

3. **Wondrous Gospel.** "The beginning of the Gospel of Jesus Christ, the Son of God" (Mark i. 1).

4. **Life-giving Gospel.** "In Christ Jesus I have begotten you through the Gospel" (I. Cor. iv. 15).

5. **Saving Gospel.** "The Gospel of your salvation" (Eph. i. 13).

6. **Peace-securing Gospel.** "Your feet shod with the preparation of the Gospel of peace" (Eph. vi. 15).

7. **Full Gospel.** "I shall come in the fulness of the blessing of the Gospel of Christ" (Rom. xv. 29).

8. **Powerful Gospel.** "I am not ashamed of the Gospel of Christ, for it is the power of God unto salvation" (Rom. i. 16).

9. **Practical Gospel.** "Only let your conversation be as it becometh the Gospel of Christ" (Phil. i. 27).

10. **Glorious Gospel.** "Lest the light of the glorious Gospel of Christ" (II. Cor. iv. 4).

11. **Everlasting Gospel.** "Having the everlasting Gospel to preach unto them" (Rev. xiv. 6).

408. THE GOSPEL PROCLAIMS

1. **Pardon** for the guilty (Acts xxvi. 18).
2. **Peace** for the troubled (Eph. ii. 17).
3. **Power** for the strengthless (Rom. v. 6).
4. **Purity** for the defiled (Acts xv. 9).
5. **Plenty** for the needy (Luke xiv. 16, 23).
6. **Pleasure** for the dissatisfied (Phil. iv. 6-11).
7. **Productiveness** of the Spirit (Gal. v. 22).

409. THE HOLY SPIRIT* IN ROMANS VIII

1. **Spirit of Life** to liberate. "The Spirit of life . . . hath made me free" (Rom. viii. 2).

2. **Spirit of God** to indwell. "The Spirit of God dwell in you" (Romans viii. 9).

3. **Spirit of Christ** to identify. "Have not the Spirit of Christ, he is none of His" (Rom. viii. 9).

4. **Spirit of Power** to raise. "The Spirit of Him that raised up Jesus" (Romans viii. 11).

5. **Spirit of Might** to quicken. "Quicken your mortal bodies by His Spirit" (Rom. viii. 11).

6. **Spirit of Leading** to guide. "Led by the Spirit of God" (Romans viii. 14).

7. **Spirit of Witnessing** to cheer. "The Spirit Himself beareth witness" (Rom. viii. 16, R.V.).

8. **Spirit of First-fruits** to pledge. "The first-fruits of the Spirit" (Rom. viii. 23).

9. **Spirit of Help** to enable. "The Spirit also helpeth our infirmities" (Romans viii. 26).

10. **Spirit of Intercession** to plead. "The Spirit Himself maketh intercession for us" (Rom. viii. 26, R.V.).

11. **Spirit of Interpretation** to make known. "The mind of the Spirit" (Rom. viii. 27).

410. THE HAPPY MAN IN PSALM XXXII

The blessed man. "Blessed is he" (verse 1).

The forgiven trangressor. "Whose transgression is forgiven" (verse 1).

The covered sinner. "Whose sin is covered" (verse 1).

The absolved perverter. "Unto whom the Lord imputeth not iniquity" (verse 2).

The guileless spirit. "In whose spirit there is no guile" (verse 2).

The silent convicted one. "When I kept silence" (verse 3).

The burdened soul. "Thy hand was heavy upon me" (verse 4).

The sapless tree. "My moisture is turned into the drought of summer" (verse 4).

The open confessor. "I acknowledged my sin unto Thee" (verse 5).

The glad witness. "Thou forgavest the iniquity of my sin" (verse 5).

---

*The word "spirit" which occurs in the rest of the chapter, refers to the new nature, as may be gathered from the R.V., where the term is given with a small s.

The godly suppliant. "For this, shall every one that is godly, pray unto Thee" (verse 6).

The safe refugee. "The floods of great waters shall not come nigh unto him" (verse 6).

The hidden saint. "Thou art my Hiding-place" (verse 7).

The preserved believer. "Thou shalt preserve me from trouble" (verse 7).

The environed singer. "Thou shalt compass me about with songs of deliverance" (verse 7).

The instructed disciple. "I will instruct thee" (verse 8).

The watched child. "Mine eye upon thee" (verse 8, R.V.).

The trustful recliner. "He that trusteth in the Lord" (verse 10).

The righteous rejoicing. "Rejoice, ye righteous" (verse 11).

411. THE LORD AROUND HIS PEOPLE

1. **Hedge to protect.** "Hast not Thou made an hedge about him" (Job i. 10).

2. **Food to strengthen.** "And He let it fall in the midst of their camp, round about their habitations" (Psalm lxxviii. 28).

3. **Deliverer to save.** "The Angel of the Lord encampeth round about them that fear Him, and delivereth them" (Ps. xxxiv. 7).

4. **Tower to shield.** "The Name of the Lord is a strong tower" (Prov. xviii. 10).

5. **Wall of fire to consume.** "The Lord will be unto her a Wall of Fire round about" (Zech. ii. 5).

6. **Mountains to shelter.** "As the mountains are round about Jerusalem, so the Lord is round about His people" (Psalm cxxv. 2).

7. **Army to fight.** "The mountain was full of horses and chariots of fire round about" (II. Kings vi. 17).

412. THE LORD AS THE HELPER

"Hitherto the Lord hath helped us." What a Helper the Lord is!

1. **Shielding Helper** (Psalm xxxiii. 20; Heb. xiii. 6); it matters not how many the enemies are, He is able to protect us by His presence, while effecting our deliverance.

2. **Supplying Helper** (Psalm xl. 17; Heb. iv. 16); He gives more than cold help; He supplies all our need, and thus helps us indeed.

3. **Sure Helper** (Psalm xlvi. 1); we need not fear that He will fail us, we can always count upon Him.

4. **Strong Helper** (Psalm liv. 4); some friends are quite willing to help us, but they have not got the strength. Not so the Lord, He is the God (Elohim, the Three in One), who can aid us whatever the emergency is.

5. **Sympathising Helper** (Psalm lxxxix. 19). The One who helps us is one of us—Christ—and therefore, understands our case completely.

6. **Satisfying Helper** (Psalm cxlvi. 5). He meets our case at every point, and satisfies all our need.

7. **Sustaining Helper** (Isaiah xli. 10). There is an arm beneath us that is able to sustain us, we may therefore lean hard.

413. THE LORD AS SHIELD IN THE PSALMS

1. **Surrounding Shield.** "Thou, O Lord, art a Shield about me" (iii. 3, R.V.).

2. **Saving Shield.** "My Shield is with God, which saveth the upright in heart" (vii. 10, R.V.).

3. **Personal Shield.** "The Lord is . . my Shield" (xviii. 2, R.V.).

4. **Appropriated Shield.** "He is a Shield unto all them that trust in Him" (xviii. 30, R.V.).

5. **Gifted Shield.** "Thou hast also given me the Shield of Thy salvation" (xviii. 35).

6. **Tested Shield.** "The Lord is my Strength and my Shield" (xxviii. 7).

7. **Victorious Shield.** "Bring them down, O Lord our Shield" (lix. 11).

8. **Anointed Shield.** "Our Shield . . . . Thine Anointed" (lxxxiv. 9).

9. **Protecting Shield.** "The Lord God is a Sun and Shield" (lxxxiv. 11).

10. **Divine Shield.** "For our Shield belongeth unto the Lord" (lxxxix. 18, R.V.).

11. **Israel's Shield.** "O Israel, trust thou in the Lord: He is their Help and their Shield" (cxv. 9).

12. **Priest's Shield.** "House of Aaron . . . . . He is their Shield" (cxv. 10).

13. **Fearing one's Shield.** "Ye that fear the Lord . . . He is their Shield" (cxv. 11).

14. **Sheltering Shield.** "My Hiding-place and my Shield" (cxix. 114).

15. **Subduing Shield.** "My Shield . . who subdueth" (cxliv. 2).

414. THE LORD'S PRAYER

THE Lord's Prayer may be summed up as follows:—

Position. A son adopted. "Our Father, which art in heaven."

Fitness. A worshipper sanctified. "Hallowed be Thy name."

Allegiance. A citizen enfranchised. "Thy kingdom come."

Usefulness. A servant employed. "Thy will be done on earth as it is in heaven."

Provision. A beggar fed. "Give us this day our daily bread."

Pardon. A sinner absolved. "And forgive us our debts, as we forgive our debtors."

Safety. A pilgrim guided. "And lead us not into temptation."

Victory. A soldier succoured. "But deliver us from evil."

Testimony. A witness's confession. "For Thine is the kingdom."

Supply. A weakling empowered. "The power."

Praise. A chorister's song. "And the glory."

Assurance. A saint's belief. "For ever."

Prayer. A believer's acquiescence. "Amen."

415. THE LORD'S PRESERVATION

I. CHRONICLES xviii. 6

1. **Lips.** The Lord preserves our *lips* from evil speaking, as the tongue is seasoned with the salt of His grace (Col. iv. 6).

2. **Eyes.** The Lord preserves our *eyes* from evil occupation, as we look unto Jesus (Heb. xii. 2).

3. **Feet.** The Lord preserves our *feet* from going into by-paths, as we walk with Him (Mal. ii. 6).

4. **Hands.** The Lord preserves our *hands* from idleness, as we are used by Him in His service (Col. i. 29).

5. **Heart.** The Lord preserves our *heart* from impurity, by His indwelling presence (Eph. iii. 17).

6. **Spirit.** The Lord preserves our *spirit* from backsliding, as we commune with Him (Song of Solomon ii. 14).

7. **Soul.** The Lord preserves our *soul* from ill, as its affection is set on Him (Col. iii. 2).

416. THE LORD'S SUPPER

THERE are three ways to which the Lord's Supper points. It bids us *look back* to the *Cross*, and reminds us of what Christ *has done;* it beckons us to *look up* to the *Throne*, and tells us of what Christ *is doing;* and it beseeches us to *look on* to the *coming* Christ, and proclaims what He is yet *going to do.* Let us look at these three looks.

I. **The backward look of Faith.** There are seven things in Mark xiv. 22, 23, that we note in relation to Christ's action with the bread and cup.

1. He "*took*" the bread and cup. The bread represents the body, and the cup the blood of Christ. As Christ takes the bread and cup we are reminded of the fact that He took upon Him human nature (Heb. ii. 16), that He might suffer for us in His divinely prepared body (Heb. x. 5, 10).

2. Christ "*blessed*" the bread, and gave "*thanks*" for the cup. In this we are reminded of the Lord Jesus as He acquiesced in the Divine plan, although it meant so much suffering to Him, for we must never forget that it pleased God to bruise Christ (Isaiah liii. 10), and to give Him the bitter cup He drank (Mark xiv. 36; John xviii. 11).

3. Christ "*brake*" the bread. In the broken bread we see symbolized the sufferings that Christ endured in His body (Isaiah liii. 5).

4. Christ "*said*," in explaining what the bread and wine represented, that they signified His body and blood. Not, as Rome teaches, that the bread and wine are actually the body and blood of Christ, but that they are symbolized by them.

5. Christ "*gave*" the bread and wine to His disciples. In like manner He has given Himself *for* us, and given Himself *to* us (Gal. ii. 20; Song of Solomon ii. 16).

6. Christ told His disciples to "*take*" the bread and wine. We take Christ by an act of faith (John i. 12), and make all He *has* and *is*, ours by so doing.

7. Christ bade His disciples, not only to take the bread, but to "*eat*" it. It is an essential that those who believe in Christ should feed upon Him, as He Himself says in John vi. 54.

As we look to the Cross and remember the Christ who suffered there, we gladly say, "His death is the *price* of our salvation" (I. Cor. vi. 20), the *pass* into God's presence (Heb. x. 19), the *propitiation* for our guilt (Rom. iii. 25), the *peacemaker* for our reconciliation (Col. i. 20), the *power* of our Christian life (Heb. xiii. 12), the *provider* of our blessing (Eph. i. 7), and the *plea* of our testimony (I. Corinthians xv. 1).

II. **The upward look of Love.** "This do in remembrance of Me" (I. Cor. xi. 25). The Lord's Supper not only reminds us of what Christ has done for us, but of the great Worker who accomplished the task. Faith leads us to rest on the work of atonement, but love leads us to praise the Atoner, and causes our heart's affection to twine around Him, even as the ivy clings round the oak. Love leads us to appreciate Christ for what He *is*, as well as for what He has done, even as Mephibosheth thought more of the king than he did of his gifts (II. Sam. xix. 30). It is the Person of Christ which gives value to the work, and, while we must never under-estimate the work of Christ on the cross, we must ever remember the Person who died (II. Tim. ii. 8), and call to mind that Christ is the living, loving Saviour, who bids us remember Him in the breaking of bread (Acts xx. 7), and says, "It is I, Myself" (Luke xxiv. 39), and as we thus consider Him (Heb. iii. 1), our heart's affection will be drawn to Him, even as the needle is attracted to the magnet, and we in turn shall influence others (Song of Solomon i. 4).

III. **The outward look of Hope.** "Till He come" (I. Cor. xi. 26). We are bidden to remember Christ in the simple and yet speaking ordinance of the Lord's Supper. Thus hope goes up the stairs of faith, and looks out of the window which love has opened, and views the coming of the Lord Jesus in His grace and glory (I. Thess. iv. 16, 17; Col. iii. 4; I. John iii. 2).

The whole triangle or trinity of Christ's work is brought before us in the Lord's Supper. What He has done, what He is doing, and what He is yet going to do, are pressed upon our attention as we gather around the Lord and sit with Him at His table. The three appearings of Hebrews ix. 24-28, are thus illustrated in remembering the Lord's death.

417. THE MAN OF FAITH

1. **Testimony of Faith.** "There shall be no loss of any man's life among you" (Acts xxvii. 22).

2. **Fellowship of Faith.** Presence of the Lord. "There stood by me this night the angel of God" (Acts xxvii. 23).

3. **Promise of Faith.** "Fear not, Paul; thou must be brought before Cæsar" (Acts xxvii. 24).

4. **Confidence of Faith.** Power. "I believe God that it shall be" (Acts xxvii. 25).

5. **Rest of Faith.** Peace. "Abide in the ship" (Acts xxvii. 31).

6. **Cheerfulness of Faith.** Praise. "They were all of good cheer" (Acts xxvii. 36).

7. **Reward of Faith.** Preserved. "They escaped all safe to land" (Acts xxvii. 44).

418. "THE MAN OF GOD"

THE title, "the man of God," only occurs twice in the New Testament, but it is of frequent occurrence in the Old Testament. If the following Scriptures are pondered, a few of the many traits which should be seen in the life of a man of God will be discovered, but the principal thought in connection with this title is, a man of God is one who is walking with God, and therefore He can speak to him, and through him to others. A man of God is:—

1. A man of blessing to cheer (Deut. xxxiii. 1).

2. A man of atonement to direct (II. Chron. xxx. 16).

3. A man of messages to speak (Josh. xiv. 6; I. Kings xii. 22; xiii. 1, 4, 5, 6, 7, 8, 11, 12, 14, 21, 26, 29, 31).

4. A man of chastisement to afflict (I. Sam. ii. 27).

5. A man of piety to witness (I. Sam. ix. 6, 7, 8, 10).

6. A man of prayer to influence (I. Kings xvii. 18, 24).

7. A man of encouragement to stimulate (I. Kings xx. 28).

8. A man of power to demonstrate (II. Kings i. 9, 10, 11, 12, 13).

9. A man of sympathy to console (II. Kings iv. 27).

10. A man of humbling to humiliate (II. Kings v. 8-14).

11. A man of warning to guard (II. Kings vi. 10).

12. A man of feeling to commiserate (II. Kings viii. 11).

13. A man of thoroughness to exterminate (II. Kings xiii. 19).

14. A man of prophecy to foretell (II. Kings xxiii. 16, 17).

15. A man of order to arrange (II. Chron. viii. 14).

16. A man of restraint to hinder (II. Chron. xi. 2).

17. A man of praise to worship (Neh. xii. 24, 36).

18. A man of holiness to separate (I. Tim. vi. 11).

19. A man of Scripture to equip (II. Tim. iii. 17).

419. THE MERCY SEAT

CHRIST, as the Propitiation or Mercy Seat, is mentioned in I. John ii. 2. The words mercy seat and atonement come from a root word which means to cover; it is a blessed fact, that not only are our sins forgiven, but we are completely covered by Him who is our Mercy Seat. As illustrating Him, let us look at the mercy seat in the tabernacle.

1. **All-gold mercy seat** (Ex. xxxvii. 6). Reminding us that God, and God alone, is the *Source* and *Dispenser* of mercy, that Christ alone is the *Channel* of mercy, and the Holy Spirit the only One that reveals this fact to us.

2. **Blood-sprinkled mercy seat** (Lev. xvi. 14, 15). On the day of atonement the blood was sprinkled once on, and seven times before the mercy seat. This reminds us of what Christ has done, namely, perfectly met the claims of God, and brought us into a perfect standing before God.

3. **Firmly-secured mercy seat** (Ex. xxxvii. 12). There was a border or crown round about it to keep it in its place. To remove the mercy seat was death (see I. Sam. vi. 19), because the ministration of death (the law) was in the ark, but the border would keep the

mercy seat on the ark, telling us that not only is Christ our Mercy Seat, but the One who maintains His position as such before God for us, because of what He is in Himself—"the righteousness of God." Thus we see in the mercy seat, mercy, and in the border, righteousness, or "mercy and truth met together, righteousness and peace kissing each other."

420. THE MOST COMPREHENSIVE VERSE IN THE BIBLE

"For God so loved the world, that He gave His only begotten Son, that whosoever believeth in Him should not perish, but have everlasting life" (John iii. 16).

Dr. A. T. Pierson calls this verse "the heart of the Gospel." Verily, every word is warm with the life of the love of God, for the blood of His compassion courses through every vein of it. But we have not merely the heart of the Gospel in this verse. We have also the height of the Gospel, for it takes us up to the throne of God, as we muse upon the term "God," from whom all love emanates; and it also carries us on to the far-reaching sea of the eternal blessedness of the redeemed in glory, as we meditate on the words "eternal life."

The comprehensiveness of this verse may be gathered if we carefully and prayerfully ponder each word, for as each leaf of the tree is a *fac-simile* of the tree itself, so each word of this verse portrays the love of God.

1. The **association of love** is found in the conjunction "*for*."

2. The **Embodiment of love** is found in the name "*God*."

3. The **expressiveness of love** is made known in the monosyllable "*so*."

4. The **fact of love** is revealed in the verb "*loved*."

5. The **exclusiveness of love** is proclaimed in the definite article "*the*."

6. The **object of love** is seen in the noun "*world*."

7. The **gift of love** is evidenced in the word "*gave*."

8. The **sacrifice of love** is discovered in the word "*only*."

9. The **becomingness of love** is unfolded in the adjective "*begotten*."

10. The **relationship of love** is made known in the noun "*Son*."

11. The **purpose of love** is seen in the conjunction "*that*."

12. The **offer of love** is made in the relative pronoun "*whosoever*."

13. The **condition of love** is stated in the verb "*believeth*."

14. The **power of love** appears in the words "*in Him*."

15. The **salvation of love** shines forth in the connection with the verb "*perish.*"

16. The **assurance of love** is revealed in the verb "*have.*"

17. The **bestowment of love** is preached in the words "*everlasting life.*"

421. THE NEW BIRTH

The new birth is the door of the Kingdom of God (John iii. 3)

1. **Necessity of the new birth.** "Ye must be born again" (John iii. 7). The "must" tells us of the absolute necessity.

2. **Author of the new birth.** "Of His own will begat He us" (James i. 18). God is the Author of the new creation, as well as of the old.

3. **Procurer of the new birth.** "Whosoever believeth that Jesus is the Christ is born of God" (1. John v. 1). The Christ, who died, is the Procurer of the new life.

4. **Effecter of the new birth.** "Born of the Spirit" (John iii. 6). The Holy Spirit is the Effective Worker in grace.

5. **Instrument of the new birth.** "Being born again, not of corruptible seed, but of incorruptible, by the Word of God" (1. Peter i. 23).

6. **Evidence of the new birth.** (See 1. John ii. 29; iii. 9; iv. 7; v. 1; v. 18, R.V.).

422. THE NEW HOME IN CANAAN

Deut. vi. 3-15

"No place like home!" is a refrain that finds an echo in most hearts. Rest and refreshment, comfort and company, are the characteristics of a true home.

1. **The blessing of home.** The home of the soul is the Lord Himself. When we are right with the Lord it is well with us. Mark the railway that may be made in the Bible in connection with the word "well."

"Well with them" (v. 29).
"Well with you" (v. 33).
"Well with thee" (vi. 3).
"Well with thee" (vi. 18).

See also the forerunners of this wellness—

"Keep" (v. 29).
"Walk" (v. 33).
"Observe" (vi. 3).
"Do" (vi. 18).

The prodigal found all his trouble, want, and misery through getting away from home, and he found all the blessings of home when he came back to his father. The moral is this: if we want the blessings of home, we must keep at home (Psalm xci.).

2. **Provision in the home** (verse 3). The land of Canaan was a land of plenty. As the Lord gave Israel plenty of earthly blessing, so He has given the believer the riches of His grace and glory. We are blest according to the riches of His grace (Eph. i. 7), supplied according to the riches in glory (Phil. iv. 19), strengthened according to the riches of His glory for spiritual life (Eph. iii. 16), and saved according to the riches of His mercy (Eph. ii. 4). Mark the *measure* of the supply, not "*out of*" the riches of the Lord, as is often said, but "*according*" to the riches of His glory.

3. **The head of the home.** "The Lord our God is one Lord" (verse 4). These words denote the Lord's supremacy, sovereignty, and strength, and because He is the one only Jehovah, He, therefore, claims the entire affection of the heart (verse 5). He will not allow any rival. Every Dagon must fall before the ark of His presence (1. Sam. v.), and the glory of every person must fade before the glory of Himself (Matt. xvii. 5-8).

4. **The rules for the home** (verses 6-9). The rules that God gave, were to be in the hearts of the Israelites; as Trapp says, "Bible men should get stamped in their heads and in their hearts, as David did (Psalm cxix. 11). Knowledge that swims in the head only, and sinks not down into the heart, does no more good than rain in the middle region doth, or than the unicorn's horn in the unicorn's head." If the word of the Lord is photographed on the heart, it will give forth its impression in the life.

Note, the *mind* is to *observe* (verse 3), the *heart* is to *treasure up* (verse 6), the *tongue* is to *teach* (verse 7), the *conversation* is to be *saturated* (verse 7), the *walk* is to be *influenced* by (verse 7), the *hand* is to be *guided* (verse 8), the *eyes* are to be *directed* (verse 8), the *house* is to be *identified* with (verse 9), and every *attitude* is to be controlled by (verse 7) the Word of the Lord.

5. **Warning to the members of the home** (verses 10-13). The children of Israel were warned not to "forget" the Lord, and charged to "fear," "serve" and "swear by His name." Trapp quaintly remarks, "Saturity oft breeds security, fulness, forgetfulness. The best, when full fed, are apt to wax wanton, and will be dipping their fingers in the devil's sauce. The moon never suffers eclipse but at the full, and that by the earth's interposition. The young mulets, when they have sucked, turn up their heels and kick at the dam. Should we with the fed hawk forget our Master? Or being full of God's benefits, like the moon, be then most removed from the sun, from whom she hath all her light? (see Prov. xxx. 8, 9). We are no sooner grown rich, but we are apt to utter that ugly word, 'This I may thank myself for.'"

6. **Remaining at home** (verses 14, 15). Israel was not permitted to go after other gods. The Lord was to be their portion. What a portion He is! We cannot be poor when we have Him. We must be poor without Him. What David said to Abiathar, "Abide thou with me, fear not; for he that seeketh my life seeketh thy life; but with me thou shalt be in safeguard" (1. Sam. xxii. 23), the Lord says to us. Let us trust and obey, and all will be well.

423. THE OBSERVANT CHRIST

"He saw"

No needy object escaped the beneficent look of Christ. "He saw" are notes which Holy Spirit plays upon continually, in drawing our attention to the swiftness of Christ's gaze in noting those who were needing His help and His readiness to aid them.

1. **Blessing.** He saw the faith of others, and blessed for their faith's sake (Luke v. 20).

2. **Calling.** He saw one who was willing to serve Him, and called him to follow after Him (Luke v. 27).

3. **Comforting.** He saw a sorrowing one, and comforted her by raising her son from the dead (Luke vii. 13).

4. **Delivering.** He saw one bound by Satan, and delivered her (Luke xiii. 13).

5. **Cleansing.** He saw those who were diseased, and cleansed them (Luke xvii. 14).

6. **Saving.** He saw a seeking one, and saved him (Luke xix. 5).

7. **Rescuing.** He saw those who were distressed, and rescued them (Mark vi. 48).

8. **Revealing.** He saw the blind man, and revealed Himself to him (John ix. 1).

424. THE PASSOVER INSTITUTED

Exodus xii. 1-14

The Lord passes over His people in judgment, but passes through the midst of those who do not belong to Him. This is strikingly illustrated in the two passings mentioned in Exodus xii. We direct attention—

I. **Jehovah passing over His people.** The Hebrew word "Pesak," rendered passover, comes from "Pasak," which means "to leap over," or "to move from one object to another." The noun "Pesak" occurs forty-eight times in the Old Testament, and is always given "passover." The verb "Pasak" is translated "pass over" in Exodus xii. 13, 23, 27, and Isaiah xxxi. 5. The same term occurs in 1. Kings xviii. 26, where the priests of Baal are said to have "leaped upon the altar," or as the Vulgate "leaped over," or as the Septuagint "ran over." The Prophet Elijah uses the same expression in I. Kings xviii. 21, when he says, "How long halt ye between two opinions?" The image is taken from birds hopping backward and forward from one branch of a tree to another. Young brings this out in his translation of the passage. He renders it:—"Till when are ye leaping on the two branches? If Jehovah is God, go after Him; and, if Baal, go after him." The Israelites, in mixing up the worship of Jehovah with that of Baal, were like lame men, who tread not firmly but dubiously.

It is of interest to know that the same term is used in describing the result of the accident which happened to Mephibosheth, who in consequence of the nurse letting him fall, "became lame" (II. Sam. iv. 4). As the priests of Baal went over the altars erected to him; as the Israelites in their sin, sought to identify the worship of Jehovah with the worship of Baal, thus were passing over from the one to the other; and as the lame man passes over the ordinary gait in his walk through his lameness; so Jehovah passed over his people when He was about to deal with the land of Egypt in judgment. The Lord uses the same word in Isaiah xxxi. 5, when He promised to defend Jerusalem from the Assyrians:—"As birds flying, so will the Lord of Hosts defend Jerusalem; defending also He will deliver it; and passing over, He will preserve it."

As an eagle, seeing a bird of prey approaching its young, passes over them to the object of danger, and in meeting and overcoming it preserves its offspring from the peril to which they were exposed; so the Lord passed over the city of Jerusalem to the army of the king of Assyria, that lay encamped against it, and by smiting him and his host, protected the earthly Zion from the destruction which threatened it.

How was it Jehovah passed over the first-born of Israel, seeing that they were mixed up with Egypt's sins and idolatry, and therefore deserved judgment as well as the first-born of Egypt? It was—

For the sake of the Lord Jesus, whose death was prefigured in the slain lamb and sprinkled blood. There can be no question about this in the light of Rom. iii. 24, 25 (R.V.), where it says, "Christ Jesus, whom God set forth to be a propitiation, through faith, by His blood, to shew His righteousness, because of the *passing over of the sins done aforetime*, in the forbearance of God." Mark the words that we have put in italics, for they say in an unmistakable manner that the ground of God's action of grace towards His people in the past, was founded on the death of Christ; as Dr. Brown says, "The sins which are here referred to, are not those of the believer before he embraces Christ, but those committed *under the ancient economy*, before Christ came to "put away sin by the sacrifice of Himself." Hence the apostle, instead of using the common word which signifies *remission*, studiously uses a very different word, nowhere else employed, signifying 'pretermission' or 'passing by'; and hence also this 'passing by' is ascribed to 'the *forbearance* of God,' who is viewed as not so much *remitting*, as *bearing with them*, until an adequate atonement for them should be made."

"In thus not imputing them, God *was* righteous, but He was not *seen* to be so. There was no 'manifestation of His righteousness' in doing so under the ancient economy; but now that God can 'set forth' Christ as a 'propitiation through faith in His blood,' the righteousness of His procedure in passing by the sins of believers before, and in now remitting them, is 'manifested,' declared, brought fully out to the view of the whole world."

The reason why God passes over the believer now is the same as that given to Israel, viz., "When I see the blood, I will pass over you" (Ex. xii. 13). Not when I see your good resolutions, your firm intentions, your earnest prayers, your much almsgiving, your zealous works, your extreme fasting, your penitent tears, your strong faith, but "when I see the blood."

> "It is not our tears of repentance, nor prayers,
> But the blood that atones for the soul."

II. **Passing through the midst of the Egyptians.** "I will pass through the land," &c. (Ex. xii. 12, 23). The expression that relates to the Lord passing through the land of Egypt is different from that which is used of the Lord passing over the Israelites. In the latter case it means a "leaping over," or "flying over from one object to another;" but in the former it signifies "a passing through the midst," as when the burning lamp passed between the pieces of Abram's sacrifice (Gen. xv. 17); or when a traveller passes through a given district. The following instances where the same Hebrew word occurs, which is rendered "pass through" in Ex. xii. 12, 23, will give us to see the above more clearly.

1. Moses and God's glory. "While My glory passeth by" (Exodus xxxiii. 22).

2. Edom and Israel. "Edom refused to give Israel passage" (Numbers xx. 21).

3. God's decree to the sea. "Waters should not pass His commandment" (Proverbs viii. 29).

4. Saul's confession to Samuel. "I have transgressed the commandment" (I. Sam. xv. 24).

5. The Psalmist's iniquities. "Mine iniquities are gone over mine head" (Psalm xxxviii. 4).

6. The frailty of man compared to grass. "The wind passeth over it" (Psalm ciii. 16).

7. Judgment. "The overflowing scourge shall pass through" (Isaiah xxviii. 15).

From the above passages of Scripture it will be gathered that the term under consideration means "to pass over the face of an object," as when the Psalmist says his iniquities have gone over him, as a wave that submerges the swimmer, or as when the Psalmist uses the figure of the wind passing over the grass and withering it. The word also signifies "to pass alongside," as when the Lord passed by Moses, and enabled him to behold His goodness. Yet, again, the expression is expressive of "passing through," as when Edom would not allow Israel passage through their country; or as when one passes through a command by going beyond its prescribed boundary; or as when an overwhelming scourge causes the inhabitants of a certain place to be destroyed because they are in the way of its onward rush. Parkhurst, in his Hebrew Lexicon, gives the following illustrations of the appellation:—

"A ferry-boat, for passing over a river" (II. Sam. xix. 18).

"A pass or passage" (I. Sam. xiv. 4).

"In Gen. x. 21, Shem, the progenitor of the holy line, is styled the father of all the children (not of Eber, his great grandson, for how was he more the father of him than of his other descendants? but) of passage or pilgrimage. The father of all those who were passengers, pilgrims, itinerants, passing from one place to another, as the holy line were, till their settlement in Canaan, and who also confessed themselves to be strangers and pilgrims on earth, plainly declaring thereby that they sought a better country. Of Abraham in particular it is written that he passed through the land (Gen. xii. 6), and during his pilgrimage from one place to another in the land of promise, wherein he sojourned as in a strange country, the epithet a pilgrim or stranger is used.

425. TOUCH OF THE LORD

THE touch of the Lord signifies His power (Daniel viii. 18; Amos ix. 5; Matthew viii. 3).

1. **Subjugation.** The touched *thigh* signifies His power to subdue (Gen. xxxii. 25).

2. **Purification.** The touched *lips* denote His power to cleanse (Isaiah vi. 7).

3. **Inspiration.** The touched *mouth* refers to His power to enable to speak (Jeremiah i. 9).

4. **Illumination.** The touched *eyes* signify His power to give sight (Matthew ix. 29).

5. **Impartation.** The touched *ear* points to His power to cause to hear (Mark vii. 33).

6. **Liberation.** The touched *tongue* indicates His ability to unloose the powers of speech (Mark vii. 33).

7. **Compassion.** The touched *hand* illustrates His power to raise for His service (Matt. viii. 15).

8. **Attraction.** The touched *heart* shows His power to mould the wills of men in causing them to follow His word and to fulfil His pleasure (1. Sam. x. 26).

God-touched hearts are sympathetic hearts to succour, steadfast hearts to influence, sure hearts to comfort, strong hearts to sustain, stalwart hearts to encourage, staunch hearts to endure, and sincere hearts to follow.

426. THE PASSAGE OF THE RED SEA

EXODUS xiv. 19-29

WE have a striking illustration in the children of Israel at the Red Sea, of what it means for the Lord to be *for* us or to be *against* us.

Israel was for God in obeying His word in relation to the Pascal lamb and Passover feast, hence the Lord is for them in protecting them in the moment of their peril. If we side with God, God is on our side.

1. **The Lord for us means that He is between us and every foe.** The "angel of God" removed from the front of the camp to the rear, and thus was between Israel and the Egyptians (verse 19). "A tradition current in the West of Scotland, tells that when one of the Covenanting preachers and his little band of hearers had been suprised on a hillside by the military, the minister cried out, 'Lord, throw Thy mantle over us and protect us.' And immediately out of the clear sky there fell a mist, which sundered and protected the pursued from the pursuers. And a Netherland tradition tells how a little army of Protestants were once saved from the King of Spain's troops by the flashing lights and noise as of an army sent by the Lord to throw confusion into the camp of the enemy. Some will remember the story of the Christian woman who, calmly awaiting in her home the approach of the enemy, was, in answer to her prayer, saved from them by a circling wall of snow. The dividing pillar is a reality yet."

When the Lord is between us and the foe, or any danger, they must touch Him before they can touch us, for "the Angel of the Lord encampeth round about them that fear Him, and delivereth them"(Psalm xxxiv. 7).

2. **The Lord for us means that we have light.** The pillar of cloud gave light to Israel at night (verse 20). As when Israel was in Goshen there was light in their dwellings when there was darkness over the land of Egypt for three days, so that the Egyptians did not rise from their places, nor saw each other; so there is light from the pillar of cloud for Israel's comfort and guidance when before the Red Sea. Those who are not the Lord's are in darkness (Isaiah lx. 2), but those who are the Lord's are called out of darkness into light, that is, from a state of sin, ignorance,

and unbelief, into a state of knowledge, faith, and holiness (I. Peter ii. 9), and are also said to be "light in the Lord" (Eph.v. 8).

3. **The Lord for us means that we have an opening through a seemingly impassable sea of difficulties.** There was no prospect, humanly speaking, for Israel to escape from the Egyptians. The mountains on either side of them, the enemy in the rear, and the sea in front, but the Lord "maketh a way in the sea" (Isaiah xliii. 16). The Lord bids His children to "go forward" into the *sea of difficulty* counting upon His guidance, into the *sea of sorrow* receiving His comfort, into the *sea of trial* leaning on His strength, into the *sea of life* trusting in Himself, into the *sea of the world* abiding in His presence, into the *sea of conflict* armed in His armour, and into the *sea of labour* looking to Him to supply all the need.

4. **The Lord for us means deliverance from the enemy.** How repeatedly we find the Lord to the front in the verses before us.

Presence—"The angel of God" (verse 19).

Power—"The Lord caused" (verse 21).

Penetration—"The Lord looked" (verse 24).

Protection—"The Lord fighteth" (verse 25).

Direction—"The Lord said" (verse 26).

Punishment—"The Lord overthrew" (verse 27).

There can be no defeat when God is warring. When any one opposes God, it is like the birds who dash against the lighthouse window as they are attracted by the light, but they do it to their own dismay and destruction.

In contrast to all that God was for Israel, and did for them, we behold in His action towards Egypt what it means for God to be against any one. It means the very antithesis of God for us. Hebrews xi. 29 gives us the reason why God was for the one and not for the other as viewed from the human standpoint. The one had faith, the other had not.

427. THE PRINCE OF PEACE

ISAIAH ix. 2-7

THE following acrostic on the title "Prince," illustrates what kind of a Prince, Christ is.

P Powerful Prince. He is "the Mighty God" (verse 6). He is mighty in many ways. His mighty acts declare His power. He is mighty to *save* (Psalm lxxxix. 19); He is mighty to *deliver* (Deut. vi. 21; vii. 8, 19); He is mighty to *conquer* (Josh. iv. 24; II. Cor. x. 4); He is mighty to *strengthen* (Gen. xlix. 24); He is mighty to use in His *service* (Col. i. 29); He is mighty in *word* (Luke xxiv. 19); and He is mighty in *work* (Mark vi. 2).

R Royal Prince. Some men have occupied princely places who have not a royal pedigree. Not so with Christ, for He is the "Son" (verse 6). His royalty is of heavenly origin, for He is the Son of God; and He is of the royal line of David, and as such will sit upon the "throne of David" (verse 7), in the time to come. Christ is royal in every sense of the word. He is royal in birth, royal in giving, royal in love, royal in grace, royal in truth, royal in action, and royal in utterance.

I Incarnate Prince. He who was the Son of God became the Son of Man that He might make the sons of men, who believe in Him, sons of God; hence we read, "Unto us a Child is born." By His birth He became our Kinsman (Heb. ii. 14), that He might have the right to redeem us. The action of Christ as the Saviour is a trinity, as seen in His incarnation, crucifixion, and resurrection. These must never be separated, for the one is essential to the other to complete the triangle of Christ's complete redemptive work as far as it relates to His atonement.

N Noble Prince. He is "Wonderful," and "Counsellor." Christ is noble in His wonderful love. David said of Jonathan's love that it surpassed the love of women (II. Sam. i. 26). We must say of Christ's love that it surpasses all other love. It is a height without a top, a depth without a bottom, a length without a measure, and a breadth without a calculation. Christ is noble in His comprehensive counsel. The Septuagint renders "Counsellor" "Messenger of great counsel." "Who teacheth like Him?" None. He eclipses all others. "Never man spake like this Man" (John vii. 46).

C Conquering Prince (verse 4). Christ is the mighty Man of valour. He goes forth conquering and to conquer. He overcomes the strong man armed (Luke xi. 22), and strips the powers of darkness (Col. ii. 15). He is the Angel that will cast Satan into the bottomless pit and set a seal upon him (Rev. xx. 1-3). He leads forth His armies and gains the victory (Rev. xix. 11-15); and as we have faith in Him we, too, overcome by His power (I. John v. 4).

E Eternal Prince (verses 6, 7). He is the "Everlasting Father," and the One of the increase of whose government there shall be "no end"; yea, "for ever" shall His righteous rule be prolonged. Unlike earthly monarchs, who come and go, this One shall remain, for His kingdom is spoken of as "the everlasting kingdom of our Lord and Saviour Jesus Christ" (II. Peter i. 11).

428. THE REPORT OF THE SPIES

NUMBERS xiii. 17-20, 23-33

THERE are certain words and expressions we may take as hubs around which the spokes of thought are found.

1. **The "Get you up" of commission** (verse 17). Moses bids the spies go search the land and see what kind of a land it was, and

what kind of inhabitants dwelt in it. It is well to know the strength and character of the enemy we have to conquer. As with Israel, so with us, when the Lord bids us to go in a given direction, it matters not how great the difficulties, or how formidable the foe, we shall have grace to surmount the one and to overcome the other. With every "*Go*" of command, He gives us the "*Lo*" of His presence (Matthew xxviii. 19, 20).

2. **The "be ye of good courage" of fortitude** (ver. 20). True courage is the outcome of the fear of God. He who fears God need fear no foe. He who has looked into the face of God can look into the face of any man. True courage has consistency as its forerunner (Joshua i. 6, 7). Ken says,

> "Stand but your ground, your ghostly foes will fly—
> Hell trembles at a heaven-directed eye ;
> Choose rather to defend than to assail—
> Self-confidence will in the conflict fail :
> When you are challenged, you may dangers meet—
> True courage is a fixed, not sudden heat ;
> Is always humble, lives in self-distrust,
> And will itself into no danger thrust.
> Devote yourself to God, and you will find
> God fights the battles of a will resign'd.
> Love Jesus ! love will no base fear endure ;
> Love Jesus ! and of conquest rest secure."

3. **The "nevertheless" of unbelief** (verse 28). Unbelief always magnifies difficulties and makes them far larger than they are. "There is always a 'nevertheless' where man is concerned, and when unbelief is at work. The unbelieving spies *saw* the difficulties—great cities, high walls, tall giants. All these things they saw ; but they did not see Jehovah at all. They looked at the things that were seen, rather than at the things which were unseen. Their eye was not fixed upon Him who is invisible. Doubtless, the cities were great ; but God was greater. The walls were high ; but God was higher. The giants were strong ; but God was stronger."

4. **The "well able" of faith** (verse 30). The man of faith who looks to God, and remembers what He is able to do, exclaims, "We are well able to overcome." C. H. M. well remarks, "Faith looks the difficulties straight in the face. It is not ignorant — not indifferent—not reckless ; but—what ! IT BRINGS IN THE LIVING GOD. It looks to Him ; it leans on Him ; it draws from Him. Here lies the grand secret of its power. It cherishes the calm and deep conviction that there never was a wall too high for the Almighty God—never a city too great—never a giant too strong. Faith is the only thing that puts God in His proper place ; and, as a consequence, is the only thing that lifts the soul completely above the influences of surrounding circumstances, be they what they may."

5. **The "not able" of despair** (verse 31). What a contrast this to the "well able" of Caleb ! "Stronger than we" is the

exclamation of despair, as the enemy is compared with the self-occupied ones; but surely the foe is not stronger than *He!* Ah! It makes all the difference whether it be "*He*" or "*We*." There is only the difference of one letter, but to take away the "*W*" and put "*H*" in its place, means the displacement of self, and the destruction of despair. If the warfare depends upon us there will be defeat, but since it depends upon the Lord there must be victory, if we trust Him. Despair is born of self-occupation and through viewing self's resources. There is only one way to get rid of self, and that is, to put Him in front of it, then self reads Himself. Or to put it in another way, the way to displace I is to put Chr in front of it and st behind it, then I is lost in Christ—

CHR-I-ST (Gal ii. 20).

6. **The "evil report" of half-heartedness** (verse 32). Half-heartedness is a worm that will kill any plant of grace. The reason why so many fail is, because there is a lack of thoroughness. Half-heartedness is the forerunner of defeat. Half-heartedness magnifies difficulties, hesitates in danger, discourages timid ones, breeds unbelief, lacks back-bone, cripples devotion, and thinks much of itself.

7. **The "we saw" of short-sightedness** (verse 33). The evil-reporters saw the great ones of earth, but they did not see the Great One of heaven. If they had looked at the great ones from God's point of view, they would have seen that they were but as "grasshoppers" in His sight (Isaiah xl. 22). Instead of this, the spies say that they are "as grasshoppers." If we look at difficulties and dangers through the medium of earth's spectacles we shall be discouraged, and a discouraged man is a defeated one; but if we stand on the mountain top of fellowship with God, earth's great ones will be pigmies.

429. THE RICH YOUNG RULER

MARK x. 17-27

LUKE tells us that the rich young ruler only lacked one thing (Luke xviii. 22), but that was a fatal defect. For a chain to lack one sound link means the danger of that which it upholds.

1. **What the rich young ruler wanted.** "Eternal life" (verse 17). Eternal life is the life which is the "life indeed" (1. Tim. vi. 19, R.V.). What it means to want this life may be gathered by noting what it is. Eternal life—

God is its Source (John v. 26).
The Risen Christ is its Channel (Hebrews vii. 16).
The Holy Spirit is its Power (Rom. viii. 2).
Faith is its Receiver (John iii. 36).
Fruit is its Evidence (Rom. vi. 22).

Christ Himself is its Embodiment (I. John v. 20).
Glory is its Manifestation (Col. iii. 4).
Eternity is its Duration (John x. 28).
Union with Christ is its Meaning (John vi. 53, 54).

Knowing God and Christ as the Sent One is its Explanation (John xvii. 3).

The one mistake the young ruler made, was that he wanted to earn this life by his doing. "What must I *do* to enherit eternal life?" is his cry. No man's doing can give Him the right to this blessing, for eternal life is the gift of God (Rom. vi. 23).

2. **What the young ruler had done.** According to the ruler's statement, he had a good record behind him (verses 19, 20). But man's estimate of the worth of his actions, and God's are two different things. God weighs man's actions in the scales of the sanctuary, and the verdict of every doing of man is "come short" (Rom. iii. 23). If there are none that doeth good (Rom. iii. 12), how can any do good in the truest sense of the word? Yea, Christ Himself said to this young man, "There is none good, but One, that is God" (verse 18). See the "*Alls*," the "*Nones*," the "*Not ones*" of Romans iii. 9-23, as to the universality of human depravity. There are degrees in sinning, but there is no degree in that all are tainted by sin. No difference as to what we *are*, there is a difference as to what we have *done*. There may be six crab apple trees in a wood, which are very different as to the apples they bear with regard to the quantity, but there is no difference as to the fact that they are all crab apple trees; so with us, there is no difference as to the fact that all are sinners, but there is a great difference as to the fruit of sin in the lives.

3. **What the young ruler would not do.** Christ told the ruler to do five things, which are associated with the five following words:—"Sell," "give," "come," "take," "follow." He was to sell what he had, give it to the poor, come to Christ, take up his cross and follow Christ. The ruler did not stand the test, for he went away sorrowful. The one great lesson in the incident is, that if anything is a hindrance to coming to Christ and following Him, it must be given up. It matters not how dear it is; if it is some earthly friend, better to separate from him than be separated from Christ (Luke xiv. 26), if it be a member of the body that is a stumbling-block, better for it to be cut off (Matt. v. 29, 30), than to be cut off from the Lord of Life and Glory.

Thank God, it is easy to be saved, because Christ by His death has removed the hindrance (Heb. ix. 26), but it is not an easy thing to live as a Christian (I. Peter iv. 18). There is a battle to be fought (I. Tim. vi. 12), a trust to be kept (II. Cor. v. 18), a talent to be used (Matt. xxv. 14, &c.), an enemy to overcome (I. Peter v. 8, 9), a watch to maintain (Mark xiii. 37), a ministry to fulfil (John xiii. 14), and a prize to win (Phil. iii. 14).

430. THE SECRET OF VICTORY

II. CHRONICLES XX

THEY who side with God are always sure of having the Lord on their side. See the case of the Levites in Exodus xxxii. 26.

1. **Seeking** the Lord is the forerunner of victory (verse 3).
2. **Praying** to the Lord is the plea for victory (verse 12).
3. **Dependence** upon the Lord is the attitude for victory (verse 4).
4. **Recognising** that the battle is the Lord's is an essential in victory (verses 15-17).
5. **Worshipping** before the Lord is praising the Victor (verses 18, 19).
6. **Faith** in the Lord is assurance for victory (verse 20).
7. **Gladness** in the Lord is the result of victory (verse 27).
8. **Rest** in the Lord is another outcome of victory (verse 30).

431. THE SON OF GOD

THE Son of God, in the First Epistle of John. Twenty-four times in this Epistle is He said to be the Son of God.

1. **What did God send His Son to be and do?**

That we might live (iv. 9).

To be a Saviour (iv. 14).

To be a Propitiation (iv. 10).

To destroy the works of the devil (iii. 8).

2. **The result of believing in Him as the Son of God**

We have eternal life (v. 12).

We know it (v. 13).

We have the witness (v. 10).

We are in Him (v. 20).

We know He has come (v. 20).

God dwelleth in us (iv. 15).

We have the Father and Son (II. John 9).

3. **The proof that we believe in Him as the Son of God.**

Believe on His Name (ii. 23; and v. 13).

Acknowledge Him as the Son (ii. 23).

Confess Him as the Son of God (iv. 15).

Have fellowship with Him (i. 3).

Continue in Him (ii. 24).

That we know His blood cleanseth us from all sin (i. 7).

Overcome the world (v. 5).

4. **Those who disbelieve that He is the Son of God,**

Make God a liar (v. 10).

Have not eternal life (v. 12).

432. THE TEMPTER

GENESIS iii

THE tempter used the serpent to tempt Eve, just as he used Judas to betray Christ.

1. **The tempter is subtle.** Thomas Watson says: "Satan did not break over the hedge where it was weakest; he knew he could more easily insinuate and wind himself about her by a temptation. An expert soldier, when he is to storm or enter a castle, observes warily where there is a breach, or how he may enter with more facility; so did Satan tempt the weaker vessel."

2. **The tempter questioning.** "Hath God said, &c.?" Bunyan, in his *Holy War*, speaks of one "Mr. Evil-questioning," who was a Diabalonian, and an enemy of Man-soul. This man went by another name, viz., "Honest-inquiry," but for all that, he was condemned and put to death. As the bait covers the hook, so the questions of Satan and his instruments hide the hook of doubt in the bait of questioning.

3. **The tempter lying.** Said a quaint New England preacher, "Beware of Bible commentators who are not willing to take God's words just as they stand. The first commentator of that sort was the devil in the Garden of Eden. He proposed only a slight change, just the one word 'not' to be inserted—'Ye shall not surely die.' The amendment was accepted, and the world was lost. Satan is repeating that sort of commentary with every generation of hearers."

4. **The tempter deceiving.** "Ye shall be as gods," but Satan only presents one side. "Martha Browning, a young woman, aged 24, was executed many years ago for murder. The fatal deed was committed to obtain possession of a £5 note, but when the tempting bait was at last really possessed, it proved not a note of the Bank of England, but a flash note of the Bank of Elegance!"

5. **The tempter cursed** (verse 14). God will not allow sin to go unpunished, either in the instrument or the one who uses the instrument. The serpent crawls along on its belly, and dust is to be its meat (Isaiah lxv. 25; Micah vii. 17); and that old serpent the devil is thrust into the abyss during the Millenium (Rev. xx. 2, R.V.), and ultimately into the lake of fire (Rev. xx. 10).

6. **The tempter hurting.** "Thou shalt bruise His heel." By these words we are told that Satan would injure Christ in some way. We know how effectually he succeeded in getting Christ to be crucified as a malefactor. The reviling, the suffering, the false

accusation, and His being esteemed smitten of God and afflicted, tell out the malice of the enemy.

7. **The tempter conquered.** "*He* (not *It*) shall bruise (crush) thy head." Christ is the Seed of the woman (Gal. iv. 4). Christ is the Stronger Man, who has overcome the strong one (Luke xi. 21, 22). Christ has been the death of death by His death (Heb. ii. 14); He has spoiled (stripped) all the hosts of hell (Col. ii. 15), and undone the whole kingdom of Satan (1. John iii. 8) for those who believe in Christ.

433. THE TEMPTATION OF JESUS

MATTHEW iv. 1-11

AFTER a time of blessing there comes a time of trial. It was after Israel had come out of Egypt that they were met by Amalek (Exodus xvii. 8). It is the same in Christian experience. When one has decided for Christ, then begins the conflict with Satan. As long as we are his, he leaves us alone, but as soon as we side with Christ, then he opposes us all he can. Bunyan pictures this in Pilgrim's Progress. As long as Christian is in the world he is unmolested, but as soon as he seeks to enter the wicket-gate then the arrows of the enemy are shot at him.

The temptation of Christ is threefold, and corresponds to the tempter's tactics with Eve in the garden of Eden.

1. The first temptation relates to **Christ's person.** Satan would get Christ to use His deity, to meet the need of His humanity. Satan had heard the voice from heaven acknowledging Christ as the Son of God, and now he says, "Being *the Son of God, it is an easy matter for You to make the stones into bread to meet Your hunger." But if Christ had done so at the suggestion of Satan, it would have been distrust of God. Christ meets the enemy with the tried and true blade of the sword of God's Word, and thus discomforts and defeats him. Satan cannot stand before the "It is written," for that is a weapon which cuts through the toughest part of his armour.

2. The second temptation relates to **Christ's work.** Christ came to lay the foundation of a kingdom that should stand the test and stress of any power that might be brought against it. The first Adam lost his position and power by sin. The last Adam had come to gain them back again by His devotion to the Father's will, in an obedience to the death of the cross. And as a result of that obedience, the Father would make the kingdoms of this world to be Christ's in crowning Him King of kings, and Lord of lords (Rev. xi. 15; xix. 16). Satan offers to Christ without the cross the

* The words "If Thou art the Son of God," express something very different from a doubt; this "*If*" has almost the force of "*Since*." "If Thou art really as it seems," &c. Satan alludes to God's salutation at the baptism.—*Godet.*

kingdoms of the world,* but Christ scorns his offer, and meets him again with the keen sharp weapon of God's truth.

3. The third temptation relates to **Christ's trust in God.** Satan takes our Lord and places Him upon a pinnacle of the Temple, and urges Him to cast Himself down, upon the plea that God will preserve Him from danger; but for Christ to do as He was bid, would be for Him to presume upon God's mercy. As Godet says, "Satan seems to say, 'If Thou art a being to whom it appertains to call God Thy Father in an unique sense, do not fear to do a daring deed, and give God an opportunity to show the particular care He takes of Thee.'"

. . . . "This is very subtle—what was the real bearing of this temptation? With God, power is always employed in the service of goodness, of love; this is the difference between God and Satan, between divine miracle and diabolical sorcery. Now the devil, in this instance, aims at nothing less than making Jesus pass from one of these spheres to the other, and this in the name of that most sacred and tender element in the relationship between two beings that love each other—confidence. If Jesus succumbs to the temptation by calling on the Almighty to deliver Him from a peril into which He has not been thrown in the service of goodness, He puts God in the position of either refusing His aid, and so separating Christ's cause from His own—a divorce between the Father and the Son—or of setting free the exercise of His omnipotence, at least for a moment, from the control of holiness—a violation of His own nature. Either way, it would be all over with Jesus, and, even, if we dare so speak, with God."

It is of interest to note that Christ quotes from the Book of Deuteronomy each time He appeals to Scripture (Deut. viii. 3; vi. 13; vi. 16). "This book, which recorded the experience of Israel during the forty years' sojourn in the desert, had perhaps been the special subject of Jesus' meditations during His own sojourn in the wilderness."

Gurnall well says, in speaking of the believer, like Christ, meeting the suggestions of the evil one with the Scriptures, "Provide thyself with Scripture answers to Satan's false reasonings, with which he puts a fair colour on his foul notions, the better to gain thy consent. He is wily; thou hadst need to be wary. He not only propounds the sinful object, but sets a fair gloss upon it, and urges the soul with arguments to embrace his offer. And when sin comes thus forth Goliath-like, it is not Saul's armour, but the smooth stones of the brook—not thy own resolution, but the divinity of Scripture argument that can preserve thee, or prostrate thy enemy. Now,

* This is no idle offer. Billy Bray used to say of this offer of Satan, "The old rascal, to offer Christ the kingdoms of the world, why he never possessed so much as a tater skin." But B. B. was wrong, for Satan is called "The prince of this world" (John xii. 31); "the god of this world" (II. Cor. iv. 4); "the prince of the power of the air" (Eph. ii. 2). And these are not meaningless and empty titles, but designations of his power and place.

thou wilt find in the Word an answer put into thy mouth to repel all Satan's sophistry. And this indeed, is to be an Apollos, mighty in the Scriptures, when we can stop the devil's mouth, and choke his bullets, with a word seasonably interposed between us and the temptation."

434. THE FIRST DISCIPLES OF JESUS

JOHN i. 35-51

As the sea is deeper the farther one advances into it, so the experience of the disciples of Christ deepens as it goes on.

1. **Looking to Jesus** (verse 36). The message of John the Baptist is, "Behold the Lamb of God." We must not forget that John had already spoken of Christ to his disciples as the Sin-Bearer (verse 29), and as the Baptizer with the Holy Spirit (verse 33). John seems to say to his followers, "I pointed you to Jesus as the Lamb of God, and as the Baptizer with the Holy Spirit yesterday, and now to-day I direct your attention to the Person of Jesus as your Example in the character of the Lamb of God. See His lowly attitude, mark His loving manner, ponder His compassionate actions, note His spotless character, meditate upon His gentle love, muse upon His righteous life, behold His lovely Person, and imitate Him, and thus follow Him. But remember, that you must first have looked to Him as the One who has removed your sins from your conscience, on the ground of His sacrificial death, and have received from Him the Baptism of the Holy Spirit, before you will have power to follow Him. And remember, all this comes by beholding Him. Gaze upon Him till you become like Him, even as the flowers reflect the glory of the sun, being beautified by the colours that they draw from it, through their being in it, and looking towards it."

The beholding that John enjoins upon his disciples is no passing glance, but as Godet says, "The word indicates a penetrating look which searches its object to its depths."

2. **Following after Jesus** (verse 37). In the disciples of John following Jesus, we have an illustration of what follows looking to Him. They who look to Christ place themselves under the charm of His personal power, and are drawn after Him, even as the needle will fly to the load-stone the moment it comes under its influence.

To follow Christ means the denial of self, and cross bearing. It is reported of Agrippina, the mother of Nero, on being told "that if ever her son came to be an emperor he would be her murderer," she made the reply, "I am content to perish, if he may be Emperor." What she said vain-gloriously, we should be willing to say and do in following Christ—Perish the self-life, so long as Christ is Lord of our life, and the inspiration of our actions.

3. **Abiding with Jesus** (verse 39). Abiding with Christ is the result of following Him. To abide with Christ means to live in the consciousness of His presence, and to have fellowship with Him. We little know how much the desciples learnt during their stay with Jesus, but it must have been very precious, for "all the sweetness of a recollection was still living in the heart of the evangelist at the moment of his writing." They who abide with Christ are sure to receive some hallowed revelation from Him, as the two disciples found, who were journeying to Emmaus, when in answer to their prayer "Abide with us," He went in to abide with them (Luke xxiv. 29, R.V.), and while in the house, at the evening meal, He made Himself known to them as He broke the bread and blessed it (Luke xxiv. 30-32).

4. **Testimony for Jesus** (verses 41-45). Both Andrew and Philip bear testimony to having found the Christ, and invite Peter and Nathaniel to the One they have found. We little know the power of individual effort. Andrew brought Peter to Jesus, and Peter was used in one day in bringing 3,000 to Christ. Let the following table speak for itself. If one hundred believers were each to bring one soul to Christ in the course of a year, and each one brought to Christ was to bring one other to Him in the course of a year, how many would be converted in the course of twenty-five years?

First year, 100.	Thirteenth year, 409,600.
Second year, 200.	Fourteenth year, 819,200.
Third year, 400.	Fifteenth year, 1,638,400.
Fourth year, 800.	Sixteenth year, 3,276,800.
Fifth year, 1,600.	Seventeenth year, 6,553,600.
Sixth year, 3,200.	Eighteenth year, 13,107,200.
Seventh year, 6,400.	Nineteenth year, 26,214,400.
Eighth year, 12,800.	Twentieth year, 52,428,800.
Ninth year, 25,600.	Twenty-first year, 104,857,600.
Tenth year, 51,200.	Twenty-second year, 209,715,200.
Eleventh year, 102,400.	Twenty-third year, 419,430,400.
Twelfth year, 204,800.	Twenty-fourth year, 838,860,800.

Twenty-fifth year, 1,677,721,600.

435. THE TEMPTATION OF JESUS

MATTHEW iv. 1-11

THE four "Thens" may be said to be like the four points of a compass.

1. **The "then" of the Spirit's leading.** "*Then* was Jesus led of the Spirit into the wilderness to be tempted of the devil"

(verse 1). It was after the blessing that Christ received from His Father that He received this buffeting from the devil.

But, mark, the Saviour was led by the Holy Spirit to be tempted of the devil. God can make the devil to be a means of grace to us. As Trapp says: "The better to fit Him thereby for His ministry. Luther observed of himself, that when God was about to set him upon any special service, He either laid some fit of sickness upon him beforehand, or turned Satan loose upon him, who so buffeted him by his temptations, that neither heat, nor blood, nor sense, nor voice remained; the very venom of the temptations drank up his spirit, and his body seemed dead. Hence it was that in his sermons God gave him such grace that when he preached they that heard him thought his own temptation enabled them to be severally touched and noted."

2. **The "then" of Satan's power.** "*Then* the devil taketh Him up into the holy city, and setteth Him on a pinnacle of the Temple" (verse 5). This is no mere figure of speech, but an actual reality, and goes to show in some measure the power that Satan has. One has only to call to mind the names and titles that are applied to him in Scripture, to understand the great power he has. Christ found the adversary no mean enemy with which to contend, neither shall we. Men often speak of Satan in contemptuous tones, but we should be careful lest we underrate his power, and thus give him an advantage over us. If he had the power to place Christ in a high place, and to tell Him to cast Himself down, and thus to presume upon His Father's care, shall we say that he has less power with us? But mark, he has no power to cast us down; he can only suggest, as in the case of Christ. Matthew Henry says: "High places are slippery places; advancement in the world makes a man a fair mark for Satan to shoot his fiery darts at. God casts down, that He may raise up; the devil raiseth up that he may cast down: therefore, those that would take heed of falling, must take heed of climbing." Satan only elevates that he may destroy. On the rocky shore of Cornwall may be seen the black cormorant seizing its prey, a shell-fish, flying up with it into the air, and then letting it fall upon some rock, that the shell may be broken in pieces. Satan's temptations are all on this principle.

3. **The "then" of the Saviour's answer.** "*Then* saith Jesus unto him, Get thee hence, Satan: for it is written," &c. (verse 10). Christ meets the temptation of the adversary each time by the sword of the Spirit. Trapp remarks: "This two-edged sword our Saviour had found to be metal of proof, and therefore holds him to it. Only the Scriptures scare the devil, as only faithful prayer can charm him (Isaiah xxvi. 16). Prayer is called a charm. Athanasius writeth that evil spirits may be put to flight by that Psalm (lxviii.), 'Let the Lord arise, and His enemies be confounded.' But this is true of the whole Word of God, which is armour of proof against the devil."

We read that Oliver Cromwell had in his army one regiment—a fine, strong regiment—called "The Ironsides." They were very religious men, and it was quite the custom for almost every soldier to carry his Bible to battle with him. They used to carry their Bible under their dress, and more than once, in a battle, the soldier would have been shot through the heart but for his Bible. The bullet went through the Bible, or it would have gone through the soldier's heart. The Bible saved the heart. Even so with the Truth of God. It is the *armour* to protect from the fiery darts of the evil one; it is the *sickle* to cut down the tares that the enemy sows among the wheat of God's truth; it is the *trumpet* to cause the walls of evil to fall before it, as the walls of Jericho fell before the blast of Israel's rams' horns; it is the *ark* to cause the dagon of iniquity to bow before it, and to topple to the ground; it is the *rapier* to pierce through the enemy's armour; it is the *stone* to cause the Goliath of hell to fall to the ground; and it is the *sword* to cut through the devil's devices.

4. **The "then" of the serpent's departure.** "*Then* the devil leaveth Him," &c. Foiled at every point by the Lord, Satan retreats like a whipped cur. Trapp says: "If Christ command him away, there is no abiding for him. Here he was foiled and quelled, and, as it were, cast down and killed, by Christ our Champion. He came into the field like another Goliath, cracking and calling craven, but ere he went thence was made to hop headless, as he first was a terror, afterwards a scorn, as it was anciently said of those chariots armed with scythes and hooks. Charles VIII., in his expedition against Naples, came into the field like thunder and lightning, but went out like a snuff, more than a man at first, less than a woman at last. Henceforth, therefore, though we are ever to expect temptations till such time as we have gotten that great gulf between the devil and us, yet fear none of those things that ye shall suffer."

436. THE THIRST OF CHRIST

"I THIRST."

1. **He thirsts for admittance.** "Behold, I stand at the door, and knock" (Rev. iii. 20; Solomon's Song v. 2).

2. **He thirsts for holiness.** "Bring no more vain oblations," &c. (Isaiah i. 13-15).

3. **He thirsts for love.** "And anointed the feet of Jesus" (John xii. 3).

4. **He thirsts for prayer.** "Let Me hear thy voice" (S.S. ii. 14).

5. **He thirsts for listeners.** "Mary, which also sat at Jesus' feet, and heard His word" (Luke x. 39).

6. **He thirsts for workers.** "Who will go for Us" (Isa. vi. 8).

7. **He thirsts for aid.** "Thirsty, and ye gave Me no drink" (Matt. xxv. 42; Judges xv. 18, 19).

437. THE THORNY GROUND HEARER

THERE are four ugly thorns that are mentioned in the different accounts of the thorny ground hearer, any one of which would kill the good seed of the Word, and these are "Cares," "Riches," "Lusts," and "Pleasures."

1. **Cares** (Luke viii. 14; Mark iv. 19; Matt. xiii. 22). The Lord Jesus knew the engrossing and enslaving character of care, hence the repeated injunction which He gave in that memorable sermon of His, when He said, "Be not anxious for your life," &c. (see Revised Version of Matt. vi. 25, 27, 28, 31, 34). When the mind is divided and distracted by anxiety, the attention is diverted from eternal realities. Anxiety is like a parasite which clings round a tree and destroys it, as when the ivy entwines itself round a young oak and eats all its life away by living upon it.

2. **Riches** (Luke viii. 14; Mark iv. 19; Matt. xiii. 22). Riches in themselves are not an evil, when they are regarded as the godly merchant looked upon them. He said that he was "handling trust funds." The evil is, when money is loved (1. Tim. vi. 10), when we make "uncertain riches" (1. Tim. vi. 17) the object of our trust instead of the Living God, and when they are a hindrance to following Christ, as in the case of the young ruler (Luke xviii. 23, 24). "Riches are like thorns; they may be touched, but not rested upon. Canst thou set thy heart upon a thorn without piercing thyself through with many sorrows?" There is a story in Greek mythology which tells of one who lost the race because she stopped to pick up the gold which was thrown in her way. Ambrose says, "In gold there is a halter; in silver there is bird-lime; in the farm there is a bond; in the love of the world there is a chain; while we search for gold we are strangled; while for silver we stick fast; while we seize upon the farm we are taken prisoners."

3. **Lust.** "Lust of other things" (Mark iv. 19). We need to remember that the word "lust" does not mean merely, that which is associated with uncleanness. Our word "desire" is more comprehensive, and is the thought that is signified here. To desire that which God forbids is sin (Gen. iii. 6).

4. **Pleasures** (Luke viii. 14). It is related of Robert Burns that he was once under serious impression. He had times of serious reflection, as recorded by his own pen. He beautifully describes himself in the review of his past life as a lonely man walking amid the ruins of a noble temple, where pillars stand dismantled of their capitals, and elaborate works of purest marble lie on the ground overgrown by tall, foul, rank weeds. As Burns thought how this illustrated his own case he was filled with great alarm. The seed of the Word had begun to grow. He sought counsel from one called a minister of the Gospel. Alas, that in that crisis of his history, he should have trusted the helm to the hands of such a pilot!

This so-called minister laughed at the poet's fears, bade him dance them away at balls, drown them in bowls of wine, and fly from these phantoms to the arms of pleasure. Fatal, too pleasant advice! He followed it, and "The lusts of other things choked the Word."

438. THE TEST

LINACRE, on his death-bed, took up a New Testament, and read the words of the Lord Jesus, "Swear not at all" (Matt. v. 34). He immediately closed the Book, with the exclamation, "Either this Book is not true, or we are not Christians." It goes without saying that the Book is true, therefore, if men do not answer to its teaching, they must come to Linacre's conclusion—they are not Christians. An old writer has said, "Christ is not only the *Root* from which we grow, but the *Rule* by which we square." What, then, is the test of a man being a Christian? In answer to the question, let us take three "*I knows*" of the Apostle Paul.

1. **Consciousness of sin.** "*I know* that in me (that is, in my flesh) dwelleth no good thing" (Rom. vii. 18). The first step towards being right, is to know that we are wrong; not merely that we have done wrong, but that the cause of wrong-doing is in the nature, which is altogether wrong. The fruit of the tree is bad because the tree itself is bad. The stream of the life is polluted because the source of the life—the heart—is defiled (Matt. xv. 19). To know that we are lost, is the initiative to seeking that we may be saved. To see that we are under the curse, will urge us to crave the blessings of the Gospel of Christ. Do we know, in the Biblical sense of knowing, that we are sinful—that is, do we not merely know it in the head, but is it a thing we have realised in our heart, so that it has made us cry out, "O, wretched man that I am!"

2. **Confidence in the Saviour.** "*I know* Him whom I have believed, and I am persuaded that He is able to guard that which I have committed unto Him against that day" (II. Tim. i. 12, R.V.).

There are many who know *about* Christ, but who do not *know Him.*

To know Christ as the *Saviour*, is to trust Him for salvation, and to deposit ourselves in His safe keeping, as the apostle says that he had done. To know Christ as our *High Priest*, is to be continually saved from sinning as we come to Him in faith and prayer (Heb. vii. 25). To know Christ as our *Prophet*, is to be instructed by Him, and to sit at His feet even as Mary did (Luke x. 39). To know Christ as our *Lord*, is to recognise that we are His property, and to submit ourselves wholly to His rule (John xiii. 13-17). To know Him as the *Christ*, is to receive Him to live and reign in us (Galatians ii. 20).

3. **Conscience void of offence.** "*I know* nothing against myself" (I. Cor. iv. 4, R.V.). The apostle did not mean to say that

he had no faults and failings. As Trapp well says, " Paul, a chosen vessel, but yet an *earthen* vessel, knew well that he had his cracks and his flaws which God could easily find out." What the apostle said was, that as far as his consciousness went, he knew nothing against himself. To be able to honestly say this, there must be (1) implicit obedience to the Word of God, (2) initiation in the ways of God, (3) instruction in the will of God, and (4) intimate fellowship with God alone.

439. THE TRANSFIGURATION

LUKE ix. 28-36

THE scene on the Mount of Transfiguration lived in the memory of Peter like a smouldering fire, for he referred to what he then saw years after, and spoke of it as a picture of the coming glory of Christ in His kingly majesty (II. Peter i. 16-18).

1. **The privileged men** (verse 28). As there are different circles among our friends, some more intimate than others, so there were different groups in relation to the disciples and Christ. There were, at least, three circles. The outer circle was composed of the seventy; the middle circle was composed of the twelve: and the inner circle was made up of Peter, James, and John. These three disciples saw the power of Christ when He raised the ruler's daughter from the dead (Luke viii. 51); they saw the agony of Christ in the garden of Gethsemane (Matt. xxvi. 37); and they saw the glory of Christ on the mount. All believers may have the privileges of grace if they will. It is not a question of withholding on God's part, it is a question of receiving on our part.

2. **The praying Christ** (verse 29). Luke makes special mention of Christ as a Man of prayer, and remarks that it was while Christ was praying that He was transfigured, as if the praying was the cause of the transformation. There is a moral transformation that the believer may know now (the same word rendered "transfigured" in Matt. xvii. 2, is translated "changed" in II. Cor. iii. 18), by prayerfully beholding the glory of the Lord; for as we prayerfully behold the glory of the Lord, we reflect His moral glory in our lives, even as the mirror reveals the face of the person who is looking into it.

3. **The pressing topic** (verses 30, 31). The topic of the conversation that Christ had with Elijah and Moses was the "decease" that He should "accomplish at Jerusalem." Moses represents the books which were written by him, namely, the Pentateuch, and Elijah represents the prophets; therefore, it is fitting that they should be with Christ and talk with Him about His atoning death, for the burden of their prophecies is the sacrificial death of Christ, as He Himself said when He journeyed to Emmaus with the two sorrowing disciples (Luke xxiv. 27), and as He also

stated to the disciples when He appeared to them in the upper room (Luke xxiv. 44). There is no topic that is of such moment to heaven, of such benefit to earth, and of such dismay to hell, as the death of Christ.

4. **The picture of the coming glory.** The transfiguration, as Peter, by the Holy Spirit, informs us, is a type of the coming glory and kingdom of Christ (II. Peter i. 16). The several persons named, are representative characters. Moses represents those believers who have fallen asleep in Christ, and will be raised when Christ comes (I. Thess. iv. 14). Elijah, who was translated to heaven without dying (II. Kings ii. 11), represents those believers who will be caught up to meet Christ in the air (I. Cor. xv. 51), when He comes. Christ is the central figure, and speaks of the One who makes the believer's glory, glory; and the three disciples on the mount, represent those who will see the glory of the heavenly saints, such as the Jews and the saved nations (II. Thess. i. 10; Rev. xxi.).

5. **Peter and the rest of the disciples asleep** (verse 32). How much Peter and his companions lost of the glory through their sleepiness we are not told, but it is significantly said, "When they were awake they saw His glory." They might have seen a good deal more if they had not gone to sleep. How much believers lose through soul-sleepiness! There are certain things to which we should always be awake, namely, to righteousness (I. Cor. xv. 34), and to strength (Isaiah lii. 1). To be awake to our privileges and responsibilities we are commanded (Rom. xiii. 11; Eph. v. 14).

6. **The proclamation of the Father** (verse 35). The proclamation is a commendation, and an exhortation. A proclamation of the worth of the Son, as the One who was specially beloved and delighted in, by the Father, and an exhortation for the disciples of Christ to "hear Him."

440. THE TWELVE SENT FORTH

MATTHEW x. 5-16

"AND as ye go, preach, saying, The kingdom of heaven is at hand" (Matthew x. 7).

There were nine things the apostles were to do, namely, "Go," "Preach," "Heal," "Cleanse," "Raise," "Cast out," "Give," "Salute," "Shake off;" and two things they were to be, viz.: "Wise," and "Harmless."

I. **What the Apostles were to do.** In Christ's instructions to His disciples we have an illustration of what all His people are to do.

1. "**Go.**" The disciples were restricted in the sphere of their labours. They were not to go to the Gentiles, but only "to the lost sheep of the house of Israel" (verses 5, 6); but believers are not so limited now, we are to go "into all the world" (Mark xvi. 15),

to "all nations" (Matt. xxviii. 19), and to "the uttermost part of the earth" (Acts i. 8).

2. "**Preach.**" The disciples had to preach "the kingdom of heaven is at hand" (verse 7), that is, Christ coming as Israel's Messiah and King. We, on the other hand, proclaim that Christ has come; hence our message is the Gospel of the grace of God. The essence of which is the death and resurrection of Christ (1. Cor. xv. 1-4).

3. "**Heal.**" "Heal the sick" was the commission of the twelve, but no man has the gift of bodily healing now, although God may heal in answer to prayer if it be His will. The spiritual health that Christ gives, as men come in contact with Him, is communicated to them as believers—being in touch with Him.

4. "**Cleanse.**" "Cleanse the lepers." One line in the message of salvation is, that the blood of Jesus Christ can cleanse from the leprosy of sin. Moral lepers are healed as we get them to come to Christ with the "If Thou wilt" of expressed need, then they can hear Christ's "I will, be thou clean" (Matt. viii. 2, 3).

5. "**Raise.**" "Raise the dead." Those who are dead in sins (Eph. ii. 1) we may quicken as the message of John v. 24, 25, is uttered in the power of the life-giving Spirit of God.

6. "**Cast out.**" "Cast out devils." As believers are walking in fellowship with Christ, He will use them in casting out the demons that possess men; for God can still use us, if it be His will, as He used Paul (Acts xix. 11, 12).

7. "**Give.**" "Freely ye have received, freely give." One rule that always holds good in the realm of Christ is, He gives that we may give. No believer must conserve to himself the blessing Christ gives, for it will be like the manna that was hoarded up by the Israelites if he does (Exodus xvi. 20). If we would have the cistern of our spiritual being ever full with the fresh and refreshing grace of God, we must take good heed that the tap of obedience, in seeking to be a blessing to others, is ever turned on.

8. "**Salute**" (verse 12). The salutation of the Christian to those with whom he comes in contact, should ever be, "Peace be unto you." The best way to bring peace to any home or heart is to tell of Christ the Peace-maker (Col. i. 20), for those who believe in Christ have peace with God through Him (Rom. v. 1).

9. "**Shake off**" (verse 14). If there were any who would not receive the messengers of Christ, then they were to shake the dust off their feet and go elsewhere. Those who are most dependent upon God are the least dependent upon men. As in the days of the apostles, so now, there are ever those who believe and those who believe not (Acts xxviii. 24).

II. **What the disciples were to be.** They were to be "wise as serpents and harmless as doves" (verse 16). There was to be the simplicity of single-heartedness and the tact of godly wisdom. Thomas Watson says, "This beautifies a Christian, when he hath the serpent's tooth in the dove's head. We must have the innocence of the dove, that we may not betray the truth, and the wisdom of the serpent, that we may not betray ourselves. In short, religion without policy is too weak to be safe; policy without religion, is too subtle to be good. When wisdom and innocency, like Castor and Pollux, appear together, they presage the soul's happiness."

Wisdom is like the rudder of the ship, it keeps the vessel on its course; and harmlessness is like the sails, which, filled with the wind, propel the ship on its way.

To possess true wisdom, that which is not the wisdom of the old serpent, is to possess Christ, who is the Wisdom of God (I. Cor. i. 24), and to be truly simple—not silly—is to keep in, what the Holy Spirit calls, "the simplicity that is in Christ" (II. Cor. xi. 3), for we are in the Divine realm of His protection and power, as we abide in Him, besides having the special promise, "The Lord preserveth the simple" (Psalm cxvi. 6).

The harmlessness of the dove is an illustration of the godly sincerity that should be the feature in the life of the child of God as he is in the world (Phil. ii. 15, margin). To be simple concerning that which is evil (Rom. xvi. 19) is to be Christ-like, for He was "harmless" (Heb. vii. 26), or "simple," as the word is rendered in Rom. xvi. 19.

441. THE WORD OF LIFE

I. JOHN i. 1

THIS title seems to bring before us Christ as the Eternal One, manifested to us on the ground of His death and resurrection by the Word and Spirit of God, and to whom we are united by the power of the Holy Spirit. The first Epistle of John speaks of—

1. The manifestation of His life to us when we were born again (i. 2)

2. Who is our Life? "The Son of God" (v. 20).

3. The character of our life—"eternal" (i. 2).

4. The gift of the life by the Father (v. 11).

5. The position He has brought us into—"out of death into life" (iii. 14, R.V.)

6. The knowledge of it through the Word of God (v. 13).

7. Where the life is—in Christ (v. 11).

,, ,, ,, ,, in us (v. 12).

8. Who have the life—believers (v. 12).

9. Who have not life—unbelievers (v. 12).

10. Future manifestation of it (ii. 25; Col. iii. 4).

Let us remember Christ is our Life. He is the Prince of Life, let us be ruled by Him; He is the Path of Life, to walk in Him; He is the Light of Life, to look to Him; He is the Fountain of Life, to drink of Him; He is the Bread of Life, to feed upon Him; He is the Tree of Life, to abide in Him; He is the Word of Life, to rest in Him.

442. THINGS THAT DIFFER

It is essential to mark the difference between salvation and service. To note the blessings that are the gifts of God's grace and those which are the reward and outcome of service.

1. **We do not run to be saved.** "It is not of him that willeth, nor of him that runneth, but of God that sheweth mercy" (Rom. ix. 16).

We are saved to run in the way of God's commands. "Run with patience the race" (Heb. xii. 1).

2. **Salvation is not a prize to be gained, but a gift received.** "It is the gift of God" (Ephesians ii. 8).

We endeavour to gain the prize of the high calling of God. "For the prize of the high calling" (Phil. iii. 14).

3. **To be accepted in the Beloved is an act of God's favour.** "Wherein He hath made us accepted in the Beloved" (Eph. i. 6).

To be acceptable (well-pleasing) to the Lord is the outcome of devotion to the Lord. "Holy, acceptable unto God, which is your reasonable service" (Rom. xii. 1).

4. **To be made meet for the inheritance of the saints in light, depends on God's action.** "Meet to be partakers of the inheritance of the saints in light" (Col. i. 12).

But to be made meet for His service is the result of allowing Him to work in us and through us. "God which worketh in you both to will and to do" (Phil. ii. 13).

5. **We do not strive for eternal life, for it is the gift of God.** "Given to us eternal life" (1. John v. 11).

But we do strive for the victory to receive the overcomer's crown. "Receive the crown of life" (James i. 12).

6. **We do not follow Christ to apprehend Him, that He may apprehend us.** "I am apprehended of Christ Jesus" (Phil. iii. 12).

But we follow after, that we may apprehend that for which we have been apprehended of Christ Jesus. "I follow after" (Phil. iii. 12).

7. **There is a difference between sonship and service.** As children of God, and as members of the body of Christ, we can never

be castaways. "I am persuaded "none can" separate us from the love of God, which is in Christ Jesus our Lord" (Rom. viii. 38, 39).

But as servants we may. "Lest . . . . I myself should be a castaway" (I. Cor. ix. 27).

443. THINGS WHICH WE OBTAIN BY FAITH

1. **Salvation.** "By grace are ye saved through *faith*" (Eph. ii. 8).

2. **Justification.** "Being justified by *faith*, we have peace with God" (Rom. v. 1).

3. **Introduction.** "By Whom also we have access by *faith*" (Romans v. 2).

4. **Adoption.** "For ye are all the children of God by *faith* in Christ Jesus" (Galatians iii. 26).

5. **Sanctification.** "Sanctified by *faith* that is in Me" (Acts xxvi. 18).

6. **Purification.** "Purifying their hearts by *faith*" (Acts xv. 9).

7. **Occupation.** "That Christ may dwell in your hearts by *faith*" (Eph. iii. 17).

8. **Progression.** "We walk by *faith*, not by sight" (II. Cor. v. 7).

9 **Preservation.** "Kept by the power of God through *faith*" (I. Peter i. 5).

10. **Expectation.** "We, through the Spirit, wait for the Hope of Righteousness by *faith*" (Gal. v. 5).

444. THORNY-GROUND HEARERS

Matthew xiii. 22

1. **Orpah** (Ruth i. 15). Orpah's decision was the result of impulsive feeing, of filial affection; it was strong suddenly, it grew up in an instant, and in an instant it perished.

2. **Demas** loved the world (II. Tim. iv. 10).

3. **Simon Magus** was not real (Acts viii. 21).

4. **Hymenæus** and **Alexander** made shipwreck of themselves (I. Tim. i. 19, 20).

5. **Phygellus** and **Hermogenes** turned away (II. Tim. i. 15).

6. The **rich young ruler** made enquiry, but got no farther (Luke xviii. 23).

7. **There were those who turned away from Christ** (John vi. 66). These are compared to a washed sow which goes back and wallows in the mire; and to a dog which licks up his own vomit (II. Peter ii. 20-22).

445. THREE APPEARINGS

HEBREWS ix. 24-28

IT must be remarked that the words rendered "appear" in Heb. ix. 24-28, are three different words in the Greek.

1. **The past appearing** (ix. 26). Here the word "appear" means, for one to be seen who had been hidden, as when one comes from behind a curtain which had concealed him.

2. **The present appearing** (ix. 24). The term here indicates appearing in an official sense. Christ now appears in the presence of God, as the Representative of His people, to plead on their behalf, and to look after their interests.

3. **The future appearing** (ix. 28). Here it signifies to see face to face, as when Paul saw Jesus, when he was on his way to Damascus (I. Cor. xv. 8).

446. THREE CROSSES OF CALVARY

THE men who were associated with Christ, are an object lesson for us, as to the difference there is between the believer and the unbeliever in relation to the question of sin. Let us look at the three men.

Upon the centre cross is Christ. Is there sin *in* Him? No. He did no sin (I. Peter ii. 22), He knew no sin (II. Cor. v. 21), and in Him was no sin (I. John iii. 5).

Was there sin *on* Him? Yes. For God made to meet upon Him the iniquity of us all (Isaiah liii. 6, M.).

Was there sin *in* the thieves? Yes. For they were, like all, conceived in sin (Psalm li. 5).

Was there sin *on* the thieves? Yes, and no.

Upon the believing thief there was no sin, for Christ was his Sin-Bearer.

Upon the unbelieving thief there was sin, for he did not look to Christ for salvation from it.

Believing thief.	**Christ.**	**Unbelieving Thief.**
Sin *in* him. No sin *on* him.	Sin not *in* Him. Sin *on* Him.	Sin *in* him. Sin *on* him.
✝	✝	✝

The relation to Christ of the thieves made all the difference as to their state before God. So is it now. They who believe in Christ have their sins borne away by Christ (I. Peter ii. 24), and those who do not are rewarded according to their works (Rev. xx. 12).

447. THREEFOLD DEATH

DEATH, THE ISSUE OF SIN.

THERE is a threefold death as the result of sin.

I. **Bodily death.** The common portion of man naturally, as a consequence of sin, is death (Heb. ix. 27).

II. **Spiritual death.** Sin has alienated man from God, hence man is dead in trespasses and sins (Eph. ii. 1).

There are three illustrations given in the New Testament of spiritual death.

1. The prodigal was dead, as long as he was separated from his father (Luke xv. 24).

2. The woman who lives in pleasure is dead, as long as she continues in a course of worldliness (1. Tim. v. 6).

3. Those who have a name to live, but who have not been quickened by the Holy Spirit, are dead in a spiritual sense (Rev. iii. 1).

III. **Eternal death.** "The second death" is eternal separation from God, from all that He is, and from all that He has to give (Rev. xx. 14).

448. THREE LOOKS

MARK x. 17-27

WE have three looks in the verses before us—"Jesus beholding" (verse 21), "Jesus looked" (verse 23), "Jesus looking" (verse 27).

I. **The look of love.** "Jesus beholding him, loved him," &c. (verse 21). Love as embodied in Christ is seen in three attitudes.

1. *Love searches.* "One thing thou lackest" is the verdict of Love, as He listens to what the young man says he has done. Christ ever turns on the search light of His penetrating gaze, for His eyes are as a flame of fire (Rev. i. 14), that the weakness in the character may be made known, or that the hidden evil may be brought out into the light. See the "*I knows*" of Christ in Revelation ii. and iii. There were many things commendable about this young man, but the one thing lacking, spoiled all. As it has been said, "What then, did this young man lack? Not right desires: he wished to inherit eternal life. Not a good moral character: all the moral law he had kept from his youth up; he had been an honouring son, an honoured citizen, a pure man. Not earnestness: he came running to Christ. Not reverence: he kneeled before Him. Not humility: he made willing and public confession of his desire and his faith, before the multitude in the open roadway. Not an orthodox belief: if words are creeds, no creed could be more orthodox than that which he compacted into the two words, 'Good Master.' Not a humane and tender spirit: for Christ looking on him, loved him. But he lacked absolute and unquestioning allegiance, entire and implicit

consecration; the spirit of the soldier who only asks what the marching orders are; the spirit of the Master Himself, whose prayer was ever, 'Thy will, not Mine, be done.' And lacking this, he lacked everything, and 'went away sorrowful.'"

2. *Love demands.* "Sell whatsoever thou hast, and give to the poor." The principle of this demand comes to all. As Dr. Lyman Abbot says, "It came to Luther when Christ bade him forsake the church of his fathers and of his childhood; to Coligny, when Christ bade him abandon his wife, and home, and peace; to William of Orange; to the Puritans; to John Howard; to David Livingstone. In one form or another it comes to every Christian; for to every would-be Christian the Master says, "Give up your property, your home, your life itself, and take them back as Mine, and use them for Me in using them for your fellow men. He who cannot—does not—do this, is no Christian."

3. *Love commands.* "Follow Me."

II. **The look of faithfulness** (verse 23). As Christ saw the rich young ruler leaving Him, He looked round on His disciples and said, "How hardly shall they that have riches enter the kingdom of God." Christ points to the retreating figure of the sorrowful rich young man, and in faithfulness reminds His disciples of the evil of riches. Old Humphrey says: "I was walking through an orchard looking about me, when I saw a low tree laden more heavily with fruit than the rest. On a nearer examination, it appeared that the tree had been dragged to the very earth, and broken by the weight of its treasures. 'Oh!' said I, gazing on the tree, 'here lies one who was ruined by his riches.' In another part of my walk, I came up with a shepherd, who was lamenting the loss of a sheep that lay mangled and dead at his feet. On enquiry about the matter, he told me that a strange dog had attacked the flock; that the rest of the sheep had got away through a hole in the hedge, but that the ram now dead had more wool on his back than the rest, and the thorns of the hedge held him fast till the dog had worried him. 'Here is another,' said I, 'ruined by his riches.'"

III. **The look of encouragement** (verse 27). Impossibilities with men are possibilities with God. The disciples are dismayed and discouraged by the words of Christ, but He at once directs their gaze from themselves to God. From man's standpoint it is impossible for man to span the great gulf which sin has made, but Christ has bridged over the impassable chasm by His death and resurrection, and now in His grace and love He says, "I am the Way," and bids all to come to God by Himself (John xiv. 6).

449. THREE REPRESENTATIVE WOMEN

THE three women are Dubious Orpah, Decided Ruth, and Disappointed Naomi (Ruth i. 14-22).

I. **Dubious Orpah.** Orpah started with her sister and mother-in-law from Moab, but she was easily persuaded to go back to the old country, the old sins, and idolatry. Her mind was never made up to go to the land of Israel, and she at once takes the bait when Naomi suggests that she and her sister should return, for it is but the expression of the desire that is in her own heart (verses 14, 15).

Many, like Pliable in Pilgrim's Progress, start well, but they soon go back.

1. The stony ground hearer received the word into his heart, and received it with joy, but he did not keep it there (Matt. xiii. 20).

2. It is not profession, but possession that is the essential thing, as is illustrated in what Peter said to Simon Magus; the latter professed faith in Christ in baptism, but, as Peter looked through the window of his soul, he saw he had no possession of Christ (Acts viii. 20).

3. The house of the soul may be swept with the broom of morality, and be garnished with the flowers of self-effort, but unless there is cleansing by the blood of Christ, and possession by Christ Himself dwelling in the heart, all else is vain (Luke xi. 25; Eph. iii. 17).

4. To be associated with Christians as Demas was (Col. iv. 14), is not sufficient; we must be associated with Christ, or we shall soon be like Demas, and go back to the beggarly elements of the world, which we had professed to leave (II. Tim. iv. 10; II. Peter ii. 21). Beware of being like Orpah! She started well, but, alas, she soon went back. Continuance is the mark of discipleship (John viii. 31), and the evidence of faith in Christ.

II. **Decided Ruth.** Ruth stands in unmistakable contrast with her sister-in-law. The latter is like a piece of wreckage tossed about by the waves, while the former is like the limpet which clings to the rock. It is a very suggestive word that is used of Ruth in verse 14, where it says she "clave unto her." The word "*clave*" is used of the clods of earth which "*cleave fast together*" (Job xxxviii. 38); of the scales of leviathian, which are "*joined one to another*" so closely that no air can come between them (Job xli. 15-17); to the bone which "*cleaveth*" to the skin (Job xix. 20); in connection with one of David's mighty men, to whose hand the sword "*clave*" when he had been fighting, so intense had been his grip in grasping his sword (II. Sam. xxiii. 10); of Naaman's leprosy "*cleaving*" to Gehazi (II. Kings v. 27); of a girdle "*cleaving*" to the loins (Jer. xiii. 11); and of the Psalmist of whom it is said he "*followeth hard*" after the Lord (Psalm lxiii. 8). From the use of the word "*clave*" we gather, how intensely in earnest Ruth was. There was no hesitation or vacillation about her. There was real grit and grip in her determination to go with Naomi, and to serve Naomi's God. There must be the like spirit with all who serve Christ. When Barnabas went down to Antioch and saw the work the Lord had been doing, in the salvation of those who had believed in Christ, he exhorted them to *cleave* to the Lord with purpose of heart (Acts xi. 23).

III. **Disappointed Naomi** (verses 19-22). Naomi is typical of a backslider. She left her native land full, like many a believer who gets away from Christ when full of gladness and power, but she came back, or was brought back, "empty." It is the same with the child of God when he gets out of communion. Naomi does not wish to be called "Naomi," that is, "pleasant;" but, she says, call me "Mara," that is, "bitter." Bitterness of spirit is born of backsliding, and is always the outcome of departure from God. David found it so, when he cried for the restoration of the joy he had lost through his sin (Psalm li. 12). Peter had the same experience, when he went out of the Lord's presence to weep, because of his denial of his Lord (Luke xxii. 62). Naomi had to learn that the cause of her emptiness, bitterness, and affliction was found in her leaving the Lord. She had thought to obtain all she desired in Moab, but she got a worse famine there than in Bethlehem, for she lost husband and sons by her self-will. If we lie on the bed of roses which the world offers, we are sure to be pricked by the thorns on the roses. We cannot have the devil's bait without the devil's hook. The world offers gifts for its advantage, and not ours, however much they may seem to promise benefits.

450. THREE SIGHTS

LUKE xix. 1-10

THE sight Zacchæus saw from the sycamore tree; the sight that the Saviour saw when He looked up and discovered the publican in the tree; and the sight which the people had, when they saw Christ condescending to be the guest of Zacchæus.

I. **The sinner's sight.** "He sought to see Jesus" (verse 3). There are many sights that the sinner seeks to have. Eve had a sight of the tree of knowledge, which led to her fall (Gen. iii. 6); and Achan looked on the Babylonish garment and the wedge of gold, which led to his death (Jos. vii. 21); but Zacchæus saw Jesus and was saved.

There are many things said about this man in his desire to see Christ.

1. It was a sight attended with difficulty, for Zacchæus was small of stature, and could not come near to Christ for the crowd, therefore he climbed up a tree. No one will be deterred by difficulty if he is truly in earnest about his eternal welfare. Difficulties are opportunities to evidence the reality of the seeker.

2. It was a sight associated with curiosity. He sought to "see who He was." Better curiosity than indifference, for indifference is like a bog which swallows up everything, but curiosity is the road that leads to the glen of interest, where the flowers of grace shall fascinate and fix us to the spot.

3. It was a sight preceded by earnestness. We read that Zacchæus "ran" and "climbed." A spirit of determination prompted him to act as he did. Earnestness is like the steam in the engine, it causes one to move with haste.

4. It was a sight from a vantage point. The publican knew that Christ was to "pass that way." There is one point of vantage where we may view Christ, and that is from the Word of God. Christ ever shows Himself through the lattice of the truth (S.S. ii. 9).

A sight of Christ is the best of all sights. A sight of Christ gives us:—

A sight of ourselves (Job xlii. 5).

Salvation (Isaiah xlv. 22).

Gladness (John xx. 20).

II. **The Saviour's sight** (verse 5). The Lord Jesus looked up as He came to the sycamore tree, and saw the anxious enquiring man hid among its branches. The Lord Jesus never passed by a person who was really desirous of knowing who He was, and what His claims were. The eyes of the Lord are as a flame of fire to search us (Rev. i. 14), but they are also as doves' eyes by the rivers of water (Song of Solomon v. 12). It is said that doves, when they drink water, do not look up till they have finished drinking. If this is so, it may be taken as an illustration of the fact that the Lord loves with an intensity that is eternal in its duration.

III. **The people's sight.** The people did not murmur as long as Christ was showing forth His power in miracle (Luke xviii. 43), but directly he went to be the guest of a man who was looked upon with contempt—for the tax-gatherers were oppressors of the people—then they began to grumble. It is the same to-day, many begin to grumble when they see one who has been noted for his wickedness converted to Christ, and if such a one is welcomed among God's people, many of the latter, instead of encouraging the one who has believed, express themselves in a cold manner, by "hoping he will hold out."

The people, if they had looked long enough and deep enough, would have seen in Zacchæus a man who was—

Called by Christ (verse 5).

Converted through Christ (verse 9).

Consecrated to Christ (verse 8).

Communing with Christ (verse 7).

451. THE WORD OF THE LORD

THE servants of God are not to speak what they like, they are commissioned to proclaim Christ. To proclaim Him:—

1. **In the saving of His grace.** "This is a faithful saying . . . Christ Jesus came into the world to save sinners" (I. Tim. i. 15).

2. **In the strength of His power.** "It is the power of God unto salvation" (Rom. i. 16).

3. **In the claim of His lordship.** "We preach not ourselves, but Christ Jesus the Lord" (II. Cor. iv. 5).

4. **In the sufficiency of His substitution.** "Preached unto him Jesus" (Acts viii. 35).

5. **In the forgiving of His love.** "Through this Man is preached unto you the forgiveness of sins" (Acts xiii. 38, 39).

6. **In the power of His resurrection.** "Preached through Jesus the resurrection from the dead" (Acts iv. 2).

7. **In the glory of His person.** "Teaching those things which concern the Lord Jesus" (Acts xxviii. 31).

8. **In the coming of His kingdom.** "This gospel of the kingdom shall be preached in all the world . . . then shall the end come" (Matt. xxiv. 14).

452. THEN

ADVERB of time, "*Then*," in connection with Christ's return.

1. **In I. Cor. xiii. 11, 12, we have the "then" of perfect knowledge.** "Now I know in part: but *then* shall I know even as also I am known." We do not know perfectly at present, for we see through an obscure glass, but when we are in the glorified state we shall see things with a perfect vision.

2. **In I. Cor. iv. 5, we have the "then" of commendation.** "*Then* shall every man have praise of God." The practical word to the Christian worker is, to "judge nothing before the time, until the Lord come."

3. **In I. Cor. xv. 54, we have the "then" of victory over death.** "So when . . . . this mortal shall have put on immortality, *then* shall be brought to pass the saying that is written, death is swallowed up in victory." Meantime death swallows up those who come under its power, but there is a time coming when it shall be defeated.

4. **In I. Thess. iv. 17, we have the "then" of union.** "*Then* we who are alive and remain shall be caught up together with them in the clouds, to meet the Lord in the air." With the loved ones who have fallen asleep, we shall be for ever with the Lord when He comes, but not till then.

5. **In Col. iii. 4, we have the "then" of glory.** "When Christ, who is our Life, shall appear, *then* shall ye also appear with Him in glory." When Christ is manifested to the world in His resplendent glory, then we, with Him, shall be seen in the glory which He has put upon us.

6. **In Matt. xxv. 1, we have the "then" of the end.** The Great Tribulation in relation to the Jewish people, who are likened to wise and foolish virgins. "*Then* shall the kingdom of heaven," &c.

7. **In I. Cor. xv. 28, we have the "then" of the eternal state.** "*Then* shall the Son also Himself be subject unto Him that put all things under Him, that God may be all in all." Meantime Christ is seen as the Son, and will be seen as such through the Millennium. After the Millennium, His Sonship will be merged into the Godhead.

453. THINGS OF CHRIST IN PHILIPPIANS

1. **Day of Christ** (i. 10). Yet to come.
2. **Gospel of Christ** (i. 27). To be preached.
3. **Work of Christ** (ii. 30). Our employment.
4. **Knowledge of Christ** (iii. 8). Our assurance.
5. **Faith of Christ** (iii. 9). Our study.
6. **Apprehended of Christ** (iii. 12). Our security.
7. **Cross of Christ** (iii. 18). Our suffering.

454. TOWARDNESS OF OUR BELOVED

"I AM my Beloved's, and His desire is toward me" (S. S. vii. 10).

1. **Peace towards us.** "Peace on earth, good will *toward* men" (Luke ii. 14).

2. **Love towards us.** "God commendeth His love *toward* us" (Romans v. 8).

3. **Life towards us.** "In this was manifested the love of God *toward* us . . . . . . that we might live through Him" (I. John iv. 9).

4. **Mercy towards us.** "Great is Thy mercy *toward* me" (Psalm lxxxvi. 13).

5. **Supply towards us.** "He hath abounded *toward* us" (Eph. i. 7, 8).

6. **Power towards us.** "God is able to make all grace abound *toward* you" (II. Cor. ix. 8).

7. **Kindness towards us.** "His kindness *toward* us through Christ Jesus" (Eph. ii. 7).

455. TREASURES OF THE NEW TESTAMENT

1. **In Christ are found "all the treasures of wisdom and knowledge"** (Col. ii. 3). The red sardius of the blessing of His atonement, the green emerald of the power of His life, the blue

sapphire of the heavenly gladness of His joy, the variegated agate of the many sidedness of His grace, and the flashing diamond of the glory of His coming, are all made known by Christ, and are found by us as we are in Him.

2. **Israel is Jehovah's peculiar treasure** (Exodus xix. 5; Psalm cxxxv. 4), which He found in the field of the nations of this world (Matt. xiii. 44), and for which Christ has given all He had (John xvii. 5), in emptying Himself of His glory (Phil. ii. 7, R.V.), and becoming poor (II. Cor. viii. 9). This privilege now applies to the Church during Israel's rejection (Ephesians i. 18-23).

3. **The Gospel is a treasure.** The apostle, by the Holy Spirit, in speaking of the "glorious Gospel," says, we have "this treasure in earthen vessels" (II. Cor. iv. 7). As the lights were in the pitchers of Gideon and his followers, and flashed forth to the discomfort of the Midianites (Judges vii. 16, 17), so the light of the Gospel of Christ, with which every true servant of Christ is entrusted, shall shine forth, as they live it truly and tell it out faithfully, and it will cause the darkness of sin to flee, the gloom of unbelief to be scattered, and the fog of iniquity to be gone.

4. **There is treasure in the heart of every man** (Matt. xii. 35). The treasure is either a blessing or a curse, according to its character. When it is the good treasure of the truth of God, then the life is beautiful with holiness, and fruitful with the graces of the Spirit; but when it is the evil treasure of the world, then the character is blighted by sin, and marred with iniquity.

5. **Earthly treasure** (Luke xii. 21). Thieves may steal it, moth may corrupt it, rust may spoil it, time will decay it, failure may take it, friends may borrow it, and death will say, "you must leave it."

6. **Heavenly treasure** (Matt. vi. 20). This is enduring in its nature, incorruptible in its texture, safe in its keeping, heavenly in its origin, holy in its character, ennobling in its possession, and worth the having.

7. **Treasures of wrath** (Rom. ii. 5). The thunderbolts of God's indignation against sin, the lightnings of His wrath, the fire of His judgment, and the putting forth of His power, are but slumbering till the self-willed sinner has filled up his cup of iniquity, when they shall burst upon him to his eternal shame, confusion, and punishment.

456. TRIAL OF ABRAHAM'S FAITH

GENESIS xxii. 1-14

There are several characters in which Abraham appears. Let us note them.

1. **The Tried Believer.** "God did prove Abraham" (verse 1,

R.V.). If the Lord gives us a special blessing, He will test our appreciation of it. If He places us in a position, He will prove our fitness for it. If He gives an Isaac, He will ask that that Isaac may be given to Him. "When a person took the first Napoleon a shot-proof coat of mail, the Emperor fired many shots at it, while the inventor had it on. Finding it answer, the Emperor gave the maker a reward. Storms of trial, sacrifices to be made, obedience required, or loving services demanded, will test us. Constantine thus tested the Christians in his household when he required them to give up their religion under a heavy penalty. Those, however, who were faithful he took into his particular favour and service."

2. **The Responsive Saint.** "Behold, here I am." When the Lord called, there was a ready response. Like Jacob (Gen. xlvi. 2, 3), Moses (Exodus iii. 4), Samuel (1. Sam. iii. 4, 5, 6, 8, 10), and Isaiah (Isaiah vi. 8), Abraham responds at once to the voice of the Lord. As the courtier stands in the Queen's presence, ready to respond to the command of Her Majesty, so the believer should ever be ready to answer in willing obedience every command of the Lord.

3. **The Loving Father.** "Thy son, thine only son Isaac, whom thou lovest" (verse 2). The heart of Abraham twined round his son in holy affection, as the creeper clings to its support. This is the first time that the word "love" occurs in the Bible, and it is suggestive of that greater love that God had for Christ, of which He speaks in John iii. 35. Mark how God speaks of Isaac—(1) "Thy *son.*" (2) "Thine *only* son." (3) "*Isaac.*" (4) "Whom thou *lovest.*"

4. **The Early Riser** (verse 3). Trapp remarks "upon Abraham rising early, to show his prompt and present obedience. He neither consulted with his wife nor with his own reason. She might have haply hung upon him and hindered him, as Zipporah did Moses, to the hazarding of his life (Ex. iv. 25, 26). He consecrates all the powers of the soul to his Creator." The early seekers are sure to find the Lord (Prov. viii. 17; Luke xxiv. 22; John xx. 1), and receive blessing from Him (Psalm lvii. 8-10; lxiii. 1; cviii. 2), even as Israel found the manna every morning before the sun "waxed hot" (Exodus xvi. 21).

5. **The Persevering Follower** (verses 4, 5). For three days Abraham plods on in obedience to the Divine word, and there is no hesitation in following out its direction. An old writer tersely says, "We must not weigh the cross, for then it will prove heavy; we must not chew the pill, but swallow it whole, else it will prove bitter; we must not plod too much, but ply the throne of grace for a good use and a good issue of all our trials and tribulations."

6. **The Confident Answerer** (verse 8). When Isaac asks the question as to the lamb, Abraham confidently answers that God will provide it. The answer of the patriarch reminds us of Him who is "the Lamb of God." Christ did not come and die to make God love us; it was because God loved us, that Christ came and died. The cause of God's grace is in Himself, even as the electric light is caused by the generating power.

7. **The Careful Priest** (verse 9). Everything is done in an orderly and careful manner. What a type this is of Christ as the sacrifice for sin! He came at the appointed time (Gal. iv. 4). He died upon a cross,—that it might be said He was pierced (Zech. xii. 10; John xix. 37)—and not according to the mode that the Jews put to death, namely, by stoning; not a bone of His body was broken, that Scripture might be fulfilled (John xix. 36; Exodus xii. 46); and He was carefully placed in a rich man's tomb that prophecy might be fulfilled to the letter (Isaiah liii. 9; Matt. xxvii. 57).

8. **The Resolute Believer** (verse 10; Heb. xi. 17-19). Who can tell the feelings of Abraham as he stands over his son with uplifted knife in hand? But he is in the line of obedience to God's will, and he has faith in God's power, even though he slays his son, that the Lord will raise him up to life. Faith looks not at consequences, but to God. "When the knife was up, the Lord came." The Lord is never too late to aid His people.

9. **The Waiting Servant.** "Here am I" (verse 11). No sooner does the Lord speak--than Abraham responds, and stands in a waiting posture to hear what the Lord wills. Our safety and blessing are found in being attentive to the voice of God in His Word. The posture of young Samuel should ever be ours, namely, that of reverent, prayerful attention to the Lord.

10. **The God-fearing Man.** "I know that thou fearest God" (verse 12). We are told how Abraham feared God, in that he was willing to give his son. All his hopes were centred in Isaac, but he yielded him at God's command, and by so doing evidenced his faith. As James says, "Was not Abraham our father justified by works, when he had offered Isaac his son upon the altar? Seest thou how faith wrought with his works, and by works was faith made perfect?" (James ii. 21, 22). As Canaan proved it was a "good land" by the fruit that came from it (Num. xiii. 23), so faith evidences its existence by its fruit. Faith receives God's "All," even Christ (John i. 12), and shows it has received Christ by giving the soul's all to Him.

11. **The Obedient Offerer** (verse 13). At God's bidding the ram is offered up in "the stead of Isaac." What a type of Christ, who has been offered up in the stead of the believer! "He gave Himself for us." Thus God answers Isaac's question of verse 7, and illustrates His title of Jehovah-Jireh in verse 14.

457. TRINITY

A SEVENFOLD light regarding the three Persons of the Godhead, is found in connection with the following truths.

1. **Death of Christ.** "How much more shall the blood of *Christ*, who through the eternal *Spirit* offered Himself without spot

to God, purge your conscience from dead works to serve the living *God?*" (Heb. ix. 14).

2. **Resurrection of Christ.** "But if the *Spirit* of Him that raised up *Jesus* from the dead dwell in you, *He* that raised up Christ from the dead shall also quicken your mortal bodies by His *Spirit* that dwelleth in you" (Romans viii. 11).

3. **Christ preaching.** "The *Spirit* of the *Lord* is upon *Me*" (Luke iv. 18).

4. **New Birth.** "*Jesus* answered, Verily, verily, I say unto thee, except a man be born of water and of the *Spirit*, he cannot enter the kingdom of *God*" (John iii. 5).

5. **Prayer.** "And *He* that searcheth the hearts knoweth what is the mind of the *Spirit*, because He maketh intercession for the saints according to the will of *God*" (Rom. viii. 27).

6. **Access.** "For through *Him* we both have access by one *Spirit* unto the *Father*" (Eph. ii. 18).

7. **Union.** "In *Whom* ye also are builded together for an habitation of *God* through the *Spirit*" (Eph. ii. 22).

458. TWELVE APOSTLES

MARK iii. 13-19

THE Lord Jesus, in choosing and ordaining the twelve apostles, had a six-fold purpose in view, as we are told in the following verses. He chose them to, and for Himself (John xiii. 18; Acts i. 2), to be with Him, to be sent forth by Him (Mark iii. 14), to be separate from the world, and to bring forth fruit (John xv. 16-19).

Many of the names of the twelve men chosen are indicative of their character. Let us note the meaning of the names, and one leading trait in the life of the persons who bear them, as suggesting what we should, or should not do, as believers in Christ.

1. **Honoured Peter.** Peter was honoured, because that to him were given the "keys of the kingdom of heaven," that is, not that he had or has the power to admit into heaven or refuse admission, but that he was privileged to open the dispensation of the Spirit to the Jews on the day of Pentecost, and to the Gentiles, as illustrated in the case of Cornelius (See Acts x). Those who believe are also honoured in that they are privileged to proclaim the Gospel of the grace of God, and offer salvation to all who will believe in Christ.

2. **Privileged James.** James, the son of Zebedee, was one of the apostles who was among the privileged three, the others being Peter and John. They were with Christ when He was on the Mount of Transfiguration (Mark ix. 2); they were with Christ when He raised the ruler's daughter to life (Mark v. 37); and they were also with Him when He went to the garden of Gethsemane

(Matt. xxvi. 37). Thus James was privileged to behold the glory of Christ, the power of Christ, and the agony of Christ. Those who believe in Christ have seen the agony of Christ, in that they have beheld Him by faith dying for them on the accursed tree; they have experienced the power of Christ, in that they have been quickened by His power from the death of sin; and they shall see the glory of Christ when He comes again.

3. **Loving John.** John was loving because he was loved, and he was loved because he was loving. He was loving because he was loved; that is, he knew the love of Christ, and that was the constraining power which moved him to love others, even as the steam in the engine is the motor that moves the train. And he was loved because he was loving; that is, the love of Christ that acted through him drew others to him, even as the law of gravitation draws things to the earth.

4. **Faithful Andrew.** The faithfulness of Andrew flashes out in more ways than one, but especially is it seen in his seeking out his brother Peter after he had found Christ for himself (John i. 40, 41). A man who is full of faith is sure to be a faithful man, and his faithfulness will evidence itself in seeking the salvation of his own kith and kin, and telling them of the Lord who can save.

5. **Friendly Philip.** Godet says: "It seems that Jesus was on terms of special cordiality with him." This is borne out by Christ's question in John vi. 5, in the action of the Greeks who came to him when they would see Jesus, and in Philip's question to Christ as recorded in John xiv. 8. He evidently was an approachable man. If the love of God is in the heart, the joy of the Lord in the countenance, and the peace of God in the mind, they will make a way to the hearts of others; so that we, in turn, shall be able to introduce others to Christ, even as Philip did (John xii. 22).

6. **Devotional Bartholomew.** "The name Bartholomew signifies son of Tolmai; it was, therefore, only a surname. It has long been supposed that the true name of this apostle was Nathanael, for in John xxi. 2, Nathanael is named amongst a number of apostles, which proves unquestionably that he was one of the twelve." The devotional spirit is the one thing that Christ commends in him, as we read in John i. 48. Prayer and praise are the lungs of the Christian life; but if we allow the congestion of neglect to set in, there will be pain and defeat. The prayer of faith is the inbreathing of God's bestowed blessing, and the act of worship is the outbreathing of the soul in thanksgiving and praise to God.

7. **Humble Matthew.** It will be noticed that the apostles are seen in pairs. Thus Matthew and Thomas are together. I draw attention to this fact for the simple reason that in the way he speaks of himself, without straining to do it, he brings out his humility. For instance, in Mark iii. 18 the name of Matthew appears first; the same order also occurs in Luke vi. 15; but when Matthew is

recording the call of the apostles he puts the name of Thomas first. Again, Mark and Luke, in speaking of Matthew, simply call him "Matthew," but when Matthew speaks of himself he calls himself "Matthew the publican" (x. 3). The epithet would remind him of the old life in sin. While God in His grace calls us His "children" and "saints," the humble soul always says "sinner" (1. Timothy i. 15).

8. **Confessing Thomas.** In looking at the doubting of Thomas, we are apt to forget the confession of Thomas after he was convinced that Christ was risen from the dead (John xx. 28). Trapp says of the confession of Thomas: "This is true faith indeed that individuates God, and appropriates Him to itself. Were it not for this possessive 'mine,' the devil might say the creed to as good a purpose as we. He believes there is a God and a Christ; but what torments him is, he can never say 'my' to an article of faith."

9. **Discriminating James.** This James is distinguished from James the son of Zebedee, by being called "the son of Alphæus." It is generally thought that this James is the one who is so often mentioned in the Acts and in the Galatians, as the brother of our Lord. He was the bishop of the Church in Jerusalem. It is in his address, as recorded in the fifteenth of the Acts, that his discrimination and holy common sense are seen (see Acts xv. 13-21). To discriminate between God's will and our own will, in whole-hearted obedience to the former, is the secret of joy; and to discriminate between the world and Christ, by being separated from the former to the latter, is the essence of holiness.

10. **Silent Thaddæus.** Godet has well remarked upon the apostles about whom little is said: "All these men have had their share in the fulfilment of the apostolic task, the transmission of the holy figure of Christ to the Church through all time." Many a Christian who has never been known, and whose name has never been mentioned, will be found to have fulfilled his mission in the day of Christ, even as the unseen stone is essential to the support of the prominent outside stone.

11. **Zealous Simon.** "The surname *Zealot*, given to Simon, is probably a translation of the adjective *kanna*, *zealous*." To be zealous in good works is the best form of zealousness.

12. **Betraying Judas.** Even Judas fulfilled his apostolic function; his despairing cry, "I have betrayed the innocent blood," is a testimony which resounds through the ages as loudly as the preaching of Peter at Pentecost, or as the blood of the martyr James. Let us be careful not to imitate the example of Judas in any way, and neither in work, look, nor action to deny our Lord.

459. TWO ADAMS

SIN is the legacy that our first parents have left the human race. Thomas Boston says: "God made Adam captain of the ship, in which were all our goods, and he ran us on to the rocks and made shipwreck of us." Romans v. reminds us that there are two great representative heads—the first and last (not second, there is no other) Adam. We can gather what we lost in the first, by pondering the following contrasts:—

In Adam		In Christ
Sin (Rom. v. 12) ...	...	Righteousness (II. Cor. v. 21).
Death (Rom. v. 17) ...	...	Life (I. John v. 11).
Banishment (Eph. ii. 13)	...	Nearness (Eph. ii. 13).
Condemnation (Rom. v. 18)	...	Justification (Rom. v. 1).
Curse (Gal. iii. 10) ...	...	Blessing (Eph. i. 3).
Judgment (John iii. 36)	...	Deliverance (II. Cor. I. 10).
Shame (Ezekiel xvi. 5)	...	Glory (John xvii. 24).
Poverty (Isaiah lv. 1)	...	Riches (II. Cor. viii. 9).
Sickness (Isaiah i. 5, 6)	...	Health (Psalm xxiii. 3).
Defeat (II. Tim. ii. 26)	...	Victory (I. John v. 4).
Sorrow (Gen. iii. 17) ...	...	Joy (Rom. v. 11).
Weakness (Rom. v. 6)	...	Power (Phil. iv. 13).
Enmity (Rom. viii. 7)	...	Oneness (Gal. iii. 28).
Bondage (Heb. ii. 15)	...	Liberty (Gal. v. 1).

The above may be illustrated by taking two books and a card—one book representing Adam, and the other representing Christ. Put the card in the book Adam, and then put it in the book Christ.

"Scripture bears witness, with the vast experience of mankind, to the depravity of men, and to their distortion universally (I. Kings viii. 46; Psalm li. 5; cxliii. 2; Jer. xvii. 9; Matt. vii. 11; Rom. iii. 19, 20; Eph. ii. 1-3)." The Chinese moralists teach that "man is born good." Yet an ancient Chinese proverb speaks of "two good men—one dead, the other unborn;" which is another way of saying, "there are none good."

The Fall was the key that unlocked the flood-gates of evil, and allowed the waters of iniquity to cut us off from God; the fall was the fatal touch that imparted to our nature the disease of sin; the fall was the hand that dropped into our cup the poison of iniquity; the fall was the robber that robbed us of the blessings of Paradise; the fall was the rust that corrupted the nature of man; the fall was the blight that marred God's fair creation; and the fall was the depositor of all the germs of evil in our nature. Watson says, "Let us lay to heart original sin, and be deeply humbled by it. It cleaves to us as a disease, it is an active principle in us, stirring us up to evil. Some think, as long as they are civil, they are well enough; ay, but the nature is poisoned. A river may have fair streams, but vermin in the bottom."

460. TWO FOLLOWINGS

I. **Coldness.** "And Peter followed afar off" (Luke xxii. 54). This is one of the seven downward steps in the fall of Peter. The first was self-confidence; the second was sleeping instead of watching; the third was doing what he had no authority to do, namely, cutting off the ear of the servant of the high priest; the fourth was following afar off; the fifth was sitting down in the company of the ungodly; the sixth was denying his Master; and the seventh was denying Him with oaths and curses (Luke xxii. 33, 45, 50, 54, 55, 57; Matt. xxvi. 72, 74). Beware of the first step, for it leads to all the rest.

II. **Cleaving.** "My soul followeth hard after Thee" (Ps. lxiii. 8), or as it might be rendered, "is glued to Thee." The Hebrew word rendered "followeth" here is the same as is rendered in Gen. ii. 24, "cleave"; in Ruth i. 14 "clave"; in Psalm cxix. 31 "stuck"; in Jeremiah xlii. 16 "follow close"; in Job xli. 17 "joined"; and in Gen. xxxi. 23 "overtook." Now if we look at the above Scriptures, we find the following thoughts:—Affection, devotion, faithfulness, attention, oneness, and earnestness. If we are following hard after the Lord there will be:—

1. Affection for Him.
2. Devotedness to Him.
3. Faithfulness to Him.
4. Attention to Him.
5. Oneness with Him.
6. Earnestness of aim to be near Him.

"Hard after Thee." As the sheep follows the shepherd; as the student his studies; as the business man his business; as the athlete for the prize; as the bird after its food; and as a hunter after the prey.

"Thee." Not theories, not dogmas, not self, not the world, or pleasure, but Thee, Thee alone, and Thee always.

461. TWO SIFTINGS

1. **Subtleness.** "Simon, Simon, behold, Satan hath desired to have you, that he may sift you as wheat" (Luke xxii. 31). Satan sifts to get rid of the wheat. Beware of the Devil's riddle.

2. **Searching.** "I will sift the house of Israel among all nations, like as corn is sifted in a sieve, yet shall not the least grain fall upon the earth" (Amos ix. 9). The Lord will bring Israel to Himself yet, but we may apply this to ourselves now. The Lord puts us in the sieve of chastisement, the sieve of trial, the sieve of humiliation, the sieve of difficulty, the sieve of disappointment, the sieve of persecution, and the sieve of wake-up-edness. What for? To get rid of the wheat? No; but to get rid of the chaff of pride, worldliness, sloth, and unbelief.

462. TWO WANTS

I. **Penury.** "Began to be in want" (Luke xv. 14). Notice the downward steps of the prodigal:—

1. His discontent. "Give me the portion of goods that falleth to me."

2. His distance. "Took his journey into a far country."

3. His dissipation. "There wasted his substance in riotous living."

4. His destitution. "And when he had spent all, there arose a mighty famine in that land."

5. His distress. "He began to be in want."

6. His disgrace. "Joined himself to a citizen of that country, and he sent him into his fields to feed swine." Thomas Fuller says, "He came from the keeping of harlots to the minding of the hogs."

7. His dismay. "I perish with hunger."

It is to the fifth downward step we draw attention now, viz., his distress or penury. "He began to be in want." The word "*hustereo*," translated "*want*" in the above passage, is rendered in Romans iii. 23, "*short;*" in Phil. iv. 12, "*suffer;*" and in Heb. xi. 37, "*destitute*." The meaning of the word is, to be behind, to be lacking, to fall short, to be last or inferior. Now, if we bear this in mind, and look at the Scriptures where this word occurs, we see the prodigal's condition portrays to the letter the condition of the sinner. Coming short of God's glory, we are bound to suffer need, that brings us into a state of destitution, and thus we are sure to be in want. He that wants Christ lacks everything; he that has Christ needs nothing.

II. **Plenty.** "The Lord is my Shepherd, I shall not want" (Psalm xxiii. 1). It has often been noticed that six of the titles of Jehovah are illustrated in this Psalm, but all ten of the titles may be seen.

1. *Jehovah-Rohi.* "Jehovah, my Shepherd" (Psalm xxiii. 1). What a Shepherd He is! The Good Shepherd who died; God's Shepherd to bear His wrath; the Great Shepherd who rose again; the One Shepherd over His flock; the Chief Shepherd, who is coming again; and last, but not least, the believer can say, "My Shepherd."

2. *Jehovah-Jireh.* "The Lord will provide" (Gen. xxii. 14 M.). "I shall not want." He has provided for our need as sinners in the death of Christ. He provides for our need as saints in the Risen Christ. He provides for our need as servants by His Word and Spirit. He provides for our need as warriors in the Truth. And when He comes again, He will provide for us for ever.

3. *Jehovah-Shalom.* "Jehovah, send peace" (Judges vi. 24). "He maketh me to lie down in green pastures. He leadeth me beside the still waters." He provides rest and refreshment, provender and peace; He does it all. We have to be careful for nothing, prayerful about everything, and thankful for anything.

4. *Jehovah-Tsebahoth.* "Jehovah of hosts" (I. Samuel i. 3, &c.). "He leadeth me." He goes before; ours it is to follow. He directs; ours it is to obey. He guides; ours it is to be led.

5. *Jehovah-Ropheca.* "Jehovah that healeth thee" (Ex. xv. 26). "He restoreth my soul," &c. He renews our strength. He brings us back if we wander, forgives our backsliding, and heals us of the causes of it.

6. *Jehovah-Tsidkenu.* "The Lord our Righteousness" (Jeremiah xxiii. 6; xxxiii. 16). "He leadeth me in the paths of righteousness." He has put us right before God. He is our Righteousness, and He keeps us right before men.

7. *Jehovah-Shammah.* "Jehovah is there" (Ez. xlviii. 35). "Thou art with me." With us to sustain, comfort, succour, cheer, sympathize, defend, save, keep, sanctify, and bless.

8. *Jehovah-Nissi.* "Jehovah my Banner" (Exodus xvii. 15). "Thou preparest a table before me in the presence of mine enemies." He is the Captain who never lost a battle. He feasts us in the sight of our foes; He furnishes with armour for the conflict; and fits us for the fray.

9. *Jehovah-Mekaddeshcem.* "Jehovah that doth sanctify you." (Ex. xxxi. 13). If we spell holiness with five letters—Jesus—we shall find that they will be like David's five smooth stones taken out of the brook, and slung in the strength of God, will kill any giant that we may meet.

10. *Jehovah-Heleyon.* "Jehovah most high" (Psalm vii. 17) "Dwell in the house of the Lord for ever."

463. TYPICAL COLOURS

Exodus xxv. 3-7

THE different things brought by the children of Israel represent the glory of the person and work of Christ.

Gold represents the divine glory of the Lord Jesus as the Son of God, and also the Lord Jesus as the Righteousness of God (Canticles v. 11).

Silver represents Christ in the value of His person atoning for sin, and the result of it to us, viz., redemption (I. Peter i. 18; Exodus xxx. 11-16).

Bronze or brass represents Him enduring the fire of God's judgment against sin (Revelation i. 15; John iii. 14).

Blue is the heavenly colour, and represents Him as the Heavenly One in the beauty of His person, dispensing heavenly blessings (Exodus xxiv. 10; Ezekiel i. 26).

Purple is the royal colour, and represents Him as the Lord and King (Judges viii. 26; John xix. 2, 5).

Scarlet represents Jesus as the suffering One; and as the glorified One—" ought not Christ to have suffered these things, and to have entered into His glory ?" (Heb. ix. 19; Matt. xxvii. 28).

Fine linen or silk (margin) represents Him as the spotless Son of Man in His person and ways (Rev. xv. 6; xix. 8; I. Pet. i. 19).

Goats' Hair. This seems to have a double meaning: *first*, it is the memorial of Jesus as the Sin Bearer, from the fact that the goats' hair covering of the tabernacle was bigger than the other coverings, the extra piece being doubled and hung down in front of the tabernacle (Exodus xxvi. 7, 9; II. Cor. v. 21); for it was a goat that was slain on the day of atonement as a sin offering (Lev. xvi. 15), thus the goats' hair covering would remind the children of Israel of the slain goat. *Second*, the hair has reference to separation, from the fact that the Nazarite was to let his hair grow long, and it would thus represent Jesus as separate from all outward evil and sin (Hebrews vii. 26).

Rams' Skins Dyed Red, which represents Christ's obedience unto death, even the death of the cross (Phil. ii. 8).

Badger Skins, which represents the outward appearance of Christ to the world. They could not appreciate the beauty of His Person and His perfect holiness. He was to them as a Root out of a dry ground, without form or comeliness (Isaiah liii. 2).

Shittim Wood, which represents Christ's holy humanity (Luke i. 35).

Oil for the Light, which represents Christ in the power of the Spirit testifying to the glory of God (Acts x. 38).

Spices for the Anointing Oil, which represent Christ acting in the power of the Spirit in His life, death, and resurrection, and the fragrance that went up to the Father as He did so (John viii. 29).

Sweet Incense. Christ's intercession for us now (Rom. viii. 34).

Onyx Stones. Job speaks of the precious onyx stone (Job xxviii. 16), therefore this represents Christ as the precious One—" Unto you, therefore, which believe He is precious" (I. Peter ii. 7).

Stones for the Ephod and Breastplate. The moral glories and beauty of the Person of Christ (Canticles v. 10-16).

As the children of Israel brought the different things to the Lord for the tabernacle, so we may bring spiritual sacrifices to Him, praising Him for all that He has revealed Himself to be in the Person and work of His Son, for having revealed Christ in us, and praying Him to reveal the moral beauties of the Person of Christ through us in our life, that glory may be brought to Him thereby.

464. UNDERSTANDING HEART

An understanding heart is a—

1. **Christ-knowing Heart.** "That we may know Him that is true" (I. John v. 20).

2. **Truth-enlightened Heart.** "The eyes of your understanding being enlightened" (Ephesians i. 18).

3. **Christ-instructed Heart.** "Then opened He their understanding" (Luke xxiv. 45).

4. **Faith-influenced Heart.** "Through faith we understand that the worlds were framed by the Word of God" (Heb. xi. 3).

5. **Bible-loving Heart.** "Daniel understood by books" (Daniel ix. 2).

6. **Word-keeping Heart.** "That I may live, and keep Thy Word" (Psalm cxix. 17).

7. **Grace-taught Heart.** "The Lord give thee understanding in all things" (II. Timothy ii. 7).

465. UNFAILING THINGS

THINGS that have to do with man fail, but the things which have to do with God, are like Himself—unfailing (Zeph. iii. 5).

Things which do not fail—

1. **The Lord's Presence.** "The Lord thy God, He it is that doth go with thee; He will not *fail* thee" (Deut. xxxi. 6).

2. **The Lord's Faithfulness.** "Nor suffer My faithfulness to *fail*" (Psalm lxxxix. 33).

3. **The Lord's Compassions.** "His compassions *fail* not" (Lamentations iii. 22).

4. **The Lord's Care.** "Neither shall the cruise of oil *fail*" (I. Kings xvii. 14).

5. **The Lord's Law.** "It is easier for heaven and earth to pass, than one tittle of the law to *fail*" (Luke xvi. 17).

6. **The Lord's Christ.** "Thy years shall not *fail*" (Heb. i. 12).

7. **The Lord's Promise.** "There *failed* not ought of any good thing which the Lord had spoken" (Joshua xxi. 45).

8. **The Lord's Love.** "Love never *faileth*" (I. Cor. xiii. 8., R.V.).

9. **The Lord's Stars.** "Not one *faileth*" (Isaiah xl. 26).

466. UNFAITHFULNESS

1. **Unfaithfulness is the Forerunner of Defeat,** as seen in the case of Achan touching the consecrated wealth (Joshua vii.).

2. **Unfaithfulness is the Extinguisher of Testimony,** as indicated in Christ's threat to the Church in Ephesus (Rev. ii. 5).

3. **Unfaithfulness means the Rod of Chastisement,** as is evidenced in the Lord's action to the chastised in the Church at Corinth (I. Corinthians xi. 30-32).

4. **Unfaithfulness means Loss of Power,** as illustrated in the lack of Church discipline in the case of the Church at Corinth, when they allowed the leaven of evil to be in their midst unjudged (I. Corinthians v.).

5. **Unfaithfulness is the Cup of Bitterness** which we fill for our own drinking, as is exhibited in King Saul when he failed to carry out the Divine behest in the utter destruction of Amalek (I. Samuel xv.).

6. **Unfaithfulness is the Napkin of Laziness,** like the man who wrapped his talent in a napkin, and was punished for his wilful neglect (Matthew xxv. 30).

7. **Unfaithfulness is the Sapper of Judgment** which undermines the house of the unfaithful one, and brings it down upon him to his destruction, as is illustrated in the house of Eli (I. Sam. ii. 27-36).

467. UNITY

THE secret of the blessing the early Christians enjoyed, and the power they were for good, may be summed up in one word—"Unity." This is seen in connection with those trite and telling words, "One accord," which occur again and again in the Acts. Mark "Accord," not "Discord." The Church should be like a well-tuned harp, upon which the Master of Assemblies can play the melodies of righteousness and holiness of life, love to each other, and glory to God in the highest.

1. **Unity in Prayer.** "These all continued with *one accord* in prayer and supplication" (Acts i. 14).

2. **Unity in Obedience.** "They were all with *one accord* in one place" (Acts ii. 1).

3. **Unity of Presence.** "They were all with *one accord* in one place" (Acts ii. 1).

4. **Unity of Purpose.** "Continuing daily with *one accord* in the temple." "Praising God" (Acts ii. 46, 47).

5. **Unity in Praise.** "Lifted up their voice to God with *one accord*" (Acts iv. 24).

6. **Unity in Service.** "They were all with *one accord* in Solomon's porch" (Acts v. 12).

7. **Unity in recognizing God's Servants.** "It seemed good unto us, being assembled with *one accord*, to send chosen men unto you, with our beloved Barnabas and Paul" (Acts xv. 25).

468. UNSURPASSED GLORY OF THE LORD

1. **His Ways are Untrackable.** "His ways past finding out" (Romans xi. 33).

2. **His Riches are Unsearchable.** "The unsearchable riches of Christ" (Ephesians iii. 8).

3. **His Love is Unknowable.** "The love of Christ which passeth knowledge" (Ephesians iii. 19).

4. **His Joy is Unspeakable.** "Joy unspeakable, and full of glory" (I. Peter i. 8).

5. **His Goodness is Unsurpassable.** "Behold therefore the goodness . . . of God" (Romans xi. 22).

6. **His Peace is not Understandable.** "Peace of God, which passeth all understanding" (Philippians iv. 7).

7. **He Himself is Indescribable.** "He is altogether lovely" (Canticles v. 16).

469. UNTO HIM

1. **Gathering.** Unto Him let us gather. "*Unto Him* shall the gathering of the people be" (Genesis xlix. 10).

2. **Listening.** Unto Him let us listen. "Then drew near *unto Him* all the publicans and sinners for to hear Him" (Luke xv. 1).

3. **Coming.** Unto Him let us bring everything. "Mary was come . . . *unto Him*" (John xi. 32).

4. **Suffering.** Unto Him let us go outside the camp bearing His reproach. "Let us go forth therefore *unto Him* without the camp, bearing His reproach" (Hebrews xiii. 13).

5. **Living.** Unto Him let us live. "Should not henceforth live unto ourselves, but *unto Him*" (II. Corinthians v. 15).

6. **Looking.** Unto Him that is able to do, let us look. "*Unto Him* that is able to do exceeding abundantly" (Ephesians iii. 20).

7. **Glory** unto Him we shall soon be gathered in the glory. "By our gathering together *unto Him*" (II. Thessalonians ii. 1).

And our song then, as now, shall be, "*Unto Him* be glory" (Ephesians iii. 21).

470. "UPON"

THE Gospel according to "*Upon*," that is, as revolving around the preposition "*Epi*," is full of instruction.

1. **The Substitute upon the Tree frees the Believer from sin's consequences.** "Bare our sins in His own body *on* (Epi) the tree" (I. Peter ii. 24).

2. **The Righteousness of God upon the Believer makes him beautiful.** "*Upon* all them that believe" (Rom. iii. 22).

3. **Being built on Christ, the Foundation makes the Believer to partake of His life.** "Build *upon* this foundation" (I. Corinthians iii. 12).

4. **To cast all care upon the Lord is the Believer's Privilege.** "Casting all your care *upon* Him" (I. Peter v. 7).

5. **The Spirit of God resting upon the Believer is his Glory and Power.** "Spirit of God resteth *upon* you" (I. Peter iv. 14).

6. **The Power of Christ upon the Believer, is the Strengthener for every trial.** "Power of Christ may rest *upon* me" (II. Corinthians xii. 9).

7. **The Grace of the Holy Spirit upon the Believer is the Outcome of Whole-hearted Surrender to Him.** "Great grace was *upon* them all" (Acts iv. 33).

471. UPPER ROOM MEETINGS

THE "upper room" in Jerusalem was a place which was memorable because of what occurred there. It was in the upper room that Christ uttered those words which we have recorded in the 14th, 15th, 16th, and 17th chapters of John. I remember a good brother at a prayer meeting in Peterhead, in the north of Scotland, praying for a mission, which was to be conducted by myself, asking that we might have "upper room meetings." I quickly responded "Amen!"

What kind of meeting did Christ have in the upper room? The following seven P's will indicate what is associated with the meeting of Christ and His disciples in the upper room.

1. **Promise** of Christ's return (John xiv. 1-7).

2. **Presence** of the Holy Spirit to comfort and help (John xiv. 16-26).

3. **Peace** of Christ to calm and still (John xiv. 27).

4. **Progress** in fruit-bearing through abiding in Christ (John xv. 1-17).

5. **Persecution** from the world through our association with Christ (John xv. 18-25).

6. **Power** of the Holy Spirit through the believer, convicting of sin (John xvi. 7-14).

7. **Prayer** of Christ for His people; an illustration of what He is doing at present (John xvii.).

472. WALK

THOSE who are saved by Christ, endeavour to fulfil His commands to—

1. **Walk in Love.** "*Walk* in love, as Christ also hath loved us" (Ephesians v. 2).

2. **Walk in the Truth.** "Thou *walkest* in the Truth" (III. John 3).

3. **Walk in the Spirit.** "*Walk* in the Spirit" (Gal. v. 16).

4. **Walk by faith.** "We *walk* by faith" (II. Cor. v. 7).

5. **Walk in Newness of Life.** "*Walk* in newness of life" (Romans vi. 4).

6. **Walk Honestly.** "Let us *walk* honestly" (Rom. xiii. 13).

7. **Walk Worthy of the Lord.** "*Walk* worthy of the Lord unto all pleasing" (Colossians i. 10).

473. WALK OF THE BELIEVER

THERE is a seven-fold walk of the child of God:—

1. **Wisely.** In the house (Psalm ci. 2).
2. **Lovingly.** In the Church (Ephesians v. 1, 2).
3. **Circumspectly.** In the world (Ephesians v. 15).
4. **Thoroughly.** In the truth (II. John iv.).
5. **Continually.** In the light (I. John i. 7).
6. **Dependently.** In the Spirit (Galatians v. 16, 25).
7. **Submissively.** In the Lord (Colossians ii. 6).

474. WATCHFULNESS

MATTHEW xxiv. 42-51

THERE are many things against which we should watch. We should watch ourselves, lest any evil arise and hurt our life (I. Thess. v. 6). We should watch against the enemy of our souls, who prowls about like an evil beast in search of prey (I. Peter v. 8). We should watch against the allurements of the world, which will fascinate the soul like the boa-constrictor does the bird, when it is held by the gaze of the serpent; and we should watch for Christ, as the watcher guards the city, for Christ may come at any time, and it becomes us to be ready.

1. **We should watch for Christ, because of the Person who commands us to do so.** "Your *Lord*" (verse 42). One of the forgotten truths of to-day, is the Lordship of Christ. His Lordship reminds us of His right to us, for we are His by purchase (I. Corinthians vi. 20), and purpose (Ephesians i. 4). Christ as our Lord tells us of His claim upon us, for since we are His we have no right to ourselves; therefore, His will should be our delight (Psalm xl. 8), His word our law (Psalm cxix. 44), and His way our pattern (I. Peter ii. 21). Further, Christ as Lord speaks of our

being His bond servants, *i.e.*, slaves. Paul ever gloried in being the "servant (slave) of Jesus Christ" (Romans i. 1). The negro Christian expressed the truth when in prayer he asked the Lord to keep him, in the following words: "O Lord, if You do not look after Your property, it will go wrong."

2. **We should watch for Christ, because we do not know when He may come** (verse 44). The coming of Christ is a subject that has been brought into ill-repute because of unholy speculation. *When* Christ may come we dare not say, but that He *is* coming, He Himself has said. Dare we question His word on the one hand, or speculate about it on the other?

3. **We should watch for Christ, for it will make us morally and holily ready for Him.** The hope of Christ's return is purifying in its effect, as we read in I. John iii. 2, 3. "Ready for either," is the inscription upon the seal of one of our Missionary Societies, which seal has also upon it an ox, standing between a plough and an altar; this at once suggests that the ox is ready for service or sacrifice. Thus all who are Christ's should be ready to do His will, whether that will means suffering or serving.

Of those who go into the marriage supper of the Lamb, readiness is the result of their righteous acts (Revelation xix. 8, R.V.).

4. **Watching for Christ is an indication of our faithfulness to Him** (verse 45). Faithfulness is only another word for obedience. King Saul lost his kingdom, through his unfaithfulness in not obeying the voice of the Lord (I. Samuel xv. 23); while Paul the Apostle has a "crown of righteousness," because he kept the faith and ran in the race faithfully (II. Timothy iv. 7, 8). The wise and faithful servant is one who gives to the household their meat in due season (verse 45). Those who act according to God's heart (Jeremiah iii. 15), ever seek to give, by life and lips, the Bread of Life to hungry souls.

5. **Watching for Christ will bring blessing now and reward hereafter** (verses 46, 47). Blessing is the gift of grace (Eph. i. 3), but reward is the outcome of service (II. Cor. v. 10).

6. Watching for Christ will preserve us from evil, and beget faithfulness to Him in every particular (verses 48-51).

475. WEAK ONES

1. The weak ones whom Jehovah uses are **tested** ones (Judges vii. 2-7).

2. The weak ones whom the Lord uses are **not anxious** about their own comfort (Judges vii. 6).

3. The weak ones whom God uses are **obedient** (Judges vii. 17-20).

4. The weak ones whom God uses are **dependent** ones (Judges vii. 18, 20).

5. The weak ones whom God uses are **united** (Judges vii. 22).

6. The weak ones whom the Lord uses are **victorious** ones (Judges vii. 21).

7. The weak ones are used as **reflectors** of God's glory (Judges vii. 2).

8. The used of God are **sure** to have their action called in question by their brethren (Judges viii. 1).

9. The instruments of God are **persevering**, although faint (Judges viii. 4).

10. The instruments of the Lord are **faithful** (Judges vii. 8).

11. The instruments of the Lord may **fall into sin** unless careful (Judges viii. 24, 27).

12. The weak ones are a **source of blessing** to others (Judges viii. 28).

476. WE HAVE

THERE are many things that the Holy Spirit says we have in Christ—

1. **Peace.** "We *have* peace with God" (Romans v. 1).

2. **Redemption.** "In Whom we *have* redemption through His blood" (Ephesians i. 7).

3. **Eternal Life.** "These things have I written unto you that believe on the name of the Son of God; that ye may know that ye *have* eternal life" (I. John v. 13).

4. **The Spirit of Adoption.** "Ye *have* received the Spirit of adoption, whereby we cry, Abba, Father" (Rom. viii. 15).

5. **Strong Consolation.** "We might *have* a strong consolation" (Hebrews vi. 18).

6. **A Sure Anchor.** "Which hope we *have* as an anchor of the soul, both sure and stedfast" (Hebrews vi. 19).

7. **A Great High Priest.** "We *have* such an High Priest" (Hebrews viii. 1).

8. **A Glorified Body in Reserve.** "We *have* a building of God, a house not made with hands" (II. Cor. v. 1).

9. **Provision.** "We *have* an Altar" (Heb. xiii. 10).

477. WELL-PLEASING

1. **Whole-hearted Presentation of Ourselves.** "Present your bodies a living sacrifice, holy, *well-pleasing* (margin) to God" (Romans xii. 1, R.V.).

2. **The Purpose in all our Life.** "Make it our aim . . . to be *well-pleasing* unto Him" (II. Cor. v. 9, R.V.).

3. **Walking as Children of the Light.** "Proving what is *well-pleasing* unto the Lord" (Eph. v. 10, R.V.).

4. **Ministering to the Need of Others.** "A sacrifice acceptable, *well-pleasing* to God" (Phil. iv. 18).

5. **Obedience to those who are over us.** "Children obey your parents . . . . . . for this is *well-pleasing* in the Lord" (Colossians iii. 20, R.V.).

6. **An Illustration of Well-pleasingness.** "Enoch . . . . . had been *well-pleasing* unto God" (Heb. xi. 5, R.V.).

7. **Holding fast Grace for Service.** "We may offer service *well-pleasing* to God" (Heb. xii. 28, R.V.).

8. **Doing good to others.** "To do good . . . . . . God is *well-pleased*" (Heb. xiii. 16, R.V.).

9. **Allowing God to Work in us.** "Working in us that which is *well-pleasing*" (Heb. xiii. 21, R.V.).

478. WENT DOWN

THE down-grade towards, and in evil and error is no modern practice.

1. **A Saint out of Communion.** "Abram *went down* into Egypt" (Genesis xii. 10).

2. **A Backsliding Worker.** "Jonah *went down* to Joppa" (Jonah i. 3); "*went down* into it" (Jonah i. 3); "*went down* to the bottoms" (Jonah ii. 6).

3. **A Self-willed Actor.** "Samson *went down* to Timnath . . . She is right in mine eyes" (Judges xiv. 1-3, M.).

4. **A Disobedient Alliance.** Jehoshaphat "*went down* to Ahab" (II. Chron. xviii. 1, 2; II. Cor. vi. 14).

5. **A Robbed Man.** "*Went down* from Jerusalem" (the place of blessing) "to Jericho" (the cursed place), "and fell among thieves" (Luke x. 30). An illustration of what sin has done for man.

6. **Cleansed Leper.** Naaman "*went down* and dipped himself seven times in Jordan . . . . . and he was clean" (II. Kings v. 14). Jordan means judgment; Christ went down into the Jordan of God's judgment, that we might be cleansed from sin (Matt. iii.; Rom. viii.).

7. **Punished Rebels.** "Korah . . . *went down* alive into the pit" (Sheol, Numbers xvi. 32, 33).

479. WHAT CHRIST WAS MADE

THE following seven Scriptures, where the word "*made*" occurs, will indicate what Christ became and suffered :—

1. **His Condescension.** "*Made* flesh" (John i. 14).

2. **His Identification.** "*Made* in the likeness of men" (Phil. ii. 7).

3. **His Humiliation.** "*Made* of a woman" (Galatians iv. 4).
4. **His Compassion.** "*Made* under the law" (Galatians iv. 4).
5. **His Obedience.** "*Became* * obedient unto death" (Phil. ii. 8).
6. **His Condemnation.** "*Made* a curse" (Galatians iii. 13).
7. **His Sin-bearing.** "*Made* Him to be sin" (II. Cor. v. 21).

480. WHAT DOES IT MEAN TO BE SAVED

1. **Submission to Christ.** "The Church is subject unto Christ" (Ephesians v. 24).

2. **Apprehended by Christ.** "I am apprehended of Christ Jesus" (Philippians iii. 12).

3. **Vitalized in Christ.** "I can do all things through Christ" (Philippians iv. 13).

4. **Enchanted with Christ.** "Whom have I in heaven?" (Psalm lxxiii. 25).

5. **Decided for Christ.** "I believe that Jesus Christ is the Son of God" (Acts viii. 37).

481. WHAT AN IMPERFECT HEART MEANS

SOLOMON'S SIN. I. KINGS XI. 4-13

SOLOMON began well, but he ended ill. The fair morning of his life is followed by the foul weather of inconsistency in the evening of his career. The rosy apple has a maggot which spoils it. As the Thames for many miles from its source is sweet and healthful, but when it passes through London it is polluted by the pollution that pours into it; so the first part of Solomon's life is beautiful with godliness, but the latter part of it is blighted with idolatry and sensuality. And all this arose from one cause, namely, an imperfect heart.

1. **An imperfect heart is a divided heart** (verse 4, 5). Solomon could give good instruction (I. Kings viii. 61), but he did not continue in following up his own precept. He thought he could share his affection with the gods of the heathen. There are many to-day who think that they can go with the world, and with Christ too. No one can serve two masters (Matt. vi. 24); we must be for Christ, or against Him (Matt. xii. 30). A friend of the world is an enemy to God (James iv. 4).

2. **An imperfect heart is a defaulting heart.** Solomon was was not like his father David (verse 4), who, in spite of his failures, was true in his loyalty to the Lord, and did not get into the meshes of idolatry. The remembrance of what David was, should have kept Solomon true to Jehovah. When the eyes of the soul get off the Lord, and look to that which is pleasing to the flesh, then it

* Same word as in the previous verses.

will not be long before we mix with the ungodly as Lot did (Genesis xix. 1), boast in self-confidence as Peter did (Luke xxii. 33), lie as Abraham did (Genesis xx. 2), get in danger as Jehoshaphat did (II. Chronicles xviii. 31), look to men as the Corinthians did (I. Corinthians i. 12), feel the chastening hand of God as Israel did (I. Cor. x. 5), and listen to the voice of the ungodly as Solomon did, when he hearkened to the voice of his wives.

3. **An imperfect heart is a distant heart** (verse 6). "Went not fully." Ah! here is the cause of his declension. If we note what it is to follow the Lord fully, we shall be better able to determine what it is, not to thus follow Him. To follow the Lord fully, signifies that we consecrate * ourselves to Him as Israel did (II. Chron. xxix. 31); we act in faith as Joshua did, when he wholly * followed the Lord (Joshua xiv. 8); we fulfil * the Word of the Lord, as Judah did unconsciously when carried away into captivity (II. Chron. xxxvi. 21); we devote our whole strength to the Lord, as when Jehu drew the bow with his full * strength (II. Kings ix. 24); we serve the Lord, as He has enjoined, as Jacob fulfilled * the specified time for Rachel (Genesis xxix. 28); we occupy the place the Lord intends, as the precious stones were set * in the breastplate of the High Priest according to His instructions (Exodus xxxix. 10); and we are guided and empowered by the Holy Spirit, as the workmen of the tabernacle were filled * with the Spirit for their employment (Exodus xxviii. 3). It goes without the saying that the antithesis to all this is, not to follow the Lord fully.

4. **An imperfect heart is a defiled heart** (verse 7). Solomon's association with idolatry would bring him into contact with the ungodly, hence, he was bound to be defiled. The breath of the world will tarnish the brightness of our faith; the contaminating touch of iniquity will blacken our life; the influence of covetousness will damp down the fire of our love; the infection of doubt will poison our confidence; the malaria of envy will fever our soul; the frost of self will chill our affection; and the leprosy of sin will infect our nature, and extinguish our testimony.

5. **An imperfect heart is a displeasing heart** (verse 9). The ire of Jehovah was kindled against Solomon, because of his back-sliding. He had received many privileges, for the Lord had twice appeared to him (I. Kings iii. 5; ix. 2). But he forgets his blessing. To displease the Lord means, that we place ourselves under His chastening hand, which will bring us sorrow of heart, and soreness of spirit.

6. **An imperfect heart is a disobedient heart** (verse 10). Solomon was disobedient in a twofold sense. First, in marrying the "strange women" (verses 1, 2), for the Lord had given plain and specific instructions that none of His people were to do this

* The words "*consecrate*" in II. Chronicles xxix. 31, "*wholly*" in Joshua xiv. 8, "*fulfil*" in II. Chronicles xxxvi. 21, "*full*" in II. Kings ix. 24, "*fulfilled*" in Genesis xxix. 28, "*set*" in Exodus xxxix. 10, and "*filled*" in Exodus xxviii. 3, are the same in the Hebrew.

(Exodus xxxiv. 16; Deuteronomy vii. 3, 4); and second, Solomon was disobedient in going after "other gods" (Exodus xx. 4). These commands have an application to us now (II. Corinthians vi. 14: Matthew iv. 10), and well for us if we follow the Divine instruction, for obedience is always the pathway of blessing.

7. **An imperfect heart is a disintegrating heart** (verse 11). Solomon's sin led to the dismemberment of his empire. He did not live to see it, but it came in God's appointed time. If God's mills grind slowly, they none the less grind surely. When we sin, we not only bring damage to ourselves, but we also bring distress to others.

482. "WHAT DOES IT MEAN TO FOLLOW JESUS?"

It is well that we should ponder the privileges of the Christian life, but we must not forget that those privileges mean corresponding responsibilities; and it is also well to remember that we cannot fulfil the responsibilities, only as we enjoy by faith the privileges. To come to Christ, and to receive from Christ, are our privileges; and to abide in Christ, and to follow after Him, are our responsibilities.

To follow Christ, means at least three things; and these are—sacrifice, suffering, and glory.

1. **Sacrifice.** In the case of the disciples it meant leaving their nets (Matthew iv. 19, 20): with Matthew, forsaking the "receipt of custom" (Matthew ix. 9); and with the rich young ruler it was "sell all that thou hast, and distribute to the poor" (Luke xviii. 22). To follow Christ, means at least two things, namely, the denial of self itself (Matthew xvi. 24); and the putting Christ and His claims first (Luke ix. 57-62).

2. **Suffering.** Christ's distinct and definite command to Peter, as He tells him that he will have to die for Him, is, "Follow Me" (John xxi. 19). Peter understood that to mean death (II. Peter i. 14). There is a "cross" for every follower of Christ (Mark x. 21), and a death to the self-life, in order that we may bring forth fruit unto God (John xii. 24-26). Jordan with its baptism, Gethsemane with its bitter cup, Gabbatha with its fiendish mockery, Golgotha with its shame, the Cross with its suffering, the darkness with its cry, and Calvary with its death, have their counterpart in our experience.

3. **Glory.** It is to His followers that Christ promises that they shall "sit in the throne of His glory" (Matthew xix. 28); who shall be with Him, and also be honoured by the Father (John xii. 26). Christ not only leads His followers to the Mount of Calvary to suffer with Him, but He also leads them to the Mount of Transfiguration, that they may be glorified with Him.

To follow Christ in holiness of life, in compassion of heart, in devotion of service, in abandonment of will, in patience of spirit, in earnestness of soul, and in loyalty to truth, is to evidence that we are His sheep (John x. 27). Surely, this is the least we can do, even as Bartimæus (Mark x. 52), and the noble band of women (Matthew xxvii. 55). Of the former we read, "He followed Jesus in the way," and of the latter we read, "which followed Jesus into Galilee, ministering unto Him."

483. WHAT EVERY MAN NEEDS

ALL men need the following seven things, among many others, whether they know it or not:—

1. **Saviour, to deliver** from the power of darkness (Col. i. 13), as Israel needed to be delivered from Pharaoh's power (Exodus iii. 8).

2. **Strength, to empower** the soul to walk in God's ways (Isaiah xl. 31), as the lame man required power to enable him to walk (Acts iii. 6).

3. **Satisfier to fill,** that the longing of the heart may be met (Psalm cvii. 9), as the need of the multitude was satisfied with Christ's provision (John vi. 11, 12).

4. **Sanctifier to separate,** that the believer may be separated from the evil, and kept to the good (II. Cor. vii. 1), as the Levites were sanctified by Aaron (Numbers xviii. 2, &c.).

5. **Succourer, to aid** in the hour of weakness and temptation (Hebrews ii. 18), as David was the succourer of Israel when he acted on their behalf (I. Samuel xvii. 50).

6. **Shield, to defend** in the time of aggressive warfare (Eph. vi. 16), as Paul indicates when he writes to Timothy (II. Timothy ii. 1-4).

7. **Sovereign to rule,** that the domain of man-soul may be kept under the rule of Emmanuel (I. Peter iii. 15, R.V.); this is illustrated in the centurion, who said that he was a man under authority (Luke vii. 8).

484. WHAT IS A CHRISTIAN?

1. **Believer in faith.** "Believeth on the Son" (John iii. 36).

2. **Servant in responsibility.** "Blessed is that servant" (Luke xii. 43).

3. **Branch in union.** "I am the Vine, ye are the branches" (John xv. 5).

4. **Friend in privilege.** "I have called you friends . . . . . I have made known unto you" (John xv. 15).

5. **Witness in testimony.** "Thou shalt be His witness unto all men" (Acts xxii. 15).

6. **Steward in trust.** "As good stewards of the manifold grace of God" (I. Peter iv. 10).

7. **Light in influence.** "Ye are the light of the world ..... Let your light so shine" (Matthew v. 14, 16).

8. **Salt in power.** "Ye are the salt of the earth" (Matt. v. 13).

485. WHAT IS A CHRISTIAN?

WHAT is a Christian? Many are the answers that have been given to the above question. The servant girl's definition of Christians was very far out, who, when asked what Christians were, replied, "People that go to church and chapel, that talk about religion, and take the parson home to tea." That was her idea of a Christian, which, doubtless, she had gathered from the *professing* Christians with whom she had come in contact, but we need hardly say that this is not the Scriptural definition of a Christian.

"Christian names are everywhere;
Christian men are very rare."

The little girl was nearer the mark when she said, "A Christian is a born-again person;" for to be born again, is to be—

Saved by the grace of God. "By grace *are* ye saved through faith" (Ephesians ii. 8).

Sanctified in the Person of Christ. "Church of God .... to them that *are* sanctified in Christ Jesus" (I. Corinthians i. 2).

Sealed with the Holy Spirit. "Grieve not the Holy Spirit of God, whereby ye *are* sealed unto the day of redemption" (Ephesians iv. 30).

Shining for the Lord Jesus. "Ye *are* the light of the world" (Matthew v. 14).

Serving with the Lord. "We *are* labourers together with God" (I. Corinthians iii. 9).

Slaves of the Lord. "Ye *are* not your own, for ye *are* bought with a price" (I. Corinthians vi. 19, 20).

Surrendering to the Lord. "To whom ye yield yourselves servants to obey, his servants ye *are*" (Romans vi. 16). Note that in the Scriptures the word "*are*" occurs against each point, and, if they are carefully looked at, we shall find that a past definite act, a present fact, and a continuous consequence are referred to. What is a Christian? One has said, in defining a Christian, that he is—

"In faith, a believer in Christ.
In relationship, a child of God.
In character, a saint.
In influence, a light.
In communion, a friend.
In conflict, a soldier.
In experience, a pilgrim.
In expectation, an heir."

486. WHAT IS A CHRISTIAN?

WHAT is a Christian? Bunyan, in his *Pilgrim's Progress*, simply defines, and in descriptive imagery depicts the path and progress of a Christian.

1. **An awakened Sinner.** A Christian is one who has been *convinced* of his sinfulness and guilt as a sinner before God, as seen in the burden on Christian's back (Psalm xxxviii. 4).

2. **A trustful Man.** A Christian is one who has *come* to the Saviour, as pictured in Christian coming up to the wicket gate, and entering into the path that leads therefrom (Matt. xi. 28).

3. **A righteous one.** A Christian is one who is *clothed* with the garment of righteousness, as we see in Christian being clothed at the cross (II. Cor. v. 21).

4. **An earnest Worker.** A Christian is one who is *concerned* about the welfare of others, as illustrated in Christian going up to, and seeking to arouse Simple, Sloth, and Presumption (Jude 23).

5. **A communing Companion.** A Christian is one who *companions* with the people of God. Talkative and Ignorance can have no fellowship with Christian, but Faithful and Hopeful are his fast friends (I. John iii. 14).

6. **A dominated Believer.** A Christian is one who is *controlled* by the Word of God, as seen in Christian consulting his roll. A true Christian receives the *whole* of the Bible as God's Word, and dares not utter such blasphemy as a Free Church Professor has recently done. He says: "A man may be a true (?) Christian (?) and yet find much in the Bible which he cannot accept." Rev. xxii. 19 is the direct contradiction to this, for what is said there may be applied to all Scripture (II. Tim. iii. 16, 17).

7. **A persevering Saint.** A Christian is one who *continues* in the way of holiness, as illustrated in the perseverance of Christian. Lions may frighten him; Doubt may lead him into captivity; and Flattery ensnare him, but he keeps on (John viii. 31).

8. **A confessing Pilgrim.** A Christian is one who *confesses* that he is a pilgrim and stranger, as depicted in Christian and Faithful passing through Vanity Fair (Heb. xi. 13).

9. **A courageous Traveller.** A Christian is one who *courageously* pushes on his way amidst surrounding difficulties, as illustrated in Christian passing through the Valley of the Shadow of Death (Psalm xxiii. 4).

10. **A conquering Soldier.** A Christian is one who *conquers* his enemies, as seen in the fight of Christian with Apollyon (I. John v. 18).

11. **An expectant Contemplator.** A Christian is one who *contemplates* with delight the prospect of heaven's glory, as represented in the pilgrims on the Delectable Mountains (Jude 21, 24).

We have thus in the book that has been said "to be next to the Bible," and next to it because so full of it, a most exhaustive and extensive description of what a Christian is.

487. WHAT IS A CHRISTIAN?

WE find that the word "Christian" only occurs three times in the New Testament. First, "If any man suffer as a Christian, let him not be ashamed" (I. Peter iv. 16). Second, "Almost thou persuadest me to be a Christian," which was spoken in contempt by Agrippa to Paul (Acts xxvi. 28, R.V.). Third, "The disciples were called Christians first in Antioch" (Acts xi. 26). It has been a matter of contention as to who called them Christians, whether it was a name applied to them in ridicule by the world, or whether God called them by that name. We believe God called them Christians, from the simple fact that the word "called" in the eight instances where it is recorded, has reference to God Himself speaking and acting. The wise men, "*being warned* of God," did not return to Herod (Matthew ii. 12); Joseph, "*being warned* of God," turned aside to Galilee (Matthew ii. 22); it was *revealed* unto Simeon by the Holy Ghost that he "should not see death before he had seen the Lord's Christ" (Luke ii. 26); Cornelius "*was warned* from God" (Acts x. 22); "She *shall be called* an adulteress" (Romans vii. 3), that is because God calls her so; "Moses *was admonished* of God" (Hebrews viii. 5); "Noah *being warned* of God" (Hebrews xi. 7); "If they escaped not who refused him *that spake* on earth" (Hebrews xii. 25). Thus in every case where the Holy Spirit uses this word,* it has reference to a communication from God, and hence we assume that the title "Christian" is God-given.

We give an acrostic on the word "Christian," as illustrating what he is—

Child of God, as to his relationship to the Lord (John i. 12, 13).

Heir of God, as to his inheritance in the Lord (I. Peter i. 3, 4).

Redeemed one, as to his being freed by the Lord (Rom. viii. 2; Ephesians i. 7).

Influence, as to his responsibility to the Lord (Matthew v. 14-16).

Soldier, as to fighting for the Lord (II. Timothy ii. 3).

Temple, as to being occupied by the Lord (I. Corinthians iii. 16).

Instrument, to be used by the Lord (Romans vi. 13).

Ambassador, as to his representation of the Lord (II. Cor. v. 20).

New man in Christ, as to his attitude towards the Lord and the world (II. Corinthians v. 17).

488. WHAT IS A CHRISTIAN?

1. A Christian is one who has **life in Christ.** "He that hath the Son hath life" (I. John v. 12).

* The words in italics are one and the same in the Greek.

2. A Christian is one who has **liberty by Christ.** "The Spirit of life in Christ Jesus hath made me free" (Romans viii. 2).

3. A Christian is one who has received **light from Christ.** "He that followeth Me . . . . shall have the light of life" (John viii. 12).

4. A Christian is one who has **likeness to Christ.** "Changed into the same image" (II. Cor. iii. 18).

5. A Christian is one who seeks **to love as Christ.** "Ye love one another, as I have loved you" (John xv. 12).

6. A Christian is one who is **under the Lordship of Christ.** "Lord, both of the dead and living" (Romans xiv. 9).

7. A Christian is one who **is learning of Christ.** "Learn of Me" (Matthew xi. 29).

489. WHAT LOVE DOES, AS ILLUSTRATED IN DAVID AND JONATHAN

I. SAMUEL XX. 32-42

DAVID'S confession about Jonathan's love for him, was that it "was wonderful" (II. Samuel i. 26). In Jonathan's regard for David we have illustrated the attitude and action of love.

1. **Question of Love.** Jonathan knew that all the hate that was burning in the mind of his father Saul against David, was born of jealousy, so he dares to ask the question, "What hath he done" (verse 32). Love will often make us bold, when under ordinary circumstances we should be timid. It was love to Christ that made Mary "early" at the sepulchre (John xx. 1), and that prompted John to run with fleetness of foot, and get to the tomb "first" (John xx. 4).

2. **Discernment of Love** (verse 33). Saul's casting the javelin at Jonathan, led Jonathan to see what he would do to David the first opportunity that occurred, yea, what he had intended to do. Love can see farther than reason. Love has long sight and insight. Love is not deceived by appearances, nor gulled by probabilities. Love is a thermometer that ascertains the temperature of things.

3. **Grief of Love** (verse 34). Jonathan is greatly grieved at the attitude of Saul towards David. The hatred of Saul to David cuts like a knife into the heart of Jonathan, and causes it to bleed with anguish for his friend. Love is always concerned for the object it loves. It was the love which Paul had to Christ and to Christ's, that prompted him to labour (I. Thess. ii. 9; II. Thess. iii. 8), yea, that made him willing to be accursed, if others might be saved (Romans ix. 3).

4. **Punctuality of Love.** At the appointed time Jonathan goes to apprise David of the state of matters (verse 35). Love is never late with its engagements. In the "fulness of the time" Christ was born (Galatians iv. 4). When "the hour was come" to keep the

Passover, "He sat down" (Luke xxii. 14); and when the hour of His death arrived, He gave Himself up to be led to the death of the cross (John xvii. 1). Believers should be equally observant in doing what the Lord enjoins on the first day of the week (Acts xx. 7; 1. Cor. xvi. 2), and in the assembling together for prayer (Heb. x. 25). This we shall do, and do constantly (Acts ii. 42), and well, if we truly love Christ.

5. **Arrangement of Love** (verses 36-40). Jonathan had previously arranged with David about the signals which should indicate Saul's feeling towards him, and these would show him whether he should return home or go away (verses 19-23). The lad who was with Jonathan and playing a part, little thought that he was a sign in his actions to the hidden David. What appears to be an ordinary event to a man of the world, is often an extraordinary event to the man who loves God (Romans viii. 28). The cross of Christ to the mob seemed to hold an impostor, but the event of all events was being carried out there (Acts ii. 23), and the arrangement that had long since been come to, was being fulfilled (1. Peter i. 20).

6. **Fellowship of Love** (verse 41). How significant are the words, "Wept one with another." Kindred hearts are beating in mutual sympathy. What a type we have here! Our divine Jonathan sympathizes with us in all our trials and afflictions, for He is "touched with the feeling of our infirmities" (Heb. iv. 15), and what He feels for us, we should feel for Him, in loving our brethren (1. John iii. 14-18) as He has bid us (John xiii. 34).

7. **Benediction of Love** (verse 42). "Go in peace," is Jonathan's benediction upon David. How these words remind us of the words of our Divine Jonathan, when He said, "Peace I leave with you, My peace I give unto you" (John xiv. 27). When we have His blessing of peace, it calms the storm of temptation and the wind of trouble, and causes a great calm in the heart, and sweet stillness in the soul (Luke viii. 24).

490. WHAT SHALL I DO?

Several times we find the above question asked in the New Testament. The following give a consecutive chain of thought:—

1. **A Dismissed Steward.** "*What shall I do?* for my lord taketh away from me the stewardship" (Luke xvi, 3). The unjust steward is commended for his thoughtfulness, and not for his sinfulness, by Christ (see Luke xvi. 9, R.V.).

2. **A Directed Son.** "*What shall I do?* I will send My Beloved Son" (Luke xx. 13). It seems as if God were uncertain what to do in the face of man's sin. We know now what He did (John iii. 16-18).

3. **A Determined Suppliant.** "There came one running, and kneeled to Him, and asked Him, Good Master, *what shall I do*

that I may inherit eternal life?" (Mark x. 17). He was determined in his pleading, but not in practising Christ's direction.

4. **A Distressed Soul.** "*What must I do* to be saved?" (Acts xvi. 30). Done is the work that saves. To believe in Him who has done the work, saves (John vi. 29).

5. **A Puzzled Judge.** "*What shall I do* then with Jesus?" (Matthew xxvii. 22). Pilate was in a quandary, and could not get out of it. He had not the moral courage to be true to his convictions.

6. **A Submissive Sinner.** "*What shall I do*, Lord*?*" (Acts xxii. 10). Saul was turned to Christ by His manifestation. He is now as much for Him as He was against Him before.

7. **A Foolish Man.** "*What shall I do?*" "This will I do." (Luke xii. 17, 18). A fool always answers his own question by a self-willed action. He never waits for God's direction.

491. WHAT WE ARE TO DO WITH THE WORD OF GOD

1. **Receive the Word with meekness,** and thus be saved from all wickedness (James i. 21).

2. **Let it dwell in us richly,** that we may teach others (Col. iii. 16).

3. **Keep it,** and thus have His love perfected in us (1. John ii. 5).

4. **Continue in it,** that it may be manifest that we are His disciples indeed (John viii. 31).

5. **Hold it fast,** that we may be able to convince gainsayers (Titus i. 9).

6. **Be doers of it,** and not deceive ourselves by thinking that hearing is enough without the doing (James i. 22).

7. **Speak it out boldly,** that the Lord may be honoured (Phil. i. 14).

8. **Hold it forth faithfully,** by living it out truly (Phil. ii. 16).

492. WHERE BLESSING IS FOUND

BLESSING from the Lord runs in the channel of obedience to Him, as we are found in the path of duty.

1. **Revelation.** The angels appeared to the shepherds, and announced the Saviour's birth, as they were watching their flocks (Luke ii. 8-10).

2. **Manifestation.** The angel of Jehovah manifested Himself to Moses as he kept the flock over which he was shepherd (Ex. iii. 1-3).

3. **Commission.** The Lord took David from the sheep-fold to be king over Israel, for as he had been faithful in the former position, so he would be in the latter (Ps. lxxviii. 70).

4. **Qualification.** It was while Gideon was threshing the corn that the Lord made known to him that He intended him to be the deliverer of Israel (Judges vi. 11).

5. **Substitution.** Elisha was called from the plough to be the companion and successor to Elijah (I. Kings xix. 19).

6. **Identification.** It was while Matthew was at the receipt of custom (Matt. ix. 9), and the disciples were following their occupation as fishermen, that the Lord called them to be His disciples and witnesses (Matt. iv. 18).

7. **Satisfaction.** The woman of Samaria little thought when she came to draw water from Jacob's well that she would there receive a drink which would satisfy her heart (John iv. 14).

493. "WHITE AS SNOW"

THE words "*white as snow*" occur in three connections in the Word of God, namely, in association with sin, the Saviour, and salvation.

1. **Sin.** Leprosy is a pronounced type of sin. There are three persons who were stricken with leprosy, "*white as snow*," and these were—Moses, for his hesitation (Ex. iv. 6); Miriam, for her opposition (Numbers xii. 10); and Gehazi, for his covetousness (II. Kings v. 27).

2. **Saviour.** When Christ was transfigured, His raiment was "exceeding *white as snow*" (Mark ix. 3); and when John saw Him, "His head and His hairs were white like wool, as *white as snow*" (Rev. i. 14). White is here emblematic of Christ's personal holiness and His righteous action.

3. **Salvation.** "Though your sins be as scarlet, they shall be as *white as snow*" (Isaiah i. 18). The one effectual cause that brings about this transformation is the blood of Christ (Rev. vii. 14).

494. "WHOSE I AM"

(ACTS xxvii. 23)

THE Christian belongs to Christ.

1. **We are His by donation.** We have been given to Christ by the Father (John xvii. 6).

2. **We are His by His death;** for He has bought us with His blood (I. Cor. vi. 20).

3. **We are His by deliverance,** for He has delivered us from the kingdom of darkness (Col. i. 13).

4. **We are His by dependence,** for by His grace we are what we are (I. Cor. xv. 10).

5. **We are His by His dwelling within us,** for our bodies are the temples of the Holy Ghost (I. Cor. iii. 16).

6. **We are His by direction,** for "as many as are led by the Spirit of God, they are the sons of God" (Rom. viii. 14).

7. **We are His by dedication,** for we have yielded ourselves to Him (Rom. vi. 16).

495. "WITH HIM"

1. **Dead with Him.** "If ye be dead with Christ" (Col. ii. 20).

2. **Buried with Him.** "Buried with Him in baptism" (Col. ii. 12).

3. **Quickened together with Him.** "You . . . . hath He quickened together with Him" (Col. ii. 13).

4. **Risen with Him.** "Ye are risen with Him" (Col. ii. 12).

5. **Seated with Him.** "Will I grant to sit with Me" (Rev. iii. 21).

6. **Suffering with Him.** "If so be that we suffer with Him" (Rom. viii. 17).

7. **Reigning with Him.** "Shall reign with Him a thousand years" (Rev. xx. 6; Rev. xxii. 5).

496. WISDOM

THE following points illustrate how we may fulfil the injunction, "Be wise":—

1. **Building.** Building on the rock in obedience to the truth (Matt. vii. 24).

2. **Receiving.** Receiving the truth of the Scriptures, and thus being wise unto salvation (II. Tim. iii. 15).

3. **Possessing.** Having the oil of the grace of the Holy Spirit (Matt. xxv. 2-5).

4. **Living.** Living a good life in meekness (James iii. 13, R.V.).

5. **Walking.** Walking carefully in the world (Eph. v. 15, R.V.).

6. **Dwelling.** Being in the environment of Christ's presence, and not being influenced by men (I. Cor. iv. 10).

7. **Seeking.** Ever seeking the good, and thus avoiding the evil (Rom. xvi. 19).

497. WHAT THE TONGUE CAN DO

JAMES iii. 1-13

THE heathen philosopher, Xanthus, expecting some friends to dine with him, ordered his servant Esop to provide the best things the market could supply. Tongues only were provided, served up with different sauces. Course after course was supplied, each consisting of tongue. "Did I not order you to buy the best the market afforded?" cried Xanthus. "And did I not obey you," replied Esop. "Is there anything better than the organ of truth, and the instrument of praise and worship?" On the next day Xanthus ordered him to provide the worst thing in the market. And lo, there was another dinner of tongue! "For," said Esop, "surely the tongue is the worst thing in the world, the instrument of strife, and the organ of lies, and blasphemy."

The Holy Spirit plainly indicates who is the perfect man; it is the man who has the mastery of his own tongue (verse 2). We have known some who have boasted of sinless perfection, who, if they were judged by this standard, would be perfect in sin, instead of being sinlessly perfect.

I. **A Suggestive Simile.** An evil tongue is compared to a fire, which is a world of iniquity (verse 6). A spark of fire is capable of immense mischief. The city of Portland, in America, was reduced to ashes from a fire, kindled by a fire-cracker, on the 4th of July. Chicago was also burnt to the ground, through a kerosene lamp, kicked over by a cow; and the great fire of London in 1666, commemorated by the monument, broke out in one house in Pudding Lane. Many a prairie fire has owed its origin to a single spark from a passing engine.

Think of the many piles of iniquity that have been lighted by the fire of the tongue! It was the devil's *insinuating* tongue that caused our first parents to sin (Genesis iii. 4); it was the *lying* tongues of Joseph's brethren, which gave Jacob so much grief (Genesis xxxvii. 32); it was the *deceitful* tongue of Jacob that robbed Esau of his blessing (Genesis xxvii. 18-20); it was the *obstinate* tongue of Pharaoh that caused the plagues to be sent (Exodus x. 28); it was the *jealous* tongue of Miriam that caused her to be smitten with leprosy (Numbers xii. 1, 10); it was the *proud* tongue of Korah and his followers that brought such swift judgment upon them (Numbers xvi. 3, 32); it was the *fault-finding* tongues of Job's friends that ministered such trouble to him (Job iv.); it was the *covetous* tongue of Judas, which caused Christ to be betrayed to His death (Matthew xxvi. 15); it was the *boasting* tongue of Peter which made him deny his Lord (Matthew xxvi. 70); it was the *unholy* tongue of Ananias that made him lie to the Holy Spirit (Acts v. 3); it was the *sectarian* tongue of the Corinthians that caused the divisions among them (I. Corinthians i. 12); and it was the *prating* tongue of Diotrephes, which caused so much trouble in the Church (III. John 9, 10).

The following maxims relating to the tongue are to the point:—

"'The boneless tongue, so small and weak,
Can crush and kill,' declared the Greek."

"'The tongue destroys a greater horde,'
The Turk asserts, 'than does the sword.'"

"The Persian proverb wisely saith,
'A lengthy tongue, an early death.'"

"'The tongue can speak a word whose speed,'
Say the Chinese, 'outstrips the steed.'"

"While Arab sages this impart,
'The tongue's great storehouse is the heart.'"

"From Hebrew wit the maxim sprung,
'Though feet should slip, ne'er let the tongue.'"

"The sacred writer crowns the whole,
'Who keeps the tongue doth keep his soul.'"

II. **A Sanctified Servant.** While the tongue may be an evil, it also can be a great good. If the tongue is sanctified by grace, held in by the Lord, and influenced by the Spirit, then there shall come forth from it the sweetness of kind and helpful words, and the "good conversation" which is commendable to the Lord (verses 10-13), for a sanctified tongue is—

A tree of life to feed (Proverbs xv. 4).
A well-spring to refresh (Proverbs xviii. 4).
An object of admiration (Proverbs xxv. 11).
A a goad to stimulate (Ecclesiastes xii. 11).
A salt to preserve (Colossians iv. 6).
A treasure to enrich (Luke vi. 45).
A jewel to beautify (Proverbs xx. 15).
As honey to please (Proverbs xvi. 24).
As silver for choiceness (Proverbs x. 20).
As food to strengthen (Proverbs x. 21).
As fruit to satisfy (Proverbs xii. 14).
As health to gladden (Proverbs xii. 18).

We only need add one letter to *words*, namely, the letter *s*, and we make words into *swords*. What a difference between the two! There is a great difference in *how* a good thing is said. Let us mark these two things—*what* we say, and *how* we say it.

498. WONDERFUL GEMS FOR SETTING

1. **Three things we are to keep from.**
   1. **Severance.** From idols (1. John v. 21).
   2. **Separation.** From the world (James i. 27).
   3. **Safety.** From the path of the destroyer (Psalm xvii. 4).
2. **Three things the Lord uses to purify or refine.**
   1. **Pruning.** The knife (John xv. 2).
   2. **Purifying.** The furnace (Malachi iii. 2, 3).
   3. **Punishing.** The rod (1. Corinthians iv. 21).
3. **Three Persons to whom the believer belongs.**
   1. **His by Purpose.** To the Father (Ephesians i. 4).

2. **His by Purchase.** To the Son (1. Corinthians vi. 20).
3. **His by Possession.** To the Holy Spirit (1. Cor. iii. 16).

4. **Threefold glory, or the Trinity in unity.**
   1. **His Worship.** The glory of the Father (Isa. vi. 1-4).
   2. **His Word.** The glory of the Son (John xii. 38).
   3. **His Warning.** The glory of the Holy Spirit (Acts xxviii. 25-27).
5. **Three witnesses in 1. John v. 8.**
   1. **Atonement made.** The blood (John vi. 50-53).
   2. **Assurance given.** The Word (John xx. 31).
   3. **Accepted Saviour.** The Spirit (Acts v. 32).
6. **Three things that are "needful."**
   1. **Work.** Needful supplies for the work of God (Ezra vii. 20).
   2. **Worship.** Needful to stir us up to our privileges (Luke x. 42).
   3. **Word.** Needful to remind us of our responsibilities (Jude 3).
7. **Three uncomely and comely persons.**
   1. **Corruption.** An uncomely sinner (Daniel x. 8).
   2. **Compassion.** An uncomely Saviour (Isaiah liii. 2).
   3. **Covering.** A comely saint (Ezekiel xvi. 14).
8. **Three illustrations of faith—taking God at His word.**
   1. **Unknown.** Noah (Hebrews xi. 7). Noah did it about a thing unknown.
   2. **Unlikely.** Abraham (Hebrews xi. 17-19). Abraham, about a thing unlikely.
   3. **Untried.** Moses (Hebrews xi. 28). Moses, about a thing untried.
9. **Three classes; or trembling saints, sinners, and devils.**
   1. **Work.** Trembling saints (Mark xvi. 8; 1. Cor. ii. 3).
   2. **Wondering.** Trembling sinners (Acts xxiv. 25; Acts xvi. 29).
   3. **Wrath.** Trembling devils (James ii. 19).
10. **An acrostic in one verse.**
    1. **A—"Ask."** Interceding Abraham (Gen. xviii. 17-33).
    2. **S—"Seek."** Importunate widow (Luke xviii. 1-8).
    3. **K—"Knock."** Indefatigable friend (Luke xi. 5-10).
11. **Threefold walk.**

1. **Uprightly.** In the house (Psalm ci. 2).
2. **Unitedly.** In the Church (Ephesians v. 1, 2).
3. **Undefiled.** In the world (Colossians iv. 5).

12. **Three things we are to obtain.**
    1. **Furnished.** Mercy, as we come to the throne of grace (Hebrews iv. 16).
    2. **Faith.** Promises, as we trust in the Lord (Heb. xi. 33).
    3. **Faithfulness.** Participation, as we endure (Heb. xi. 35).
13. **Three things we shall obtain.**
    1. **Appointed to full salvation.** Salvation (I. Thess. v. 9).
    2. **Association with Christ.** Glory (II. Thess. ii. 14).
    3. **Acknowledged by Christ.** Eternal glory (II. Tim. ii. 10).
14. **Three things which cannot be found.**
    1. **Blotted out.** The sins of the believer (Jer. l. 20).
    2. **Blessed in Christ.** The life of the saint (Col. iii. 3).
    3. **Buried by God.** The body of Moses (Deut. xxxiv. 6).
15. **Three things God cannot do.**
    1. **Foundation.** He cannot lie (Titus i. 2).
    2. **Faithfulness.** He cannot deny Himself (II. Tim. ii. 13).
    3. **Firmness.** His word cannot be broken (John x. 35).
16. **Three things we have need of.**
    1. **Empowered.** We need grace to help us (Heb. iv. 16).
    2. **Endurance.** We need patience to endure (Heb. x. 36).
    2. **Enabling.** We need one another (I. Cor. xii. 21).
17. **Threefold meetness.**
    1. **Participation.** God rejoicing over returning prodigals (Luke xv. 32).
    2. **Position.** Believer made meet for God's presence (Colossians i. 12).
    3. **Purification.** Servant made meet to be used (II. Tim. ii. 21).
18. **Three impossibilities in connection with the sinner.**
    1. **Bondage.** Cannot please God (Romans viii. 8).
    2. **Barrenness.** Cannot bring forth fruit (Matt. vii. 18).
    3. **Banishment.** Cannot enter the kingdom (John iii. 5).
19. **Three impossibilities in connection with the believer.**
    1. **Separation.** Cannot serve God and Mammon (Luke xvi. 13).

2. **Shining.** As a light he cannot be hid (Matt. v. 14).
3. **Suffering.** He cannot escape cross-bearing (Luke xiv. 26, 27).

20. **Three things we are to strive to obtain.**
    1. **Winning.** An incorruptible (victor's) crown (I. Cor. ix. 24, 25).
    2. **Warring.** A good report (Hebrews xi. 39).
    3. **Walking.** Joy and gladness (Isaiah xxxv. 10).
21. **Three things we have obtained.**
    1. **Righteousness.** Precious faith (II. Peter i. 1).
    2. **Redemption.** Redemption (Hebrews ix. 12).
    3. **Riches.** An inheritance in Christ (Ephesians i. 11).
22. **Three things the believer cannot do.**
    1. **Implantation.** Cannot sin (I. John iii. 9).
    2. **Indwelling.** Cannot bring forth fruit of himself (John xv. 4).
    3. **Identification.** Cannot do without fellow-saints (I. Corinthians xii. 21).
23. **Three things marred.**
    1. **Sin.** The potter's vessel—sinner marred by sin (Jeremiah xviii. 4).
    2. **Substitute.** The Saviour marred for us (Isaiah lii. 14)
    3. **Service.** The girdle marred by neglect—slothful servant (Jeremiah xiii. 7).
24. **Threefold proving.**
    1. **Obedience.** Obedience, the proof of love (II. Cor. ii. 9; viii. 24).
    2. **Overcoming.** Faithfulness, the proof of being God's (Philippians ii. 22).
    3. **Obtaining.** Endurance in life and doctrine the proof of faithfulness (II. Timothy iv. 5).
25. **Threefold transfiguration.**
    1. **Glory.** Christ transfigured * on the mount (Matt. xvii. 2).
    2. **Grace.** Moral transformation (Romans xii. 2).
    3. **Gazing.** Spiritual transformation, as we gaze on the Lord (II. Corinthians iii. 18).
26. **Three things we "need not," as believers in Christ.**
    1. **Translation.** We need not be washed again (John xiii. 10).

* Same word in Greek—*metamorphoomai*—translated "transfigured," "transformed," and changed," in the three Scriptures.

2. **Teaching.** We need not any man to teach us (I. John ii. 27).

3. **Testimony.** We need not be ashamed (II. Tim. ii. 15).

27. **Three things we are not to neglect.**

1. **Attention.** Not neglecting to stimulate believers to add to their faith (II. Peter i. 12).

2. **Activity.** Neglect not any gift of grace (I. Tim. iv. 14).

3. **Apprehension.** Neglect not the great salvation (Hebrews ii. 3).

28. **Threefold quietness.**

1. **Peace.** Quietness of conscience (Isaiah xxxii. 17).

2. **Power.** Quietness of heart (Isaiah xxx. 15).

3. **Plenty.** Quietness of soul, led by the Lord (Psalm xxiii. 2, margin).

29. **Three things we are to buy.**

1. **Salvation.** The wine and milk of the Gospel (Isa. lv. 1).

2. **Security.** The truth of God, by obedience (Proverbs xxiii. 23).

3. **Separation.** The gold tried in the fire (Rev. iii. 18).

30. **Three things we are to find.**

1. **Refreshment.** Pasture, as we go *in* to the Lord's presence for communion, and *out* in service (John x. 9).

2. **Rest.** Rest, as we take the yoke of Christ (Matt. xi. 29).

3. **Reward.** Grace, to help in time of need (Heb. iv. 16).

499. WORKMEN'S MATERIAL

1. **Four stages in fruit-bearing in John xv.**

1. **Pruning.** Fruit (verse 2).

2. **Progress.** More fruit (verse 2).

3. **Proficiency.** Much fruit (verses 5, 8).

4. **Perpetuity.** Fruit that remains (verse 16).

2. **Four laws in Romans vii. and viii.**

1. **Just. Holy. Good.** The law of God (vii. 12).

2. **Jeopardising. Polluting. Bad.** The law of sin (vii. 23).

3. **Judging. Reminding. Accusing.** The law of conscience (vii. 23).

4. **Justifying. Sanctifying. Enabling.** The law of the Spirit of Life in Christ (viii. 2).

3. **Four things the Lord Jesus is made to the believer in 1. Corinthians i. 30.**
   1. **Salvation.** "Wisdom," to enlighten us.
   2. **Standing.** "Righteousness," to justify us.
   3. **Separation.** "Sanctification," to separate us.
   4. **Security.** "Redemption," to complete us.
4. **Four things in Exodus xiv. 13-15.**
   1. **Lord.** Faith's object—"The Lord."
   2. **Looking.** Faith's attitude—"Stand still."
   3. **Led.** Faith's advance—"Go forward."
   4. **Liberty.** Faith's victory—"The Lord shall fight."
5. **Four points in connection with the palsied man in Mark ii.**
   1. **Grand Contrivance.** Four men bringing one to Christ.
   2. **Grievous Case.** Man sick of the palsy.
   3. **Gracious Cure.** The man and Christ.
   4. **Glorious Consequence.** The man forgiven. Healed. Walking.
6. **Four men in connection with trees.**
   1. **Covering.** Adam *behind* a tree (Genesis iii. 8).
   2. **Curse.** Christ *upon* a tree (Galatians iii. 13).
   3. **Conversion.** Zacchæus *in* a tree (Luke xix. 4).
   4. **Communion.** Nathaniel *under* a tree (John i. 48).
7. **Four words * that are of frequent occurrence in John's Gospel.**
   1. **Object of God's Love.** "*World*" occurs seventy-seven times.
   2. **Outflowing of God's Love.** "*Love*" occurs fifty-six times.
   3. **Obedience to Love.** "*Believe*" † occurs one hundred times.
   4. **Ordination by Love.** "*Life*" occurs thirty-six times.
8. **Four things of God in Acts xx. 24-28.**
   1. **Salvation. Service.** "Grace of God" (verse 24).
   2. **Standing. Success.** "Kingdom of God" (verse 25).
   3. **Scriptures. Simplicity.** "Counsel of God" (verse 27).

* In Matthew the word "*world*," occurs *nine* times; the word "*love*," *twelve* times; the word "*believe*," *eleven* times; and the word "*life*," *seven* times. In Mark the word "*world*," occurs *three* times; "*love*," *five*; "*believe*," *fifteen*; and the word "*life*," *four* times. In Luke the word "*world*," occurs *three* times; "*love*," *fifteen*; "*believe*," *eight*; and the word "*life*," *six* times.

† Translated once, "commit" (John ii. 24).

4. **Shepherding. Supply.** "Church of God (verse 28).

9. **Four times the words "for us" occur in Rom. viii.**
   1. **Indwelling.** The Holy Spirit for us (verse 26).
   2. **Immovable.** The Father for us (verse 31).
   3. **Intention.** The death of Christ for us (verse 32).
   4. **Intercession.** The Son for us (verse 34).

10. **Four aspects of righteousness in Romans x.**
    1. **Uncleanness.** Man's righteousness (verse 3).
    2. **Unsparing.** The righteousness of the law (verse 4).
    3. **Unspotted.** The righteousness of God (verse 3).
    4. **Unity.** The righteousness of faith (verse 6).

11. **Four heads of an old sermon on "He shall see His seed" (Isaiah liii. 10).**
    1. **Implantation.** He shall see them "*born* and brought *in*."
    2. **Instructed.** He shall see them "*educated* and brought *up*."
    3. **Irremovable.** He shall see them "*supported* and brought *through*."
    4. **Identification.** He shall see them "*glorified* and brought *home*."

12. **Four Gospels are four pictures of Christ.**
    1. **Position.** Matthew. The King. The lion.
    2. **Patience.** Mark. The Servant. The ox.
    3. **Perfection.** Luke. The Son of Man. The man.
    4. **Power.** John. The Son of God. The eagle.

13. **Four (k)nots (to untie).**
    1. **Encouragement.** "Fear not" (Revelation i. 17).
    2. **Enlightened.** "Fret not" (Psalm xxxvii. 1).
    3. **Endurance.** "Faint not" (II. Corinthians iv. 1).
    4. **Enumeration.** "Forget not" (Psalm ciii. 2).

14. **Four aspects of the will of God.**
    1. **Protection.** The will of God carried out by the Father, our protection (John vi. 37-40).
    2. **Pattern.** The will of God carried out by the Son, our pattern (Heb. x. 9; John iv. 34; Matt. xxvi. 39).
    3. **Power.** The will of God carried out by the Spirit, our power (Romans viii. 27; Philippians ii. 13).
    4. **Practice.** The will of God carried out by the believer, our practice (John vii. 17).

15. **Four references to idolatry in the New Testament.**
    1. **Decree.** No idolaters have part in the kingdom of Christ (Ephesians v. 5).
    2. **Departure.** The believer is to flee away from (1. Corinthians x. 14).
    3. **Death.** Mortify all tendency to (Colossians iii. 5).
    4. **Decision.** Keep from (1. John v. 21).
16. **Fourfold command to "watch" in Mark xiii. 33-37.**
    1. **Regard.** Watch for your own sake (verse 33).
    2. **Responsibility.** Watch for His word's sake (verse 34).
    3. **Reward.** Watch for Him (verse 35).
    4. **Remember.** Watch for His own sake (verse 37).
17. **Fourfold Prayer in Psalm xxviii. 9.**
    1. **Save thy children. Relationship.** "*Save* Thy people."
    2. **Sanctify Thy Redeemed. Redemption.** "*Bless* Thine inheritance."
    3. **Supply Thy sheep. Refreshment.** "*Feed* them also."
    4. **Support Thy Saints. Regard.** "*Lift* them up for ever."
18. **Four times we have the words in Revelation, "I come quickly."**
    1. **Contending.** "Behold, *I come quickly:* hold that fast which thou hast," &c. (Revelation iii. 11).
    2. **Cleaving.** "Behold, *I come quickly:* blessed is he that keepeth the sayings of the prophecy of this book" (Revelation xxii. 7).
    3. **Compensation.** "Behold, *I come quickly;* and My reward is with Me," &c. (Revelation xxii. 12).
    4. **Certainty.** "Surely, *I come quickly*" (Rev. xxii. 20).
19. **Four "Beholds" in Genesis xxviii.**
    1. **Pathway.** "Behold a ladder set up on the earth" (verse 12).
    2. **Performing.** "Behold the angels of God ascending and descending on it" (verse 12).
    3. **Promise.** Behold, the Lord stood above it" (verse 13).
    4. **Presence.** "Behold, I am with thee" (verse 15).
20. **Four times in Hebrews Christ is said to be seated at the right hand of God.**
    1. **Vicarious Work.** As the Sin-Purger (i. 3).

2. **Vital Work.** As our great High Priest (viii. 1).
3. **Valorous Workman.** As the Accomplisher of His work (x. 12).
4. **Victory Won.** As the Conqueror (xii. 2).

21. **Four times the words "The just shall live by faith," occur.**
    1. **Recognition.** In contrast to sin (Hab. ii. 4).
    2. **Righteousness.** The persons—the just, *i.e.*, the justified (Romans i. 17).
    3. **Repose.** In contrast to works (Galatians iii. 11).
    4. **Responsibility.** The life of faith (Hebrews x. 38).

22. **Four "Lets" in connection with the word "alone."**
    1. **Supplication.** "Let *us* alone" (Mark i. 24). Demons.
    2. **Searching.** "Let *it* alone" (Luke xiii. 8). Fig tree.
    3. **Separation.** "Let *him* alone" (Hosea iv. 17). Ephraim.
    4. **Self-sufficiency.** "Let *them* alone" (Matthew xv. 14). Blind guides.

23. **Four times the words "gift of God" occur in the New Testament.**
    1. **Ignorance.** "If thou knewest the gift of God" (John iv. 10).
    2. **Interposition.** "The gift of God is eternal life" (Romans vi. 23).
    3. **Impossibility.** "Thou hast thought that the gift of God," &c. (Acts viii. 20).
    4. **Interest.** "It is the gift of God" (Ephesians ii. 8).

24. **Four words full of meaning, viz., "God is my salvation" (Isaiah xii. 2).**
    1. **My Saviour.** "God"—the person mentioned (Luke i. 47).
    2. **My Strength.** "Is"—a fact stated (Psalm xviii. 1, 2).
    3. **My Shield.** "My"—a personal interest (Psa. xxviii. 7).
    4. **My Song.** "Salvation"—the blessing obtained (Exodus xv. 2).

25. **Four places unto which Elijah and Elisha went together, in II. Kings ii.**
    1. **Sin's reproach removed.** "Gilgal." It means "Rolling away" (Joshua v. 9).
    2. **Spirit indwelling.** "Bethel." It means "The house of God" (Genesis xxviii. 19).

3. **Separated from the world.** "Jericho." It means "City of the Moon" (Joshua vi. 26).

4. **Security and oneness.** "Jordan." It means "Judgment" (John v. 24).

26. **Four things we are to roll or cast on the Lord.**

1. **Consecration.** Roll thyself on the Lord (Psalm xxii. 8, margin).
2. **Committal.** Roll thy burden on the Lord (Psa. lv. 22).
3. **Courage.** Roll thy way on the Lord (Psalm xxxvii. 5, margin).
4. **Confidence.** Roll thy works on the Lord (Prov. xvi. 3, margin).

27. **Four stages prefigured in Ezekiel xlvii. in connection with the waters.**

1. **Walk.** The water to the ankles (verse 3).
2. **Worship.** The water to the knees (verse 4).
3. **Work.** The water to the loins (verse 4).
4. **Progress.** A river to swim in (verse 5).

28. **Four "togethers" in Ezra.**

1. **Oneness.** "Gather together" (iii. 1).
2. **Power.** "Stood together" (iii. 9).
3. **Worship.** "Sang together" (iii. 11).
4. **Work.** "Build together" (iv. 3).

29. **Four gardens of Scripture.**

1. **Sin destroying.** Garden of Eden (Genesis ii.).
2. **Saviour's Agony.** Garden of Gethsemane (John xviii. 1).
3. **Servant's Joy.** Garden of Joseph of Arimathæa (John xix. 41).
4. **Satisfaction to Christ.** Garden of the Beloved (S.S. v. 1).

30. **Four "nots" in Psalm 2, or contrast 'twixt saint and sinner.**

1. **Manliness.** "Blessed is the man that walketh *not*," &c. (verse 1).
2. **Meditation.** "His leaf also shall *not* wither," &c. (verse 3).
3. **Misery.** "The ungodly are *not* so," &c. (verse 4).
4. **Mourning.** "Shall *not* stand in the judgment" (verse 5).

31. **Four references to God's faithfulness in Psalm lxxxix.**

1. "Make known Thy *faithfulness* to all generations" (verse 1).
2. "Thy *faithfulness* shalt Thou establish in the very heavens (verse 2).
3. "Thy *faithfulness* also in the congregation of the saints" (verse 5).
4. "Thy *faithfulness* round about Thee" (verse 8).

500. WEDGES FOR DRIVING

1. **A threefold picture in Psalm xxiii.**
   1. **Activity and Dependence.** Shepherd and sheep (verses 1 and 2).
   2. **Attention and Direction.** Traveller and guide (verses 3 and 4).
   3. **Attentive and Delighted.** Host and guest (verse 5).
2. **A threefold secret in Psalm xxiii.**
   1. **Provided by the Lord.** Secret of a happy life (verses 1-3).
   2. **Presence of the Lord.** Secret of a happy death (verse 4).
   3. **Perpetually with the Lord.** Secret of a happy eternity (verse 6).
3. **A threefold answer to the first question in the New Testament, viz., "Where is He?" (Matt. ii. 2).**
   1. **Atonement for Sin.** On the cross (John xix. 17-19).
   2. **Advocacy for the Saint.** On the throne (Heb. x. 12).
   3. **Advancement by the Spirit.** In the heart (Eph. iii. 17).
4. **Threefold supply in Philippians.**
   1. **Renewing of the Spirit.** Of the Spirit (i. 19).
   2. **Regardless of Self.** Of service (ii. 30).
   3. **Riches in the Saviour.** Of our need (iv. 19).
5. **Threefold delighting of three persons.**
   1. **Source.** The Father—"Delighteth in mercy" (Micah vii. 18).
   2. **Submission.** The Son—To do the Father's will (Psalm xl. 8).
   3. **Searching.** The believer—In the Word of God (Psalm i. 2).
6. **Three companions of mercy.**
   1. **Cross.** Mercy and *truth* met together (Psa. lxxxv. 10).

2. **Crook.** *Goodness* and mercy following (Psalm xxiii. 6).
3. **Crown.** *Faithfulness* and mercy sustaining (Psalm lxxxix. 24).

7. **Three times we read of Israel keeping the Passover.**
   1. **Protected.** In Egypt (Exodus xii. 11).
   2. **Provision.** In the wilderness (Numbers ix. 5).
   3. **Praise.** In the land (Joshua v. 10).

8. **Three things Israel fed upon.**
   1. **Christ the Lamb of God.** Roast lamb in Egypt (Exodus xii. 9-11).
   2. **Christ the Lowly One.** Manna in the wilderness (Exodus xvi.).
   3. **Christ the Living One.** Old corn in the land (Joshua v. 11).

9. **Israel seen in three positions, illustrating our positions.**
   1. **Position.** In Egypt—In the world, not of it (Ex. viii. 23).
   2. **Path.** In the wilderness — Experience, or progress (Deut. xxxii. 10).
   3. **Possessions.** In the land — Fulness of blessing (Joshua v. 12).

10. **The Bride's conception and progress in relation to her Beloved.**
    1. **Safety.** "My Beloved is mine, and I am His" (S.S. ii. 16).
    2. **Surrender.** "I am my Beloved's, and my Beloved is mine" (S.S. vi. 3).
    3. **Satisfaction.** "I am my Beloved's, and His desire is toward me" (S.S. vii. 10).

11. **Three precious "I will's" in Exodus xxv. 22.**
    1. **Openness.** "There *I will* meet with thee."
    2. **Oneness.** "*I will* commune with thee."
    3. **Obedience.** "*I will* give thee in commandment."

12. **Three things used in the consecration of Aaron and his sons.**
    1. **Salvation.** "Water" (Exodus xxix. 4). Regeneration (Titus iii. 5).
    2. **Spirit.** "Oil" (Exodus xxix. 7). Indwelling (1. John ii. 27).
    3. **Sanctification.** "Blood" (Exodus xxix. 20). Separation (Hebrews xiii. 12).

13. **Threefold condition for the Lord's workers to be in, in Exodus xxxv.**

1. **Freewill offering.** Willing-hearted (verse 5).
2. **Fitted for the Work.** Wise-hearted (verse 10).
3. **Fired to the Work.** Warm-hearted (verse 21).

14. **Three freely's.**
    1. **Salvation.** "Take the water of life *freely*" (Revelation xxii. 17).
    2. **Standing.** "Justified *freely* by His grace" (Rom. iii. 24).
    3. **Service.** "*Freely* ye have received, *freely* give" (Matthew x. 8).

15. **Three things the Lord requires of us in Micah vi. 8.**
    1. **Righteousness of Life.** To "do justly."
    2. **Regarding the Lowly.** To "love mercy."
    3. **Respecting the Lord.** To "walk humbly with thy God."

16. **Three distinguishing words in connection with the Saviour.**
    1. **Sin.** *A* Saviour. Shows the need (Luke ii. 11).
    2. **Saviour.** *The* Saviour. Shows there is but one (I. John iv. 14).
    3. **Saved.** *My* Saviour. Shows that He is mine (Luke i. 47).

17. **Three things we are to do in relation to those who are over us in the Lord, in Hebrews xiii.**
    1. **Remembrance. Imitating. Consider.** "Remember them" (verse 7).
    2. **Recognition. Instructed. Consent.** "Obey them" (verse 17).
    3. **Regard. Identification. Comply.** "Salute them" (verse 24).

18. **Three things we are to make, or accomplish.**
    1. **Attention.** Straight paths for our feet (Heb. xii. 13).
    2. **Addition.** Our calling and election sure, by adding to our faith what the Lord commands (II. Peter i. 10).
    3. **Advancing.** Full proof of the work God has given us to do (II. Timothy iv. 5).

19. **Three W's in Psalm vi.**
    1. **Distress.** "I am *weak*" (verse 2).
    2. **Discomfort.** "I am *weary*" (verse 6).
    3. **Deliverance.** "The Lord hath heard the voice of my *weeping*" (verse 8).

20. **Three things the Lord will do for him that considereth the poor (Psalm xli. 1-3).**

1. **Protection.** "The Lord will deliver him in time of trouble."
2. **Preservation.** "The Lord will preserve him."
3. **Provision.** "The Lord will strengthen him."

21. **Three times God is said to be our "Refuge" in Psalm xlvi.**

1. **Encompassed.** "God is our *Refuge* and Strength" (verse 1).
2. **Empowered.** "*God* of Jacob is our Refuge" (verse 7).
3. **Encouraged.** "God of *Jacob* is our Refuge" (verse 11).

22. **Threefold deliverance in Psalm lvi. 13.**

1. **Praise.** "Thou hast delivered my soul from death."
2. **Prayer.** "Wilt not Thou deliver my feet from falling?"
3. **Practice.** "That I may walk before God in the light of the living."

23. **Three steps in Psalm lxiv. 10.**

1. **Rejoicing.** "The righteous shall be glad in the Lord."
2. **Resting.** "And shall trust in Him."
3. **Recognition.** "And all the upright in heart shall glory."

24. **Three times the Psalmist refers to his soul, in Psalm lxiii.**

1. **Longing.** "My *soul* thirsteth for Thee" (verse 1).
2. **Loving.** "My *soul* shall be satisfied" (verse 5).
3. **Leaning.** "My *soul* followeth hard after Thee" (ver. 8).

25. **Three things we are to do all the day, as seen in Psalm lxxi.**

1. **Thanking.** "Let my mouth be filled with Thy praise . . . all the day" (verse 8).
2. **Trusting.** "My mouth shall show forth Thy righteousness," &c., "all the day" (verse 15).
3. **Testimony.** "My tongue shall talk of Thy righteousness all the day long" (verse 24).

26. **Three good things in Psalm lxxiii. 28.**

1. **Telling all to the Lord.** "It is good for me to draw near to God."
2. **Trusting in the Lord.** "I have put my trust in the Lord God."

3. **Testifying of the Lord.** "That I may declare all Thy works."

27. **Three precious "buts" in Ephesians ii.**
    1. **Rebellion and love.** "*But* God, who is rich in mercy" (verse 4).
    2. **Distance and nearness.** "*But* now in Christ Jesus" (verse 13).
    3. **Foreigners and citizens.** "*But* fellow-citizens with the saints" (verse 19).

28. **Three things we are to do with the Word of God in II. Timothy.**
    1. **Tenacity.** Hold it fast (i. 13).
    2. **Teaching.** Rightly divide it (ii. 15).
    3. **Testimony.** Preach it (iv. 2).

29. **A threefold contrast in Psalm cxxvi. 6.**
    1. **Service and Return.** "Goeth forth"—"Come again."
    2. **Sadness. Rejoicing.** "Weepeth"—"Rejoicing."
    3. **Seed time. Reward.** "Seed"—"Sheaves."

30. **Three precious "I will's" in Isaiah xli. 10.**
    1. **Encouragement.** "*I will* strengthen thee."
    2. **Empowered.** "*I will* help thee."
    3. **Endurance.** "*I will* uphold thee with the right hand of My righteousness."

31. **Three persons whose visage is described.**
    1. The *sinner*'s visage blackened by *sin* (Lam. iv. 8).
    2. The *Saviour*'s visage marred for the *sinner* (Isa. lii. 14).
    3. The *Sovereign's* visage altered towards the *saints* (Daniel iii. 19).

501. WHETSTONES TO SHARPEN

1. **Threefold Finding.**
    1. Found *by* Him a sinner (Luke xv. 5).
    2. Found *in* Him a saint (Phil. iii. 9).
    3. Found *of* Him a servant (II. Peter iii. 14).

2. **Threefold salvation.**
    1. Saved from the punishment due to sin (Eph. ii. 8).
    2. Being saved from the power of sin (Rom. v. 10).
    3. Shall be saved from the presence of sin (I. Peter i. 5).

3. **Threefold appearing.**
    1. Atonement by His past appearing (Heb. ix. 26).
    2. Advocacy by His present appearing (Heb. ix. 24).
    3. Appearing the second time (Heb. ix. 28).
4. **Threefold gain.**
    1. Gain of grace (Phil. iii. 7).
    2. Gain of godliness (1. Tim. vi. 6).
    3. Gain of glory (Phil. i. 21).
5. **Three "Yet Not I's" of Paul.**
    1. "Yet not I" of walk (Gal. ii. 20).
    2. "Yet not I" of word (1. Cor. vii. 10).
    3. "Yet not I" of work (1. Cor. xv. 10).
6. **Three "No differences."**
    1. "No difference" of salvation and sinnership (Rom. iii. 22).
    2. "No difference" of standing as to place (Rom. x. 12).
    3. "No difference" of sanctification as to mode (Acts xv. 9).
7. **Three handwritings of Scripture.**
    1. On stone (Ex. xxxii. 15, 16). Justness of the law.
    2. On the wall (Dan. v. 5). Judgment on a sinner.
    3. On the Cross (John xix. 19, 20). Judgment of Man.
8. **Three feasts.**
    1. **Finished work of Christ.** Feast provided (Luke xiv. 16).
    2. **Faith in Christ.** Feast enjoyed (Luke xv. 23).
    3. **Folly of sinner.** Feast lost (Luke xvi. 19-25).
9. **Three aspects of death and sin.**
    1. Dead *in* sin (Eph. ii. 1). Sinner.
    2. Death *for* sin (1. Peter iii. 18). Saviour.
    3. Dead *to* sin (Rom. vi. 2). Saint.
10. **Threefold power against our threefold enemy.**
    1. The Father is opposed to the world (1. John ii. 15-17).
    2. The Son is opposed to the devil (1. John iii. 8).
    3. The Spirit is opposed to the flesh (Gal. v. 17).
11. **Threefold power for us.**
    1. The Father as our Protector (Rom. viii. 31, 32).
    2. The Son as our Pleader (Rom. viii. 34).
    3. The Spirit as our Power (Rom. viii. 26).

12. **Threefold name—Lord, Jesus, Christ.**
   1. **Jesus.** Saviour *for* me (Matt. i. 21).
   2. **Christ.** Sanctifier *in* me (Gal. ii. 20).
   3. **Lord.** Sovereign *over* me (John xiii. 13).

13. **Threefold service of Christ.**
   1. **Past.** "He came to minister" (Mark x. 45).
   2. **Present.** "He girded Himself" (illustration) (John xiii. 4).
   3. **Future.** "He will come forth" (Luke xii. 37).

14. **Three spiritual things of Ephesians.**
   1. **Christ, the Depository.** Spiritual blessings (i. 3).
   2. **Christ, the Delight.** Spiritual songs (v. 19).
   3. **Christ, the Defender.** Spiritual enemies (vi. 12).

15. **Three persons with their mouths stopped.**
   1. The sinner (Rom. iii. 19).
   2. The Lord Jesus (Isa. liii. 7).
   3. The man without the wedding garment (Matt. xxii. 12).

16. **Thrice threefold contrast**—Ps. xxii., xxiii., xxiv.

1. Cross.	1. Grace.	1. Wrath.	(Ps. xxii.)
2. Crook.	2. Guidance.	2. Wealth.	(Ps. xxiii.)
3. Crown.	3. Glory.	3. Welcome.	(Ps. xxiv.)

17. **Three perfect things.**
   1. God's work is perfect (Deut. xxxii. 4).
   2. God's way is perfect (Ps. xviii. 30).
   3. God's will is perfect (Rom. xii. 2).

18. **Threefold manifest union between the Father and Christ, as illustrating what our union is, and should manifestly be.**
   1. Union of will (Luke xxii. 42).
   2. Union of work (John ix. 4).
   3. Union of walk (John viii. 29).

19. **Three aspects of eternal life.**
   1. Present possession (1. John v. 11-13). Gift.
   2. Present aim (1. Timothy vi. 12). Growth.
   3. Future manifestation (Colossians iii. 4). Glory.

20. **Three aspects of grace.**
   1. Saved by grace (Ephesians ii. 8). Salvation.
   2. Standing in grace (Romans v. 2). Standing.
   3. Growth in grace (II. Peter iii. 18). Strength.

21. **Three times Christ took Peter, James, and John with Him.**
   1. Saviour and death (Mark v. 37). Sympathy.
   2. Saviour and disciples (Mark ix. 2). Suffering.
   3. Saviour and Divine glory (Mark xiv. 33). Splendour.

22. **Three times the words, "Be it known unto you," occur in Acts.**
   1. Wholeness (Acts iv. 10). Power of His name.
   2. Forgiveness (Acts xiii. 38). Power of His blood.
   3. Salvation (Acts xxviii. 28). Power of His grace.

23. **Threefold singing of the angels.**
   1. At the Creation (Job xxxviii. 7).
   2. At the coming of Christ (Luke ii. 13).
   3. At the coming of the sinner to Christ (Luke xv. 10).

24. **Threefold rest.**
   1. Rest of salvation (Matthew xi. 28).
   2. Rest of service (Matthew xi. 29).
   3. Rest in suffering (II. Thessalonians i. 7).

25. **Three aspects of faith.**
   1. Believing in the Word of God (I. John v. 9).
   2. Accepting the Person of Christ (John i. 12).
   3. Committing the soul to the Lord (II. Timothy i. 12).

26. **Three precious facts in Colossians iii. 3.**
   1. A treasure—"Life is hid with Christ."
   2. The Treasurer—"Christ."
   3. The treasury—"Hid with Christ in God."

27. **Threefold choosing.**
   1. Chosen to salvation (II. Thessalonians ii. 13). Salvation.
   2. Chosen to holiness (Ephesians i. 4). Separation.
   3. Chosen to service (Ephesians ii. 10). Service.

28. **Threefold cleansing.**

1. Our conscience by the blood (I. John i. 7). Redemption.
2. Our ways by the Word and Spirit (Ephesians v. 26). Renewing.
3. Ourselves (II. Corinthians vii. 1). Responsibility.

29. **Threefold aspect of God's mercy in Psalm ciii.**

1. Plenteous in supply (verse 8).
2. Great in saving (verse 11).
3. Everlasting in securing (verse 17).

30. **Threefold deliverance in II. Corinthians i. 10.**

1. Who *hath* delivered (II. Corinthians i. 10). Death.
2. Who *doth* deliver (II. Peter ii. 9). Danger.
3. Who *will* yet deliver (I. Thess. i. 10). Destruction.

31. **Twice threefold contrast in Psalm i.**

UNSAVED.	SAVED.
1. Separated from God.	1. Separated to God.
2. Sinning against God.	2. Serving only God.
3. Scorning at the truth of God.	3. Searching the truth.

502. WEAPONS FOR USING

1. **Three facts in connection with the words "IT IS."**

1. *It is* written, "There is none righteous" (Rom. iii. 10). State of the sinner.
2. "*It is* finished" (John xix. 30). Sacrifice of the Saviour.
3. "*It is* I" (Matthew xiv. 27). Succourer of the Saint.

2. **Threefold picture of Enoch.**

1. His walk (Genesis v. 24). Fellowship with God.
2. His faith (Hebrews xi. 5). Faith in God.
3. His testimony (Jude 14). Faithfulness to God.

3. **Three times Christ is said to be glorified in His saints.**

1. By what He *has* done *for* us (John xvii. 10). Grace.
2. By what He *is* doing *in* us (II. Thess. i. 12). Growth.
3. By what He will *yet* do *for* us (II. Thess. i. 10). Glory.

4. **Three unspeakable things.**
   1. Unspeakable gift (II. Corinthians ix. 15). Redeemer.
   2. Unspeakable joy (I. Peter i. 8). Rejoicing.
   3. Unspeakable words (II. Corinthians xii. 4). Revelation.

5. **Three things about Christ as the Rock.**
   1. *On* the Rock (Psalm xl. 2). Stability.
   2. *In* the Rock (Isaiah xxxiii. 16). Security.
   3. *From* the Rock (Deuteronomy xxxii. 13). Strength.

6. **Three times we read of Paradise.**
   1. Promise to the dying thief (Luke xxiii. 43).
   2. Place where Paul was caught up to (II. Corinthians xii. 4).
   3. Provision for the saint (Revelation ii. 7).

7. **Three "must's" of John iii.**
   1. A necessity for the sinner, "Ye *must* be born again" (verse 7).
   2. A necessity for the Saviour, "*Must* be lifted up" (verse 14).
   3. A necessity for the saint, "I *must* decrease" (verse 30).

8. **Three times we read of the mixed multitude.**
   1. "A *mixed multitude* went up also with them" (Ex. xii. 38).
   2. "*Mixed multitude* . . . fell a lusting" (Numbers xi. 4).
   3. "Separated from Israel all the *mixed multitude*" (Nehemiah xiii. 3).

9. **Three things the Lord does in Deuteronomy xxxiii.**
   1. Saves by His grace (verse 29).
   2. Satisfies with His favour (verse 23).
   3. Separates to Himself (verse 16).

10. **Threefold manifestation of God in Titus.**
    1. His goodness in giving us His Word (Titus i. 3).
    2. His grace in giving us His Son (Titus ii. 11).
    3. His glory, which we shall share with Christ (Titus ii. 13).

11. **Three men who went down.**
    1. Abraham *went down* to Egypt (Genesis xii. 10). Saint out of communion.
    2. Jonah *went down* to Joppa (Jonah i. 3). Servant shirking his work.
    3. Man who *went down* to Jericho (Luke x. 30). Sinner straying.

12. **Threefold abiding.**
   1. Abiding *in* Christ is deliverance (John xiv. 20).
   2. Christ abiding in us is power (John xv. 1-11).
   3. Abiding with Christ is communion (Luke xxiv. 29; John i. 39).

13. **Three things essential to the Christian for power.**
   1. Clean heart for worship (Psalm li. 10; lxxiii. 1).
   2. Clean hands for work (Psalm xxiv. 4; Job xvii. 9).
   3. Clean feet for walk (John xiii. 10).

14. **Three things not to be done to the Holy Spirit.**
   1. The sinner is not to *resist* Him by refusing Christ (Acts vii. 51).
   2. The saint is not to *grieve* Him by looseness in walk (Ephesians iv. 30).
   3. The servant is not to *quench* Him by despising others (1. Thessalonians v. 19).

15. **Three Persons we are to walk worthy of.**
   1. The Father, who has called us (1. Thessalonians ii. 12).
   2. The Son, who has redeemed us (Colossians i. 10).
   3. The Holy Spirit, who indwells us (Ephesians iv. 1).

16. **Three aspects of judgment in relation to the Christian.**
   1. Our judgment as sinners, as to our persons (John v. 24; Romans viii. 3).
   2. Our judgment as saints, as to our walk (1. Cor. xi. 31, 32).
   3. Our judgment as servants, as to our work (1. Cor. iii. 13-15).

17. **Three "every whit's."**
   1. "Clean *every whit*" (John xiii. 10). Regeneration.
   2. "*Every whit* whole" (John vii. 23). Recovery.
   3. "*Every whit* uttereth His glory (Ps. xxix. 9, M.). Reflection.

18. **Threefold comfort.**
   1. The Father comforts by His Word (Psalm cxix. 50).
   2. The Son comforts by His work (Luke xxiv. 37-40).
   3. The Holy Spirit comforts by His presence (John xiv. 16).

19. **Three last things in 1. Corinthians xv.**
   1. The last enemy—death (verse 26).
   2. The last Adam—Christ (verse 45).
   3. The last trump—coming (verse 52).

20. **Three important truths.**
   1. Justification, or accounted righteous in Christ (Rom. iv. 5).
   2. Sanctification, or association with Christ (Heb. x. 14).
   3. Glorification, or assimilation to Christ (I. John iii. 2).

21. **Three persons who were said to be dead.**
   1. Prodigal, while separated from his father (Luke xv. 24).
   2. Pleasure seeker, while living in the world (I. Tim. v. 6).
   3. Professor, who had only a name to live (Rev. iii. 1).

22. **Three times the Father acknowledged Christ from heaven.**
   1. At His baptism (Matt. iii. 17).
   2. At the transfiguration (Mark ix. 7).
   3. In praying to the Father (John xii. 28).

23. **Three times the question was asked "Where is He?"**
   1. The wise men inquire (Matthew ii. 2).
   2. The Jews inquire (John vii. 11).
   3. The neighbours of the blind man inquire (John ix. 12).

24. **Three visits of Christ to the home at Bethany.**
   1. As the Teacher (Luke x. 38-42).
   2. As the sympathising Friend (John xi. 18-45).
   3. As the suffering Saviour (John xii. 1-9).

25. **Three times Nicodemus is mentioned in John's Gospel.**
   1. As the inquirer (John iii. 1).
   2. As the confessor (John vii. 50).
   3. As the worker (John xix. 39).

26. **Three times the words "Who hath believed our report," are mentioned.**
   1. By the prophet (Isaiah liii. 1).
   2. By the Lord Jesus (John xii. 38).
   3. By the apostle Paul (Romans x. 16).

27. **Threefold covering.**
   1. Grace. "Clothed, and in his right mind" (Luke viii. 35).
   2. Godliness. "Clothed with humility" (I. Peter v. 5).
   3. Glory. "Clothed upon with our house which is from heaven (II. Corinthins v. 2-4).

28. **Three attitudes of the believer in Ephesians.**

1. *Seated* with Christ (chapters i. and ii.). Identification.
2. *Walking* as Christ) chapters iv. and v.). Illumination.
3. *Standing* against the enemy (chapter vi.). Infestation.

29. **Three things we are crucified to in Christ.**

1. Self—"*I* am crucified with Christ" (Galatians ii. 20).
2. The flesh —"They that are Christ's *have* crucified the *flesh*" (Galatians v. 24).
3. The world—"The world *is* crucified unto me, and I unto the world" (Galatians vi. 14).

30. **Three "spared not's."**

1. God *spared not* the angels (II. Peter ii. 4).
2. God *spared not* the old world (II. Peter ii. 5).
3. God *spared not* His own Son (Romans viii. 32).

31. **Three conditions to be in to realise the power of God.**

1. Powerlessness (II. Corinthians xii. 9, R.V.).
2. Prayerfulness (Acts iv. 31, 32).
3. Progressing in knowledge (Philippians iii. 10).

503. WEIGHTY WORDS OF COMFORT

1. **The "shall not" of sin.** "Ye *shall not* surely die" (Genesis iii. 4). Here we see the devil's lie. The Lord had said in the previous chapter (Genesis ii. 17), "Thou shalt surely die." Man fell by believing the devil's lie.

2. **The "shall not" of safety.** "When I see the blood, I will pass over you, and the plague *shall not* be upon you" (Exodus xii. 13). They were *safe* because the blood was sprinkled on the door-posts and lintel; and they were *sure* of it, because they had the word of God for it. Every believer in Christ is *safe* because resting in the *work* of Christ, and *sure* of it because resting in the *Word* of God.

3. **The "shall not" of separation.** "*Shall not* eat of them" (Lev. xi. 4, 8, 11, 41, 42). The children of Israel could only eat of clean things; of beasts, only those that chewed the cud and divided the hoof. The divided hoof speaks to us of the separate walk; and chewing the cud, of meditation upon the Word. We are only to feed upon those things in a spiritual sense that will enable us to walk in separation from all that is evil.

4. **The "shall not" of freshness.** "His leaf also *shall not* wither" (Ps. i. 3). The Lord's trees are all evergreens, and always fruit-bearers. This is the result of separation from the world and its worldliness, and meditation *in*, and practice *of* the Word of God.

5. **The "shall not" of remembrance.** "For the needy *shall not* alway be forgotten: the expectation of the poor *shall not* perish for ever" (Psalm ix. 18). The wicked may flourish for a time, and many of God's saints may be, and are poor as far as this world's goods are concerned; but if it is only Christ and a crust here, there is the unchanging inheritance hereafter.

6. **The "shall not" of stability.** "The Lord . . . is at my right hand: I *shall not* be moved" (Psalm xvi. 8; lxii. 2). The realised presence of the Lord beside us is the cure for unstableness. He is beside us as the *Strength* to uphold, as the *Companion* for fellowship, as the *Friend* to counsel, as the *Guide* to direct, as the *High Priest* to succour, as the *Comforter* to cheer, and as the *Teacher* to instruct.

7. **The "shall not" of supply.** "The Lord is my Shepherd; I *shall not* want" (Psalm xxiii. 1). If—and it all depends on the if—the Lord is our Shepherd, we shall not want for rest, good, satisfaction, guidance, restoration, renewing, righteousness, companionship, defence, care, comfort, provision, anointing, joy, goodness, mercy, and a home for ever, as the above Psalm testifies.

8. **The "shall not" of Fatherly care.** "They that seek the Lord *shall not* want any good thing" (Psalm xxxiv. 10). Alexander Peden, in a sermon of his, says: "I remember as I came through the country, that there was a poor widow woman, whose husband fell at Bothwell. The bloody soldiers came to plunder her house, telling her that they would take all she had. 'We will leave thee nothing,' said they, 'either to put in thee or on thee.' 'I care not,' said she; 'I will not want as long as God is in the heavens.' That was a believer indeed."

9. **The "shall not" of courage.** "They *shall not* be ashamed in the evil time" (Psalm xxxvii. 19). We read in Isa. l. 7 of the Lord Jesus saying in prophecy, "Therefore have I set My face like a flint, and I know that I *shall not* be ashamed." As Christ was not ashamed to go to the cross for us, although He despised the shame of it, so let us not be ashamed to take up the cross after Him, and boldly, yet humbly, confess Him.

10. **The "shall not" of preservation.** "Though he fall, he *shall not* be utterly cast down; for the Lord upholdeth him with His hand" (Psalm xxxvii. 24). "Do you believe in the *perseverance* of the saints?" was a question that was once asked. "No," was the reply; "but I believe in the *preservation* of them."

11. **The "shall not" of protection.** "God is in the midst of her: she *shall not* be moved" (Psalm xlvi. 5). God in the midst, or the Holy Spirit in the believer, is the power for *walk*, *worship*, *warfare*, *witnessing*, and *work*. He is also within us as the *Spirit of Life*, *Light*, *Liberty*, *Leading*, and *Love*.

12. **The "shall not" of confidence.** "He only is my Rock and my Salvation; He is my Defence: I *shall not* be moved" (Psalm lxii. 6). Three precious things the Lord is to us here—(1) Our Rock for *stability;* (2) our Salvation for *safety;* (3) and our Defence for *security*. Verily, if He is this *only*, we shall not be moved.

13. **The "shall not" of trust.** "He *shall not* be afraid of evil tidings: his heart is fixed, trusting in the Lord" (Psa. cxii. 7). The one whose heart is stayed upon God is above circumstances, and in all disappointments he takes away the "D" and puts the "H" in, and says they are His appointments.

14. **The "shall not" of holiness.** "And an highway shall be there, and a way, and it shall be called 'The way of holiness;' the unclean *shall not* pass over it" (Isaiah xxxv. 8). What is holiness? 1. *Position*—"*highway*"—"sanctified in Christ." 2. *Separation*—"way of holiness"—sanctified by blood. 3. *Purification*—"The unclean shall not pass over it"—"Cleanse ourselves from all filthiness of the flesh and spirit" (II. Corinthians vii. 1).

15. **The "shall not" of unerring.** "But it shall be for those (margin, 'for He shall be with them'): the wayfaring men, though fools, *shall not* err therein" (Isaiah xxxv. 8). How can they err when, as the margin puts it, He is with them? They have to submit to, and trust in their God, and His is the responsibility to bring them safely through.

16. **The "shall not's" of Christ as the perfect Servant"** "He *shall not* cry, nor lift up, nor cause His voice to be heard in the street. A bruised reed *shall* He *not* break, and the smoking flax *shall* He *not* quench; He shall bring forth judgment unto truth. He *shall not* fail nor be discouraged," &c. (Isaiah xlii. 2-4). In the first, we have the humility of Christ; in the second, the patience of Christ; in the third, the tenderness of Christ; and in the fourth, the perseverance of Christ.

17. **The "shall not" of presence, promise, and protection.** "When thou passest through the waters, I will be with thee; and through the rivers, they *shall not* overflow thee: when thou walkest through the fire, thou shalt not be burned; neither shall the flame kindle upon thee" (Isaiah xliii. 2). He is *between us and the danger*, as He was with Daniel in the lion's den; or He is *with us in the danger*, as He was with the three Hebrew young men in the fire.

18. **The "shall not" of faith.** "For the Lord God will help Me; therefore *shall I not* be confounded" (Isaiah l. 7). Here we hear the Lord Jesus as the Confident Man speaking. He is the Prince and Pattern of faith, and it is our privilege to trust in God as He did.

19. **The "shall not" of food.** "Man *shall not* live by bread alone, but by every word that proceedeth out of the mouth of God" (Matt. iv. 4). These words the Lord Jesus spake to and overcame Satan by. The Word of God is the Christian's food, and if we would be *strong* in soul, *useful* in service, *victorious* in conflict, and *glorify* God, we must continually feed thereon.

20. **The "shall not" of endurance.** "And I say unto thee, thou art Peter" (a stone), "and upon this rock" (the Rock—the Christship of Jesus) "I will build My Church; and the gates of hell (*hades*) *shall not* prevail against it" (Matt. xvi. 18). What a contrast we get in Rev. i. 18! Although the unseen world could not prevail against Christ, He has prevailed against it.

21. **The "shall not" of continuance.** "Heaven and earth shall pass away, but My words *shall not* pass away" (Matt. xxiv. 35). What *consolation* this brings to the believer in Christ! but what *consternation* it ought to bring to the unsaved! See the following Scriptures, where we find the words, "It is written":—*Sinner* (Rom. iii. 10-18); *Saviour* (Heb. x. 7); *servant* (Rom. x. 15); *child of God* (1. Peter i. 16); *neglecter* (Isaiah lxv. 6).

22. **The "shall not" of reward.** "For whosoever shall give you a cup of water to drink in My name, because ye belong to Christ, verily I say unto you, he *shall not* lose his reward" (Mark ix. 41). The least thing done to any of Christ's, He reckons as done to Himself.

23. **The "shall not" of communion.** "Martha, thou art careful and troubled about many things; but one thing is needful; and Mary hath chosen that good part, which *shall not* be taken away from her" (Luke x. 41, 42). The Lord did not find fault with Martha for serving, but He did find fault with her for being *cumbered* with it, and *commended* Mary for putting Him first. The Lord wants of us the *worship* of Mary, and the *work* of Martha.

24. **The "shall not" of provision.** "But there *shall not*" ('not, not, a double negative'—*Newberry*) "an hair of your head perish" (Luke xxi. 18). We may well sing—

"He who has fed, will feed;
He who has led, will lead;
He who has kept, will keep;
He who has saved, will save."

25. **The "shall not" of no condemnation.** "Verily, verily, I say unto you, he that heareth My word, and believeth on Him that sent Me, hath everlasting life, and *shall not* come into condemnation, but is passed from death unto life" (John v. 24). The very things that God would have had to judge the believer for at the great white throne, He has judged in Christ on the cross.

26. **The "shall not" of illumination.** "He that followeth Me *shall not* walk in darkness, but shall have the light of life" (John viii. 12). Darkness symbolises sin, unbelief, and ignorance; and light, holiness, faith, and knowledge. If we are following Christ, we shall be like Him, trust Him, and know Him.

27. **The "shall not" of freedom.** "Sin *shall not* have dominion over you" (Romans vi. 14). To say that we have no sin, is to contradict the Word of God. To say we must sin, is to destroy the whole work of Christ, and to utter a gross libel upon the indwelling Spirit. To say that we need not sin, is to state a blessed privilege.

28. **The "shall not" of confidence.** "Whosoever believeth on Him *shall not* be put to shame" (Romans x. 11, R.V.). If God be for us, there is no fear of being put to shame; for our interests are His.

29. **The "shall not" of glory.** "We *shall not* all sleep, but we shall all be changed" (I. Corinthians xv. 51). The Lord Himself coming *for* His people, was a truth the Old Testament knew not of, but it is the mystery now shown to us, if we have eyes to see it.

30. **The "shall not" of liberty.** "Walk in the Spirit, and ye *shall not* fulfil the lust of the flesh" (Galatians v. 16). There will be purity of heart and life, confidence towards God, and power with men, if we are walking in the Spirit.

31. **The "shall not" to the unsaved.** "The ungodly *shall not* stand in the judgment, nor sinners in the congregation of the righteous" (Psalm i. 5). Who shall be able to stand in the Lord's presence? Only those who are standing in His grace (Rom. v. 2). All others will be banished from Him. If hell is nothing else, it is this—eternal separation from God, and from all He is and has to give.

SCRIPTURE TEXT INDEX

The Scripture verses listed below are those upon which the author has based his outline.

GENESIS

3:1-15 216, 285
3:5-19 237
9:1-17 110
12:1-9 35, 243
14:18-20 177
17:1 105
17:2 107
18:17-21 2
18:22-23 4, 107
22:1-14 308
25:27 139
25:27-32 82
28:10-19 141
28:12-15 347
28:15 102
32:9-11, 24-30 203
32:9-12 143
32:25-30 140
37:28-36 157

EXODUS

1:1-14 136
6:6-8 138
12:1-14 274
14:13-15 345
14:19-29 278
24:3-7 317
25:8 123
25:22 351
31:1-6 114
35:5, 10, 21 352

NUMBERS

8:6-19 215
13:17-20, 23-33 280
14:24 32
24:5-9, 17-19 194

DEUTERONOMY

1:33 146
6:12 25
6:3-15 208, 272
18:15-18 61
33:16, 23, 29 359
33:29 194

JOSHUA

3:5 215
3:5-17 70
6:8-20 89
14:5-14 34
24:13-25 160

JUDGES

7:17 50

1 SAMUEL

7:12 265
17:38-51 71, 73
20:32-42 334

2 SAMUEL

2:1 134
5:1-12 74
22:44 167

1 KINGS

11:4-13 327
20:1-30 204
20:31-43 66
21:1-29 69

1 CHRONICLES

18:6 267

2 CHRONICLES

15:1-10 237
16:1-12 80
16:9 153
17:3-16 242
19:9 121
20:1-13 144
20:3-30 284
25:1-16 118
25:17-28 220
26:16-23 205

NEHEMIAH

8:10 162

JOB

1:10 63

PSALMS

2:1-5 349
19:7-10 232
23:1-6 232, 350
27:1-14 145
26:2, 6, 8 352
28:9 347
30:1-11 233
32:1-11 264
32:7 203
41:1-3 353
46:1, 7, 11 353
56:13 353
63:1, 5, 8 353
64:10 353
71:8, 15, 24 353
73:28 353
78:8-10, 17-19 25
89:1-8 349
103:1-5 6
103:8, 11, 17 358
119:89-112 115
126:6 354
132:11-18 139

PROVERBS

1:1-15 190

SONG OF SOLOMON

2:3 234
7:10 307

ISAIAH

5:11-14 245
9:2-7 279
9:6 179
11:1-9 53
12:2 348
41:10 354
52:13-15 47
53:1-12 47
53:10 346
57:5 111

JEREMIAH

38—39 81

MICAH

6:8 352

ZEPHANIAH

3:5 319

MATTHEW

2:2 350
4:1-11 286, 289
6:13 78
10:1-16 221
10:5-16 295
13:22 299
18:1-14 39
21:1-7 17
24:42-51 323

MARK

1:30 199
2:3 98
3:13-19 311
6:14-29 154
6:30-44 92
10:17-27 282, 301
13:33-37 347
14:22-23 268
14:32-42 249
14:53-63 150
16:4 187

LUKE

2:8-20 217
2:25-34 46
2:36-37 18
5:6-7 101
8:15 164
9:28-36 294
10:30-37 262
19:1-10 304

JOHN

1:35-51 288
1:51 61
2:11 46
2:13-25 152
3:3 272
3:7, 14, 30 359
3:16 420
6:27-35 57
9:4 59
9:5 59
9:7 219
11:4-56 147
11:35-44 149
12:26 95
14:3-30 139
14:15, 21, 23 164
14:21 176
15:16 20

ACTS

2:38 102
5:28 28
6:5 176
6:8 175
11:23 39
17:24-25 60
20:24-28 345
26:5-26 191
27:23 337

ROMANS

5:10 22
8:2-27 264
8:26-34 346
10:3-6 346
13:8-10 172
13:8-14 183

1 CORINTHIANS

1:30 345
5:26, 45, 52 360
15:48 121

2 CORINTHIANS

1:10 358
2:16 219
4:4 27

GALATIANS

5:22-23 101

EPHESIANS

2:4, 13, 19 354
5:18 62

COLOSSIANS

3:3 357

HEBREWS

9:7—10:2 185
9:24-28 300
11:1-12 87
11:13-22 88
11:23 122
11:23-31 90
11:32 88
13:5 6
13:6 259
13:7, 17, 24 352

JAMES

3:1-13 338

1 JOHN

1:1 297
2:2 270
3:1 177
4:8, 16 172

REVELATION

3:7 41, 42
4:5 230